RABELAIS AND THE FRANCISCANS

TWO ASPECTS OF THE
RELIGIOUS VOCATION

Der Predicant.

THE PREACHER
(From HOLBEIN, *Bilder des Todes*)

THE THEOLOGIAN, NICHOLAS OF LYRA, OFM
(From HOLBEIN's illustrations to
ERASMUS' *Stultitiae Laus*)

RABELAIS
AND THE FRANCISCANS

BY

A. J. KRAILSHEIMER

CLARENDON PRESS · OXFORD
1963

Oxford University Press, Amen House, London E.C.4

GLASGOW NEW YORK TORONTO MELBOURNE WELLINGTON
BOMBAY CALCUTTA MADRAS KARACHI LAHORE DACCA
CAPE TOWN SALISBURY NAIROBI IBADAN ACCRA
KUALA LUMPUR HONG KONG

PRINTED IN GREAT BRITAIN AT THE VILLAFIELD PRESS
BISHOPBRIGGS, GLASGOW

ACKNOWLEDGEMENTS

This book has taken a very long time to write, and rewrite, and but for the help and encouragement of one or two friends and colleagues it would probably never have been finished at all. The bulk of the work was done at Glasgow, during the eight years when I had the good fortune to belong to the French Department of the University. For the constant kindness and encouragement of Professor Alan Boase I shall always be deeply grateful. No less profound is my gratitude to Mr. J. G. Dawson, who read several preliminary drafts of the work, and whose unfailing patience and unsparing criticism helped more than anything else to bring it to completion. When I came back to Oxford, Mr. C. A. Robson was kind enough to read the MS and offer some good advice, which greatly helped me in composing the final draft. I should particularly like to thank Mr. Iain Macdonald, himself a Glasgow graduate, for much practical advice and encouragement over a number of years, and for reading more than one draft of this book. Whatever defects and blemishes may still remain, I hope that these friends at least will recognize how much the finished work has been improved, thanks to their help. They are, of course, in no way responsible for my opinions, conclusions or vulgar errors.

This is an appropriate place to record my thanks to the University of Glasgow for assisting me on two occasions to pursue research in Paris.

The Editors of the *Modern Language Review* have kindly allowed me to reproduce Chapter II (Pan), which appeared in slightly modified form as an article, 'The Significance of the Pan Legend in Rabelais' Thought' in vol. lvi, January 1961.

It is fitting that my debt to the two Universities of Glasgow and Oxford should be symbolized by the fruitful collaboration of Glasgow printers and Oxford publishers. I am most grateful to both for making the final stage of the work so speedy and smooth.

A. J. K.

Oxford,
January, 1963.

CONTENTS

NOTE

Page references to Rabelais's text are to the complete edition of his works by J. Boulenger, in *Bibliothèque de la Pléiade*, 1934. The following abbreviations are used:

TL   *Tiers Livre*   CL   *Cinquiesme Livre*
QL   *Quart Livre*   BD   *Briefve Declaration*

Reference to the sermons are by the folio number for sixteenth-century editions (recto unless otherwise stated) and by page reference for modern editions, in each case following a letter which indicates the series:

A   Maillard, *Sermones de Adventu* (1494)
F   Maillard, *Œuvres Françaises*
P   Menot, *Carêmes de Paris* (1517, 1518)
Q   Maillard, *Sermones Quadragesimales* (1498)
R   Messier, *Sermones de Quadragesima* (before 1531)
S   Maillard, *De Stipendio Peccati* (before 1500)
T   Menot, *Carême de Tours* (1508)

Details of editions will be found in the Bibliography.
Other abbreviations are as follows:

AFH   *Archivum Franciscanum Historicum*
BHR   *Bibliothèque d'Humanisme et Renaissance*
RER   *Revue d'Etudes Rabelaisiennes*
RHF   *Revue d'Histoire Franciscaine*

In quotations from the sermons the often considerable eccentricities of spelling and syntax in the original have been reproduced, but punctuation has sometimes been slightly modified, some accents have been supplied for French words and the distinction between 'u' and 'v', 'i' and 'j', 'ae' and 'e' has been introduced throughout. For Rabelais, Boulenger's text has been followed, but with a much more sparing use of accents.

INTRODUCTION

Some of the greatest difficulties in understanding the men of the Renaissance result from their own prejudices. As a consequence of their passionate rejection of the medieval legacy and all it stood for, we tend to accept them as the torchbearers of a new age, and to echo them in treating the antithesis 'medieval and Renaissance' as if it were as valid as 'ancient and modern'. Even now, when a supreme semantic irony has made the originally pejorative 'Gothic' a respectable and even admirable epithet, the tendency persists to take seriously the protests of such men as Rabelais against the 'tenèbres des Gothz'. Though there is less excuse today than formerly for misunderstanding the Middle Ages, and the true significance of the Renaissance, critical work on some of the greatest authors still betrays strange blind spots.

Rabelais is an outstanding case in point. His work frequently and vigorously expresses his contempt for previous centuries and admiration for the ancient world and contemporary humanism, but by its very form and existence demonstrates the impossibility of breaking with the past. In his life as in his work Rabelais shows the paradoxical, and sometimes anomalous, situation into which history had thrust him. His early training, up to the age of twenty-five or so, had been in the order which led the attack on the New Learning, and yet while still a member of that order he began his own classical studies and made contact with Budé and other leading humanists. His first published works were erudite essays in law and medicine, but he first achieved literary immortality as the anonymous author of a book written in the popular and medieval tradition.

When one considers the enormous mass of critical work devoted to Rabelais, much of it of the highest quality, it is, to say the least, curious that an element universally recognized as important should have received so little attention. There are countless studies of Rabelais's classical sources and humanistic affinities, of his friends and enemies, of his literary antecedents and successors, but he must be almost unique in having no full study devoted to his formative years. Many years ago now Gilson's admirable essay 'Rabelais Franciscain' showed how much of Rabelais's work only makes sense when considered in its proper context. Gilson wrote then: 'Pas une des expressions dont il use qui ne porte et qui ne prouve la survivance d'un théologien fort compétent chez l'auteur de *Pantagruel*',[1] and later critics have always accepted this expert testimony. Though Gilson gave a number of examples to show the Franciscan provenance of Rabelais's thought, and made some suggestive remarks about 'le sel franciscain', his work has never been seriously followed up. There are some excellent pages in Febvre,[2] some acutely perceptive observations by Auerbach,[3] odd references by other scholars,[4] but still no proper study of the *années de moinage* and their influence on Rabelais.

The main purpose of the present work is to fill this gap, but this involves more than one problem. One of the main reasons for the failure of otherwise sound scholars to do justice to this question is the common tendency to lump together a broad variety of elements in Rabelais's work, scholastic, medieval or monastic, which have little or nothing to do with his personal experience, but are simply philosophical or literary commonplaces. A single example of this will suffice: though Rabelais's training in scholastic and monastic ways was Franciscan, with his brief Benedictine phase no more than an interlude, it is nearly always the Benedictine Frère Jan who is taken as the accredited representative in the book of the *années de moinage*. No real progress towards understanding Rabelais can be made until something concrete can be established regarding life in a specific branch of the Franciscan order at a specific time. This is what the first part of this book tries to do.

It happens that the years during which Rabelais was an Observant friar were precisely those of greatest moment within the order. The province to which Rabelais belonged, like the other French Observant provinces, was ruled by statutes far more rigorously observed than those of the ordinary unreformed

---

[1] E. Gilson, 'Rabelais Franciscain' in *Idées et Lettres*, p. 231.

[2] L. Febvre, *La Religion de Rabelais*, pp. 179–81.

[3] E. Auerbach, *Mimesis*, p. 238.

[4] The first person who seems to have thought about this seriously was A. Méray, but his two books *La Vie au Temps des Libres Prêcheurs* and *Les Libres Prêcheurs Devanciers de Luther et de Rabelais* are highly tendentious and adopt a method of selection that makes them of very little use. Later came L. Thuasne, with a quite good chapter on 'Les Sources monastiques de Rabelais' in his *Études sur Rabelais*, and a much less good section in *Villon et Rabelais*.

Cordeliers, and new legislation, of which records survive, was enacted and enforced while he was still at Fontenay. The picture of his career is still far from complete, but we can reconstruct its essential lines.[1]

One of the most fruitful sources of information regarding Franciscan methods and attitudes in Rabelais's time is the considerable amount of sermon material which happily has come down to us. The main function of the Friars Minor has always been preaching, the career for which Rabelais was being trained up to the time he left the order, and the models which were current in his time have a great deal to reveal. Several critics have compared the style and language of the preachers with that of Rabelais, and this is in itself a rewarding field of study, but one can go further. Rabelais like his brethren inherited a long tradition which included more than 'le sel franciscain'. The sermons which were being studied while he was at Fontenay offer more points of comparison with the book he was to write some ten years later than any other Franciscan production. They show in the first place how the technical and academic training in theology, canon law and philosophy was adapted to the pastoral needs of a popular and, at least partly, illiterate audience, corresponding closely to the public at which Rabelais aimed his first books. They show too which points of doctrine and which authors received most notice from the preachers. Above all they show which aspects of social and religious life the preachers wished to stress, and in what sense. Since virtually all the extant sermons are penitential, usually for Advent or Lent, there is obvious distortion, over and above the normal prejudices of the order, so that the mirror held up to the public should be as unflattering as possible, and thus inspire the desired contrition. Even so, the distortion is in itself a feature of the religious atmosphere in which Rabelais and his readers grew up, and is thus directly relevant to the picture eventually presented in his work.

From a literary point of view the imagery, narrative technique, vocabulary and satire of the preachers offer a priceless store for any intending popular writer, and in the matter of invective they are second to none. Any serious evaluation of Rabelais's irreverence or audacity must take into account the standards set by the preachers.

[1] See Chapters 2 and 3 below.

Something like three hundred sermons, all preached between 1490 (that is just before Rabelais's birth) and 1531 (the year before *Pantagruel*), all by French Observants of high standing in the order, provide the material analysed in Chapters 3–6. With the sole exception of Messier's series, they were all in print at the time Rabelais was at Fontenay, and are thus strictly relevant to his training. It should be made clear that these printed sermons are not simply records of the spoken word (though they are always that) but were published specifically as models for other, less resourceful, preachers to follow. Constant directions to the intending preacher remind the reader of their function. This was also a reason for reproducing the sermons in Latin, liberally sprinkled with French, although they were originally delivered in the vernacular, for the Franciscan order was international, its missionary role was important and the same Latin text might serve as basis for translation into a variety of tongues.

While the first part of this book attempts to reconstruct from Franciscan history, and the sermons, the life and training represented by the phrase *années de moinage*, the second part is concerned with the wider implications of Gilson's remark quoted earlier. It is clear that such theological competence as Rabelais had must have come to him in the first place through his Franciscan training, and there is no real problem in discovering what doctrines and methods prevailed in the order at the time. The difficulty arises from the fact that there exists no generally received statement (let alone interpretation) of Rabelais's thought with which Franciscan teaching can be compared. The question goes far beyond theology, involving as it does attitudes and interests which are sometimes scarcely intellectual. The second and much the longer part of this book deals therefore with what Rabelais has to say under a number of headings, ranging from metaphysics to politics. Each chapter groups together references to a given subject scattered throughout the work, and though the selection is not exhaustive it can fairly be claimed as representative. There are obvious disadvantages in using such a method; it tends to be scrappy and repetitious; there will be inevitable gaps where the available material fails to supply the answer to some vital question, and there is a real danger of distortion when texts are taken out of context from a work largely in dialogue form. Despite all this, a systematic analysis of what

Rabelais actually says has long seemed overdue, and this is an attempt to supply it. The habits of mind thus revealed tell us more about Rabelais's debt to his Franciscan masters than could any piecemeal comparison between texts by Rabelais and by the Scholastics.

So that the evidence from formal Franciscan teaching should be as directly relevant as the sermons, only the most characteristic and accessible doctrines of the two great doctors of the order, Bonaventura and Scotus, have been considered here. Their teaching always formed the basis of Franciscan instruction, and whatever else Rabelais may have read, it is safe to assume that this was his grounding.

Scientific and medical knowledge is the one major deliberate omission from this analysis of Rabelais's work, because whatever odd bits of such information he may have picked up as a friar, he is known to have started his medical studies in earnest only after he left the order.

Finally it should be said that there is no intention in this book of denying or minimizing the humanistic influences in Rabelais's work. So much has been written on this by other scholars that it seemed more profitable to concentrate here on a neglected aspect of Rabelais. By presenting Rabelais's Franciscan background in more concrete terms than usual, this study has tried to redress the balance, hitherto weighted heavily on the side of humanism, where Rabelais himself would probably have preferred it always to remain.

There is not room in such a work as this for even the briefest examination of theories advanced by other scholars on general questions to do with Rabelais, but certain debts cannot be passed over in silence. Of all the books on Rabelais perhaps none has proved more helpful and stimulating to this study than that of L. Febvre. In the specific field of this book by far the greatest debt is to Gilson,[1] whose regrettably brief incursions into Rabelais scholarship have been invaluable, and who has been the surest of guides through the whole realm of medieval thought. For the sermons it is a pleasure to pay tribute to the now distant work of Samouillan[2] and La Borderie[3] on Maillard and

---

[1] See also 'Notes médiévales sur le TL de Rabelais' in RHF ii, 1925, pp. 72 seq.

[2] Abbé A. Samouillan, O. Maillard, sa Prédication et son Temps.

[3] A. de la Borderie, Œuvres Françaises d'O. Maillard.

Nève[1] on Menot, as well as the excellent work of Owst,[2] who though concerned with England and an earlier period has much of value to suggest about preaching in general. On more general aspects of the early sixteenth century the work of Renaudet[3] and Imbart de la Tour[4] continues to be indispensable. Many other lesser debts are acknowledged in their place.

[1] J. Nève, *Sermons Choisis de M. Menot.*
[2] G. R. Owst, *Preaching in Mediaeval England* and *Literature and Pulpit in Mediaeval England.*
[3] A. Renaudet, *Pré-Réforme et Humanisme à Paris.*
[4] P. Imbart de la Tour, *Origines de la Réforme.*

PART I

THE FRANCISCANS AND THEIR TRAINING

1 : CHRONOLOGY

APART from Rabelais's own formal communications with the Papal Chancery, neither detailed nor wholly impartial, the only direct and reliable evidence concerning the *années de moinage* is to be found in the letters written by Guillaume Budé to Fontenay, first to Pierre Amy and then to Rabelais as well. Unfortunately all of Amy's letters, all but one of Rabelais's and probably several of Budé's have perished, but despite this and some difficulties of dating, there is still a good deal to be learned from what survives.[1]

The first extant letter from Budé to Amy was written in February 1520,[2] and alludes to the fact that Budé had just been reminded by his friend and fellow humanist, François Deloynes, that he owed Amy a letter. It is hard to judge from the extremely formal style how well Budé knew Amy at that time, but it is clear that he already knew something about him, perhaps through Deloynes, had perhaps met him briefly, and certainly showed enthusiastic approval for his devotion to the New Learning. Budé commends Amy's zeal for classical studies, and says that while he realizes how many religious duties and cares hinder Amy's pursuit of learning, he envies him his quiet life, free from the cares of the Court and the world. He ends by remarking that Amy is probably the only one of his community to be interested in such studies.

A few weeks later Budé writes again,[3] the first letter having

---

[1] For notes and comments on these letters, L. Delaruelle, *Répertoire de la Correspondance de G. Budé*, remains the most complete account, though later scholars have had to modify details, especially of dating.

[2] Budé, *Epistolae Latinae* i, p. 267.

[3] Ibid., p. 301: 'Ac tibi . . . contigit ut, in utriusque linguae officinis egregie inchoatus, reclamante, ut memini, parente tuo faceres, ut in istam sodalitatem dares nomen primum, deinde profiterere . . .' There is a real difficulty of translation here; it has always been accepted (apparently since Delaruelle) that these words mean that Amy was forced by his father to enter religion. This interpretation seems to depend on taking the father's reaction to refer to protests against Amy's studies. A much more natural translation would completely change the picture by applying the idea of parental protest to Amy's abandonment of studies for a career in religion, and in view of Amy's subsequent religious history this seems right. However, as an additional complication, the word 'reclamare' can also mean 'demand insistently' in classical Latin, though less commonly than 'protest'. It is time the whole question of Amy's career was reopened, but for the moment it is enough to indicate that the standard account must be accepted only with great caution.

apparently gone astray, and develops much the same themes at greater length. He speaks warmly of Amy's knowledge of theology, praises his intellectual gifts and early devotion to learning and finds it providential that, 'after an excellent start in both Latin and Greek, in spite [?] of your father's protests, you came first to put down your name for that [Franciscan] order and then to be professed'.

The reference to Amy's early progress in *Philologia*, and his abrupt change of life apparently against paternal wishes, rather suggests that he may have been a little older than most novices when he joined the order and that his vocation may have been rather sudden. At all events, Budé does not go on to commiserate, but to extol the religious life:[1]

Hence those holy orders of yours, composed of men who not only have withdrawn by the very fact of their vow from the imaginary goods that are subject to the whims of fortune, but have turned their backs on three things that man peculiarly calls his own, country, family and freedom, seem to me to be nurseries for blessed spirits, founded purposely by Providence to supplement the ranks of the heavenly armies, once so notably depleted through pride.

This unsolicited testimonial from the leading humanist of France (which he never retracted) shows how dangerous it is to assume that men like Budé were, as leaders of intellectual progress, necessarily opposed to the monastic ideal, as distinct from its contemporary abuses. The Stoic, and Christian Stoic at that, undertones of the phrase just quoted no doubt explain some of Budé's sympathy.

Budé ends the letter (in Greek) by approving Amy's studies, which embrace both religion and mathematics, and then (in Latin) agrees with him that Aristotle is excellent on human and scientific subjects, though not on eternal and divine matters, as can be seen from the *Metaphysics*. He briefly refers to translations by Bessarion and Argyropoulos, and to Themistius's paraphrases. This is indeed the only specific reference to the books Amy (and Rabelais) was studying at Fontenay, apart from a few books from that period bearing Rabelais's *ex libris*.

[1] 'quo fit ut vestrae illae piae sodalitates non modo bonis imaginariis fortunaeque cedentium ipsa professione, sed etiam tribus rebus animum abdicantium, quae maxime cuiusque sunt propriae, civitate, cognatione, libertate, mihi velut seminaria esse videantur animarum beatarum, a providentia utique instituta ad supplementum caelestium exercituum quondam per superbiam luculenter imminutorum.'

Neither of these letters to Amy mentions Rabelais, and as subsequent letters link the two friends together in greeting, it seems more than likely that Rabelais had not yet arrived at Fontenay. However that may be, in the autumn of the same year, about November 1520, it seems that Amy persuaded Rabelais to write to Budé. The experiment was not at first successful, for Rabelais's next (and only extant) letter to Budé[1] complains in rather pained fashion that Amy has misled him. All was soon well, however, for Budé wrote back in April 1521,[2] the following month, taking all the blame on himself and commenting that Rabelais should have more confidence in a fellow priest and religious than to attack Amy for something of which he was in any case innocent. The main interest of this letter is that it confirms that Rabelais was in priest's orders by 1521.

In later letters to the two friends Budé shows considerably less enthusiasm for the religious life and expresses his indignation at the vigorous measures of repression being taken against all those suspected of sympathy with the new Lutheran heresy. He speaks[3] of the superiors of the Mendicants and 'all those who make a superstition of ignorance and call it orthodoxy', and deplores the personal attacks on Erasmus and the tendency to brand as heretics all those whose only innovation is the study of Greek. He puts the blame for all this on the Mendicant doctors in the Sorbonne, on whose orders Greek books are being seized, and says that the Franciscans are above all responsible.

The second of Budé's two letters to Rabelais[4] refers to some commission with which Rabelais had been entrusted on behalf of the brother of André Tiraqueau, and then goes on to discuss the result of the repressive measures as they have been felt at Fontenay. Budé knows that Amy and Rabelais are bound by ties of friendship and common devotion to learning, and for this they have suffered when they deserved reward. He continues:

I gathered from one of the more civilized and honourable members of your order that you have had returned to you what we both love

---

[1] *Œuvres,* p. 959.　　　　[2] *Epist. Lat.,* iii, p. 325.

[3] *Epist. Graecae,* in translation by A. Pichon, pp. 134-7: 'omnes porro imperitiam superstitiose observantes sub nomine orthodoxae disciplinae.'

[4] Ibid., p. 142: 'accepi a quodam elegantiorum ipsius sodalitii et honestatis observatorum, vobisque redditas fuisse delicias nostras, libros inquam, quos isti suo arbitrio a vobis subduxerunt, vosque restitutos esse in priorem libertatem et tranquillitatem.'

so much, that is the books which they [your superiors] took it on themselves to remove from you, and that you have yourself been restored to your former peace and liberty.

The most likely explanation of the last word is that the friends had suffered imprisonment in the convent, a form of punishment laid down by the rule. Budé adds that his informant confirmed this report on oath, and though he is not sure at the time of writing where the friends are, it is clear that he assumes the storm to have blown over. This letter is generally agreed to date from January 1524, so that the events leading up to the confiscation and later return of the books must have taken place a month or two earlier. Since the books can only have been returned by the superiors at Fontenay who confiscated them, and since the letter Budé had just received from Rabelais spoke of Tiraqueau, Rabelais can have been away from Fontenay only temporarily, if at all. The case of Amy[1] seems to have been quite different, for after his release he apparently had wind of another impending attack. Rabelais himself recalled long after how Amy fled (*TL*/x), and a letter of July 1524 speaks of Amy's being in correspondence with Conrad Pellikan and currently sheltering with the Benedictines at Saint-Mesmin, near Orleans.[2] From there he seems to have made his way to Basle early in 1525, where he lived in poor health under Pellikan's protection until he died some months later. From a reference in Budé's last letter to Amy, as also from Erasmus's much later recollection of Amy's end, it looks as though persecution at Fontenay had brought on an illness from which he never recovered. Amy's connexions with Pellikan, who was soon to pass over to the Reform, indicate that the superiors at Fontenay may not have been so unreasonable after all in suspecting him of Lutheran leanings as well as Hellenic interests.

This is all we know for certain of Rabelais's career as a Franciscan and of his friendship with Amy, and but for Budé we should not know even this. The fact that Rabelais moved only a few miles to Maillezais, and in fact joined a monastery-cathedral

---

[1] See H. Meylan, 'La mort de Lamy', in *Fr. Rabelais* 1553–1953, p. 248.

[2] Amy may well have had connexions at Orleans, for Deloynes (*ob.* 1524), who reminded Budé to write to him, was the son of the Bailli of Beaugency and had professed law at Orleans before going on to Paris and high legal office, and the Abbot of Saint-Mesmin was Fr. du Moulin, seigneur de Rochefort, Grand Almoner of France (*ob.* 1526) who belonged to the same circles. See Delaruelle, op cit. p. 6 n. 5 and Renaudet, *Pré-Réforme et Humanisme*, p. 688, n. 2.

of which his diocesan bishop was abbot, contrasts strongly with Amy's flight into distant exile, and supports M. Marichal's view that the main reason for Rabelais's transfer was his desire to study medicine.[1] Then, as now, no stigma attached to a religious who wished, for good reason shown, to move to a canonically higher order, and the papal dispensation for Rabelais's assumption of the Benedictine habit proves that he had made out his case.

It seems highly probable from these letters of Budé that Rabelais came to Fontenay from another house some time in 1520; Franciscan communities were not so large that Amy could have failed to refer to a fellow humanist if Rabelais had already been there at the time of the first letter. By 1521 at latest he is a priest, and from his *Supplicatio* to the Pope[2] we learn that he entered the order as *juvenis* and regularly took minor and major orders before being ordained priest. According to statutes in force in Rabelais's time,[3] and in conformity with canon law, no person could take the habit before the age of sixteen or be ordained priest before twenty-five. Before profession a full year's noviciate had to be served, and during this time every opportunity was to be given on both sides for the novice to return to the world if his vocation proved unsuitable. The normal course of studies for the priesthood lasted about six years, though one cannot speak with full assurance of conditions in the early sixteenth century, and the rule laid down that a friar remained subject to the *magister juvenum* until he was twenty-five. Dispensations of a year or two from this programme were quite common, and in the case of a man as intelligent as Rabelais would have been granted without difficulty. The most natural time for Rabelais to be transferred to another house would be after the completion of his studies for the priesthood, and it would be entirely consistent with Franciscan practice that he should move, for, unlike monks, friars take no vow of stability to the house of their profession and are normally moved anywhere within the province. Moreover the chapter held

---

[1] R. Marichal, 'Rabelais devant le néo-Platonisme' in *Fr. Rabelais* 1553–1953, p. 183.

[2] To Paul III, in 1536, recapitulating the démarche made at an earlier, unspecified, date to Clement VII. In *Œuvres,* ed. H. Clouzot vol. i, p. LIII.

[3] *Monumenta Franciscana,* vol. ii, 'Statuta Generalia . . . apud Barcinonam 1451', pp. 83 seq. It is specifically stated that during the probationary year the novice is to learn the Divine Office by heart, but not to engage in any kind of study, nor to have any contacts with the world outside the cloister except under strict supervision.

at Lavaur in 1539[1] passed a rule whereby young friars would change houses every three years, which suggests that in some quarters at least the idea of frequent and regular movement had found favour for some time before receiving actual legislative expression. The question of when and where Rabelais entered religion must be answered in the light of known Observant practice at the time. Given the intensity of the struggle between the reformers within the order and their Conventual opponents, one may reasonably assume that the Observants took some care to follow their own rules at this time. Every house then had a noviciate,[2] so that on that account Rabelais could have entered any one of the twenty-four houses of the Observant province of Touraine[3] (after 1518 renamed Touraine-Pictavienne). The rule laid down[4] that as far as possible every house, and certainly every province, should provide a place 'where the brethren can be duly instructed in basic studies and theology', but there is no information as to how this was arranged in Rabelais's province at this time. An old, but quite unconfirmed, tradition[5] has it that Rabelais joined the Franciscans at La Baumette, just outside Angers, in 1511. In favour of this theory one may note that Rabelais's mother had at least one brother living there,[6] and that the university would certainly offer such facilities for study as an intending priest might need, though Observant regulations allowed only one friar from the province to read for a degree at a time. It is interesting to know that if Rabelais were a member of the community at La Baumette[7] he would almost certainly still

---

[1] A. de Sérent, OFM, 'Statuts des quatre provinces françaises des Cordeliers', in RHF, vii, 1930, p. 25: 'Fratres juniores unoquoque saltem triennio relegentur ex uno ad alium conventum, ut sic consuescant juxta Regulam neque domum neque locum neque aliquam rem in hoc mundo habere.'

[2] 'Pendant plusieurs siècles [until 1600] chaque couvent eut son noviciat où etaient formés à la vie religieuse les sujets recrutés ordinairement dans les environs.' Max Courtecuisse, Tables Capitulaires des Frères Mineurs de l'Observance . . . de Bretagne, p. LXVIII.

[3] See RHF, vi, 1929, p. 304 for complete lists with analysis of all Franciscan houses in the West of France at different periods.

[4] Monumenta Franciscana, vol. ii, p. 94: 'per quae fratres in primitivis scientiis et in sacra theologia debite instruantur.'

[5] Cf. Chronology in Œuvres, ed. Lefranc, vol. i.

[6] The Frapin, seigneur de Saint-Georges, of the Ancien Prologue to the Quart Livre.

[7] Wadding, Annales Minorum, vol. xii, p. 559. The convent had been founded by René d'Anjou in 1457, and is said to have had (in the sixteenth century) a normal complement of twenty friars, including a Guardian, a Lector, five Preachers. It enjoyed considerable prestige and a reputation for piety, and at the end of the century was one of the first houses to accept the stricter rule of the Recollects.

have been there to participate in the ceremony on Easter Eve
1518, when by special papal dispensation the friars sang divine
office for the first time, having up till then been prohibited by
their royal founder's insistence that they should only say the office
and thus leave themselves more time for prayer and meditation.
On the assumption that Rabelais did in fact enter religion in
1511, he would have finished his probationary year by 1512, and
then after six years' study be ready to be ordained in 1518 or,
more strictly, 1519. By that time he would be twenty-five, no
longer subject to the *magister juvenum*, and ready to start on his
active ministry of preaching. Before arriving at Fontenay he may
have gone home on leave, he may have been posted briefly to
another house, he may have made a tour of the province, but it is
certain that his years of formal instruction were behind him.
Wherever Rabelais received his first training, he was a fully
fledged Friar Minor of the Observance, and a priest, by the time
he wrote to Budé from Fontenay.

By a most happy chance the Franciscan sermons which have
survived are exactly relevant to this period of Rabelais's life, and
one can confidently assert that all but the last collection were
included in the library at Fontenay. Olivier Maillard[1] died in 1502
after a long and distinguished career, and there were several
editions of his sermons. In 1518 his body was ceremoniously
transferred to the Franciscan church in Toulouse as a mark of
respect, and his prestige was never so high as at that time, when
he seems to have enjoyed, at least locally, the cult of a Beatus.
Michel Menot[2] preached Lents at Tours in 1508, and in Paris

[1] Maillard was born c.1430, probably near Nantes, where he apparently began his
preaching career with a Lent c.1460. He held the office of Vicar-General of the
Ultramontane family of the Observants (second only to the Minister-General of
the whole order in Rome) for the maximum permitted tenure of three trienniates,
and in the course of his duties visited the Low Countries, Germany and Spain.
He quarrelled several times with Louis XII, and in 1500 was briefly exiled, but
welcomed at Bruges by the Emperor. He was bitterly disappointed by his failure
to reform the Paris house (see next chapter), but was actively preaching to the last
when he died at Toulouse. He is reckoned to have composed well over five hundred
sermons, of which four main editions survive. See A. de la Borderie, *Œuvres
Françaises d'O. Maillard.*

[2] There are some indications that he was born in Beauce, and he tells us he studied
at Orleans. Reminiscences of Louis XI at Arras (1477–9) and of his funeral (1483)
are the only clue to his age. In 1496 he gave a Lent at Amiens, and from his sermons
there are hints that he may have visited Provence and Italy. Appointed Guardian
of the dilapidated house at Chartres in 1514, he rebuilt the convent and found time
to give two Lents in Paris, but died soon after the second series and was buried in
his own church. See J. Nève, *Sermons Choisis de M. Menot.*

in 1517 and 1518, in which year he died. He had been Guardian of Chartres since 1514, and died at the height of his fame. The first of several editions of his sermons appeared in 1519.

Again in 1518, a true *annus mirabilis* for the Franciscans, the sermons of Antoine Farinier[1] on the seven deadly sins were published at Lyons, though he had been dead for many years. The last of the preachers, Robert Messier,[2] did not publish his sermons until 1531, so Rabelais cannot have known them in print at Fontenay, but as Messier was Guardian of the great Paris house from 1526 to 1529, during which time Rabelais is known to have been in Paris, he may have had Rabelais in his audience on occasion. In any case his sermons are particularly interesting, for they show that the preaching tradition continued unbroken right up to the time that *Pantagruel* was published, and probably later still.

The preachers are not all equally informative, largely because only twenty-one sermons survive of Farinier and one series of Messier, as against three of Menot and several of Maillard, but as far as possible the selection made here is representative, despite the temptation to quote extensively from Menot, whose modern editor has done all the hard work.

---

[1] Farinier (or Fradin) came from Villefranche in Beaujolais. Louis XI imprisoned him for over-bold preaching, and even when popular protests secured his release he was forbidden to preach again. Exiled in 1478, he distinguished himself at the siege of Rhodes in 1480, and seems to have died soon afterwards. F. de Sessevalle, *Hist. Générale de l'Ordre de S. François*, vol ii, ch. vii, p. 128 seq.

[2] Messier preached a Lent at Amiens in 1497, the year after Menot, and again in 1503 and 1517. As Guardian of Amiens he was charged in 1503 with another friar by the Minister-General with the task of reforming houses in the province of France (i.e. Northern France) and next year was appointed Guardian of Troyes. In 1523 he was elected Minister-Provincial of the province of France, in 1526 to the great house in Paris, an even more exalted post, and in 1529 Provincial again. In 1535 he was Custos of Vermandois (i.e. with jurisdiction over several houses forming a sub-division of the province called a custody). He died in 1546, confessor to the Clarisses at Longchamps, where Isabelle de France was buried, and made himself active in his later years in promoting her cause for canonization. See *AFH* iii, p. 535, viii, p. 145, xxxvii, p. 30.

2 : THE FRANCISCAN PICTURE

THOUGH other orders, notably the Benedictines, have in the course of time produced more offshoots, and have allowed a greater measure of autonomy to individual houses, none has shown a greater internal disunity than the Franciscans.[1] The genesis of the order is in itself partly responsible for this; St. Francis was not merely an unlearned man, he distrusted study and even forbade it to his followers. Before he was dead this negative attitude had already been challenged and modified within the order; the rapid expansion of universities in the thirteenth century and the example of the Dominicans together forced the issue. From then on the Friars Minor shared with the Friars Preachers a leading, and often decisive, position in the intellectual world, but there was always latent or overt opposition to this breach of the founder's prescriptions and many saw in humble ignorance a surer way to salvation than the arguments of the schools.

Coupled with this fundamental split on the question of learning was an equally fundamental disagreement over poverty. So much depended on this rule that from the first the orders of friars had been called Mendicants, to distinguish them from the older orders of monks who grew up within the feudal system and enjoyed fixed revenues based on possession of property, that is land and feudal dues in kind. However the increasing complexity of urban life, where from the first the Mendicants found their sphere of action, and the needs of administration and discipline within a loosely knit order scattered in small communities throughout Europe (and even in Asia and Africa) forced the issue again. Various forms of property tenure were accepted, and progressive deviations from the strict rule of no possessions soon led to the inevitable abuses connected with religious ownership.

---

[1] A convenient, though rather superficial, account of the order from its foundation until the sixteenth century is by Sessevalle, *Hist. Générale de l'Ordre de S. Francais* A much more incisive description is in M. D. Knowles, *Religious Orders in England,* especially the brilliant last volume, (iii), where in a few pages he sketches (pp. 10–13) the origins and character of the Observants, and in the chapter on their suppression (pp. 206–11) gives so vivid a picture of them in action that, though it applies primarily to English friars, it could be transposed almost complete to fit the French. Professor Knowles indeed makes the point that these English Observants came nearest to the Catholicism of Latin countries.

The opposition to this development was still more bitter, and persists to some extent even today.

These two persistent conflicts within the order were accentuated from time to time, as in the unhappy affair of the Spirituals, so that it is fair to say that the Franciscan body was never free from internal strain and stress, and that on every plane and every question opinions were divided, often sharply. At worst this led to open conflict, at best to a peculiarly elusive spirit compounded of tendencies which sought to be complementary when really they were contradictory. The effective result of these tensions could lie anywhere between the extremes of sanctity and depravity.

This permanent disunity within the order was complicated by a variety of factors during the period 1500–18, at which time Rabelais was making his first acquaintance with the religious life. On the purely doctrinal level the conflict between the more conservative partisans of Scotus and those who preferred the nominalism of Ockham had led to bitter disputes of a highly technical nature, involving the clash of personalities and parties which every academic argument provokes.[1] Though Bonaventura and Scotus stand at opposite poles in temperament and approach, the spirituality of the one and the subtlety of the other had been adopted throughout the order as complementary aspects of a single truth. The same could not be said for Ockham, even if he claimed to be expounding the same truth as Scotus, since the implications of his teaching proved excessively formal in practice and assorted ill with the older tradition. Though nominalism had long been officially prohibited in the schools of Paris, the Scotists had not made much of their monopoly, and by 1518 the most lively aspect of Franciscan teaching was the disagreement between rival schools of thought.

This particular dispute primarily affected university circles, which meant in effect the very small minority of Franciscans connected by past or present ties with the great house at Paris, but its repercussions must have been felt more distantly throughout the order. A far more serious dispute, in which the Paris house played a leading part, was that waged between the reforming group, who wished to impose the strict observance, in other words the return to the ideals of the founder (hence their name Observants), and the more easygoing old guard, known as

[1] For the doctrinal issues see Renaudet, *Pré-Réforme et Humanisme*, passim.

Conventuals. The position of the Paris house[1] in university and capital was from the first a threat to discipline, and attempts to reform it met with the most determined and picturesque opposition. A contemporary chronicler has left a graphic account.

In 1502 Olivier Maillard, Vicar-General of the Ultramontane branch of the Observants for the third time, attempted to introduce fifty friars of good character into the Paris house as a nucleus of reform. The community refused to submit, and on the orders of Georges d'Amboise, Cardinal Legate, two bishops paid a solemn visit to the convent to enforce the reform. At news of their coming the friars exposed the Sacrament on the altar and began to sing their office: 'Domine non secundum peccata nostra facias nobis,' and as the bishops entered 'Adjuva nos, Deus salutaris noster.' At every attempt that the bishops made to speak a new chant began, and after four hours of this liturgical filibuster, they withdrew in defeat.

Next day the bishops reappeared, accompanied this time by a royal official with a hundred archers in reserve. The performance of the previous day was prudently not repeated in view of the archers, and the bishops were finally able to read out the orders laying down the reforms to be applied. A house containing so many doctors of theology and canon law was not so easily nonplussed: 'Ils deffendoient leur querelle en montrant titres, règles, auttorités, raisons et examples et firent apporter en leur chapitre les Decretales et Clementines, dispenses et privilèges, et tous les droicts dont aider se purent.' Still more ingenious, they protested that while they were ready to accept a higher standard of religious life, they preferred apostasy to a reform executed by Maillard and his companions, whom they hated. In the end they won, and though a commission was nominally set up to reform them, Maillard withdrew, and in fact died only three months later with his design frustrated.

If this episode shows vividly the bitterness of feeling en-

[1] The Paris house, reported by Pellikan to number some three hundred and fifty in 1516, came directly under the Minister-General of the whole order. After the changes of 1517 the Guardian ranked as a Minister Provincial, and was provided in turn by the three French reformed provinces (i.e. France, Touraine-Pictavienne, and Bourgogne). The events of 1502 are described by Jean d'Auton, *Chroniques de Louis XII*, quoted by A. de Sérent in *France Franciscaine*, iii, 1914–20, p. 342; see also Renaudet, op. cit. pp. 331 seq. and p. 688. Similar incidents, often involving violence, are described at length in I. de la Tour, *Origines de la Réforme*, vol. ii, Book ii.

gendered by religious questions (and the Franciscans were by no means alone in having such incidents) it also illustrates a fact of great significance for the appreciation of Rabelais's background; the tone of high farce in which some of the most momentous historical events were played out. The monks of Seuillé (*Garg./* xxvii) and the friars of Paris use the same weapon of plainchant at a distance of thirty years. This struggle between Observants and Conventuals affected the whole order, and was working up to a climax of bitterness during Rabelais's youth.

Besides these domestic quarrels the order, through its preachers, was incessantly engaged in campaigns against every kind of abuse, social, moral and religious. The constitution of the Mendicants permitted them at once greater freedom of movement and a wider audience than either the monks, who had never been primarily preachers since before 1200, or the parish clergy, unfitted by talent or inclination for effective work in the pulpit. As a result, the recorded sermons of the friars offer a picture of local and contemporary conditions throughout Christendom which is both critical and detailed.[1] The financial independence of men who by their vow of poverty had nothing to lose, and their virtual autonomy within the Church, allowed them to be as outspoken as they pleased. By 1500 the Franciscans in particular had long established a reputation for commenting pungently and disrespectfully on any class of society, or any abuse, which seemed to deserve criticism.

This policy in an age when no attack was answered by simply turning the other cheek led to some drastic reprisals. Maillard's disapproval of royal policy over Cerdagne and Roussillon, and still more of Louis XII's divorce from Jeanne de Valois, led to his exile.[2] One of his best known sermons, preached in Bruges on Passion Sunday 1500 before the Imperial Court, shows that exile from France did not deter him from making similar criticisms of the Empire. One of Maillard's predecessors, Antoine Farinier (or Fradin) incurred the displeasure of Louis XI, and despite popular riots in his favour was exiled in 1478, being lucky to escape with his life. Ten years later Erasmus's friend, Jean Vitrier, then Guardian of Saint-Omer, found himself censured by the Sorbonne

---

[1] Owst and Knowles both give a good idea of the situation in England which, *mutatis mutandis,* is largely applicable to that obtaining in France in the Middle Ages.
[2] The following three examples are discussed in Sessevalle, op. cit. vol. ii, ch. vii.

for bold preaching at Tournai. Many more examples of official disapproval of Franciscan preachers could be cited, and it is no accident that many of the most active recruits to the cause of Reform came from the ranks of the Mendicants, though, of course, they also supplied some of the most effective opposition to the new heresy. From protest to Protestant is a fatally easy step. Kings and prelates, even Popes, had learned over the centuries that Franciscan preachers were no respecters of persons. Though no individual Franciscan ever achieved the notoriety of the Dominican Savonarola, as an order the Friars Minor were probably without rivals for consistent indocility. This tradition of independence in the face of authority and even danger would be learned by every member of the order, though it would hardly have figured in official teaching.

After 1518 all these tendencies took a slightly different direction.[1] Luther's Ninety-Five Theses appeared in the same year as the decisive General Chapter of the whole order finally convened in Rome by the Pope in 1517, and though the two events were unconnected their consequences could not for long remain separate. As a result of this Chapter the constitutions of the order were changed so that the feud between Observants and Conventuals was, if not healed, at least regulated. The autonomy of the two branches (to which the Capuchins were added as a third a decade later) persists to this day. By the new constitutions the Observants were divided (as before) into Cis- and Ultramontane families or branches, which would alternate in providing a Minister-General for six years, the Cismontanes to start. The head of the family not currently supplying the Minister-General was known as Commissarius-General. The French houses were divided between the Observants and Conventuals, and new provinces designated, so that the former Observant province of Touraine became Touraine-Pictavienne to distinguish it from the Conventual province of Touraine, and in certain towns where each branch had a house amalgamation was ordered (not always with satisfactory results.)

By the time we know Rabelais to have reached Fontenay the most important effects of this reorganization within the order

---

[1] The fullest account of these events is in Wadding, *Annales Minorum*, vol. xvi, under the appropriate years. He not only provides the documents but some revealing judgements as well.

were being manifested. In 1520 the General Chapter of the Observants was held at Bordeaux under the second Minister-General, an Italian, Franciscus Lychetus (Lychetti)—the first had been promoted cardinal and had to resign office after a few months. From Bordeaux he went via Poitiers to Paris, and it is not inconceivable that he may have made the detour to Fontenay on his way. In Paris Lychetus took steps to restore discipline both of life and learning (this was a perennial need). We are told that he laid down strict rules of study and conduct, and directly ordered the students in theology to read only the text of Scotus and commentaries upon it which most faithfully interpreted his thought.[1] This meant, it appears, his own unfinished commentary on Scotus, and dealt an official blow against the Nominalists.

In the course of an energetic tour of France, Germany and Austria Lychetus deposed as many as seventy superiors, but before his work could be consolidated he died the same year at Buda. His epitaph[2] describes him as 'a most learned and devout man, but not used to administration, and thus not enjoying universal approbation', and adds that one of his special worries was caused by those over-zealous reformers of the Observants who found the former Conventual houses awarded to them by the new settlement too luxurious, and who consequently took unauthorized steps towards what they regarded as a more Franciscan way of life by disposing of surplus property. This detail gives some insight into the sort of dispute likely to be provoked by the changes.

Next year, 1521, another Italian, Paulus Soncinas, became Minister-General, with a Spaniard, Franciscus ab Angelis Quiñones, as Commissarius-General of the Ultramontanes. Only four years after Luther's revolt the Franciscan authorities showed themselves very sensitive to the danger, and the most energetic measures were taken to combat heresy, notably by the German Franciscan, Thomas Murner, one of Luther's most redoubtable adversaries. This double assault on heresy and intellectual devi-

---

[1] 'In conventu Parisiensi multa ordinavit circa studia ac regimen studentium, ac lecturam textus Scoti, cuius doctrinae erat peritissimus ac fidelis interpres: "Mando etiam quod studentes in theologia tantum se occupent in lectionibus Scoti, et commentariis eiusdem quae precise sunt ad mentem ipsius."' He had himself written a commentary on the first three books of the *Sentences.* Wadding, op. cit., p. 120.

[2] 'Doctissimus et religiosus, sed in regimine inexpertus, neque adeo a plerisque probatus.' Ibid., p. 121.

ation, with strict orthodoxy and Scotism as the only permitted line, was accompanied in France by an event of no less importance. In 1521, at the request of François I, two friars, Jean Morlin and Alexandre Rosseti, were named 'Commissarii Apostolici ad reducendos omnes Conventuales ad modum vivendi Observantium'. The final reform of all the French Conventual houses[1] took some time to accomplish, but the last phase under royal patronage can have done nothing to improve internal relations within the order, in which unwilling recruits were constantly being absorbed into the Observants. When in 1523 Quiñones succeeded as Minister-General he was able to ensure continuity of this stricter policy.

It will be seen that Rabelais's time as a Franciscan fell wholly within the period which culminated in these drastic reforms, and that his period at Fontenay coincides with the most vigorous phase of all. In the light of what has just been said it is especially significant that Rabelais should have chosen an Observant house in the first place, and his choice makes it much easier to reconstruct the atmosphere in which he lived than if he had gone into the laxer Conventuals.

A corrective must be added to this rather bleak picture of squabbles and Scotism. St. Francis had specifically allowed for foreign missions in his rule, and had set the example by his own visit to the Holy Land, and from the beginning of the sixteenth century the annals of the order pay more and more attention to missionary activities. The discoveries in the New World, and those in the Far East, offered an opportunity for mass conversion which the Church seized with vigour, using the friars as the special apostles of the faith. Since the new lands were mostly claimed by Spain and Portugal, except for those Asiatic realms too strong for colonial treatment, most of the missionaries came from Iberia, but the intense activity in these distant and fabulous lands cannot have failed to stir the imagination of every Franciscan who knew what was going on.

Besides the stimulus of these travellers' tales the order was not so barren of good learning as the humanists were wont to claim. Vitrier, Erasmus's friend already mentioned, was a notable

---

[1] The Conventuals of the province of France were in fact never brought under the Observance, but the position is exceedingly complicated. See H. Lippens, OFM, 'De Observantia in Prov. Franciae,' in *AFH*, xxxvii, 1944, p. 3.

scholar. So was another friend of Erasmus, Conrad Pellikan, sometime Guardian of the Basle house in which Amy died and a Hebraist of note. Budé's own testimony in his letter to Rabelais[1] that his news comes from 'one of the more civilized members of the order' proves that all friars were not as ignorant and reactionary as those who confiscated the books and censured Erasmus. The special interest of the Franciscans in the great Complutensian Bible of Ximenes reminds us that Erasmus was not alone in bringing new light to the task of exegesis. It would certainly be a mistake to suppose that any perceptible degree of humanist enlightenment was officially encouraged by Rabelais's superiors, but to keep a sense of perspective one should imagine a background less crudely obscurantist than Rabelais's own 'tenèbres des Gothz' might suggest.

This picture gives some idea of the turbulence which characterized the Franciscans at this time; with internal struggles to put their house in order, campaigns against external abuse, missions to far countries, the friars offered a restless and even adventurous prospect to the young novice. The history of the Observant house at Greenwich[2] shows that the reforming ideal of such men as Maillard could be realized with the most inspiring results. Just because the superiors at Fontenay repressed Greek study and heresy with an equally heavy hand there is not the slightest reason to suppose that the religious spirit was any less lively there than at Maillezais[3] where, from such evidence as we have, amiable torpor had long prevailed. The idle, ignorant, venal, lecherous Cordeliers of popular legend are a part of the Franciscan image which cannot be dismissed as pure invention, but the Observants were doing their best to replace the image by something closer to the model of their founder. What they stood for can be seen most clearly in the sermons through which above all they exercised their active ministry.

---

[1] See note 4, page 5.
[2] See note 1, page 11.
[3] See abbé Lacurie, *Histoire de l'Abbaye de Maillezais*.

3 : CRITICISM OF THE LAITY AND THEIR RELIGION

IN 1531 there appeared in Paris a collection of Lenten sermons by one Robert Messier, sometime Minister Provincial of the Observants in Northern France. It seems likely that this series had been heard in Paris, or elsewhere, at some time during the previous ten years, when Messier first made a name for himself in the capital. By the time the sermons were published the German Reformers had sympathizers all over France, Rabelais, Calvin and Loyola, each in his own way the herald of a new age, had all passed through the University of Paris and the beginnings of the Collège de France were receiving royal encouragement, but the sermons of Messier give no hint of new things, and except in style differ hardly at all from those of his brethren Menot and Maillard, two, and even three, generations back. The preachers at least knew no 'great divide'.

Next year, 1532, at Lyons, there was published anonymously a little book offering the story of Pantagruel, whose father Gargantua had been the eponymous hero of a recent best-seller. The *Grandes Chroniques de Gargantua*, and this their sequel, had an ancestry at least as old as that of Messier's sermons, and again the voice of the past is rarely interrupted by any newer tone, though decisively when it is. In the old tradition, Rabelais addressed his first literary venture in popular style to 'très illustres et très chevalereux champions, gentilzhommes et aultres.' Two years later his own version of the father's story, *Gargantua*, adopts a more familiar tone: 'Beuveurs très illustres, et vous verolez très precieux.'

It is not just idle speculation to wonder how many of those who heard or read Messier's sermons (perhaps Rabelais among them) helped to make the *Grandes Chroniques* so successful a few months later. The preachers often refer to the reading habits of their audience in terms which strongly suggest that substantially the same public is concerned in each case. To some extent they were consciously competing with such popular authors as Rabelais. In considering some of the things they have to say about the religious life of the laity one needs first to ask how the preachers conceived their task and the nature of their audience, and then what kind of religious discipline, sacramental and otherwise, they recommended to the laity. Charges of laxity and abuse are mainly interesting for the light they throw on what people were accustomed to hear. It is clear that any popular work will keep fairly closely to familiar ground in its social or religious allusions, which might otherwise be missed, and for this reason the teaching and chiding of the sermons are both directly relevant to Rabelais's primary aim of getting the public on his side.

References to the congregation are so uniform in all the preachers, regardless of time or place, that the words of one may safely be applied to all. Menot begins his Lent at Tours with the words: 'Honorable et à mon semblant devot auditoire' but, like Rabelais, once he is sure of his audience he tends to be less complimentary. One important difference between the composition of sermon audience and reading public is graphically described in Menot's sermon on Laetare Sunday, which interprets the feeding of the five thousand in contemporary style. Whereas Rabelais addresses himself to his male readers, who will pass on the tale to their ladies, Menot's remarks explain why the women in the audience are so much more frequently addressed than the men. According to him (P/416) the number fed, 'sans les femmes et les petitz enfans', was far above five thousand, for experience showed him that for every man at a sermon there were always four women. He thinks too that there must have been a throng of children, if the women of Palestine were anything like those of Tours, who only come to hear sermons when they have a child hanging at their breast and a crowd of small children at their heels ('post caudam'), who never stop howling throughout the sermon, to the annoyance of preacher and congregation.

This vivid picture of noisy and numerous children is no doubt equally applicable to most public assemblies of the time, and illustrates the practical difficulties the preachers had to face. Despite such difficulties, however, Farinier condemns those so dead in spirit, or so weary, that they find a sermon which lasts more than an hour too much for them.[1] There is no other internal reference to the length of sermons, but this, from a sermon on 'Tepiditas',

---

[1] 'De auditione verbi dei quid dicam? Quia videntur esse mortui vel ita attediati quod unus sermo unius horae durat eis multum.' (19 v.)

certainly suggests that the preachers would have liked to go on for more than an hour. The standard expected by the preachers was not a comfortable one but it must be seen in the context of the time. For instance, Menot condemns (P/242) 'domina burgensis' who is in bed at 8 a.m. when the bells are ringing for the sermon, and is found still there by neighbours returning from their morning duties. Rabelais too felt strongly about sloth, condemning the old regime under which Gargantua 's'esveilloit entre huict et neuf heures' (*Garg.*/ XXI) and making him get up at 4 a.m. under his new masters (*Garg.*/XXIII).

Even when people did come to sermons it was not always for good reasons, and Menot asks (T/26) his female hearers if they do not go just to see 'le maintien du prescheur' and whether he would say something they might 'tourner en gaudisserie'. He refers to the fact that the sermon was often, especially in Lent, given in two parts, the second coming after the midday meal. As he says, many no doubt came along out of curiosity; after dinner, when they have eaten and drunk their fill they say 'Let's go to hear that preacher so that we can have a bit of amusement'.[1] Gargantua offers another example of the habit of going out for afternoon entertainment, for when bad weather prevents exercise he goes out after dinner: 'ouir les leçons publiques, les actes solennels, les repetitions, les declamations, les concions des prescheurs evangeliques,' all put in the same programme and on the same plane as the visits to craftsmen, apothecaries and street entertainers (*Garg.*/ XXIV).

While there is ample evidence that the sermons satisfied, not always intentionally, the desire for entertainment, there is also a grimmer side to the picture of the preachers' reception. Both Maillard and Farinier had personal experience of the reprisals a preacher might expect if he offended those in power, but it is Menot who expresses most bluntly the occupational risks of his calling. When fervent preachers take truth into the pulpit with them, he says (P/435): 'on les menasse de les mener fieri cardinales, faire cardinaulx sans aller à Romme et de leur faire porter le chapeau ruge.' Frère Jan, escaping from his captors uses the

---

[1] 'Sic certe multi hodie veniunt ad sermonem tantum curiose. Postquam fecerunt prandium et quod sunt saturati et repleti, dicunt: Eamus ad audiendum illum praedicatorem, ut audiamus aliquid quod nos laetificet.' (P/421)

same gallows-jest: 'Je vous feray icy cardinal . . . vous aurez un chapeau rouge à ceste heure de ma main.' (*Garg.*/XLIV.)

For Menot it is so important that the layfolk should attend sermons that without them he says (T/26) they would be worse than infidels and Saracens, even devils, and this is a serious matter. Preaching is not intended for entertainment like a player's flute ('fistula histrionis') but must be rough and harsh in denouncing vice;[1] the preacher's tongue must be like the barber's lancet (P/267). This spiritual surgery was not to everyone's taste. According to medieval belief the toad swells up when it smells the vine-flower, so, says Menot (T/32), the 'gros godons', poisonous and swollen with sin, croak in protest when they are exposed to the sweet odour of truth from the pulpit.

This all shows that the preachers were competing for attention with popular entertainers and sometimes stooped to use the same methods, but those who took their vocation seriously scorned all considerations of personal prestige or material advantage. As ever Menot is forthright (P/299) in condemning great preachers who use their talents for the sake of worldly honours, or for the collection, and not for the salvation of souls and glory of God. Their time will come, though, and when on Judgement Day they ask God for their reward they will be told: 'Verily I say unto you you have received your reward.' (cf. Matt. vi.2).

Sacraments

To think of sacramental discipline in post-Tridentine terms is to invite anachronism when dealing with these critical years of the early sixteenth century. Although Messier actually lived to see the opening of the Council of Trent, he, and all the others, are much closer in spirit to the Lateran Council of 1215, which continued to set the norm of practice until the forces of the Counter-Reformation came fully into play. One should, therefore, not compare our preachers with those of the Counter-Reformation but rather with those whose inertia and laxity had helped to provoke the Reformation. In this respect the Franciscans lead, rather than follow, con-

---

[1] 'Sancta praedicatio non est ut fistula histrionis, quae non est facta nisi ut homines recreet, ut hodie dicunt mundani . . . Sed debet esse rudis et aspera in reprehendendo vitia.' (P/229)

temporary opinion, both in their practical exhortations and their doctrinal exposition.

Sermons are not catechisms, but it is a little strange that while so many points of doctrine and practice, elementary as well as erudite, are discussed in the sermons, there should be a single instance of all seven sacraments mentioned together, and another in which five of them occur. For the rest there are countless references to every aspect of Penance, many fewer on the Eucharist, passing mention of Baptism and Unction, a bare word on Ordination and nothing on Confirmation (except one legal reference) or Matrimony as a sacrament, though the married state frequently comes up for discussion.

The most detailed reference comes from a sermon by Maillard 'De Justitia', delivered after Easter as a pendant to his Lenten series.[1] He says that there are only seven sacraments, not all of which are necessary for salvation, for Matrimony and Orders are not received by everyone. Baptism after original sin and Penance after mortal sin are necessary always, but apart from these the other sacraments are not necessary, or if they are, are 'satis facilia'; that is, Confirmation, Eucharist, Extreme Unction. The second reference comes also from Maillard (s/121) and consists of the briefest catalogue of sacraments as means of grace, this time omitting, perhaps accidentally, Matrimony and Unction.

As far as Baptism was concerned there was no need of exhortation. Everyone accepted that the sacrament was essential, and in an age when registration of births was unknown Baptism was probably the only formal event which the life of every person would be bound to include. The status of Confirmation, on the other hand, was not very clearly defined, and in some places it seems to have been a matter of chance whether the sacrament was ever conferred at all. This was perhaps not the case in France, but the sermons do not suggest that parents, or godparents, or indeed anyone else, should encourage or prepare children to be confirmed. The only reference seems to be a quite incidental remark by Farinier (40), who after denouncing the horrors of

---

[1] 'Non enim habet nisi septem sacramenta; quae etiam omnia non sunt christianis necessaria; quare non omnes recipiunt matrimonium nec ordines. Baptismus autem post peccatum originale et Penitentia post peccatum mortale sunt necessaria. Alia autem sacramenta a baptismo et penitentia non semper sunt necessaria; aut si sunt necessaria sunt satis facilia; puta confirmatio, eucharistia, extrema unctio &c.' (Q/221)

physical incest goes on still more violently to condemn what he calls spiritual incest, that is a union between a person and his godparent or sponsor at Confirmation. The reason for the prohibition was, of course, spiritual in origin, but Farinier seems to have a purely legal interest in the subject.

Extreme Unction is another sacrament which is virtually ignored. Deathbed scenes are described quite often, but in every case the emphasis is on the need for a full confession, and nothing is said of the last rites. Thus Maillard sternly warns doctors not to lay a hand on a patient until he has made his confession.[1] According to him, their practice is not to urge a patient to confess lest he should despair of recovery, but once he is so stricken that he can scarcely speak or even breathe they recommend confession and holy water. Such a confession Maillard finds almost worthless, for the sick man has almost lost the power of reason, and this explains his insistence on the need for spiritual before physical ministrations.

Perhaps this is what Rabelais was thinking of when he made Frère Jan exclaim: 'Vous me semblez les prescheurs decretalistes qui disent que quiconques voyra son prochain en dangier de mort il le doibt, sus peine d'excommunication trisulce, plustout admonester de soy confesser et mettre en estat de grace que de luy ayder.' (*Garg.*/XLII.)

These examples bear out Maillard's distinction between Penance, for an adult always necessary to salvation, and the other sacraments, which even when necessary are 'satis facilia'. It has always been true that no Catholic should communicate in a state of mortal sin, and that a good confession removes any obstacle to Communion, which may in that respect be called 'satis facile', but in modern times, and really since Trent, Communion has played an ever increasing role in the life of the laity. Since nearly all our sermons belong to the penitential seasons of Advent and Lent it is only to be expected that sin and confession should be stressed, but it might also be expected that the approach of

---

[1] 'Domini medici, vobis loquor. Cum accedetis ad aegrotum non debetis apponere manum nisi primo fuerit confessus et contritus . . . Sed forte dicetis: Pater, practica est talis quod numquam persuademus confessionem ne forte infirmus dubitet de morte. Sed quamprimum videmus quod infirmus est afflictus adeo quod non potest loqui nec emittere anhelitum; tunc dicimus quod oportet habere confessorem et aquam benedictam . . . O Deus meus, haec confessio penitus nulla est. Tunc enim infirmus paene usum rationis perdidit.' (Q/125 v.)

Christmas or Easter would prompt some reflections on the Eucharist and Communion in which all would (or should) share. There is no question of doctrinal innovation; Corpus Christi had been kept as a great feast for centuries, veneration for the Blessed Sacrament was universal, and the obligation to attend Mass on Sundays and holidays was, so far as we know, observed by the vast majority of people. As far as Communion is concerned, however, the injunctions of the Lateran Council to confess and communicate in one's parish church at Easter seem to have been everywhere obeyed as a sufficient, not a minimum, requirement. Thus to stress the need for confession without any compensating emphasis on Communion entails the most profound devotional implications, as the Council of Trent was not slow to recognize. The sermons give some idea of the pastoral consequences of this lack of balance, and it should be noted that they have as little to say about the communion of the laity as about the eucharistic significance of the Mass. Once again it is with discipline, not sacramental devotion, that they are concerned.

Time after time the preachers complain that the one obligatory confession a year is not enough, and they even suggest that some people found this too much. One tale describes how a soldier who has not kept his fast is told that he should confess his sin:[1] 'Oh, what is confession? and what have I done?' Menot comments: 'Ecce incredulitas.'

Maillard three times quotes Gerson, the great fifteenth-century churchman, in support of his own view that confession should be more frequent and conscientious, and that Communion should be received only after the most thorough preparation. A man once told Gerson (A/17) that even daily confession did not keep him pure from sin. Again, according to Gerson (Q/139), a priest would need a whole day to hear one man's confession properly, and if there were not sufficient time before Easter, the penitent should wait until St. John's Day (23 June) before receiving the Lord's body. He says too (A/75) that if he were a parish priest he would rather keep a parishioner waiting for absolution from one year's end to the other and thus make sure of a good confession, even though it meant missing Communion, than expedite him as so many clergy do. The emphasis on the solemnity of Communion

---

[1] 'Veniet ung gendarmeau, et dicetur ei; Tu non jejunasti; oportet confiteri— O et quid est de se confesser? et quid feci? (T/65)

is normal, and so is the insistence on the need for confession as preparation, but somehow the preparation seems to receive so much attention that the means becomes an end in itself.

Observations on the perfunctory discharge of pastoral duties by parish clergy are typical in the sermons of the friars' general attitude. Relations between Mendicants and secular clergy had seldom been cordial, and sometimes became exacerbated. It must be remembered though that most of the sermons discussed here, and many others like them, belong to what would now be called missions, and were preached by invitation not in conventual churches, but in great parish churches and cathedrals (e.g. Maillard at Saint-Jean de la Grève), where they were addressed as much to the secular clergy as to the laity. In fairness to the parish clergy one should not overlook the statistical side of their pastoral problem. Today, when even in Catholic countries the categories of *incroyants, croyants, pratiquants* are familiar, it is hard to visualize the sixteenth-century scene just before Easter, when every single man and woman, and even quite young children, had to discharge a whole year's burden of sin in the confessional, while others thronged impatiently in the queue, or else risk sanctions both social and religious which would effectively make him an outcast. Even though the proportion of clergy to laity may have been much higher then than now, and though the regular clergy lent a hand, it is obvious that in the time available the pastoral burden must have been overwhelming. All this needs to be borne in mind when one considers the ordinary person's attitude to confession, and thus the context in which Rabelais's references to the subject were written and read.

Menot condemns both priest and penitent, using sometimes irony; 'You see, for blaspheming against God, for bearing false witness, c'est tout ung. By having Father John to dinner you can go to confession and come away as clean as if you had just had your tunic washed,'[1] and sometimes threats: 'Messieurs, you who go to confession once a year and stick to the rule of the canon "Omnis utriusque sexus" (ii/887), you come to your priest with a great *mea culpa* and say: "Father, I confess all these my sins and all those which I have now forgotten—Why forgotten?—Father,

---

[1] 'Ecce, pro blasphemando Deum, pro dicendo falsum testimonium, c'est tout ung. Habendo dom. Johannem et dando sibi prandium, confiteris, et inde recedis ita mundus sicuti si primo posuisses tunicam in lixivio.' (T/156)

I haven't been to confession this year, so I can't remember half
my sins."—What a great abuse!'
'Then there is the priest who only wants to get it over and
pocket his fee. He sends you off straight away, and absolves you,
saying "Go my friend".—And where will he go with an absolution like that? To all the devils, and there he will keep a place
for his confessor.'[1]

Menot accuses both priest and penitent of negligence and urges
more frequent confession as the only remedy.

'You go a whole year without confession and at the end of the
year spend four hours in the box and still can't remember everything . . . you keep back a lot of things and only confess what you
want the priest to know . . . In my view it is impossible that a
person who has not been to confession for half a year should be
safe . . . You are blind, the priest is negligent et n'en demande que
la depesche.'[2]

'Are there some of you here who have decided to confess on
Easter Eve and communicate next day? To fast next year and not
this one? Car ceste caresme est trop fascheuse.'[3]

Maillard and Menot both give examples showing the need for
real amendment and not mere formal regrets followed by relapse.

Speak up you men who keep concubines; three or four days before
Easter you put away your concubines and say to them 'Come back
three days after Easter'. Then you go to confession. To all the devils
with such a confession; it is not confession but mockery.[4]

---

[1] 'O Domini qui itis ad confessionem semel in anno et regulatis vos secundum
canonum: "Omnis utriusque sexus" (11/887) venitis ad sacerdotem et dicitis magnum
mea culpa, et dicitis: Pater confiteor de omnibus peccatis, tam de his etiam quae
dixi, quam de oblitis.—Cur de oblitis?—Pater, hoc anno non fui confessus; sic
non possum recordari mediam partem peccatorum meorum O magna abusio!'
'At ergo sacerdos ille qui non quaerit nisi expeditionem et pecuniam, expedit te
immediatae horae; dat tibi absolutionem, et dicit tibi: O, amice vade.—Et quo
ibit cum tale absolutione? Ad omnes diabolos, et confessori suo servabit locum.'
(P/257)
[2] Stabitis per annum sine confessione, et in fine anni eritis per iv horas à confesse,
et tamen omnium recordari non poteritis . . . multa retinebitis et non confitebimini
nisi quae velitis quod presbyter sciat . . . Volo dicere quod impossibile est quod
persona quae a medio anno non fuit confessa sit secura . . . Tu es caecus, presbyter
est negligens . . .' (T/135)
[3] 'Sunt ne in societate qui determinaverunt confiteri in vigilia Paschae et com-
municare sequenti die? jejunare anno futuro et non isto anno?' (T/35)
[4] 'Loquamini mihi vos concubinarii: per tres vel quattuor dies ante festum
Paschae mittetis concubinas vestras extra; et dicetis eis: Veniatis feria tertia post
Pascha: postmodum vaditis ad confessionem. Ad omnes diabolos confessio talis;
non est confessio, sed potius irrisio.' (Q/156 v.)

Take the case of a girl who has been led astray and has spent a whole year shut up with a priest, à pot et cuiller. Today she comes to confession. Do you mean to say that tomorrow she is to go off and sleep with a canon or some other priest and go on like that for the whole of her life? It would certainly be a serious heresy to say so.[1]

Maillard endorses the parochial obligation laid down by the Lateran Council, and reminds (Q/130 v.) his hearers that they are not allowed to receive the sacraments anywhere but in their own church except with the permission of their parish priest. He recalls that the Mendicants had won the right to shrive anyone, but says that it is only right (honestum) to attend divine service on great festivals in one's own church. The sermons certainly do not support the view sometimes advanced that confession to an unknown friar was a soft option compared to facing a parish priest who met you daily. The advantages of the parochial rule are illustrated neatly by an exemplum. Maillard tells the tale of a certain parish priest who has just heard a sermon on the lines of those quoted above, and so takes the lesson to heart that he refuses Communion on Easter Day to a known harlot. She protests that she has been properly shriven and exclaims: 'Why should I not receive my God just as well as the preachers and priests who celebrate Mass, go to confession and have their harlots every day? Which is the greater evil?—The priest was indeed a wise man and said to her: 'Madame, they are not under my jurisdiction.'[2]

The parish priest's knowledge of his flock gave him the responsibility for seeing that the sacrament was not administered to notorious sinners, but Menot reminds his hearers that the recipient too has an absolute responsibility not to 'eat and drink to his own damnation'. He tells the parish priest he must not give the sacrament to anyone he does not know and supposes a dialogue: 'Tu es une garce orguilleuse. Are you of this parish? . . . What is it publicly to give the body of Christ to a harlot? Believe me it is worse than handing Christ over to the gentiles to be crucified.'[3]

---

[1] Sit casus: Est filia seducta quae fuit per annum inclusa cum sacerdote, cum poto et cocleari, à pot et cuiller. Hodie venit ad confessionem. Vis dicere quod cras debet ire ad dormiendum cum canonico vel cum alio sacerdote et sic perseverare toto tempore vitae suae? Certe esset magna haeresis hoc dicere. (P/300)

[2] ' "Quare non recipio Deum meum ita bene sicut faciunt praedicatores et sacerdotes qui celebrant, confitentur et habent singulis diebus meretrices suas? Quod est majus malum?" Vero curatus erat sapiens et dixit illi: "Domina, illi non sunt in subjectione mea." ' (S/121)

[3] 'Es tu de ista parrochia? . . . Et dare publice corpus Christi publicae meretrici, quid est? Pejus, mihi credite quam Christum gentilibus crucifigendum tradere.' (T/171)

He speaks (T/215) of a man who fulfils his Easter duties outside his parish, because if he did it there he would have to take back his wife, whereas now he goes back to his mistress for another year. Some men and women, he says (T/171), will receive the sacrament on Easter Day in such a state that it might have been better for them if the devil had strangled them in front of everyone, and once again he addresses his words to adulterers, fornicators and procuresses.

Even when they are specifically talking of Communion the preachers have nothing to say of the spiritual joy awaiting the truly penitent recipient. Advent and Lent are seen not so much as seasons of preparation for the celebration of the Incarnation and Resurrection as preliminaries to the Last Judgement. Only one sermon, from the latest of the series discussed, gives any hint of a more positive attitude to Communion. Messier recalls (135 v.) that the early Christians took Communion together daily, that by St. Augustine's time Sunday Communion was normal, later still it became restricted to Christmas, Easter and Whitsun, and since 1215 to Easter alone. He comments that many people have become so negligent and hardened in evil will that they do not merely fail to communicate once a year, but go for years and years without Communion. This is a most grave charge, and would be of great importance if it could be proved, but unfortunately there are no other references in the sermons and without supporting evidence it would be imprudent to make too much of it. It is none the less significant that the only reference to more frequent Communion, independent of the context of more frequent confession, should come from the series preached after Luther's revolt.

Conduct

Besides these remarks on sacramental discipline the preachers have some interesting and sometimes strange things to say about the conduct of the laity in religious matters. They all deplore behaviour in church, sometimes in lurid terms. Farinier speaks (3) of men leaning on the altar, relics being bought and sold, dogs coming into church and falcons being actually brought in. He says that layfolk go into the choir even during the singing of the office, and that they do not go down on both knees even at the Elevation of the Host. Maillard accuses (f/104) young people of both sexes of damning themselves by lascivious and blasphemous behaviour in the very presence of their Saviour. In one sermon (f/127) he cries: 'O pescheur, meschant voleur, fils degeneré, tu as devant les yeux le gibet [la croix] où pend ton père et ton maistre et tu ris et tu plaisantes, et tu voys ès banquetz de 30,000 diables!' He has been (q/90) in Jewish and Ethiopian (Moslem?) temples and found there more reverence than in Christian churches. Menot says (p/426) that when people want a place to tell stories, strike bargains or make false promises they choose the church. All through Mass, he says (p/483), the jokers (*gaudissores*) never stop their noisy laughter, and keep walking about. He repeats Farinier's charge that they only bend one knee at the Elevation, and hardly bare their heads even then. The church is described inevitably as the resort of lovers and wantons. Against the background of such complaints Panurge's nasty tricks in churches seem less incredible (*Pant.*/xvi, xvii, xxi, xxii).

There are rather few positive prescriptions. Maillard attaches great importance to almsgiving, and assures (a/35 v.) his hearers that pious exercises alone will not earn them salvation unless they also give generously, but in general one has the impression that contributions to the Church in tithes, dues and so on were so exactly regulated by law and so numerous that the question of giving was treated with comparatively little urgency.

Private prayer is not a subject one would expect to find discussed very often in sermons, but there is one reference to it by Farinier (31 v.) of some interest. He describes what should be the standard practice (*ordinarium*) for the good Christian; immediately on rising, and when dressed (for people slept naked), he should kneel down, make the sign of the cross, say the Apostles' Creed, the Lord's Prayer, the Ave and commend himself to his guardian angel, and all this before going to Mass lest death might catch him unprepared on the way.

Menot has some pointed remarks about fasting and abstinence. To those who believe that a minor infraction of the fast does not matter, he retorts (t/36) that to cook and eat an apple is no light thing, for on account of a single apple thousands upon thousands have been damned who might otherwise have been saved. He has no use either for those who claim that their state of health prevents them from observing the fast, and who then abuse their dispensation:[1]

Tomorrow you will feel ill because you feasted this evening. You will be drunk this evening, and in the morning your head will be shaking and you will have to stick it en ung seau d'eau. You would have done well to abstain, you could have done it without risk, in fact to the advantage of your health. I say that you are sinning grievously.

The hangover is theological as well as physical.

It should not be thought that the preachers make no concessions to human frailty; in fact they were too experienced to make impossible demands. Maillard quotes (A/23 v.) the example of St. Louis, who gave up marital relations with his wife throughout Advent, and says that he does not expect his hearers to do as much, but if the saint could thus give up a legitimate act, how much the more should others give up their sins, which are not very creditable (*multum honesta*). Again in Advent he says he does not wish to lay too heavy a burden on them because the flesh is weak. He does not expect (A/38) them to wear a hairshirt throughout Advent, to fast on bread and water, to get up every day in the small hours for matins, he only asks them to serve God as they have hitherto served the devil. As usual the sting is in the tail, but it is interesting to see that Maillard expressly declares that it would not be reasonable to impose on ordinary folk the austerities laid down for members of religious orders in Advent (and Lent).

Some remarks on the apparently common preoccupation of some women with theology throw a curious sidelight on the religious life of the laity. On the whole the preachers do not approve and treat the women with some irony. Maillard invites (A/2 v.) them to lift up their hearts for he has heard they are 'semi-theologales'. There are some odd references (A/6 v., A/58 v., T/199) to French Bibles, and both Maillard and Menot condemn the women for having these as they have love stories and romances. This might possibly (but improbably) refer to those parodies of Scripture which were so popular in the Middle Ages, or might simply be disapproval of a literary fad which did not discriminate between the Bible and light reading, but there is some

---

[1] 'Cras te invenias lasche quia sero cenasti. Eris sero ebrius; mane caput tremet et oportet quod ponas caput en ung seau d'eau. Tu bene abstinuisses et sine periculo, immo cum majori sanitate. Dico quod graviter peccas.' (T/116)

evidence that the preachers found some women altogether too enthusiastic in their amateur study of theology.

Menot gives a very odd account of a woman who doubts whether one should buy eggs in Lent: 'Here are our ladies with a whole library of theology in French. Off they go to Carmelites and Augustinians and other convents and get advice all round, but don't do anything about it: y font tant de charivariz et courir les rues for a minor problem, in fact for nothing at all.'[1]

He continues with the extraordinary story of a woman who has taken a vow never to eat tongue, and who refuses Communion on her deathbed in literal fulfilment of her vow after a discussion with her priest on the full implications of the doctrine of Transubstantiation. Such perverse ingenuity can never have been common, but it must have been a sufficiently live issue to warrant comment from the pulpit.

One would like to know more about this theology in French, and there may well be something in it, for it was not very long before Marguerite of Navarre, as well as the Meaux group, was taking theology very seriously.

Common folk learned less from theological books than from the sermons in stones which had for centuries helped to instruct the illiterate. Menot justifies (T/213) the images of the Virgin and saints and says 'ce n'est pas pour adorer les pierres' but to recall the saints and their virtues.

It is appropriate to end on a more recognizably Franciscan note. Sympathy for the humble and meek had been a feature of the order from the days of the founder himself, and simple faith earned respect. Messier tells (88) of a confessor who asks a soldier during his confession if he knows the creed. The soldier says he does not. The confessor then asks him whether he would renounce God if in the course of war the enemy tried to compel him to do so. Again the soldier answers no. To this the confessor replies that he can see the man indeed knows his creed.

---

[1] 'Ecce nostrae dominae qui habent totam theologiam in gallico et librariam. Ecce ibunt ad Carmelitas et Augustinenses et ceteros conventus et tot habebunt consilia, et nihil facient de omnibus; y font tant de charivariz et courir les rues, pro modico, immo pro nihilo.' (T/157)

4: CRITICISM OF THE CLERGY AND THEIR RELIGION

WHAT has just been said about the religion of the laity, as represented in the sermons, gives some idea of the atmosphere in which Rabelais and his readers were brought up. The picture is admittedly one-sided, but one-sided in a way that suits the present purpose. Conduct and discipline can hardly be expected to qualify for praise in penitential sermons, but equally there would be no point in setting up a target for attack which bore no resemblance to reality. In terms of what religion meant to the ordinary layman, the sermons constantly exhort him to beat his breast rather than to lift up his heart. This may or may not have been what the layman needed; this is what he got. Presumably if the laity had followed the specific exhortations of the preachers they would have earned commendation, but it is questionable whether, in the view of the preachers, laymen had it in their power to amend their lives as instructed. Up to a point they obviously could do something about their shortcomings, by more regular and conscientious confession, by more reverent conduct in church and by a greater awareness of their Christian duty outside church. Even this brief list entails something beyond the unaided power of the laity, and brings us directly into contact with the preachers' main theme: the clergy.

Already in speaking of the sacraments we have seen how sharply negligent confessors are criticized, and it must now be emphasized that such criticism is very much more frequent and more vehement than attacks on the laity. Taking laymen to task is a natural part of the penitential preacher's brief, but in our period, whatever may have been the case at other times, this formed a quite secondary element in the friars' sermons. Only when Maillard has developed (A/89 v.) a long and scathing attack on clerical abuses does he preface a much milder assault with the words: 'veniamus ad laicos'. Statistics are not available, and might be dangerous if they were, and analogies, though tempting, could be misleading, but the facts speak for themselves. By their own logic the preachers could not blame the sheep for the negligence of the pastors, though the same wolf would eventually carry off both, and in seeking to improve the situation they concentrated on that smaller body of men on whom all the rest depended. By just the same logic, prelates, higher but fewer, are attacked even more vigorously than parsons. It is important to stress not only the attack but also the logic behind it, for this has had repercussions whose effect has not yet worn off. The attacks on prelates are on unworthy prelates, not on prelates as such, and formed a traditional part of Mendicant sermons throughout the later Middle Ages. The aim of such attacks was reform in the head and in the members, not decapitation or dismemberment, but the time came when drastic surgery seemed to some the only cure. By then the preachers had been overtaken by events.

From the first the friars had assumed the duty of castigating whatever evils or abuses seemed to threaten the health of the Church. In the course of their history they spared no one in the hierarchy of Church or State in whom they thought to find fault, and only the humble and meek remained secure from their attacks. Though this criticism sometimes brought down on them the strongest marks of official displeasure, often exile, sometimes death, it must be remembered that their right to criticize was not only never challenged as such, but was actively encouraged by their invitations to preach in great churches packed with distinguished congregations. The friars were largely independent of local hierarchies, though they could preach only with permission, and to that extent enjoyed greater freedom of expression than secular clergy, but as religious they were bound by the vow of obedience, so that a word from a superior within the order, let alone from the Pope, could restrain or even silence them. Such officially recognized and controlled criticism doubtless acted as an effective antidote against corruption, but at the same time the very strength of the medicine was a potential danger to a body which might one day be too enfeebled by decay. Ockham, Farinier, Maillard each fell foul of authority in his day, but up to the time of Luther the limits of permissible criticism were generally recognized and respected.

It is difficult, and in the state of present knowledge perhaps impossible, to chart the signposts of change in this matter of criticism, but some obvious stages can be noted. Throughout Rabelais's youth and up to the time of his ordination the wind of reform blew uninterruptedly in spiritual affairs, and his own Observant branch of the Franciscans played a leading part in word and deed. The Lutheran crisis coincided with Rabelais's post-ordination years, and also with the major crisis within the order. The drastic purge of officials which followed the re-organization of 1518 was designed to strengthen discipline but we know that it also exacerbated internal relations, and it is not unreasonable to assume that the effect on a young friar of Rabelais's temperament was unsettling. Outside the order, the inner logic of centuries of criticism was now being followed through by Luther. If the faults of the laity are largely due to the negligence of the clergy, especially the prelates, and if the ultimate source of authority is the Pope as head of the Church, and if he refuses to change things, or call a council which will, can a conscientious Christian stand passively by? Luther's solution, when all else failed, was decapitation. Thus at exactly the same moment the two main pillars of authority for a Franciscan had been shaken, by quite different agents and with quite different results, but in such a way as to call in question the basis of the right to criticize freely.

Lacking mass media of communication, ideas in the sixteenth century spread unevenly, and with a considerable time-lag, but even so, what was still possible (and actually done) in Messier's sermons of 1531 was not necessarily so in 1542, the year of the first definitive edition of Rabelais's first two books, when the Placards had been followed by Calvin's emergence and triumph, still less in 1552, when the full *Quart Livre* appeared in a world which can almost be called post-Tridentine. Ten years later still, when religious differences had flared up into war, Huguenot exploitation of Rabelais's posthumous last book shows how rapidly the shibboleths were changing. Effect is no longer a safe guide to intention, as can be seen from Estienne's polemical use of texts from our preachers; in half a century officially tolerated criticism of Catholics by Catholics had become a major weapon in the Protestant armoury.

We can be wise after the event, but such considerations as those just quoted must have been acutely hard to apply in contemporary practice. The preachers' comments which follow were certainly not meant as ammunition for heretics, though that is how they were eventually used, nor was Rabelais's training intended to make him the hammer of the papacy, though this is what he became. He was trained to utter criticisms of the kind reproduced here to an audience which expected to hear them, and no doubt continued to expect as much, long after Luther and Calvin had gone their own way. Past a certain age people tend to be conservative, and this sometimes leads to an anachronism that can be dangerous. One can see an example of this in the belated Erasmians of the 1540's, but in Rabelais's case at least one strongly formative influence preceded even that of Erasmus.

All the examples which follow are very similar in form and content, and it is clear from internal evidence that the sermons criticizing ecclesiastical abuses were delivered to a congregation which included clergy of all degrees. At an interval of ten years Maillard in Paris and Menot in Tours deplore the present state of the Church. Maillard, directly (Q/190 v.) addressing 'ecclesiastici', charges them with simony, lechery, hypocrisy and, worst of all, lack of devotion. Never were there so many priests and so little piety, so many books and so many ignorant, so many religious and so few who keep the rule. Menot uses (T/16) the same words to deplore the lack of devotion in the Church, and goes on to claim that while the Church has never before enjoyed such material prosperity the clergy have never before been more simoniacal.

Maillard cautiously condemns papal authorization of unnecessary indulgences, protesting his obedient submission to Pope, cardinals and prelates, while pointing out that even the Pope may err if wrongly advised.[1] Menot is a little more outspoken, but he too has very little to say about the Pope. In one rather entertaining story (T/67) he tells how a monk returned from the next world to report what he found in Hell. The actual words deserve quotation and recall Epistemon's similar report in *Pantagruel*: 'Ecclesia enim saepissime regitur per reprobos. Ecce, fuerunt multi papae, damnati ad omnes demones, episcopi, judices, consiliari et de toute telle maniere de billon.' Elsewhere Menot laments (P/294) the fact that not all Peter's successors are worthy, quoting the example of the heretical Pope Liberius, as well as others whose evil hearts are

---

[1] 'Nolo tamen revocare clavem ecclesiae, sed dico quod quando Papa et cardinales cognoscunt quod non est aliqua necessitas aut justa et rationabilis causa, non debent dari indulgentiae. Nolo loqui contra potestatem Papae nec cardinalium nec prelatorum ecclesiae . . . Papa enim saepenumero decipitur in his quae facti sunt; errare potest Papa (ex. de consti. lib. vi. c. licet): Indulgentiae . . . de quibus Papa non est sufficienter informatus parum valent.' (Q/110)

masked by an appearance of virtue. He refers too to the scandal of nepotism, and does not shrink from quoting (P/322) the opinion that the Franciscan Pope Sixtus IV was a notable offender, promoting his disreputable nephew who later became Julius II. While such references show that out preachers were no Papimanes, they can not safely be pushed further.

No inhibitions of any kind govern the criticism of prelates. Maillard bluntly asserts (Q/130) that the sinfulness of prelates does more harm than anything else, and (Q/110) that the Church's ruin is directly attributable to the scant respect earned by the clergy. Menot takes the view (P/375) that bad prelates are a scourge sent from God, or rather from the devil, to destroy the Church. In his picturesque way he puts the blame squarely on the prelates:

O quel esclandre! j'en dis à la pure et realle verité. Mille prelati sunt causa quod pauper et simplex populus peccat et quaerit infernum, que le povre simple peuple peche et se damne ad omnes diabolos; . . . quant le maistre est tabourineur et menestrier, communiter les varletz sont danseurs. (P/409)

The violence of the language is striking and stage directions to shout ('*Hic exclama*') suggest that the effect on the audience may have been startling. Maillard asks (F/107) the rhetorical question 'who goes into the Church', and answers himself: 'chasseurs, ruffiens, ribaulx, paillars, ignorans, ambitieux, aveugles, les yeux bandez,' ascribing their introduction into the Lord's house to 'sacrilegi presbyteri putridi! spurcissimi ecclesiastici!'

Half a century later Menot finds things no better, and compares (P/245) those prelates who ought to be as the pillars holding up the Church to the effigies of baboons held up by the building itself. The familiar accusation that asses are now crowned and sit in the seats of the apostles occurs time after time. Messier, the only one preaching after Luther, is if anything the most violent. The greater part of his Lenten series is devoted to a detailed and relentless criticism of clerical deficiencies. It is not known where he first preached these sermons, but if they were in Paris, as is almost certain, and in his own Franciscan church, near the Sorbonne, which is probable, there must have been more clergy in the congregation than would normally be the case.

All the preachers frequently use a direct vocative, condemning 'vos domini episcopi, vos domini prelati' for negligence, absenteeism and so on, and leave no room for doubt as to the outcome of such a pastorate, saying that souls, alas, are lost through such negligence. Messier is rather more circumstantial and the recurrent references to Paris suggest an identifiable attack *ad hominem*. Like most Lenten preachers he develops (15) the text of Christ's temptation by the devil, especially the scene on the pinnacle of the Temple. In the past the sure flight of prelates has borne them safely out of danger, but now that appointments are made regardless of youth and for family reasons, their modern successors, mere fledgelings, are too feeble to fly at all. He quotes (31) the popular text from Isaiah lvi (as Menot does more than once) about dogs who no longer bark; to gain preferment, doctors of theology have been ready to preach the word, but once established in some fat canonry they fall silent, 'on leur a gecté ung os en la gueulle.' Study is used as a pretext for going off to Paris: 'the shepherds abandon the sheep'[1] and the wolves prowl ready. Ignorance is the rule among the 'asini coronati', but those who actually do study in Paris are accused (47) of reading Ovid, Virgil, Terence and the like instead of Scripture, the basis of truth and knowledge. The choice of pagan authors is interesting in 1531, for it is obvious that Messier is thinking of the same range of purely entertaining literature as that enjoyed four centuries before by the humanists whom St. Bernard condemns, and not at all of the new authors, Greek as well as Latin, cultivated by the New Learning, by then well under way. He condemns (133 v.) those who take service in noble households and are content to perform the most menial tasks, such as cooking, rather than devote themselves to their sacred ministry. Rabelais's description of Basché's *sommelier*, Maître Oudart (*QL*/XII), who was also parish priest, illustrates what then used to be the custom.

Speaking (71 v.) of the three ways of serving God in a cathedral church, Messier inevitably invites local comparison, though, unlike Maillard, he does not actually name the Paris chapter. The three categories are the canons, who spend most of their time in choir asleep, 'la jambe estandue en hault', until they become bored and go off into the nave for a chat; then the vicars choral, who sing their descants and despatch their masses so rapidly that the middle is cut out, serving God not with their hearts but with 'la patenostre du singe', a mere movement of the lips; last come 'les

---

[1] 'Dimittunt oves in ore luporum et dicunt quod stant Parisius ad studendum.' (46)

petiz enfans du cueur', in whom he alone finds some devotion and good conduct. Rabelais's 'mocquedieu non oraison' is a rather less picturesque version of the same idea.

The simian comparison was a popular one, as the discussion on monks in *Gargantua*/XL shows, and it is put most pungently by Menot (T/31): 'Quaeratis hodie à ces gros godons et escornifleurs d'offices, invenietis in eis tantam devotionem sicut in simia xxx annorum.' Rabelais does not take up the simile of the thirty-year-old monkey, but clearly his description of Frère Jan as 'beau despescheur d'heures, beau desbrideur de messes, beau descrotteur de vigiles' (*Garg.*/XXVII) is in the same tradition.

Many of these sins of omission are tracable, and traced by the preachers, to faulty methods of selection. The reiteration of attacks on the higher clergy has already been discussed, and it may be relevant to note that no office in the Franciscan Order, unlike the monastic orders, was permanent, except in the rare cases, frequent only in the mission field, of friars promoted to bishoprics. The sense of being constitutionally outside a hierarchy which was constantly under attack, of being a professional critic of the establishment, is a major factor to be considered in Rabelais's training. Anti-clericalism is a French characteristic of great antiquity, and though the Franciscan position was at the opposite extreme, the preachers are often remarkably similar to anti-clerical writers in their targets and means of attack.

In the same way *gauloiserie* has often been linked with anti-clericalism, and it is not surprising to find the preachers treating sexual themes in a manner more reminiscent of popular tales than the pulpit. Ammunition and target are the same in fabliau and sermon, though the batteries are differently sited. St. Nicholas's Day always falls in Advent, and Maillard makes the most of the occasion in his penitential series. He recounts (A/34) the familiar legend of how the saintly bishop, passing one night by an inn, heard lamentations from within, and on inquiry learned that three young girls were there awaiting the morning, when their parents, too indigent to support them, were going to sell them into prostitution. He thereupon threw three bags of gold through the window and saved them from infamy. Maillard drily comments that modern prelates also give money to girls, but for different reasons and with different results. Nicholas did not hoard his wealth, he did not keep concubines 'à pain et à pot', he did not provoke to lust by exacting a shameful price from women wanting to be married, but the same cannot be said of modern churchmen.

Not all Maillard's charges were meekly accepted, and there is a record[1] of at least one official protest, when in 1491 the canons of Notre Dame sent a deputation to the Bishop of Paris to protest against Maillard's recent accusation from a Paris pulpit that they kept concubines in the cloister. Since his most outspoken comments on clerical concubinage date from later years, Maillard must have given the chapter a dusty answer.

No great indignation would be roused in a congregation listening to attacks on clerical concubinage, real social and spiritual evil though it undoubtedly was, for by the sixteenth century it had acquired the status of a very old and not very good music hall joke. A subject closer to French hearts, and one on which the Mendicants' stand was constitutionally determined, was that of clerical venality. Both in quantity and quality of denunciation this may be reckoned the preachers' principal target among contemporary abuses. The indulgence dispute which first incensed Luther and Rabelais's satire thirty years later on the financial implications of the Decretals show how live and varied a topic this was. Passions are infallibly aroused as soon as the profit motive comes into religion. After the long battles of the Middle Ages the Mendicants were wholly committed to the cause of apostolic poverty, and here, as on the subject of sex, their treatment of abuses has close parallels in anti-clerical, and indeed anti-Mendicant, popular literature. The money-changers in the Temple provide an irresistibly suitable text for Maillard's sustained attack on venality in his Advent series. Time after time he reverts to the charge that priests are selling the sacraments. Detailed accounts of clerical transactions occur in many of the sermons (A/2, A/87 v., A/89 v.), and we hear how the tariff for confessions or masses is arranged on a commission basis (s/103), how poor priests are exploited, and, worst of all, how the sacrament is denied to the poor man who cannot pay for it.[2] Similarly marriage and even

---

[1] Renaudet, op. cit. p. 15: 'Ipse male locutus est et in scandalum dominorum canonicorum in claustro commorantium, vocando eos concubinarios in praedicatione quam fecit dominica praeterita in ecclesia parisiensi.'

[2] 'Non communicat pauperi non habenti; quia dominus his opus habet pro canibus nutriendis et avibus pascendi et equis parandis.' (R/127 v.)

burial become a real problem for the poor who cannot afford the price.[1]

The accumulation of wealth through pluralism and the failure of rich clergy to give alms to the needy sets off Maillard's eloquent fury.[2] 'O gros godons damnati infames et scripti in libro diaboli', did they think, thieves and sacriligious men that they were, that those who originally founded their benefices did so to promote lechery, whoring, gambling? Where they should be giving religious money to the afflicted they are spending it on horses and hounds, harlots and players. Many times modern luxury is contrasted with evangelical poverty, and in this the friars were assured of a sympathetic audience, for the richest layman could feel a glow of self-righteousness at the thought of so much clerical cupidity and avarice.

There is a remarkable long passage in Menot (P/376) in which he describes how the contemporary traveller would frequently find on his way ruined or abandoned churches and monasteries. Asking why the proper funds had not been applied to arrest this decay, he hears that they have been consumed by three phrases ('trois cordelieres') of the Ave Maria, viz. 1. 'Benedicta tu', 2. 'in mulieribus', 3. 'fructus ventris'. This is interpreted as meaning first pomp and show, second 'les donnes[3] die et nocte', third banquets, by which three means absentee priors and abbots waste the substance of their charge. The accusation is common enough, but such a gloss on the Ave is not, and illustrates the use to which sacred texts could be put. In comparison Rabelais's parody of a commentary, when Lasdaller glosses the psalm (*Garg.*/XXXVIII) is completely harmless.

Venality begins before ordination, and three of the evils most consistently denounced are simony, nepotism and pluralism. Some, the preachers say, owe their election not to the Holy Spirit but to force of arms, (P/321) 'à force d'armes, par la pointe de l'espée, et à moyen de gensdarmes, espées, hacquebuttes et

---

[1] 'Committuntur ne multa sacrilegia in hac villa? venduntur ne sacramenta? quid dicitis domini ecclesiastici? Si pauperrima filia velit nubere in aliam parrochiam nonne oportet eam solvere summam certam pecuniarum? Et de sepulchris, quid dicendum est? Non enim sepelietur quis in ecclesia nisi solvat unum francum.' (A/89)

[2] 'Fures et sacrilegi (ut dicit Bernardus) creditis vos quod fundatores beneficiorum vestrorum dederint vobis beneficia ad luxuriandum, ad meretricandum, ad ludendum au glic gallice?' (A/23 v.)

[3] This is apparently the Italian word 'donna', a rare borrowing.

hallebardes', some enjoy the highest preferment through nepotism, promoted by relatives who have reached the top (P/322) 'voyre feust il filz d'ung savetier ou sorty de la maison d'ung bostelier de foing.' All the preachers speak of the grammar of preferment, in which the only legitimate one of the six cases is the vocative, for those called by God. (A/33 v., A/66 v., T/164, R/73).

Menot touches on a delicate point when he speaks (P/355) of boys of ten being appointed to parishes of 500 hearths; his interlocutor is made to say in defence of the deed: 'O frater, vos nescitis verbum bonum, le mot du guet. Dominus Papa dispensavit nos . . .' Menot answers that the day will come when the poor wretch will wish that a wolf had strangled at birth the sheep on whose skin the dispensation was written and the goose from which the quill was taken. Like his brethren he was perfectly submissive to papal authority, but like them he does not hesitate to question appeals to this authority which seem to him spurious or ill-conceived.

The language used in condemning abuses is very often zoological, and Messier surpasses all the others in one particular sermon in which he successively describes delinquent clergy as 'reptiles and worms rather than men . . . moles, serpents and horned asses.'[1] He tells (127 v.) the fabliau of the fox and the monkey, equating the tailless monkey with the priest without a benefice, while the abundantly tailed fox is the one with four or five benefices. When such language and sentiments were commonplace in the pulpit, full allowance must be made in assessing standards of reverence and respect obtaining when Rabelais first wrote.

Another aspect of this highly critical attitude to authority, which some critics seem to find peculiar in Rabelais, is the preachers' view on excommunication, the stock sanction of those empowered to invoke it. They all condemn abuse of this power,

---

[1] Isti venditores in ecclesiam Dei calidos et versutos repletos veneno peccati: adulatores, latrones, praedones: qui reptilia et vermes magis quam homines dici possunt, introducunt. Et sicut maximum damnum fieret homini si sponsa sua sic per artem magicam incantaretur; quod loco prolis produceret talpas, serpentes, vel asinos cornutos; ita fit in parte ista irrecompensabile damnum per ecclesiae venditores.

Quando enim aliquis avarus qui totus inhaeret terrae in ecclesia canonizatur vel praeficitur in prelatum; possunt ecclesiae filii dicere: Mater nostra genuit nobis serpentem. Et quando praeficitur unus episcopus illiteratus vel laicus, merito possunt dicere quod ecclesia peperit unum asinum cornutum.' (R/23 v.)

especially for temporal offences (Q/145), and they find it a terrible thing that a soul should be damned for frivolous reasons (P/433), 'pour ung fagot, pour une paire d'esperons'. Messier goes further, and after speaking (47) of excommunicating a man for four *sous*, deals with ecclesiastical justice, which for the least offence will consign a man to jail on bread and water. One thinks of Villon at Meung, and also of the vindictive threats of Homenaz a century after him.

A not uncommon image of the pre-Reformation Church associates friars and pardoners, indulgences, relics and pilgrimages, as all forming part of the same superstitious amalgam. The briefest glance at the sermons should dispel that illusion. The very words recall Rabelais, and the attitude requires no comment.[1] 'Domini bullatores et portatores reliquiarum' . . . 'les jargonneurs, caphardi et mensuratores vultuum ymaginum' (A/37) (i.e. image-kissers) are accused of fraudulent speaking; 'les porteurs de rogatons' are said (P/406) to instruct poor widows to spend their money on indulgences rather than the bare necessities of life; preachers of indulgences are described (R/71) taking the saints' bones back to the tavern where they spend their gains, and the comment is made that the saints whose relics now lie on the table had probably never in their lives been inside such a place. Disgust, contempt and indignation inform the numerous references to this squalid fringe of ecclesiastical hangers-on. The question of false relics, 'pigges bones', is not at issue, for the texts make it clear that the authenticity of the relic or the technical legality of the indulgence is accepted. What is condemned so bitterly is the cash tariff applied to piety and the unscrupulous exploitation of poor and simple people too ignorant to resist this form of moral blackmail. The gross unworthiness of the pardoners and the base ends to which they turned their profits had long been a theme of popular literature, but the persistence of the evil in the face of all attacks shows what can be achieved by what might be called spiritual market-research.

The historical importance of this abuse is partly fortuitous, since Luther's quarrel with Tetzel was not in itself a major issue until forced to its logical conclusion, but it is worth noting that

---

[1] 'Estis hic domini bullatores et portatores reliquiarum? Vos dicitis vos habuisse de bullis c scuta et curatus x pro vino suo. Et licet essent rubea; vous les avez abattuz à tous les diables.' (A/26 v.)

the preachers state their views on the subject with some precision. Maillard condemns (Q/110) the traffic in indulgences, charges bishops who permit it with criminal complicity, and explicitly dissents from current teaching on the theological machinery of indulgences. He says quite plainly that the doctrine is not to be found in the fathers, and is regarded by modern doctors as 'semper dubia'. Formally protesting his submission to the Pope and the Church's authority, he goes on to ask whether it is credible that some great usurer, vicious and laden with sin, can earn remission of all his sins by putting six coins in the box. For himself he finds it hard to believe and harder to preach.

Menot goes into great detail on the same subject, only a few months before the Ninety-Five Theses were nailed up, and evidently found it more than usually delicate, for there are two alternative versions of the main passages and more stage directions than usual to guide the wary preacher following him. In one version he speaks (P/258) of Mary Magdalene as having gained the '*magna indulgentia*' through her tears of true contrition, and ends by saying that the Lord did not bid her put money in the box, but said 'thy faith hath made thee whole' (Luke vii). The other version is a good deal more violent, pointing out that many who have been lulled into a false sense of security by indulgences had bought them to their own damnation. He concludes with the direction to develop and amplify ('*practica et dilata*') the abuse of these indulgences, and to speak against the '*caffardi*' who delude the people by telling them they can win salvation through vows and pilgrimages.

All this could have been written, and very probably was said from time to time, by Rabelais, and we find the attack on the same 'caffards' developed in *Gargantua*/XLV, where they are accused of deceiving the people in just the same context of votive offerings and pilgrimages. It has in the past been sometimes rather lightheartedly assumed that the 'caffards' and friars were equally anathema to Rabelais because they stood for the same things. Such a view cannot be sustained in the light of this evidence.

The summary of evidence would not be complete without a word on Rabelais's other favourite target, the sophists of the Sorbonne. Here too he is only echoing Maillard. (A/44 v., A/46) Scholars would be better employed studying the book of conscience than sophisms, students of civil and canon law will not be saved by all their learning unless they have a good conscience. (Q/141) (cf. 'science sans conscience n'est que ruyne de l'âme.') The vain disputes between Nominalists and Realists are dismissed (s/125) as sophistry, and distinguished from the true theology which confounds heretics and is based on Scripture. All this may be compared with what Rabelais has to say on the same subjects, and notably on Hippothaddée, 'le bon theologien' (TL/xxix).

The most common charge made against Rabelais's brethren by modern critics is that of ignorance and hostility to learning, and it seems that Maillard, for one, was conscious that such opinions as those just quoted might be interpreted in that sense. He specifically answers the point on one occasion (Q/143) when he is speaking of a true religious vocation, and emphasizes that he means an order of regular observance, like his own branch. Some priests, he says, object that if they joined the Observants they would not be able to study, but he replies by referring them to SS. Thomas and Bonaventura (the sermon was preached on the feast of St. Thomas) as men who combined profitable study with regular observance. There is no need to claim that the subjects offered for study would have appealed to Rabelais, though Bonaventura probably did, but the traditional picture of crass ignorance seems to derive from too literal an interpretation of such objections as that here answered by Maillard.

Also interesting are some remarks by Menot on the religious vocation. There are those, he says (P/307), who enter the order of St. Benedict, St. Francis or others not for the sake of God and his saints, not to save their own souls, but for riches, or to live in comfort and idleness: 'Paix et aises sans rien faire, à tous les diables telles entrées.' This is just the point made by Rabelais in the discussion on monks (Garg. xxl) and the main merit of Frère Jan is said to be that he is not one of the 'moines ocieux'. In talking of encouraging boys to follow the religious vocation Menot is at pains to insist on 'religio bene observata', otherwise there is no merit in the vocation.

As a footnote to the discussion of religious life it is interesting and not altogether expected to find Maillard on at least five occasions (A/7, A/21 v., A/36 v., Q/107 v., Q/122 v.) offering as an example of excellence that of the order least like his own, the Carthusians. Apart from its proverbial integrity ('Numquam re-

formata quia numquam deformata') the Carthusian order exemplifies more than any other the pure monastic spirit, with its austerity, rule of silence and remoteness from the world. It is a little surprising that a man so intensely active as Maillard, belonging to an order which stood for a very different conception of the religious life, should thus hold up the Carthusians as an ideal, for theirs could truly be called a fugitive and cloistered virtue. It may be coincidence, but it is also odd that Rabelais, whose dislike of the monastic ideal can hardly be disputed, omits from an otherwise comprehensive list of religious targets all mention of the Carthusians. This is odder still if it is recalled that Erasmus chose a Carthusian as spokesman for the contemplative life in one of his most celebrated *Colloquia*, which Rabelais cannot have failed to know.

This is perhaps the place to note the single reference to Luther made by Messier (57 v.). As his sermons were published in 1531, fourteen years after the Ninety-Five Theses and only three before the Placards, it cannot be contended that the significance of Luther was still obscure, but Messier treats Lutheranism as a casual phenomenon barely worthy of mention. Using the zoological language to which he is so addicted, he compares 'noster Leutherus' (sic) to a fox; the pointed muzzle represents Luther's eloquence, the fine pelt the fine-seeming knowledge, which is actually worthless, as witness the only example given, namely that it is lawful for priests to marry. The fox has a brush 'bien tofue', corresponding to Luther's following of heretics, and his breath is fetid, like Luther's knowledge, foul and nothing worth. A popular sermon may not be the place for technical theological discussion of heresy (though other theological points raised are technical enough) but this seems extraordinarily inept as a judgement passed in 1531, and typically obsessive in its sole specific reference to clerical marriage. One can only conclude that the friars were out of date and did not know it.

The relevance of the material discussed here to Rabelais should be obvious. Whatever his later views on the Franciscans, he had joined in his youth the branch of the order most conspicuous for its criticism of current abuses; all his formal training had been carried out in a reforming atmosphere, and together with the vow of obedience he had learned the Franciscan duty of plain speaking. The prevailing attitude in the Order may be summed up as a passionate defence of poverty and the poor against extravagance and exploitation by ecclesiastics; an almost obsessive preoccupation with spiritual wickedness in high places; a plea for return to evangelical simplicity both in material and intellectual things; a monotonous insistence on sexuality as a source of sin; perhaps most of all a deep conviction that religion means the love and service of God, who rewards the faithful with salvation, and is not to be seen just as a career or even an institution.[1]

[1] It is worth pointing out that on one occasion when Menot actually has something good to say for the clergy, he himself finds this so exceptional as to deserve comment; as usual, there is a sting in the tail: 'Domini ecclesiastici, malui de dignitate vestra hodie praedicare quam vos arguere majori verborum acrimonia et dicere sicut quidam dicunt quod des corones des prestres seront pavées les rues d'enfer.' (p/354)

5: CRITICISM OF SOCIETY AND MORALS

NATURALLY enough the sermons are more concerned with religious questions than anything else, but it is not to be expected that they would altogether abstain from social comments, especially in view of the Mendicants' teaching on poverty. Medieval history shows more than one example of how such teaching could be pressed to the limit and provoke actual revolt, and dissident friars were not uncommon among the ranks of the proletariat from whom they were often recruited. Our preachers were no rabble-rousers, nor would their invitations from local authorities have been so regularly received if they had been, but they belong unequivocally to what would now be called the left wing on social questions. With no property of their own to lose (at least in theory) they had no personal stake in the existing economic order, and were to that extent disinterested critics. Their consistent championship of the weak and oppressed, however, obliged them to speak out against any form of exploitation and their burning desire for social justice is one of their most marked features. All this is popular in the sense that most people liked to hear it, and also in that it was one of the few legitimate channels through which the people's feelings could be made articulate. In appealing to the same people Rabelais had every incentive to follow the preachers, and there is besides every reason to suppose that in this their views were his.

Reading sermon after sermon one has the distinct impression of a well-defined area of criticism very different from that which might be encountered in similar circumstances today or indeed in the seventeenth century. There are inevitably complaints of public depravity, often localized or so framed as to allow a place-name to be supplied as appropriate; these show few interesting variations on a perennial theme. There are observations on the bourgeoisie in general, for neither nobles nor peasants figure with any frequency in the sermons, and especially on women, reminding them of their moral (i.e. sexual) and social obligations. Finally, and most prominent, there are detailed attacks on individual groups and professions, in which lawyers occupy by far the most conspicuous place.

Rabelais's father was a lawyer of some repute, and we know that it was the protracted lawsuit between Antoine Rabelais and his friends and Gaucher de Sainte-Marthe that inspired the Picrochole episode. Moreover his early friends at Fontenay included the distinguished lawyer, Tiraqueau, and throughout his life he mixed much with men of law. All this is undeniably relevant to a study of the legal elements in his work, but it does not seem adequately to explain the often violent hostility shown to members of the legal profession. Every book has something to say about the law; Baisecul and Humevesne in *Pantagruel*, Picrochole in *Gargantua*, Bridoye in the *Tiers Livre*, Chiquanous in the *Quart Livre*, Chats Fourrez (almost certainly authentic) in the *Cinquiesme Livre*, are major episodes, and there are numerous scattered references as well. Without questioning the importance of experience and family background in helping to form such passages, one cannot reasonably ignore the resemblance, often verbal, between Rabelais's criticisms and those of the sermons.

Unpopularity is often a lawyer's lot in a country where most litigants are relatively uneducated, and in France, where litigation has always been a national pastime, the unpopularity was probably even more marked than elsewhere. Even so, Maillard seems to be unduly harsh in delivering a considered opinion which recalls the proverbial medieval question as to whether an archdeacon can be saved: 'I do not wish to deny, Messieurs, that an advocate can be saved if he does what he ought, but I say it will be difficult.'[1]

His indictment ranges over all branches of the profession, which he accuses of living on chicanery, extortion and fraud.[2] The members of the Bar, the Parlement, the procurators of the Châtelet and of the bishop's court, are all accused (A/35) of eating whole platesfull of the devil's favourite dish, the tongue of deceit. The notaries who record proceedings by which the poor are oppressed will meet the same judgement as the rest on that dread day of wrath. (Q/107) He does not stop at professional conduct, but further charges them with unprofessional attentions to women. (Q/134)

---

[1] 'Ego nolo dicere domini quin advocatus, si faciat quod debet, possit salvari, sed dico cum difficultate.' (A/77)

[2] 'Et vos domini in Parlemento, quum fecistis aliquam deceptionem, numquid dicunt vobis socii vestri: Vous luy avez bien faict desploier ses escuz. Il semble ung grant papelart gallice.' (A/26 v.)

Of all dangerous callings he finds advocacy the most dangerous. (F/122)

Menot explicitly relates their peril to their oppression of the poor, and says (T/8) they have a name for 'ronger le povre peuple'. Unless the poor man's property is restored and justice satisfied, all concerned with the case, judge, lawyers, witnesses and scribes will go 'ad omnes diabolos in infernum.' (T/64) He explains that 'avocasserie' is a specially dangerous profession on account of the gifts that blind many lawyers to truth. He even accuses (P/324) (and shouts his charge) members of the Parlement for leasing house property to brothel-keepers: 'Vela bel honneur pour gens de judicature.'

There is in Messier (34 v.) a passage extraordinarily reminiscent of the Chats Fourrez and told with equal verve. He tells how a little client ('clientulus') comes to the wicked advocate, who says 'or dictes', demanding gold before he speaks. Then when he does speak he keeps breaking off to say 'or sa', and unless he sees gold will allow the case to be aggravated. When the poor man pulls out the coin, the advocate takes it and puts it in his purse, saying 'or bien'. All is indeed well once the gold is tucked away.

Such attacks emphasize the venality of lawyers, and once again the profit motive inspires the fiercest indignation. Justice, like religion, should be a duty, not a business. Nor can one miss the similarity of the attacks on pardoners and venal clergy and those on the men of law, for both groups choose as their victims the same poor and simple folk who know no better and can least afford the price. Those who should set the example do not, those who have the power shirk the responsibility, those who have the knowledge use it for deception, once again 'science sans conscience n'est que ruyne de l'âme.' The characteristic feature of these and other social criticisms is that they are directed at the class which represented wealth, the bourgeoisie, not that which nominally exercised power, the nobility. One has to look hard for references to the king or the Second Estate.

One brief text from Menot shows how the line of argument might have proceeded.[1] The king, he says, allows markets on feastdays, the king allows brothels. 'I do not know if the King

---

[1] 'Rex permittit nundinas in festis; Rex permittit lupanaria. Sed nescio si Rex habuit revelationem quod qui mercatur in festa et dominica non peccat mortaliter. Nescio si Rex habet bene istam auctoritatem permittendi tuam usuriam.' (T/84)

has had a revelation that anyone trading on Sunday or a holy day is not sinning mortally. I do not know if the king really has the authority to permit your usury . . .' That sort of irony could have led to trouble and is in fact exceptional. All the same, Maillard too was no respecter of persons, as his exile shows, and in his earliest extant series, preached at Nantes, there is a fair amount of political discussion. His references to excessive taxation (F/111) must have been popular with everyone but the king and his fiscal officers; 'comestores populi . . . predatores excoriatores populi . . . spoliatores qui escorchez Dieu et le monde' is strong language by any standards. His later occasional reminiscences of Louis XI and his hated minister, Tristan l'Hermite, show that he had specific examples in mind. It should be added that his views on taxation were perfectly orthodox, and he stressed the obligations of ruler and subject respectively for fixing and paying taxes, always provided they were assessed 'rationabiliter'.

The subject of trade and commerce comes up with some frequency, largely no doubt because most of the sermons were preached in big towns, like Paris or Tours, with large and prominent legal and mercantile communities. Since trade and profit are closely identified it is natural that the preachers should show little indulgence to occupational weaknesses, but some of the detail sounds a little incongruous for the pulpit. A recurrent feature of the attack is the apparently indiscriminate collection of persons denounced in a single phrase, as when Maillard calls to account 'vile harlots, usurers inscribed in the devil's book, craftsmen and mechanics who practise infinite deceptions in business.'[1] He asks if they are present, and what they expect to show for so much profit, concluding with a sinister pun that they seem to be playing 'aux oublies'. Elsewhere he describes (A/28 v.) some of the tricks of the trade, as when apothecaries put their packets of ginger, pepper, saffron, cinnamon and other spices on the cellar floor so that they should absorb damp and weigh more, and wool merchants are said to soak their wares for the same reason. A dramatized anecdote (Q/175) of immediate popular appeal tells of a worthy citizen of Paris who wanted to buy just one ounce of equity and good faith. He visits the different trades-

---

[1] 'Estis hic viles meretrices; et vos usurarii scripti in libris diaboli; et magistri artifices et mechanici qui facitis infinitas deceptiones in negociis? Quam recognitionem facietis de tot beneficiis susceptis? Ego credo quod vos luditis aux oublies.' (A/34 v.)

people in turn, and having failed to find the required ounce at goldsmiths, innkeepers and so on, finally gives up, deciding that such a commodity is nowhere to be found in Paris. Yet another charge is that of Sunday opening (Q/155), and in making it Maillard invokes a familiar saint in Rabelais's calendar: 'You are keeping the feast of St. Pansart which is the devil's feast.'[1]

The main interest of these criticisms of trade and commerce is social, and the very circumstantial accusations made, as well as the general tone, correspond quite closely to what would in a later age be a function of the popular press. In terms of potential audience and mass circulation the friars probably constituted the most powerful advertising medium of the age, so that their identification with the generally inarticulate masses in social and economic matters is a factor of major importance. Though their attitude derives partly from their vow and pursuit of poverty, it is one that can readily be adopted by others whose poverty is no less real for not being the subject of a vow.

Another urban phenomenon on which the preachers have a word to say is academic life. Considering the prominent role played by their order in the University of Paris, the remarks of Maillard and Menot show very little confidence in that institution. Things do not seem to have changed much since Villon's day, and Rabelais's heroes have a very similar report to make of academic activities. We hear (A/86 v.) that St. Louis ordered that brothels should not be sited in the neighbourhood of a college, and now the first thing the students see as they come out of their college is a brothel. Masters and regents are accused of showing their pupils night haunts, and one passage (S/96) actually addresses the rectors who lead their students to the brothel. The violence of rectorial elections is deplored (A/87), and the charge of rowdiness, and worse, is made (T/73) against the students of Orleans, Paris and Poitiers. Even the booksellers are not spared (A/62), for, not satisfied with damning themselves, they take others with them by printing erotic and lustful books. Taken in conjunction with the attacks on sophists already discussed, these comments on university life cover the range from Janotus de Bragmardo to Panurge and the Limousin scholar. Caricature as it doubtless is, the picture of the sermons offers a recognizable popular image.

---

[1] 'Et vos domini qui tenetis domos vestras apertas diebus dominicis et venditis sicut aliis diebus. Vos colitis festum sancti Pansardi, qui est dies diaboli.' (Q/194)

So far the topics dealt with have fallen mainly within the public sector, and have been more concerned with money than with sex, though that is always lurking round some oratorical corner. When women are considered it is just the reverse, and the catalogue of sexual aberrations is only occasionally varied by the introduction of allied weaknesses. To say that the preachers are anti-feminist is almost like saying that they are against sin. One must not forget the predominantly masculine bias of society, which may not have felt so strongly against sin but was committed to the view that women are inferior by nature. To that extent many of the preachers' observations are addressed to the converted, and it would be rash to assume that a majority even of their female hearers, who allegedly outnumbered the men, dissented from the attacks on their sex, or at least from the basis of such attacks. It must have been more embarrassing for the women than for the men to listen to these remarks from the pulpit; everyone may be able to think of some bad lawyer or merchant, but to identify a given man with a particular attack is a different matter, whereas some of the female victims are described by visually recognizable features. Thus at Tours Menot speaks (T/39) of the bourgeoises of the town who carry velvet covered books of hours and 'grosses patrenotres', though they do not know the service and 'ne font que barboter' like monkeys (cf. Messier's 'patrenotre du cinge'). The young Gargantua had just such devotional equipment, put to just such a use (*Garg.* XXI). In any case some of them are said (A/6 v.) to have the Bible in French for the same reason that they have books 'de amoribus fatuis et secretis mulierum', for the sake of fashion and frivolity.

Even more easily recognized than the prayer books is the dress denounced by the preachers. There is a good deal said about feminine vanity, changing fashions, the sinfulness of cosmetics and so on, but the particular article of dress which seems to annoy the preachers, who animadvert upon it several times, is the train, and also, curiously, gloves. One quip from Menot on this point must have gone down very well, for he plays on the word for train ('cauda = queue') and wishes that the women had all the tails of the cows in Brittany and a page to carry them.[1] It may be said that such details are too trivial to take up time in a sermon,

---

[1] 'Una mulier vult facere unam caudam in tunica. Utinam haberent omnes caudas vaccarum Britanniae et unum servulum ad portandum.' (T/78)

but the analogy of the popular press is relevant again here, and it is also relevant that people had come to expect this sort of thing. It goes without saying that there is hardly a word about masculine vanity, for this is not serious comment but a skirmish in the eternal war of the sexes. Vanity is only brought in to prove a point against women, their inherent frivolity and desire to attract, which it is not required to prove against men.

There is not much left unsaid on the subject of sexual licence and the only interest to be found on this score is in the limits to which a preacher was prepared to go. In language the limit does not stop short of vulgarity and violence. Mesdames are asked (A/42 v.) about their erotic reading, and how they have 'embureli-qoqués illos gaudisseurs'. Pre-marital intercourse between engaged couples is denounced (A/76) for practical as well as moral reasons, for after marriage the husband may accuse his wife of showing equal favours to others, calling her 'paillarde, meretrix etc.' Marriage may be only the beginning of trouble (Q/131 v.), for if a husband's purse does not run to his wife's extravagant fancies, she may choose to earn the money for clothes by selling her favours. Adultery is constantly condemned, sometimes with reasoned arguments. One of the most concise statements (P/415) against it gives the arguments under two heads; first, uncertainty about any offspring resulting, in which case the responsibility is heaviest on the women, second, the fragility of each sex, when the man is the more responsible, since he must show himself stronger and more virtuous than the woman. Such unquestioning accept-ance of man's superiority, and thus greater responsibility, is fundamental in all thinking about the sexes at this time, and can only very loosely be classified as anti-feminist.

Even marriage is a pitfall, and we are told (P/353) that many husbands and wives will be damned more swiftly for 'inhonestas' within marriage than even adulterers and harlots. Farinier, in a course on the seven deadly sins, comes to a point in a sermon on Lust (43) when he ought to speak of sodomy, but finding the subject too abominable for public discussion turns instead to marital relations, which conceal a wealth of dangers unless ruled by the sternest austerity. A reasoned view on the whole question of sexual relations is given (T/112) by Menot, speaking for all his colleagues; as gold is more precious than silver, so virginity is more noble than widowhood, and as silver is more precious than lead, so widowhood is more precious and noble than marriage. The gift of continence alone ensures safety.[1] There are some grim reminders of what used to happen in an age when contraceptive methods were rudimentary, so that abortion or even infanticide might be the only way to remove unwanted children. One sermon wishes (A/76) that the audience had their ears open to the cries of children thrown into rivers or latrines, and deplores the practice, allegedly approved by some priests, of bringing about a miscarriage before the foetus was canonically deemed to have acquired an 'anima rationalis'. Another speaks of errant wives going in their husband's absence for abortions, and adds 'I know what I am saying: there may be some women who understand me very well; the case concerns them.'[2] This sounds like the sort of information learned in the confessional, and it is not difficult to imagine the effect of such a public condemnation on a tender conscience.

The preachers occupy themselves to a remarkable extent with the most intimate details of family life, showing a realism which no student of contemporary ways can afford to ignore. Some parents are accused, morally speaking, of giving their children a rope with which to hang themselves, and they are censured for allowing their boys and girls to share the matrimonial bed, where they witness what they should not, 'secreta matrimonii'. The preacher adds[3] that he does not want to go into details, for a little is enough for those who know what he is talking about. The subject of modesty is dealt with in some detail (P/261) and the custom is condemned whereby a woman after childbirth bathes in the presence of other women. Such shameful nudity is found deplorable, for it provokes immodest looks, shameful gestures, unseemly words. What is worse, the young daughters come too. Not thus the chaste Susanna . . .

Nudity, like vanity, seems to be judged by a double standard, for the several references to the chaste Susanna (a predictably popular pulpit story) in the context of female immodesty can be

---

[1] Cf. the 'prescheurs de Varennes' who oppose second marriage (TL/VI)

[2] 'Quando fecerunt peccatum suum et sunt pregnatae et maritus est extra, vadunt se facere eventer . . . Ego scio quid ego dico; forsan aliquae bene intelligunt; casus eas tangit.' (P/430)

[3] 'Vos domini burgenses datis pueris cordam damnationis eorum. Hoc dico propter illos qui filios suos ponunt in lectis qui vident secreta matrimonii. Et filii et filiae vident ea quae vos mutuo facitis. Taceo particularia, quare intelligenti pauca sufficiunt.' (Q/96 v.)

balanced by a single passing reference to male nudity. Men are mildly condemned, seculars as well as religious, for going to the baths and there showing each other what should be concealed,[1] but women doing likewise, especially in front of their daughters, are consigned to the everlasting sulphur baths.[2] Cleanliness may be a virtue, but nudity is the shortcut to damnation, and the '*estuves*', public baths, are treated by the preachers as if they had all developed into the same thing as the etymologically cognate 'stew' of contemporary England.

The duty of parents, especially mothers, to their children is a recurrent theme, and if the proportion of men to women and children attending the sermons were really like that quoted earlier,[3] the children must have had plenty to talk about when they got home. In this connexion, the duty of a mother to feed her own child is mentioned more than once (A/71, Q/180), and the example of Mary at the first Christmas quoted. It may be recalled that Erasmus makes similar play with this point. One of the alternatives to such dutiful maternity is to abandon the child in the gutter, where it often finds a new foster-mother in the Church. These waifs, superfluous to their parents' wishes or 'tropditeulx' as Rabelais calls them, often rise to the highest honours in the Church, which they love and respect as a true mother. Messier compares them (27) with the ostrich eggs, which according to medieval belief were left in the sand to be hatched out by the sun. When they have been raised up by God, their sun, their parents who once left them in the dust are only too glad to recognize them. Messier tells the exemplum of Maurice de Sully, Bishop of Paris, who was willing to acknowledge his mother only clothed in rags, not in fine raiment.

As will be seen, there are few positive recommendations to parents, and the negative ones generally come back to some aspect or other of sex. Indeed women seem to be brought into the sermons at all only in a sexual context, and therefore almost never with approval. The causes and effects of this preoccupation with

---

[1] Vadatis ad stuphas, ad banqueta; vos dicitis quod ad termas mulieres non vadunt cum hominibus; sed homines vadunt et religiosi, et quod honestum est ire . . . Vos manetis exuti in termis et ostenditis verenda vestra aliis.' (A/56 v.)

[2] 'Utinam bibuli hoc considerarent et mulieres qui se stuphant. Ego invito vos ad stuphas sulphureas. Quid exemplum pro filiabus vestris quae vident vos nudas.' (Q/171 v.)

[3] See above, chapter 3.

sexuality need no comment, but it does lead to the slightly paradoxical situation that one finds proportionately greater emphasis
on sex in the sermons than in Rabelais, who is popularly (and
wrongly) associated with bawdy. It may be that the friars had
earned so disreputable a reputation in popular tradition that these
members of a reforming body felt themselves obliged to express
themselves fiercely and frequently on the subject, but it is not
very long before any given topic harks back to the familiar theme
of sex.

It seems hardly credible that drunkenness and gluttony were
less conspicuous in France then than now, but they are barely
mentioned. One passing reference to the fate awaiting drunkards
links them in the same sentence with the women who go to public
baths. Apparently reducing all places of public resort to the same
formula, the preachers find the tavern as dangerous as the baths,
and for the same reason (T/56). The cleric or advocate who goes
to the tavern ostensibly for a drink is really going there because
that is where the brothel is. A serving-maid is bound to end up
as a harlot, 'elle est baisée, tastée etc.' Carnival (T/28) brings shame
and dishonour to girls in the taverns. Sometimes (T/81) a foretaste
of eternal punishment is visited upon men in this life, and then
they contract 'la verrolle de Naples', leprosy or some other sick-
ness.

Dancing is not forbidden to the laity, though it is a mortal sin
for clergy. Menot cries out (P/271) his indignation at the custom
whereby a priest publicly dances with a woman the day he
celebrates his first Mass. As ever, the sexual element is not long
absent. It is obvious, according to Menot, that dancing is the
devil's first invention, for it involves circular movement, the
movement proper to demons. This serious piece of demonology
goes on at some length, to be concluded with the proverb: 'I do
not know which is worse, a monk at a dance or a fly in the milk.'[1]
He ends a whole sermon on dancing with some practical advice
addressed (as always) to his female listeners. He has studied dancing at Orleans, but that is not the way he is going to teach them;
first they must go to maître Fifi (the nightsoil man) and borrow
some of his thick cloth to veil their eyes against vain glances,
then they must put on their hands the gloves used by peasants
rooting out thorns, finally they must go and stand three hours in

[1] 'Monachus in chorea et musca in lacte, nescio quid vilius.' (P/273)

the coldest pond they can find. Thus prepared they can go and dance as much as they like.

The only other social evils denounced at all often are swearing and gambling, often connected, and sufficiently serious to have been the subject of particularly ferocious legislation under St. Louis. Playing (A/79) for fun or a pint of wine is no worse than a venial sin, so long as there is no swearing, when it becomes mortal. The bad language of gamblers was proverbial, and Rabelais devotes a whole chapter to the twin evils (TL/xi). Apart from the obvious social dangers of gambling and biblical injunctions against swearing, there seems to have been a theological association too, for Menot, in his Paris Passion (P/513), quotes the text on casting lots for his garments and adds 'Comment on dicing' ('Nota de ludo taxillarum'). It was incidentally the practice of clinching a deal with an oath that led Menot to condemn (T/94) clerical ventures into commerce. Even oaths are no proof of good faith, and we are told of the Jews in Avignon, Moors and pagans who keep their word better than so-called Christians. (P/332)

To complete the picture witchcraft and sorcery must not be forgotten. There are attacks on diabolical astrology and necromancy, and a whole sermon by Maillard (F/96) against 'sorciers, charmeurs, devins, chiromanciers' and the like. We are in the Her Trippa country with this sort of thing, but the preachers naturally did not spend much time on abuses which the great majority of their audience would, at least with their lips, condemn.

Penitential sermons never paint a rosy picture, nor do the weaknesses of human nature change so very much over the years, but it is none the less easy to see what distinguishes these Franciscan preachers from other penitential preachers of other orders and other centuries. The outstanding impression, confirmed abundantly by friend and enemy alike, is the tremendous vigour of their performance and the high degree of direct appeal to the audience. The preachers themselves recognize, and regret, that the sermon is a social occasion with an intermission for lunch, but they make the most of it. The next most striking feature is the sustained assault on the moneyed classes, rather than the landed gentry or men of war. This is largely a consequence of the composition of the town audiences known to have heard them first, and also reflects the substantially increased importance of merchants and bankers in the period. Perhaps more than either of these factors it is due to the Franciscan sense of social justice already mentioned, and to the order's general tendency to support the poor and exploited, to succour the humble and meek and put down the mighty from their seat. The accumulation of wealth for its own sake, beyond necessity, is a matter for divine justice, which will exact the price for avarice, but the justice of this world need not await the Day of Wrath. Thus the rapacious clergy who deprive the poor man of the spiritual attentions he cannot pay for are condemned like the extortionate lawyers who care only for their fee and nothing for justice and the poor man's rights. The weight of the attack is on a heedless and entrenched establishment, abusing power and shirking responsibility.

The key to the Franciscan attitude is to be found in their three vows of poverty, chastity and obedience, and in that order. If cupidity is the root of all evil, lust is not far behind. The equation of sin and sex is as old as the first puritan, and the monotony of the theme is varied only by literary or social novelties. Clerical lapses, female depravity and the profit motive in sex are the main features of the attack. Women come very badly out of the sermons, and it must be remembered that though the friars had no family life of their own, they had unrivalled experience, as itinerant confessors, of the whole range of human behaviour. The preoccupation with sex dominates most of what they have to say of family life, and if they recognize its biological function it is without enthusiasm and with the obvious desire to ration what cannot actually be prohibited. This leads to some curious results; there are several comments of a traditional kind on female propensity to gossip, but compared with pages on sex there is hardly a word on envy or malice resulting from such gossip; similarly, students are more often rebuked for lechery than idleness, a more familiar occupational disease. In general sins of violence, anger, greed, jealousy, sloth, even pride are almost ignored in comparison with those of lust and avarice.[1]

Obedience is the only remedy offered for this state of affairs, and no sermon fails to make the point at length and in detail that the guide to right conduct is no mystery, but is laid down in

[1] It is interesting to compare this with some figures compiled by Owst, *Preaching in Mediaeval England,* p. 323, n. 2, for references to particular sins occurring in the treatise by Waldeby: Avaritia 56, Luxuria 33, Superbia 32, Invidia 23, Gula 19. Even in the fourteenth century, and in England, the themes were the same: poverty, chastity and obedience in that order.

Scripture, in the Church's laws, based on Scripture, and, to some extent, the laws of the land, which should ultimately reflect divine justice. They offer no Utopia, and their examples of good living are nearly always Christ and the Apostles, and then the saints, especially those whose feast they are commemorating. Their own, or other orders, are not held up as models except in the most special cases. It is no part of their purpose to preach an easy virtue within the reach of all, but rather man's complete dependence on God, whose grace he must strive to earn, though it can come only as a free gift.

This was the atmosphere in which Rabelais and his readers were brought up. In his reactions both to lawyers and to women he shows many of the same feelings as his former brethern, and his choice of language cannot fail to evoke echoes of the sermons. It is fitting to conclude this tableau of the contemporary scene with a text from Maillard, which not only shows how gloomy a view he takes of the world around him but is an admirable example of his oratorical skill, comparable with the Prologue to the *Tiers Livre*:

Quis enumerare sufficeret quot perjuria, passim, dietim, communiter ac indistincte bibendo, comedendo, ludendo, fabulando, emendo, vendendo, eundo, redeundo, in domibus, in ecclesiis, in theatro, in foro, in curiis et aliis quibuslibet locis, ab omnibus personis cujuslibet status, gradus, sexus aut conditionus, committuntur?[1] (F/100)

---

[1] 'Who would be competent to enumerate how many perjuries, constantly, daily, commonly and indifferently, whether eating, drinking, playing, gossiping, buying, selling, going, coming, at home, church, theatre, in the market, at the courts and anywhere else you like are committed, by all persons of every rank, position, sex or condition?'

6 : STYLE AND TECHNIQUE OF THE SERMONS

WHEN the majority of people are unable to read the influence of the spoken word in forming popular literary taste is naturally very great. All through the Middle Ages, and well into the sixteenth century, many people must have made their first acquaintance with organized literary form of any pretentions through hearing sermons, especially those preached in a series for Advent or Lent by friars invited for their fame and skill. At any rate until the invention of printing sermons could maintain a more consistent standard than any other form of popular literature simply because of their origin and purpose; though they rarely achieved literary excellence, the average level of the sermons is respectable. While there were no schools of writing for story-tellers, dramatists and so on (at least in a formal sense), the sermon was the product of a particular order or group, carefully prepared according to a set plan and carrying on the tradition of centuries with conscious fidelity. As with all examples of the spoken word, ultimate success depended on the individual speaker, but delivery was as much a matter of training as composition, and a high degree of uniformity could be assured. All in all the sermon preserved a continuity of popular appeal, style and technique for centuries until the Counter-Reformation changed the fashion. For Rabelais the sermon offered a double source of inspiration; first in the oral tradition, and then in the peculiar visual appeal of the printed versions, which combined the oddest Latin with bursts of very colloquial French.

The main characteristics of the genre had long been fixed;[1] the use of *prothema* (a miniature sermon introducing the main one) and *thema*, the usual practice ('more solita') of choosing a point ('quaestio') of theology or canon law for the body of the sermon, the division and sub-division of the sermon, often with remarkable virtuosity, according to the words, and even the letters, of a

---

[1] Nève, in the preface to his edition of Menot, gives an excellent study of the technique of the medieval sermon, and Gilson in his review article on this book adds some details, 'M. Menot et la technique du sermon médiéval' in *Idées et Lettres*.

Scriptural text. Up to a point particular occasions, like the feast of St. Mary Magdalene, or particular liturgical gospels and epistles, like the casting of the money-changers out of the Temple, would provoke more or less similar reactions from different preachers, but otherwise the unexpected, not to say incongruous, treatment of texts makes for considerable variety. Some whole series have a single theme (e.g. Maillard's *Stipendium Peccati*), others continue the same theme through several sermons in a series, sometimes a bewildering range of questions occurs within a single sermon. While it is true to say that the ultimate key to each series and each sermon is scriptural, it is also true that the mechanical division of texts robbed the word of much, if not all, of its meaning by the time the final subdivision was reached. None the less, the finished product of a Maillard or a Messier represents a very considerable feat of organization, and for all its artificiality communicates its message clearly enough.

All this is true of the sermons as they have come down to us, but the directions included for intending users of the texts are valuable in showing the sort of variation which was recognized as advisable or not according to circumstances. Maillard, or his editor, on several occasions recommends a still ampler illustration of legal or theological points than the already generous version of the printed text. 'Preacher at the end of the question repeat the cases of the law to which Maillard briefly referred.'[1]

Other remarks make it clear that the appetite of the listeners, not of the preacher, was to be the deciding factor. Menot, speaking of the Donation of Constantine, adds the note: 'Here resolve, if you wish, that difficulty',[2] namely the authenticity of the donation and Constantine's right in any case to dispose of the powers in question.

Later on he leaves it to the discretion of the preacher whether or not to appeal directly to the audience: 'Preach, if you wish, about despising the world, inducing youths to forsake it for a religious vocation.'[3] A more curious case concerns discretion on a matter where Menot evidently felt a little unsure: 'Tell the story, if it seems consistent with chaste speech ("castum eloquium") of

---

[1] 'Tu praedicator in fine quaestionis repete casus legis per Maillardum summarie allegatae.' (A/2 v.)

[2] 'Resolve, si vis, hic difficultatem illam.' (P/374)

[3] 'Praedica, si vis, de mundi contemptu, saeculares adolescentes ex hoc inducens ad ingressum religionis.' (P/452)

the procurator who, finding his wife with another man and the door open, drew the curtains, closed the door and went off feeling wretched.'[1]

Number LXXI of the *Cent Nouvelles Nouvelles* amplifies the rather tantalizing reference, and one would very much like to know how many preachers managed to fit this story into their personal conception of 'castum eloquium'.

On another occasion Menot's misgivings are more pronounced: 'Beware, preacher in case you scandalize simple minds by saying this.'[2]

The warning is certainly not superfluous and concerns the bizarre theory of another Franciscan, Huet, to the effect that Mary so dearly desired the redemption of humanity that 'she would have crucified her Son with her own hands' had no one else been there to do it.

Similar injunctions, 'sed de hoc sobrie' and the like, show that the preachers were well aware of the reactions of different audiences and were bold within well defined limits. These, it should be said, never applied to actual language, where complete freedom seems to have been the rule. With this freedom of language went on occasion a notable disregard for convention in outward behaviour. An often quoted example is almost certainly based on a misunderstanding;[3] the celebrated cough, 'Ahem!', of the Bruges sermon is most likely an indication to Maillard's reader that the audience might be expected to cough and fidget at just that point, though the episode of Janotus de Bragmardo suggests that coughs were exploited deliberately for rhetorical ends. Still more striking, and unimpeachably attested, are the songs based on popular melodies which Maillard sang, and perhaps even improvized, from the pulpit just before the end of his long life. A contemporary of equal fame, Jean Bourgeois, had no less striking pulpit methods, and in order to stir his hearers' hearts would carry into the pulpit a death's head to remind them of their final end.[4]

---

[1] 'Dic, si videtur castum eloquium, de illo procuratore qui uxore sua cum alio inventa et ostio aperto, cortinas clausit et ostium camerae, et sic recessit miser.' (P/413)

[2] 'Cave, o tu praedicator, ne hoc dicendo scandalizes intellectus simplicium.' (P/453)

[3] This sermon, and the songs, are to be found in *Œuvres Françaises*.

[4] See Sessevalle, op. cit., pp. 128 seq.

In actual methods of exposition too the sermons employ devices calculated to arouse and maintain attention. Maillard is specially fond of dramatizing his points by creating personages to debate them. Thus a debate (A/40 v.) on the Immaculate Conception (preached on that feast) presents the argument through the mouths of Domina Mendacium and Veritas, and on another occasion (Q/119 v.) to reinforce a point he cries: 'Hear Paul on the right, Peter on the left, two most powerful witnesses', and proceeds to quote from their epistles. Maillard is also fond of puzzles and ingenious etymologies. In one sermon he asks who were the two women who lived together for five thousand years without composing their quarrel, and answers that they were Virginitas and Maternitas, only reconciled in the person of the Virgin Mother.

Elsewhere (Q/176) he offers some learned diabology, quoting a gloss on the word 'dyabolus', which derives, according to this authority (apparently Bonaventura), from '*dya*', that is 'two', and '*bolus*', meaning 'a lump', thus '*dyabolus*' means 'making two lumps of body and soul'.

Messier's diabology brings him, perhaps by accident, to a more accurate interpretation, recalling one of Rabelais's favourite words for the devil: 'In the first place the devil reckons like a claimant with the tax-collector. For like a claimant, French *contreroleur*, like a false accountant, he counts most carefully those expenses which he sees the official has overlooked.'[1]

In the main, however, the devils who figure so largely in the sermons are conventional, almost automatic, performers. The formulas are all similar and all come as the culminating piece of invective against some class of evildoer: 'Ad mille diabolos . . . Ego invito vos ad omnes diabolos . . . Ibitis ad omnes diabolos in infernum . . . Multi papae, damnati ad omnes diabolos . . . Ad 30,000 diabolos talis poena.' The most extravagant of all: 'Sed si moriaris in peccato mortali semper et in perpetuum eris

---

[1] 'Primo diabolus computat sicut calumniator cum receptore instituto. Sicut enim calumniator, gallice contreroleur, sicut falsus auditor computi, . . . illas expensas diligentissime computat in quibus vidit receptorem neglexisse.' (67 v.) The Greek word 'diabolos' does mean 'calumniator' in Latin, which is why Rabelais and other humanists so often use the latter word for the devil. In medieval Latin 'calumniator' is the usual word for one making a claim or challenge, both in a legal and a general sense, and it is clear that this is how Messier is using the word. It had no necessarily pejorative sense either in legal or fiscal contexts until the Renaissance restored its original Latin meaning of deception.

demoniacus in inferno et possessus a cent mille pannerées de diables.' (P/389)

This sort of language may have added a picturesque touch to doctrine, but it is hard to believe that such repetition, or such statistics, can have produced a very deep impression. In the matter of personal invective the sermons show more imagination, and indeed fervour. The English 'goddam' survived as 'goddon', quite a favourite term of abuse with the preachers. Maillard addresses rapacious clerics: 'O gros goddons, damnati infames et scripti in libro diaboli, fures et sacrilegi.' (A/23 v.) Menot speaks in like fashion to negligent clergy: 'Gros goddons, escornifleurs d'offices.' Corrupt prelates are 'grossos goddons venenos et inflatos per peccatum'. (T/31)

Very many of the sermons deal with sexual licence of one sort or another, but it is not only the concubines and harlots who are attacked, in fact they are treated if anything less harshly than those who procure their ruin. The word *macquerelle* occurs very often, not always with a precise meaning, but invariably with violent scorn:

O puantes maquerelles, inhonestae maritatae, quomodo potestis pro foeti ditate tam horribile dare animas vestras? (T/76)
O mauldicte macquerelle, impudens et inhonesta paillarde, puis après que tu auras gaudy et prins tes faulx plaisirs et voluptez, jusques au bout de l'aulne, mundus cui scrivivisti impediet ne te damnari? Leno tuus, o paupercula et misera paillarde, impediet ipse te a damnatione? (T/92)

Most precise and most picturesque is this menace:

Est una macquerella quae posuit multas puellas au mestier, ad malum, ibit, elle s'en ira le grand galot, ad omnes diabolos. Est totum? Non, non, elle n'en aura pas si bon marché, non habebit tam bonum forum, sed omnes quos incitavit ad malum servient ei de bourrées et de cotteretz pour luy chauffer ses trente costés. (P/367)

These extracts give a good idea of the direct, often brutal and vulgar, methods of the preachers, who expounded their lessons in the language of the streets and the taverns.[1] It is impossible here to give an exhaustive list of all the French colloquialisms to

---

[1] Samouillan, himself a priest, has some interesting observations on this point: 'le fond celtique d'humour qui constitue l'esprit gaulois est profondément philosophique et humain, et n'offre d'ailleurs aucune incompatibilité avec l'esprit chrétien' (O. Maillard, p. 280), and, speaking of obscenity in the Middle Ages: 'sagesse, amour du vrai, détachement et mépris du monde, sentiment plus profond du néant universel . . . en harmonie avec l'esprit chrétien.'

be found in sixteenth-century sermons,[1] and it is abundantly clear that the preachers not only did not make any effort to create a separate style and vocabulary peculiar to their calling, but indeed went further in familiarity than many secular contemporaries. They combine colloquial expressions with animal similes, they quote proverbs and make puns, they refer to popular songs, and all this with such insistence that the original French is more often than not reproduced with the approximate Latin translation lest the point be lost. A few examples give some idea of the effect:

'Vos gaudisseurs, meretrices, macquerelles, lusores et telle manière de billon.' (A/32 v.)

'. . . et habetis embureliqoqués illos gaudisseurs.' (A/42 v.)

'Invenietis in eis [escornifleurs d'offices] tantam devotionem sicut in simia xxx annorum.' (T/31)

'Ces escornifleurs de bona dies, qui sunt ita innocentes sicut simia xxx annorum.' (P/330)

Menot compares the clergy to 'those baboons which are set up on towers or pillars. We see not just in spirit but with our eyes asses crowned and sitting in the place of the apostles.'[2]

Messier too turns to zoology for his illustrations, and explains a popular fabliau thus: 'Morally the monkey without a tail is a priest without a benefice . . . The fox with his abundant tail is the one with numerous benefices.' and 'How many asses are crowned today who know nothing.' He compares the unworthy prelates currently produced by the Church to 'moles, serpents, or horned asses' (i.e. the horns of the mitre).[3]

On several occasions a quotation from Isaiah is used to effect against the clergy of the day. Thus Menot: 'There are many now of whom it could be said as in Isaiah lvi: They are all dumb dogs and cannot bark, for they have a bone in their mouths.'[4] 'For our modern doctors [of theology] in France are gagged, they have a bone in their mouth.'[5]

---

[1] Nève gives an impressive list drawn from Menot (pp. lxii–lxix) and Samouillan gives some from Maillard.

[2] 'Sunt sicut isti babouini qui ponuntur in turribus seu pilariis. Videmus non spiritu sed ad oculum asinos coronari et sedere loco apostolorum.' (P/245)

[3] 'Moraliter simia carens cauda est sacerdos carens beneficio . . . Vulpes autem abundanter caudata est multipliciter beneficiatus. . . . O quot hodie sunt asini coronati qui nil sciunt . . . talpas, serpentes, asinos cornutos.' (R/127 v.)

[4] 'Sed nunc de multis potest dici illud Esaiae lvi: Universi canes muti, non valentes latrare; habent enim os in ore.' (P/230)

[5] 'Doctores enim nostri qui sunt in Francia sunt embaillonnez, habent os in ore,' (P/329) because they do not denounce the monstrous abuses caused by the Roman Curia.

Messier elaborates the same theme: 'But there are some dumb dogs who cannot bark, and these are those doctors who are now canons or beneficed and used to preach at the beginning; but on leur a geté ung os en la gueulle and so they are silent.'[1] As a variant on his monkey's lack of devotion Menot takes another animal: 'Scribae et Pharisaei ... tantam habebant ad Deum devotionem que ung chat à nager, cattus ad navigandum. (P/405) Finally a farmyard image: 'Numquam poule n'ayma chapon, nec castus meretricem.' (T/106)

These animal examples are only a few of the striking expressions that occur, many of a proverbial nature and found also in Rabelais. By a curious coincidence Maillard brings into one sentence two words which at once recall the *Tiers Livre*: 'Dominae burgenses ... habetis ne tunicas vestras à la *grant gorre*? Et vos qui ponderatis gressus vestros et vaditis gressu inconsueto; alias *au gros bis*; quibus videtur quod nullus est dignus vos aspicere.'[2]

The old poet Raminagrobis had married 'la Grant Gorre', according to *Tiers Livre* XXI, and though it cannot be proved that Rabelais had this text in mind, the coincidence is extraordinary.

In his sermon on the Prodigal Son Menot describes the plight of the penniless young man: 'Il n'y avoit que frire et que mettre soubs la dent.' (P/382)

Speaking of the Five Thousand Menot recalls the famous open-air banquet in *Gargantua*: 'Sedebant ibi sur la belle herbe verte et post comestionem habebant licentiam eundi ad bibendum in mari *à tyre larigot*.' (P/417)

The grim jest about 'faire cardinal sans aller à Romme' has already been mentioned; another jest which recalls Rabelais is connected with a famous saint, not found in the Church calendar but no less honoured for that: 'Numquid loquimini vos mulieres de amatoribus vestris quando estis in festo *sancti Pansardi*?' (Q/189) 'Vos colitis festum *sancti Pensardi*, qui est dies diaboli.' (Q/194)

Referring to Hell, Maillard quotes a popular jingle: 'Non est jocus, non est fabula. Il n'y a ne si ne qua car il faut passer par là.' (Q/222 v.)

---

[1] 'Sed sunt aliqui canes muti qui non possunt latrare, et sunt illi doctores qui modo sunt canonici et beneficiati et in principio praedicabant: sed on leur a geté ung os en la gueulle et ideo tacent.' (31)

[2] 'Mesdames, ... are you wearing your sumptuous tunics? And what about you who walk with measured tread and unaccustomed gait, all stuck up, thinking nobody fit to look at you.' (A/10)

There are other popular sayings: 'De troys choses Dieu nous garde. De cetera de notaires. De qui pro quo d'apothicaires. Et de bouchon de lombard friscaires.' (A/72) 'Monachus in chorea et musca in lacte, nescio quid vilius.' (P/273)

We hear of an unprepared death: 'Sacerdos suadetur ei [morienti] ut faciat testamentum porci, quia non dicet nisi: ouy, ouy, en.'[1] and of God's justice: 'Deus non est remunerator nominum sed adverborum, i.e. non remunerabit opus quod fit, sed quod bene fit.'[2]

One sermon tells of the wailing of the damned in Hell, and describes their song as having: 'Sex notas valde miserabiles, scil. Ut, Re, Mi, Fa, Sol, La.' (P/246) presumably demonstrated in the pulpit, and then expounded at great length by scriptural quotation introduced by the respective syllables of the scale.

Menot's humour has much verve: 'Melius esset leprosam esse quam pro pulchritudine frangere matrimonium—O frater, dicetis, non frangimus, mais nous le ployons.'[3] but not always much taste, as in the play on words which the Latin disguises, but which in the original was 'saints-seins': 'O vos Dominae . . . videbitis quod abscondimus sanctos. Amore Dei abscondatis sinus vestros, quia macellum est clausum in Quadragesima.'[4]

A suggestion of misogyny appears in this unexpected comparison: 'Citius evacuaretur fimus stabuli in quo fuissent XLIV equi quam domina esset disposita et posuisset toutes ses espingles.'[5]

His description of good living is effective too: 'Facientes salisas si friandes qu'on y mangeroit une vielle savate.' (P/362)

Maillard is equally skilful in finding the right phrase: 'Garrula lingua sicut babillator qui non potest tacere; sed semper clamat. Sicut ung tracquet gallice; latine vero tara tara unius molendini.'[6]

---

[1] 'The priest persuades him to make a pig's testament on his deathbed, because he can only say ouy, ouy, en.' (P/459)

[2] 'God rewards not nouns but adverbs; that is, he does not reward the deed done, but the deed well done.' (P/299)

[3] 'It would be better for you to be leprous than break your marriage vows because you are beautiful—O Father, you say, we are not breaking it, only bending it.' (T/12)

[4] 'Mesdames, you see we hide the saints [veiled in Lent]. For God's sake hide your breasts, because there is no flesh on show in Lent.' (literally: 'the butcher's shop is closed') (P/468)

[5] 'It would be quicker to muck out a stable where forty-four horses had been than for Madame to be ready with all her pins in place.' (P/331)

[6] 'A wagging tongue is like a babbler who can't keep quiet but cries all the time. Like a mill-clapper.' (A/35) 'Babillator' probably represents some popular name for a bird in French; cf. modern French 'fauvette babillarde', a whitethroat warbler.

Even taken out of their context, as here, these brief extracts are striking in themselves, but in order fully to appreciate their impact one must read them with their background of laborious Latin, where the lapses into French always come as a slight shock. Allowing for the original French of their actual delivery, one must remember that every one of these phrases is used to press home a point of doctrine or exhortation, often quite technical. Numerous as these examples of familiar speech are, they form a very small proportion, though a highly important one, of the total volume of the sermons, and thus each provides the occasion for a sudden contrast of style, an unexpected trick of oratory, which cannot be conveyed by any means short of reading the original. The point to be emphasized is the immediate value to any literary artist of such well-tested precedents, and also the value to us of so clear a criterion of what was normal and accepted practice in sacred contexts. It would need a far more detailed study than lies within the scope of the present work to assess adequately the stylistic debt owed by Rabelais and others to the sermon tradition, but even these few extracts should show how closely related are the styles of all those whose appeal was deliberately popular, whether sacred or profane.[1]

On the question of literary models, there is a final point of great importance: the exempla. These anecdotes and illustrations occupy a leading part in the sermons, and vary from traditional to topical, from scabrous to hagiological. In content and narrative technique they provide a most valuable comparison with secular story-tellers, and indeed borrowing is sometimes reciprocal, as with Menot and the *Cent Nouvelles Nouvelles*.

Numerous collections of exempla still survive covering various periods, regions or orders, and a very varied picture of medieval tastes can be built up by following the fortunes of particular specimens. The Classical Renaissance showed how enduring the fashion of exempla had become; Rabelais and Montaigne are equally typical of their respective generations in this. The actual position of the exemplum in the different sermons varies according to the context, and some sermons consist indeed of a single extended exemplum, like Menot's impressive Prodigal Son. Maillard uses them particularly to illustrate points of law and doctrine, Menot and Messier are more literary in their choice, both having

[1] Both Owst's books deal with just this point.

a notable predilection for zoology. Literally any source could, and did, provide exempla and the selection which follows is representative but only a fraction of the total to be found in these sermons. A large and important group of exempla is drawn from hagiology. Many come from the *Golden Legend*, and in Franciscan sermons the saints of the order figure fairly prominently, though less than one might have expected. It is, however, a point of some interest that in one case, that of Farinier's twenty-one sermons on the seven deadly sins, the third sermon on each sin is devoted to examples of the saints, and especially of St. Francis, through whom we may derive comfort and inspiration. It may well be that this rather mechanical, but useful, formula was more common than the sermons examined here suggest. The conversion of Alexander of Hales, responsible more than anyone else for the entry of the order into the universities, occurs at least twice at some length in Menot, but hardly at all in the others, who mention him mainly as an authority. Bonaventura is not mentioned in exempla either, and inspires only one passing remark (Q/143) from Maillard, who links his name with that of St. Thomas as an example of a good religious who was also a good scholar. Very surprisingly the founder himself is seldom mentioned at any length, despite the ready-made exempla of the *Fioretti*, not to mention the *Liber de Conformitate* to which Henri Estienne later took such exception. Menot, for instance, speaks of him only half a dozen times, mostly to stress his humility, but also to show him thanking God for the beauty of His creatures. Other references are more general, such as regrets for a more worthy age in which such saints could flourish.

Menot, like the others, is a habitual *laudator temporis acti*, and in one sermon at Tours speaks of his predecessors in the order, saintly men all:

What holy religious man in the last hundred years has preached in France and has not preached to you? You surely remember such holy men as Friar Antoine Farinier, Tisserand, Friar Jean Bourgeois.[1]

What was true of Tours was true too of Paris:

Mesdames, Messieurs, how many good religious preach and have preached the truth to you and told you what you do not do? I don't mean those who lived in the time of King Clothair, I am talking about

---

[1] 'Quis sanctus religiosus a centum annis praedicavit in Gallia qui non praedicaverit vobis? Habetis bene memoriam sanctorum virorum . . .' (T/55)

those you have seen in your own time preaching, especially of our order. You have seen Friar Antoine, Friar Richard, Friar Jean Tisserand, who brought back poor penitent girls, Friar Jean Bourgeois, Friar Olivier Maillard who are renowned for miracles and whose life and doctrine is approved by all.[1]

These two references give a good idea of the continuity of tradition within the order, and bring out clearly which names were most held in honour by the contemporaries of Rabelais. For the rest, Franciscan propaganda is conspicuously lacking from the sermons. Many of the more popular saints provide material for the sermons. Apart from the *pièces de circonstance* produced for the saint's actual day, such as the remarkable sermons on St. Mary Magdalene, there are anecdotes about the saints which evidently formed part of the preachers' stock in trade. Some are bizarre, some moral, some historical, and at times it seems as though the familiar principle of epic invention is at work, whereby incidents are attracted from one figure to another more prominent. The French patron, St. Denis, provides a particularly rich store of legend, for he was identified not only with the person martyred in Paris, but also with the Denis (Dionysius) whose name was appropriated by the author of the works of pseudo-Dionysius the Areopagite and who was supposed to have been one of St. Paul's first converts. The story of this triple saint's reaction to the natural phenomena observed in Athens at the time of the Passion had immense influence, and is quoted by Maillard and Menot (twice):

Then Saint Denis, who was at Athens when he saw this [eclipse] and when all were amazed, said: 'Either the god of all nature is suffering or the whole machine of the universe is being destroyed.' And then they made an altar at Athens in memory of him who suffered and it was called the altar of the unknown god.[2]

[1] 'O Domini et Dominae quot sunt et quot fuerunt boni religiosi praedicantes vobis veritatem et id quod non facitis? Non capiemus eos qui fuerunt a tempore Regis Clotharii; loquamur de eis quos vidistis tempore vestro praedicantes, et specialiter de ordine nostro: Vidistis fr. Antonium, fr. Richardum, fr. Joh. Tisserand, qui reduxit pauperes filias penitentes, fr. Joh. Bourgeoys, fr. Olivier Maillard qui clarent miraculis, quorum vita et doctrina ab omnibus approbatur.' (P/329)
  Cf. 'Panurge . . . preschoit eloquentement, comme si feust un petit frère Olivier Maillard ou un second frère Jan Bourgeoys.' (*QL*/viii)
[2] 'Tunc beatus Dionysius qui erat Athenis quando vidit hoc; et omnes mirabantur: dixit: Aut deus totius naturae patitur, aut tota machina mundi destruitur. Et tunc Athenis fecerunt unum altare in memoriam illius qui passus est et vocabatur altare dei ignoti.' (Q/211)

Originally from the *Golden Legend*, this story seems to have become for Franciscan preachers at least an essential part of the Passion recital, and its importance in the later development of Rabelais's thought may have been decisive.

The lesson drawn (A/33) from St. Nicholas's action in favour of the three young girls has already been mentioned, and comes in fact from a sermon preached on his feast. A variety of moral lessons is drawn from the life of the saintly bishop, contrasted with his less saintly successors.

Another exemplum of particular popularity concerns conversion. There is a whole group of similar tales, all aimed at showing the vanity of academic pursuits, even theology, unless a godly life goes with them. Menot twice refers to the conversion of Alexander of Hales in this connexion, but the most famous because of its dramatic qualities, and the one most familiar in iconography, is that of Bruno. According to legend (Q/122 v.) Bruno's Parisian master, Raymond, was being carried to burial when his corpse suddenly rose up on the bier and cried out that he was damned, for having devoted his life (very successfully) to the pursuit of knowledge instead of his own salvation. Though young Bruno is never supposed to have led the dissolute life which so often precedes legendary conversions, the experience was enough to turn him away from the world and make him found the Carthusian order, for which Maillard had such admiration. This particular tale is typical of certain elements specially dear to the Middle Ages, in profane and sacred literature alike: the voice from the dead. Leaving aside the special case of Lazarus, always a source of much interest, these elements include the unmasking from beyond the tomb of a character whose life had been generally assumed to be blameless, the violent conversion from what is usually a thoroughly worldly life to one of frightening asceticism, and the general suspicion of what St. Augustine had so eloquently condemned as '*libido sciendi*'. The very similar episodes in *romans courtois*, and indeed as late as Epistemon's resurrection in Rabelais, suggest a permanent psychological pattern.

A remarkable variation on the voice from the dead theme is ascribed by Maillard to St. Bernard. It will be remembered that Menot has an even more pungent tale told by an anonymous monk. According to Maillard, the Abbot of Clairvaux returns from Heaven and speaks to one of his former brethren:

Eo die quo ante tribunal summi judicis fui vocatus, 35,000 obierunt; de quibus tantum tres salvati sunt; scil. ego et quidam heremita; et quidam mercator, qui nondum est in paradiso sed in purgatorio. Alii omnes aeternaliter sunt damnati.[1]

Such vital statistics, coming from a source so reliable, were not to be ignored, but one wonders why so modest a figure as 35,000 was chosen, even in the comparatively small medieval world.

The most hair-raising exemplum of all, and almost certainly the longest, occupies the greater part of a sermon which comes at the end of Maillard's Lenten series, though not actually forming part of it. (Q/222 v.) This occupies six closely printed columns, and tells the whole horrific life and death of Eudo, Bishop of Magdeburg. This man after a promising beginning, rose to high office in the Church at the price of his own soul, and the latter and most lurid part of the tale describes how devils come to seize him, and how attempts were made, on the evidence of those who had seen the infernal visitations, to depose the wretch. The story in this case is so long and so detailed, that one has the impression that even the preacher was more fascinated by the events than anxious to point the hardly obscure moral.

The type of exemplum which the sixteenth century particularly favoured and of which the pattern is to be seen in Erasmus's *Aphorisms*, is very rare in the sermons. Classical authors are quoted quite frequently, but almost always for some moral sentence, and not for any actual episode. Menot (T/31) exceptionally speaks of Demosthenes, to whom he attributes the maxim 'sapientiam auro meliorem', but Greek and Roman antiquity is represented almost exclusively by books and not by people.

In much the same way the world of epic and romance makes incidental appearances in the sermons. Maillard and Menot both speak in general terms of the romances, which they condemn, and Menot (T/37) refers to his hearers' familiarity with the *Roman de la Rose* and *Melusine*. Messier (52 v.) gives an exemplum of King Arthur, but this should rather be accounted history than epic, for he ascribes to the '*Historia Britonum*' the legend that Arthur bore on the inside of his shield a picture of the Virgin at which he would look when needing fresh strength in battle.

---

[1] 'On the day I was called before the tribunal of the supreme judge 35,000 died; of these only three are saved: myself and a certain hermit, and a certain merchant, who is not yet in Paradise but in Purgatory. All the rest are eternally damned.' (Q/174)

Somewhat more historical (William of Malmesbury for one includes both stories in his history) is the anecdote (66) of William the Conqueror stumbling as he disembarked on English soil, but interpreting the omen favourably by exclaiming that he had begun by clutching a handful of the land he was soon to conquer. It is not very clear why Messier took this interest in English history, but he goes on to link William's experience in England with a very popular exemplum, used by the other preachers as well. According to this, men betray their origin by their accent, and different preachers illustrate the point by choosing various provinces, and going on to show how we betray our origin, divine or diabolical, by our spiritual accent. Messier relates this exemplum and emphasizes it by a quite lengthy account of how William succeeded in replacing native Saxon in England by French, and by Latin for his clerks. It looks as though his references to English history reflect some recent reading or perhaps even a visit, but it is an indication of the variety of subjects which the preachers were prepared to introduce into their sermons.

Rather more interesting is the use made both by Maillard and Menot of personal reminiscences of an age already quite far distant. Maillard refers briefly on several occasions to Louis XI, the harsh ruler of a former epoch whose terrors effectively prefigure the harshness of the Day of Judgement. One phrase of Maillard's recalls Louis's hated and evil minister, Tristan l'Hermite, who, according to Maillard, was wont to say: 'By St. Catherine, that is neither man nor woman, hurry him off to the gallows.'[1]

It is quite certain that the bogy of a figure vividly and painfully remembered by the older generation would impress men more deeply with the inexorable nature of divine justice than some of the fanciful statistics more common in sermons.

Menot too finds in Louis XI a potent reminder that even earthly justice can give a faint picture of that awful day to come. He tells (T/24) in some detail how the king avenged himself on those citizens of Arras who persisted in their loyalty to the Duke of Burgundy, and like Maillard draws a grim parallel between what is after all only a finite punishment and that which threatens us hereafter.

---

[1] 'Per sanctam Katherinam iste nec est vir nec mulier, festinanter ducatis ad patibulum.' (Q/187)

The most characteristic feature of Menot's style is, as has often been mentioned, the vivid and varied range of zoological references. One which caught Estienne's fancy describes the procession of the Carnival ox through the streets of Paris, and is used in Menot's Lenten series of both Tours and Paris (T/11, P/346). The lively picture of the animal decked out in all its finery, being led through the merry crowds apparently in triumph, only to be felled mercilessly while still in its trimmings, impresses the reader and must have been even more effective in the pulpit.

In a different vein is the fabliau (T/17) of the mule, boasting of its high connexions, of the prelates and princes borne by his kinsfolk, only to be reminded brutally by a peasant of his lowly antecedents. This particular story, from Aesop, was later adapted by La Fontaine.

Another very graphic description is that of the magpie hunt, also repeated at Tours and Paris. In a few strokes Menot fills in the picture of the terrified bird, pursued by the hawk from above, dogs from below, and finally flushed from refuge in a bush by the huntsman. The very involved moral, comparing the situation of our souls with that of the bird, is less impressive than the story as a literary performance.

A good example of Menot's style is an animal exemplum, which involves the monkey and the fox so often alluded to by other preachers:

Cum simiae tenebant statum et habebant uxorem et assessores, et aliquis babouin transivit. O, dicit dominus, et transitis sic, sine faciendo honorem curiae?—Et de quo teneor vobis facere honorem, qui estis ita infectae personae et inhonestae?—Et le babouin fut empoigné et scinditur ejus cauda.—O, dicitur domino, O quam felix est qui est in curia vestra. Ecce, hoc dixit vulpes, et statim data est ei cauda longa et tunica magna et authoritas faciendi quaecumque vellet.[1]

Accompanied by the appropriate gestures the story could not have failed to register.

Another type of illustration, not necessarily an exemplum, is the deliberately topical or local allusion. Menot makes Solomon

---

[1] 'When the monkeys were holding court with their wives and assessors a baboon passed by. "O, said the lord, that is how you pass by, without paying your respects to the court?"—"And for what reason should I pay respect to you, unclean and disreputable persons that you are?"—And the baboon was seized and his tail cut off.—"O, said someone to the lord, how happy is the man who dwells in your court."—Now this was the fox, and at once he was given a long tail and authority to do whatever he liked.' (T/59)

say to the two women he is judging. 'As I can see, you never studied at Angers or Poitiers so that you could plead your case well.' (P/265)

Maillard speaks (A/36) of a man claiming to be a burgher's only son, sent some time before to study medicine at Montpellier, and Menot's comments on student behaviour at Orleans and Poitiers belong to the same class. So, perhaps, does Maillard's story of matrimonial discord which begins: 'A certain noble once told me in Angers . . .' (A/51 v.)

Many stories are set in Paris, as one would expect, whether in university, cathedral or city, and some evidently belong to well-established local folklore, like those of Pierre de Coignet and Philippe, subject of a minatory exemplum (Q/139) on the perils of pluralism.

Maillard seems, though the impression is only a subjective one, to range further for the locale of his exempla than others, and almost invariably gives a time and place to the more striking ones. Of these, one exceptionally well told (Q/215 v.) relates how a young beauty of Vendôme ignores her confessor's counsels and persists in her vanity. She asks him to bring back from a visit to Paris a really good mirror for her; he, determined to teach her a lesson, goes to the cemetery of the Innocents, looks round the remains of mortal men, and chooses the head of a beautiful woman who had died only a week or two before. Bringing back his gift carefully wrapped, he watches the young woman collect all her friends to admire this new witnesss to her beauty, and then suddenly uncovers it, exploiting the general horror to point the moral. That this story is well within the bounds of possibility is shown by the practice of Jean Bourgeois, mentioned earlier, of bringing a deathshead into the pulpit.

All these exempla, numerous as they are, are specialized in comparison with the greater number of what might be called pattern anecdotes. These are equally applicable to all situations and all audiences and in some cases details of location or identity can be seen modified from one preacher to another.

Maillard tells (Q/140) the story of a parish priest in Normandy, mocked by his bishop for keeping a nominal roll of his flock. The priest replies that the bishop can afford to take chances, since he has hawks and dogs enough to bring back any sheep who might wander from his diocese. When Menot tells (T/82) the same story, the details are slightly changed. In his version the parish is no longer specified as Norman, and the occasion for the priest's remark is the bishop's offer to him of a parish of two or three hundred souls, which the priest hesitates to accept.

Another very popular story is found in Farinier. (42 v.) It tells how a certain person spied on the general chapter of the demons, who are scolded one after another for having taken too long over their mission of securing various souls for damnation. At last one appears who says that he has finally corrupted a hermit, though it has taken him eleven years, far longer than any of his colleagues in their respective tasks. The achievement is recognized as remarkable, and this demon alone wins commendation and sympathy from his master. In Maillard's version (s/96) the worthy demon is he who has taken nine years to make a bishop fall in love with a maid in his household.

Another popular tale (s/99) concerns a young girl with a single precious ring, which her five brothers, all evildoers of various kinds, try to win from her, with offers of different disreputable rewards. She defends her virtue to the end, until a prince, as virtuous as he is handsome, appears, and to him she voluntarily surrenders her treasure. In the sermon this is used as an exhortation to young girls to keep their precious jewel for the Heavenly Bridegroom. When Messier tells (77 v.) the same story it is without pointing this particular moral.

The theme of five attempts and a jewel is transposed in another favourite story, of five women visited in turn by an *entremetteuse*, who on behalf of her master offers them a ring in exchange for certain favours. Maillard tells (A/7 v.) the tale as a dramatic dialogue, and makes the women respectively natives of Picardy, Poitiers, Tours, Lyon and Paris, in descending order of virtue. The first answers nothing, the second hesitates a moment until the ultimate of misconduct is reached with the Parisienne, who says that her husband will be out the following Wednesday. The story is accompanied by lively comments, and is used to show the different degrees of resistance to temptation. As Messier tells (98 v.) it, the story is very similar, but he says nothing of the origins of the women in question, a point stressed by Maillard, who constantly attacks the wickedness of Paris.

Sometimes the exemplum or illustration is exploited at great length throughout a whole sermon or even group of sermons.

Thus Menot begins a detailed exposition, comparing Our Lord's nature with the signs of the Zodiac, with the words: 'Astrologers say the sun passes through many signs.' (P/269)

Towards the beginning of his Advent sermons (A/7) Maillard proposes to examine 'ten sins of will, twenty of word, thirty of deed', and links all the sins of speech to a single exemplum. This describes how the devil fell ill and refused all the dainties offered to him, saying that only 'le pâté des langues' could restore him: 'I want to eat the food on which I was brought up. What women eat when they are in the baths. That food is tongue pâté.'[1]

The devil comes into many of these exempla, notably one in which Menot tells (T/52) of a notorious evildoer at whose death there was loud wailing from the demons, mourning the loss of one who had brought them so many damned souls and could now no longer serve their cause. It is interesting that Menot (or his editor) openly acknowledges the debt for this exemplum to an Advent series by one Grith, a Franciscan of Basle.

One of the few other directly acknowledged borrowings is from Valerius Maximus, who provides the well-known story (T/86) of the patrician Roman girl who nourished her mother, condemned to die of starvation in prison, from her own breast.

Maillard and Menot both have good stories on the theme of silence, though rather different in treatment. Menot describes how a talkative woman received from her confessor the simple penance of keeping silence through the length of a rosary, but who found even this more than feminine frailty could bear: 'How difficult it is to keep silent, I shall never accept the penance of silence!'[2]

Maillard starts from a legal maxim: 'The law says: "Silence signifies consent" . . . If you women ask your husbands' permission to go to banquets and they say nothing you interpret this as signifying their consent. And if they give you a great slap they might be said to dissent.'[3]

Finally two exempla set in church may be quoted. They have obvious emotional appeal, and may be based on fact. In a sermon preached at Christmastide Maillard goes to the *Golden Legend*

---

[1] 'Volo comedere de esca de qua fui nutritus. Quam comedunt mulieres in balneis existentes. Illa esca est pastillus de linguis.' (A/26)

[2] 'Quam difficile est silere, numquam sumam penitentiam silentii.' (T/200)

[3] 'Lex forensis dicit: Qui tacet consentire videtur . . . Si vos mulieres quaeratis licentiam maritis vestris ire ad banqueta, si nihil dicant, interpretative consentire videntur. Et si darent vobis unam magnam alapam, dicerentur dissentire.' (A/7 v.)

for the story of a dissolute woman who at last repents, but does not immediately find any hope of salvation. In a sermon more than usually full of tenderness he strikes the final note of comfort by making her say (following his source): 'I dare not have recourse to Your Passion, but to Your Nativity.'[1]

More than one of these Christmas sermons stress the helplessness of the Infant Jesus, and appeal to the maternal instinct of the hearers.

The other exemplum, from Farinier, is meant to urge not only the necessity, but also the efficacity of repentance. He recounts how a preacher produced such an effect by a sermon on penitence that at the end of it a woman flung herself at the foot of the pulpit and publicly confessed her wretchedness. Violated by her father, she had first poisoned her mother, then her father, and immediately after this horrible avowal fell dead before them all. The preacher at once calls for the prayers of all those present on behalf of this unfortunate soul, but is stopped by a voice from above: 'O preacher, do not pray for her, but ask her to pray for you for she is already with God.'[2]

It should be added that this is from a sermon on *Accidia*, spiritual sloth and despair. People, then as now, need perhaps to be jolted out of complacency more often than to be reassured, but the preachers were too experienced in psychology to omit all counterweight to their normal threats and recriminations.

The preceding selection represents only the smallest fraction of the vast fund of anecdote and exemplum to be found throughout the sermons. It should, however, be enough to give some idea of the richness of the field and also the public appetite for stories of all kinds. From the point of view of style and technique the exceptional value of such models is obvious.[3]

---

[1] 'Non audeo recurrere ad passionem vestram, sed recurro ad nativitatem vestram.' (A/82)

[2] 'O praedicator, noli orare pro ea, sed rogate eam ut oret pro vobis, quare jam cum Deo est.' (18 v.)

[3] The following judgement, though written with fourteenth-century England in mind, is no less appropriate to sixteenth-century France:

'The friars' blend of fact and fancy influenced English literature more than their scholarship did. It is a truism to say that lay writers would replace them as story-tellers and that the exemplum would find a new setting. More important was the friars' share in accustoming the public to listen to Classical and pseudo-Classical sayings and stories. Demand and supply stimulated each other. My study of the problems has filled in a corner of the old generalisation: When Chaucer mocked at the friars, he was biting the hand that fed him. They educated his audience.' Beryl Smalley, *English Friars and Antiquity in the early Fourteenth Century*, p. 307.

In the case of Rabelais, of course, they educated him too.

7 : LITERARY AND PSYCHOLOGICAL EFFECTS OF THE FRANCISCAN YEARS

BY 1532, when Rabelais published *Pantagruel*, he had already made his name as doctor and humanist, and it has always intrigued critics that he should at a relatively late age (about forty) have launched suddenly into a form of authorship unlikely to increase his prestige with his fellow scholars, and in any case behind the mask of a pseudonym. The motive commonly proposed for this departure is financial need, and this is almost certainly right. If the question 'why?' can thus be answered with fair assurance, the same cannot be said for 'how?', to judge from the suggestions usually put forward. We know that he deliberately imitated contemporaries with recent success in the same field, notably Merlin Coccaie (the ex-monk Folengo) and the anonymous author of the *Grandes Chroniques*, of which his own book was ostensibly a sequel, but the most casual glance at these two models reveals the vast gap between them and Rabelais. One might claim that genius has its own rules, and that first books often do show an astonishing sureness of touch, not always sustained later. It may well be that Rabelais had tried his hand at authorship before he risked publication, and that his efforts were either read aloud to chosen friends or circulated in manuscript, and there is nothing inherently improbable in such a hypothesis. The one explanation which seems never to have received the attention it deserves is also the most obvious; Rabelais's immediate success in a popular genre is partially at least a consequence of his Franciscan years.

He had been trained throughout his formative years for a specific career, which would eventually have involved him, if all went well, in intimate and constant contact with people of all classes, from the illiterate masses to the Court. His order had developed and perfected a style which we know to have been immensely effective and popular, and the wide diffusion in print of sermons by acknowledged masters must have helped to maintain standards amongst friars, not all of whom could deploy such talents. Rabelais was trained in an order whose main function was preaching, and though it cannot be proved that he ever preached himself (a certain time would first normally elapse after ordination) he undoubtedly had an orator's ear. A point to be made with insistence is the predominance of an oral style in an age of sporadic literacy, when many people became acquainted with popular literature through hearing it read aloud. This stylistic feature is very marked in Rabelais, and certain passages lose considerably unless they are read aloud (e.g. the quarrel over the cakes in *Gargantua* or the story of Diogenes and his tub in the Prologue to the *Tiers Livre*). The discursive style, full of anecdotes and exempla, all ostensibly pointing a moral, is another technique with which Rabelais had long been familiar and which he practises in his turn. Since his principal concern was to make money, he would have been unnaturally obtuse had he not exploited to the full the literary capital he had for so long put aside. As it is the popularity of the friars was matched by that of Rabelais's first books, and a comparison between the two invites the suggestion of cause and effect.

The question of how Rabelais formed his style and won immediate popular appeal is answered so well by a proper combination of the influences of models, always admitted, of personal experience in various milieux and of the hitherto neglected Franciscan training, in ascending order of importance, that it seems unnecessary to press the point. Beyond style, however, there is the larger, and perhaps more interesting, question of artistic creation. Here some very odd views have long prevailed. It has been pointed out by every critic of Rabelais that in all his books, and especially in the early ones, there are numerous reminiscences of his early years. Plattard and others have done valuable work on the role of Touraine and Poitou in the novel. To some extent the adoption of the epic pattern of birth, childhood, education and so on, especially when applied to the father after the son, quite naturally leads Rabelais to evoke his own childhood memories of Chinon and La Devinière, student days in Paris and the rest, and within this pattern of reminiscence critics have set aside a place, with somewhat perfunctory piety, for the *années de moinage*. We are told that Frère Jan and Seuillé belong to these memories, odd anecdotes about Cordeliers are thrown in for good measure, and a passable chapter of bits and pieces can be put together for any study of life and works. There is no need to acquiesce in accepting so obviously inadequate an approach.

One aspect of the problem, the psychological one, has apparently been ignored. When the work has been sifted for all references to Fontenay, or other Franciscan associations, the harvest is found to be very meagre; among members of the Fontenay cenacle, André Tiraqueau and Amaury Bouchard, both friends of long standing, and their near neighbour, Jean Bouchet, are mentioned, together with a few others from time to time; Amy, alone of all the friars Rabelais knew, comes up once or twice, but of conventual life, of the other brethren, there is not a word, apart from vague snarls at '*farfadets*'. The argument from silence has been rather overworked of late in Rabelais studies, and it is only with some reluctance that it is brought up here. In view of the admitted place of reminiscence in the work, the silence concerning formative years is very strange, and stranger still if one accepts the theory of Rabelais's implacable hostility to his former order. An angry dog might be expected at least to bark, if not to bite, and if he does neither it is time to ask why. The negative fact that names and incidents of Franciscan life are, apart from Amy's flight, not mentioned can hardly be explained without reference to Rabelais's career as a friar, but there is first a positive point concerning his creation.

It is not very easy to describe just what sort of a book Rabelais wrote, because it contains elements both of the fairy-story it was supposed to continue and of real life. It is fantasy and fact, based on truth, and comic in essence. In comic creation a frequent device is the exploitation of obsolescence, with middle-aged characters as the comic victims, or the middle past a setting for events. Chaucer, Shakespeare, Molière all use this technique; so does Rabelais. For the writer embarking on creation and wishing neither to recount autobiographical facts in the first person, real or assumed, nor to revive the historical past in a chronicle, a particularly fruitful theme is that of the private world. By this means the writer sees a certain section of the past, of which he has direct experience, as an organic whole, and writes about the recreated world, now gone beyond recall except in his memory, with the double advantages of temporal detachment and personal involvement. Proust is the extreme example of this technique (Wodehouse is another in a less exalted medium), and others will readily come to mind. Certain situations lend themselves particularly well to this form of creation, which ideally demands a state or phase to which the subject never expects to return, and which has produced a deep and lasting impression, further enhanced by memory. Such states are prison, schooldays, or active service, to name but three. There is nothing specifically comic about this phenomenon, though distance blunts a temporary anguish which in retrospect may well appear ridiculous. Life as a friar must for Rabelais have had elements of all three of the examples just given. It is submitted now that he made use of this closed chapter of his life to create for himself as an author an autonomous persona, distinct in time, place and mood from the respected scholar and doctor of Lyons, though, of course, engaging in dialogue with the latter at points in the book.

It has often been noted that successive editions of the early books tend to add archaisms to the style, that references to the past, for instance to the long dead Reuchlin affair, do not diminish through the work, and that the *Quart Livre* reflects an anachronistic approach to many current problems. If, as has already been suggested, Rabelais drew on Franciscan training for style and technique, it is surely likely that he also drew on his experience as one who had been inside the enemy camp. The element of parody is strongly marked in Rabelais, and it should be seriously asked whether this is not sometimes self-parody, in the context of his past identity. If this is so, one would expect echoes of formal intellectual training in the same context, and this point will be examined in the second part of this book.

It is time to return now to the negative problem of silence. The pseudonym, which he dropped only fourteen years later for the intellectually more pretentious *Tiers Livre*, the banal financial motive, and Rabelais's known cultural and scientific ambitions (and reputation) at the time of writing, all make it probable that he was not at first anxious to be identified with a book of which he may even have felt a little ashamed. Success no doubt helped him overcome this diffidence, but he claimed right up to the end to be writing only in his leisure moments, and it would be wrong to discount automatically such traditional protestations. Since it is generally claimed that Rabelais looked back on his career as a friar with feelings such that he was normally unwilling to talk about it except with hostility, the economic hypothesis is that for a work whose authorship he was not proud to acknowledge he should choose a persona, an identity, which was eminently expendable. To anticipate conclusions a little, there is a good deal to commend the idea that the emergence of Pantagruel as a serious hero in the later books coincides with Rabelais's success in emancipating himself effectively from a past compounded of much fruitless trial and error. This hypothesis is economical also in that it does not leave the *années de moinage* as a silent desert in the middle of a rich field of reminiscence extending from childhood to Montpellier. Rabelais speaks of what he likes to remember, and works out of his system what he wants to forget by exploiting and transforming it.

Both the first two books contain a wealth of disparate material, ranging from the popular appeal of the picnic following Gargantua's birth to the high-flown Ciceronian oratory of Ulrich Gallet. Some of the chapters are almost entirely borrowed from earlier models, and as such offer slight interest here, some draw copiously on the humour of the Latin Quarter, and are popular only in a limited social sense, some again are wholly serious in theme and treatment, like the letters from Grandgousier and Gargantua to their respective sons. Any interpretation which claimed to reduce all these, and other, different elements to a simple or single formula would quite properly be rejected; there is no one master key to Rabelais's creation.

The suggested picture looks something like this: Rabelais's first avowed intention was to continue and imitate a popular story-book, this was an activity beneath the dignity of one in his intellectual position, so he drew upon popular techniques learned in his youth, and could claim to have wasted no time on new apprenticeship for such unscholarly work. Then, for reasons of literary construction, it became necessary to show how the successive generations of giants were in the forefront of progress, each in his time, and for this he drew on his own experience when, as a young friar, he first came into contact with the New Learning, and eventually with his heroes, Erasmus and Budé. 'Bliss was it in that dawn to be alive' is the message of Gargantua's magnificent letter, and this early thrill of discovery can be firmly located in the *années de moinage*. This journey into the past took him back beyond organized Protestantism to the age of Erasmus—and indeed Maillard—when reform without schism seemed a perfectly feasible ideal, and when all men of good-will could still have been kept within the same fold. In those happier days it was enough to come to terms with one's local superiors, international forces had not yet been ranged on either side. Similarly the targets were fixed, and largely traditional, so that the social and religious satire was as straightforward as the demon-king of pantomime. Sorbonne-baiting had its dangers, but all the best people enjoyed the sport. The world of the child, the world of giant fantasy, the intoxicating vista of new horizons for the young friar who had nothing to lose but his cowl, are related ingredients in Rabelais's creation, of which they form the underlying structure. The wealth of ornament, grotesque and solemn, is what one sees first, but without the architectural framework of a comprehensive vision it would not be there at all. Rabelais's age of innocence is the period he spent as a friar, his '*temps perdu*' was the age in which a letter from Budé seemed to be a combination of manna in the cultural wilderness and the tablets of the law. The real life into which he had longed to escape is that from which his fantasy releases him ten years later. The second part of this book attempts to demonstrate the persistence of certain habits of mind in Rabelais up to the end, and a major factor in this persistence is the journey into the past thus understood. This is not to minimize the place of the future in Rabelais's vision, but one has only to think of the detailed blueprint for Thélème, his own brave new world, to realize that it represents the wish-fulfilment of a monk named Frère François rather than Frère Jan. As late as the Isle Sonnante chapters of the *Cinquiesme Livre* (accepted as mainly authentic) there are whole episodes which only make full sense when related to a monastic context.

There remains the fascinating, but singularly difficult problem of Rabelais's vocation. The picture of Franciscan life given in most critical accounts, like Rabelais's own occasional references to friars, is so remote from the evidence of such sources as the sermons, histories of the reform movement and so on, that it is not surprising that Rabelais's Franciscan career should so often be treated as a tragi-comic disaster. The more one ponders the evidence the less convincing such a simple solution seems to be.

It is perhaps easiest to start at the end, with as little prejudice as possible, and ask why Rabelais left the Franciscans. Marichal and sixteenth-century documents together conclusively prove that if Rabelais wanted to pursue medical studies professionally he could not do so as a friar. How or why Rabelais became interested in medicine one can only surmise, but once this interest had been aroused it dominated all others and, as events prove, lasted out his life. In these circumstances it is simply not necessary to seek any other reason for Rabelais's transfer from an order where he could not study medicine to one where he could, though other reasons undoubtedly existed as well. It is relevant to note that he did not give up sacerdotal duties, that he obtained papal dispensation for the transfer, that he remained a religious until his irregular departure for Paris (*c.* 1528) and took care as late as 1534 to regularize his position once more so that he could enjoy the benefices for which his new, legal status of secularized canon now made him eligible. His attachment to Geoffroi d'Estissac at Maillezais seems to have been more secretarial than monastic, but, such as it was, he shared the Benedictine life until his so far unexplained removal to Paris, where his medical progress was so rapid and remarkable as to make a medical rather than a religious motive perfectly plausible. It would be hard to sustain the argument that he left the Franciscans mainly or simply to have a good time.

Much play has been made with the affair of the books, and this is clearly crucial. The facts, however, are not altogether simple, and, as already noted, the defection of Amy more than justifies the action of local superiors enjoined from above to stamp out heresy. Budé's letter speaks of the Greek books being restored to Rabelais and the restitution of his former liberty, but if he had really been in trouble with the authorities they would certainly have confiscated his books for good and either kept him under house arrest or transferred him to some other house, beyond the reach of his suspect contacts. The fact that they did none of these things, and that papal authority was eventually forthcoming for Rabelais's transfer to the Benedictines, despite his association with a suspected heretic, is a strong argument in favour of Rabelais's good standing at Fontenay and in the order generally. The suggestion that Rabelais may have been a passably good religious will undoubtedly strike many readers as a heresy more obnoxious, and much sillier, than any for which Amy suffered, but it cannot just be dismissed. So far the traditional view of Rabelais's lifelong antipathy for his order has been tacitly assumed to be correct, but if this view could be shown to need modification, the idea that he was by no means a bad friar would appear less eccentric.

Thélème reminds us that Rabelais's ideal community would be ruled by a reversal of the canonical vows of poverty, chastity and obedience. It is tempting to conclude from this that Rabelais's dislike of religious life can be traced back to these vows, and there is no better hypothesis from which to start. Of the three vows, that which seems most clearly unsuited to Rabelais's temperament is the last. Obedience to other men and to man-made regulations is not an idea to awaken Rabelais's enthusiasm. There are forms of obedience he not only recognizes but commends; above all, filial obedience, then, in the young giants' case, obedience to parentally approved tutors, later there is much stress on feudal obedience to one's lawful lord. All these he would regard as examples of natural obedience, and thus essential to the maintenance of order, discipline and morality. Ecclesiastical obedience, whether to members of a hierarchy or religious superiors, he regards as stunting, arbitrary and eventually leading to revolt, as one may judge from the chapter on 'Fay ce que voudras', which also of course applies to restrictive regulations of any kind. It should not be overlooked in this connexion that the order Rabelais joined had been notoriously free, and often undisciplined in the past, so that a young man with genuine religious convictions but a strong desire for independence might hope to find there greater opportunity for self-expression than in other orders. Criticism of the establishment can be found in other orders, but by none was it carried to the same lengths as by the Observants. The career of a Maillard or a Menot could fire a young man to follow the same path of uncompromising criticism. In practice it it did not work out like that, and though one can see how Rabelais might have hoped to reconcile the vow of obedience with his turbulent disposition, he was disappointed. One result of this is perhaps to be seen in his individualism, and the fact that he neither offered nor followed the programme of a group or party. After leaving the Franciscans he never again entrusted his ideals or his fate to an organization, for his Benedictine phase was clearly one of convenience.

As far as chastity goes, Rabelais's illegitimate children show that he found this vow uncongenial as well. It is impossible to say, and pointless to speculate, how he lived before contracting the liaisons of which these were the fruit. One must, however, ask how he was affected by years of hearing warnings against women, against sex, against sin. For all the connotations of the adjective 'rabelaisian' it is plainly untrue to say that he stands for open licence, let alone sexual aberration. The plea against chastity at Thélème is for marriage, not promiscuity, the lengthy discussions in the *Tiers Livre* are again on marriage, and against the past promiscuity of Panurge, and numerous other passages, including the opening sentences of Gargantua's letter to his son, tell the same story. For Rabelais sex is ordained for procreation, but of legitimate offspring in the bonds of matrimony. One might as well claim that the friars' talk of bawds and pimps reflects their sympathy with such persons as to adduce Panurge or Frère Jan as proof of Rabelais's advocacy of sexual freedom. There had always been within and without the order plenty of friars and ex-friars to set a precedent of indulgence, but until he went to Paris Rabelais does not seem to have been one of them. If the vow of chastity repelled him it was because it deprived him of one of the rights he later most bitterly regretted giving up; the right to found a family and bring up children bearing his name. It is significant that Luther himself only claimed this right after long theological and spiritual questioning, and that his view on clerical marriage is the only specific error imputed to him by Messier. It was no light matter, and Rabelais does not treat it as such. He shows no patience with the agents of sexual licence, prostitutes and adulterers, and does not react noticeably against Franciscan teaching on women, as we shall see later. Long conditioning as friar and monk and secular priest reinforced in him the Pauline view that it is better to marry than to burn. From this standpoint it is fair to ask whether his own lapses, however commonplace by worldly standards, did not leave in him some feeling of guilt and resentment at women in general, as well as a deeper resentment at the tyranny of a vow (albeit taken voluntarily) which deprived him of freedom to live as a whole man. Nothing inclines one to the view that revolt against Franciscan demands of chastity played the slightest part in causing him to leave the order, or in making him fall foul of authority. It is at the same time certain that he found the obsessive identification of all sex with sin unhealthy and harmful.

Poverty has always been the most characteristic Franciscan vow, and that which was most stringently interpreted. Physical conditions in friaries tended to be less good than in monastic houses, which were often very wealthy, and preferment within the order was only temporary and brought with it none of the material rewards enjoyed by priors and abbots elsewhere. For whatever reason Rabelais became an Observant these must have been the most immediately obvious considerations before him. With this view of poverty went a sympathy and contact with the poorer classes unsurpassed by any other order. Prohibition on owning land or property was also a major factor in fitting friars for mission work far afield, and for travel in general. Here it looks as though one could say with confidence that Rabelais would find this attitude congenial, and that indifference to material goods, as well as sympathy for the poor and humble, forms an integral part of Pantagruelism as it finally evolved. In this love of evangelical poverty, in contrast to the cupidity and luxury of many of the contemporary clergy, the Franciscans stood for something of which Rabelais can only have approved.

Taking it all in all, it seems as though Rabelais may have joined the Franciscans with some reasonable hope of realizing ideals which the Observants represented more explicitly than anyone else at the time. Even if he were forced, or persuaded, to become a friar by parental or other pressure, a perfectly sound hypothesis, the possibility cannot be rejected out of hand that he was for a time a satisfactory religious. In many ways his life as an Observant was the best preparation then available for the evangelical movement to which he later gave his sympathies. The trouble seems to have been that ideals of social and religious reform which had been appropriate a century or two before were no longer adequate to the needs of the day, and that the standards even among Observants fell short of those set by men as distinguished as our preachers. Fontenay was not a very important place, unlike La Baumette, for instance, and the atmosphere could easily have been very narrow and parochial. All the evidence points to intellectual rather than spiritual frustration as being the first symptom of Rabelais's mistaken vocation, but even here one must be careful, for in some houses at least there was room for humanist scholarship, witness Vitrier at St. Omer, Pellikan at Basle and Amy, until he was suspected of heresy. The simplest explanation of Rabelais's long-term attitude to his former order is probably the best; he just grew out of it, as a schoolboy or student grows out of an environment which may once have absorbed his interest. Disillusionment, frustration, resentment at petty restrictions and obsolete attitudes are what one might expect from Rabelais if this were so, but not hatred, contempt or vindictiveness. Only in speaking of Amy does he show any personal emotion, but neither there nor elsewhere does he name the persecutors. Compare this with the real virulence with which he refers to the Sorbonne in all his books, and even with the gibes at Calvin. He does not satirize St. Francis or St. Bonaventura, but keeps his scorn for Scotus and the theologians. It is the intellectual, not the spiritual side of the order he attacks. Had the Observants really won the day and cleaned up the French provinces of the order, they might have become less repressive, but they were overtaken by events.

The Franciscan training stood Rabelais in good stead and put him further along his chosen path than other religious educations of the time could have done, but it was too little and too late. It is not contended that Rabelais spent the rest of his days nostalgically or guiltily regretting a vocation he had betrayed; apart from anything else his medical vocation would justify his transfer in his own and other people's eyes. Perhaps one way of stating the case as it appears from all the available evidence on both sides is that Rabelais joined the right order at the wrong time. Rather than speak of lifelong antipathy we should speak of a feeling of relief at timely release. However the situation be formulated, one always comes back to the first principle; in the beginning was the friar.

PART II

RABELAIS AND HIS WORK

8 : INTRODUCTION TO
THE INTELLECTUAL BACKGROUND

To complete the picture of Rabelais's debt to the Franciscans, the more formal intellectual training he received as a friar must also be taken into account. His world picture, his standards of truth and goodness, his logical axioms and so on all belong to what one may call the infrastructure of his thought, and as such affect his assimilation of new ideas. It is in this underlying mental structure that the effect of early training will ultimately be revealed.

At two points in his life Rabelais pursued a course of study of which we know the outcome. At some time before 1520 he followed the course in Arts and Theology prescribed by the Franciscans for those seeking ordination and duly became a priest. Then after an interval of some obscurity, during which he transferred to the Benedictines and later lived as a secular, he undertook whatever preliminary studies were necessary for him to matriculate in 1530 at Montpellier, and be received only a few weeks later as Bachelor of Medicine, graduating as Doctor in 1537. In between the two milestones of ordination and baccalaureate we know that his interests were classical, and soon orientated specifically towards medicine. With Amy's help he taught himself Greek from about 1520, and seems to have become rapidly quite proficient. At the same time we know him to have frequented the humanist cenacle at Fontenay, where he met Tiraqueau, Bouchard and others, many of whom remained his friends for life. Several of these Poitevin humanists were lawyers, and Rabelais's family background may have encouraged their common legal interests. It is known too, that Platonism was a topic of discussion, and it is surely safe to assume that medicine was soon another. First as a Franciscan and then as a Benedictine, Rabelais had ample opportunity over a period of perhaps five years for conversation with men of culture, and access to books which would not normally come the way of a friar dependent on his house's library. There can be no doubt that Rabelais's formation as a humanist progressed very far in these years.

It is not known for certain what formal training he would have had to undergo to be accepted so quickly as a Bachelor at Montpellier, but it is generally thought that he performed the appropriate academic exercises at Paris, presumably in both Arts and Medicine. Since he had already satisfied his Franciscan examiners, whom one must not assume to have been either lenient or incompetent, in Arts and then in Theology, the Arts qualification demanded of him at Montpellier may have been satisfied quite formally, and can neither have taught him much that was new nor proved very onerous. On the other hand his medical proficiency is attested by his rapid attainment of the degree of Bachelor, followed in 1532 by appointment to the responsible post of doctor at the Hôtel-Dieu at Lyons, and finally by his nomination, after his doctoral exercises in 1537, as professorial supervisor of two students at Montpellier, though the assignment did not last very long. It is true that his work on Galen and Hippocrates displays as much expertise in philology as in medicine, but his professional standing is solidly attested and can only have been acquired by long and hard study. Such study is quite sufficient to account for any time spent under formal instruction at Paris or elsewhere.

This all means that Rabelais absorbed whatever knowledge he ever had of Scholastic methods and doctrines in the first instance when he was a friar, and subsequently only at a time when his interests were dominated by medicine and kindred subjects. The impact of such training would naturally have been greater when he was younger, and it seems therefore safe to ascribe to the *années de moinage* all traces of formal instruction in subjects other than medicine and science. Of the many ways in which this training may have been reflected in his work the only one of immediate concern is that which shows some signs of system and arrangement. In examining as wide a range as possible of Rabelais's thought one must look not so much for evidence of knowledge as principles of organization.

At this point a complicating factor arises, for Rabelais did not wait to leave Fontenay before beginning his humanist education and affecting to despise Scholastic ways. For purposes of prestige, and perhaps conviction, he had to show himself emancipated from medieval habits of mind against which his new friends revolted. While still at Fontenay he was seeking in the pages of the authentic Aristotle, and still more of Plato, that truth which he had failed, or refused, to find in the authors prescribed by his order. For thirty years he continued to read voraciously, and naturally absorbed a great many new ideas and facts. The quantity of his reading is not in dispute, but the way he interprets it in his work is more controversial. From Rabelais's point of view, he had forsaken a way of life and thought, both comprehensive and exact, for the road of freedom. He was not strictly speaking a convert from one faith to another, unless his brand of eclectic synthesis is to be called a faith, and in abandoning the Scholastic system he certainly did not adopt any other *system*. This does not mean that his new road had no guiding marks, but that these were more random than systematic, and depended on the person or author currently in view. At the age of thirty, let alone forty or fifty, there is seldom any adequate substitute for the formal training of one's youth, and Rabelais was not of such a temperament as to find or even seek one.

The following analysis of Rabelais's thought has tried to observe certain principles which should reduce arbitrary distinctions to a minimum. Wherever Rabelais refers openly to Scholastic doctrines as such, whether seriously or for intentions of archaism or parody, it is pointless to invent any source other than his early training. When he refers to classical sources, their status can be checked. Patterns of thought revealed by scattered classical references can be established with fair precision, to indicate which authors are quoted in particular contexts and also the broader trends emerging from Rabelais's selection. Finally these trends and patterns can be compared with what is known of Rabelais's Scholastic training, so that one can form some idea of what is new and what is merely a version of long familiar notions. Allowing for the elements of parody and archaism, it is fair to assume that Rabelais wished as far as he could to dissociate himself from Franciscan habits of mind, but it is an open question how far this was possible at all. In any case it must be considered whether his early years did not predispose him in favour of one set of ideas rather than another. It may be that there was in Rabelais something of M. Jourdain, and that he had for years as a friar been studying Platonism without realizing it. It cannot simply be accepted that Rabelais discarded old habits of thought as completely as his friar's habit; 'cucullus non facit monachum' works both ways; much of the friar persists in the '*moine défroqué*'.

It is essential for a true picture to separate Rabelais's ideas from their alleged authors, for prestige accrues from dropping the right name in the right place, while the ideas themselves may turn out to be of quite different provenance from that advertized. Only when the veils of prejudice and prestige have been stripped can one hope to see Rabelais's mind as it really was, and thus to assess the influence of his first masters.

The first group of chapters examines his world picture, extending from God through spirits to the world of nature, and may be called largely formal. It is followed by another group of chapters dealing with the practical problems of life, moral and religious, adding up to a detailed picture of Pantagruelism. On the basis of this summary of Rabelais's thought one can then scrutinize the classical authorities to whom he appeals and come to a juster appreciation of their role. Lastly the salient Franciscan doctrines relevant to these ideas must be considered before one draws a conclusion.

There are two major omissions from this review: first medical and scientific subjects, as already explained; second in the sphere of religion. It is very hard to say just when Rabelais began thinking along evangelical lines in a partisan sense, but by the time he came to write he seems to have had ideas which commended him both to Marguerite and to Calvin. Part of the chapter on 'Authorities' deals with Scripture, but it is quite impossible to say that such and such an interpretation of a given text first occurred to him at a given date. The staple diet of all students of theology, of whatever shade, was the Bible, and the Fathers; and the only fact of which one may be certain is that Rabelais knew his Bible well before he came to know any Protestants as such. Under these circumstances the only profitable course is to compare what Rabelais actually says on religious questions with the appropriate Franciscan teaching, noting points of similarity or divergence. In the world of black and white, Catholic and Protestant are irreconcilable antitheses, but in the less clearcut world of reality there is room for overlapping as well as for contradiction. There is, as one might say, still 'matière de breviaire' in a Protestant prayer-book. The most such an inquiry as this can aim at is probability on balance, not irrefutable proof.

9 : GOD

SUPREME in the hierarchy of Rabelais's universe is God, and it is logically with God that any examination of his world-picture must begin. Ignoring for the present specifically doctrinal questions, we find a surprisingly detailed conception of God in the work. There is hardly a page where the name of God is not, in a Mosaic sense, taken in vain, and with these we are obviously not concerned. There are besides innumerable references to God in various contexts, illuminating in themselves, but mentioning '*Dieu*' only without any particular attribute, and these are of no immediate concern. In this chapter we shall deal only with the definitions of God, of which there are two given actually as definitions, and with His names, of which more than a dozen occur in the four books, sometimes alone and sometimes combined with one or more others. More than a literary habit is at stake in the choice of God's names. The sixteenth century had seen an increase, if anything, in the interest shown from the earliest times in Dionysius's work on the Divine Names, translated early in the century by Lefèvre d'Etaples.

The first of these definitions comes in the *Tiers Livre* (XIII, 393):'—ceste infinie et intellectuale sphaere, le centre de laquelle est en chascun lieu de l'univers, la circunference poinct (c'est Dieu scelon la doctrine de Hermes Trismegistus) à laquelle rien ne advient, rien ne passe, rien ne dechet, tous temps sont praesens—' The context is a long exposition by Pantagruel, always Rabelais's most reliable witness, of divination by dreams, which he explains by the participation of the soul during sleep 'de sa prime et divine origine', and the contemplation of the sphere just described. Coming as it does in an unusually coherent and detailed chapter, the definition carries even more weight than if it were isolated. That it was found striking is certain; the author of the *Cinquiesme Livre*, Rabelais or another, repeats it almost identically (but without the attribution to Hermes) in the final chapter, and M. Lefranc[1] quotes other sixteenth-century

---

[1] A. Lefranc, *Grands Ecrivains Français de la Renaissance*, p. 174.

instances of the same definition. The question of source can probably never be solved in this case, and as usual Lefranc argues more brilliantly than convincingly. The only certain facts are that the definition is not by Hermes, but is first found in the pseudo-Hermetic and anonymous thirteenth-century *Liber* xxiv *Philosophorum,* quoted by Alain de Lille and used thereafter by very many authors,[1] including notably SS. Thomas and Bonaventura, and Cusa, usually giving Hermes as their source. The most economical hypothesis is that Rabelais saw the comparison in Bonaventura,[2] if not in other Scholastic authors as well, while still a member of the order which derived its chief spiritual nourishment from the Seraphic Doctor. On what occasion, if any, this quotation was recalled to Rabelais's mind is surely irrelevant; its Scholastic ancestry is so large and well-established that attempts to explain Rabelais's version in the same way as that of Marguerite de Navarre ignore completely their respective backgrounds. Apart from the fascinating, but quite otiose, speculation as to its source, this definition of Rabelais's is extremely interesting in itself. The neo-Platonic inspiration hardly needs the pseudo-authority of Hermes for us to recognize it. God's place outside space and time, His independence of matter, His omniscience, all come out from this comparison of the sphere. The definition is, of course, incomplete in that it makes no mention of God's active powers, and for this very reason it is especially interesting in this book of action.

The other definition is less complicated and more obviously Christian. Arriving at the island of Papimanie, Pantagruel and his companions are asked: (*QL*/xlviii, 690) 'L'avez-vous veu?', referring to 'Celluy qui est', who is shown subsequently to be the Pope. Once more it is Pantagruel himself who speaks: 'Celluy qui est par nostre theologicque doctrine est Dieu. Et en tel mot se declaira à Moses. Oncques certes ne le veismes, et n'est visible à oeilz corporelz.' No ingenious arguments or painstaking research are necessary to prove the outstanding importance of this definition for the Scholastics. Today perhaps no more than a familiar quotation from Exodus, for the sixteenth century as for the whole Middle Ages 'Celluy qui est' would at once be re-

---

[1] G. Paré, *Le Roman de la Rose et la Scolastique Courtoise,* pp. 184–5, and Gilson, *La Phil. au Moyen Âge,* p. 231.

[2] St. Bonaventura, *Itinerarium Mentis ad Deum,* cap v.

cognized as the mainspring of Scholastic philosophy.[1] A curious coincidence, but one of a kind extremely frequent in Rabelais, is that only a couple of pages further on Homenaz, Bishop of Papimanie, quotes another text from Exodus and immediately afterwards the Delphic inscription 'EI', subject of one of Plutarch's dialogues. That Rabelais consciously or unconsciously put these ontological texts so near is the strongest indication of a deeply rooted training in Scholastic philosophy. Since the 'EI' quotation is passed without comment from either side, it is not possible to judge how far Rabelais wished to draw attention to one of his fundamental beliefs, the continuity and identity of pagan and Christian (or Jewish) ideas, but the coincidence should be noted.

These two definitions, one from each of the *Tiers* and *Quart Livres,* have nothing obviously in common except that they occur a few lines apart in Bonaventura's best known work. It remains to see how far the various names and attributes accorded to God throughout the work fit in with these definitions.[2] Statistics can be used to demonstrate almost anything, and no finality is claimed for those which follow, but they do at least show a remarkable degree of consistency. God is called '*bon*' about eleven times in the work, '*seigneur*' or '*souverain*' the same number of times, both results to be expected. More surprising is the fact that '*servateur*' occurs no less than twelve times, about half of the references being to Christ, as well as '*saulveur*' (twice) and '*conservateur*' (twice). An odd detail is that *Gargantua* is the only book in which '*saulveur*' is to be found and the only one in which '*servateur*' is not. More than half the instances of '*servateur*' are in the *Quart Livre.* Next in order of frequency is '*createur*' (or '*plasmateur*'), found eight times evenly spread through the work, and found also in the minor works of the early period. Other names are '*eternel*' (three), '*protecteur*' (three), '*juste*' (three), '*grand*' (five), '*tout puissant, omnipotent*' (three), and such particular titles as '*dateur de tous biens*' (three), '*le Dieu Sabaoth*', '*le très hault Dieu des cielz*'.

This not inconsiderable list is mildly surprising in itself in view of the general tone of Rabelais's work and the fact that his age

---

[1] Cf. Gilson, *L'Esprit de la Phil. Médiévale*, ch. ii, where he quotes these texts side by side, in a discussion of the basic importance of the 'Ego sum' theme to the whole medieval concept of existence.

[2] Cf. L. Febvre, *La Religion de Rabelais*, pp. 260–5. Neither the method nor the conclusions are quite the same as ours. See Appendix. p. 106.

was hardly one in which excursions into theology could be undertaken lightheartedly. The most evident feature of this catalogue is that attributes of essence are far outnumbered by attributes of activity. Indeed, *'bon, grand eternel'* with a single mention of *'vivant'* are about the only ones, and the first two are often linked with another active name. The contrast with the two definitions just quoted comes from the complementary, not contradictory, nature of the list.

Much the most interesting title of all is *'servateur'*, for which Rabelais clearly had a marked predilection. The word is very rare in French (Cotgrave does not even give it and he knew his Rabelais well), and is an obvious Latinism. In Latin, however, the word is also restricted in use. Medieval and contemporary Church Latin used either *'Salvator'* (whence the usual French *'saulveur'*) or *'conservator'* (found Gallicized in Rabelais) and we have to go back to classical Latin to find *'servator'* used at all frequently. The linguistic authorities equate the word with the Greek Σωτήρ, but theologically this is not much help. At least six times Rabelais uses the word of Christ (and as we have seen avoids *'saulveur'*). A very fine shade of meaning is suggested by one instance (*QL*/LXV, 743) of 'le bon Dieu, nostre Createur, Servateur, Conservateur', and elsewhere the idea of preservation rather than salvation seems to be indicated. Rabelais's choice of the word is doubtless prompted by his desire to use classical instead of medieval forms, and was very probably encouraged by some such humanist practice as that recommended by Budé (apparently following Gregory Nazianzen): 'Jesus autem ipse Christus numquam sine praefatione Servatoris hominum a nobis appellandus.'[1] A definition by Polydore Vergil goes even further: 'Jesus, id est servator, et Christus, hoc est rex . . .'[2] Unfortunately the ideas which this classical word has to express are foreign to its history, and despite such statements as these, we are left with only a partial theory of Rabelais's attitude to God. On balance, it looks as though eternal salvation was more in Rabelais's mind than just preservation from earthly ills, either of which meanings the word could bear.

The frequent incidence of *'seigneur, souverain, roy'* (altogether equalling *'servateur'*) is not strange and the context (often political)

---

[1] Quoted by J. Bohatec, *Budé und Calvin*, p. 54.
[2] Polydore Vergil, *De Inventoribus Rerum*, lib. IV, p. 224.

as well as the form of Rabelais's book (modelled on the *romans de chevalerie*) account for it. More interesting is '*createur*', of which the theological and philosophical significance cannot be overlooked. In fact, '*createur*' and '*servateur*' together (a combination found three times in the work) supply the active complement of the ontological definitions. It is particularly in *Gargantua*, the most unequivocally evangelical of all the books, that the creative power of God is emphasized, and we find such phrases as 'à Dieu rien n'est impossible' (VI, 46), 'Dieu seul peult faire choses infinies' (XX, 83), 'Dieu nous faict en telle forme et telle fin . . . que faict un potier ses vaisseaulx' (XL, 142) with similar expressions in the minor works of the period. It is not suggested for a minute that any doctrinal, or rather sectarian, significance is to be attached to this emphasis, but simply that Rabelais at a period of some religious fervour (Calvin seems to confirm this in *De Scandalis*) was particularly conscious of the creative power of God, certainly a revelation he did not owe to the Reformers.

In all these names there are surprising stresses and surprising omissions. God as Father of all is not mentioned, though there are two references 'Dieu par son cher fils' (*Garg.*/LVIII, 186) 'Dieu le Père' (*Pant.*/VIII, 225); God as Truth is never mentioned (this is very surprising: cf. next chapter), though his omniscience is brought out in the definition of the sphere. Taken as a purely factual record over so long a period (1532–52) in so many contexts and usually unpremeditated, these names show a considerable degree of consistency, and seem to tally more closely with a constant attitude of mind than with a random selection.[1]

Though the Trinity itself is nowhere mentioned—outside purely religious writings one could hardly expect it—Our Lord is mentioned several times, and the Holy Spirit at least once. The

---

[1] Cf. V. I. Saulnier, *Maurice Scève*, pp. 430 seq., where Scève's treatment of the same question in his *Microcosme* is analysed. The Holy Spirit is mentioned once, the Son five times and the following names of God are found:

tout connaissant	1	vivant eternel	2
designateur	1	architecteur	1
ouvrier	1	plasmateur	1
createur	4	auteur de tout savoir	1
Dieu aymant	1	juge	1

Cf. also Maillard, who in his Bruges sermon speaks of 'Dieu le Createur' thirteen times, referring both to Father and Son, e.g. 'se presenta Dieu le Createur, le jour du grant vendredy, pour faire sacrifice à Dieu *son* père pour noz pechiez.' (*Œuvres Françaises*, p. 7.) In his first *Chant Royal en l'Honneur de la Vierge* we find 'la Vierge, mère du Redempteur/Son plasmateur, d'amour preordonné'. (ibid.)

greatest number of references is in *Gargantua*. There are three
references all together in the chapter (x) which discusses white
as the symbol of joy: 'la Transfiguration de Nostre Seigneur'
and 'la Resurrection du Saulveur et son Ascension'. Frère Jan
in a sincere and not at all farcical speech recalls Our Lord's
seizure by the Jews in the garden (xxxIx, 138). Gargantua
himself, in the last chapter, speaks of: 'celluy qui tousjours
tendra au but au blanc que Dieu, par son cher Filz, nous a
prefix' (LVIII, 186). In addition, the first editions of *Gargantua*
include a mention not repeated in later editions (vi, 44): 'Dieu
(c'est Nostre Saulveur) dict on l'Evangile Joan. 16 . . .'; the
phrasing is interesting as applied to Christ. In *Pantagruel* the only
reference is in Gargantua's famous letter to his son: 'l'heure du
jugement final, quand Jesu-Christ aura rendu à Dieu le père son
royaulme' (VIII, 225), and this has been fully commented on by
Gilson.[1] To the same period belongs the Almanach for 1535
where we read (930): 'vous convient souhaiter (comme S. Pol
disoit Philipp. I: Cupio dissolvi et esse cum Christo) que vos
asmes soient hors mises cette chartre tenebreuse du corps terrien
et joinctes à Jesus le Christ'. All these references of the early
period are either scriptural quotations or paraphrases, and reflect
the same phase of religious preoccupation which also produced
the texts on God's creative power. The significance of these texts
is not great, except in that they show the most normal orthodoxy,
and all we can say from them is that Rabelais gives every sign of
having been a devout Christian at the time.

Very different is the tone of the *Tiers* and *Quart Livres*. By
then scriptural quotations tended to be taken as a shibboleth of
the now established Reform, and St. Paul in particular was a
dangerous authority. Friendly references to the Reform (that, at
least, of Geneva) are quite absent, replaced by one or two pointed
attacks. With the crystallization of the religious situation into two
powerful opposing factions, Rabelais's earlier fervour gives way
to caution, if not disillusionment. All the more valuable are the
rare indications of his thoughts concerning Christ. In the *Quart
Livre* there is a completely anodyne reference to Zaccheus, who
wished to see 'Nostre benoist Servateur autour de Hierusalem'
(Prol/547), with a gibe at the supposed relics of Zaccheus, alias
St. Sylvain, preserved at St. Ayl near Orleans.

[1] *Idées et Lettres*, p. 231.

Apart from this there seem to be only two references to Christ, one in each book. By one of those coincidences which it is almost axiomatic to demand in Rabelais, the two references deal with the same problem, but are so widely separated that the connexion must be assumed to lie only in Rabelais's subconscious mind. In the *Tiers Livre* the question arises of consulting oracles for advice in Panurge's marital problems. The erudite Epistemon gives a list of some of the better known oracles of antiquity and comments (xxiv/437): 'Mais vous sçavez que tous sont devenuz plus mutz que poissons depuys la venue de celluy roy servateur on quel ont prins fin tous oracles et toutes propheties.' There will be more to say in a later chapter about the oracles and their silence, but the point is that this is the first time that we find Rabelais linking Christianity and paganism. Christ, 'celluy roy servateur', is an historical figure, not the hero of a particular religion's devotional chronicles. At his coming the pagan oracles and the Jewish prophets alike lost their *raison d'être* and were silent. The idea that the Christian era fulfilled and supplanted the pagan era, with all that was best in it, is not original, nor even a discovery of the Renaissance. The classic, and in the sixteenth century recently repopularized, treatment of this theme is in Eusebius's *Praeparatio Evangelica*, whose choice of texts is quite parallel with Rabelais's own and from whom Rabelais may have derived more than textual borrowing. Thomism, too, is built primarily on such an assumption. This single sentence is more significant and suggestive of a personal philosophy than all the previous texts just mentioned.

What confers on it quite unique importance is its relationship to another text published some six years later: the Pan chapter which marks in many ways the highest point of Rabelais's thought. The Pan story with its many implications will be examined in another chapter but in its direct bearing on Rabelais's ideas about Christ something may be said of it here. The titles used are (xxviii, 640) 'celluy grand Servateur des fidèles', 'nostre unicque Servateur', 'le grand Pasteur'[1] and the eloquent elaboration of the name Pan: 'le nostre tout, tout ce que sommes, tout ce que vivons, tout ce que avons, tout ce que esperons est luy,

[1] Du Cange gives as one of the meanings of 'servator' in medieval Latin 'pastor gregarius', and though it is not clear how common the usage was, it is not inconceivable that Rabelais had the connexion in mind.

en luy, de luy, par luy'. There are two points relevant to the present question. First, the greatly expanded but essentially similar treatment of the theme just seen in the *Tiers Livre* of the continuity between pagan and Christian eras, whereby a pagan author (Plutarch) is quoted as providing unwitting testimony of the historicity of the gospels. The other lies in the unusually devout apostrophe to Our Lord. The place of Christ in the universe is affirmed here in philosophical, not religious, terms and brings out the transition effected in Rabelais's thought between the first two and second two books. If the religious fervour is less evident in the second period, such passages as this show that the deepest intellectual foundations underlie Rabelais's faith, where it may be suspected a more partisan spirit had earlier prevailed. At all events, this chapter of the *Quart Livre* blends all the elements to be found scattered elsewhere into a carefully reflected attitude to Christ. The use of pagan authors, even of pagan religions, in confirming the universality of Christ's power, the historical concord between gospels and independent pagan witnesses, finally the supreme place of Christ in the existence of those who profess His faith.

For the sake of completeness, the single mention of the Holy Spirit should also be recorded. That there is but one such reference is not very strange; even in religious contexts, the third person of the Trinity, by definition the most abstract, is seldom mentioned. It is not altogether unexpected that this reference should come during a religious discussion in *Gargantua*. Frère Jan's presence has prompted a debate on monks, whom Gargantua declares quite useless in the world. He denies that, even if they did pray as they should, their prayers would be of any use (XL, 141): 'Tous vrays christians . . . en tous lieux, en tous temps, prient Dieu et l'Esperit prie et interpelle pour iceulx, et Dieu les prent en grace.' The attack on monasticism and the value of intercessory prayer is unmistakably partisan, but the same cannot very well be said of the role assigned to the Spirit, which appears perfectly orthodox (and Pauline).

Several other aspects of Rabelais's theology do not properly belong to this chapter, and will be considered in others. What one may call the ways of God to man, His providence and His grace, as well as the ways of man to God, in prayer and reverence, are more conveniently treated separately under the headings of

'Providence' and 'Religion'. If general conclusions can be drawn from these scattered texts about God, first of all must come their consistency. Emphasis changes in a man's work just as it does in his life, and the twenty years of Rabelais's literary output saw changes of the most fundamental nature in the life of all civilized Europe, let alone of his own. Nevertheless, such contrasts as there are seem to spring from complementary, not contradictory, ideas. The development of the work, to be seen in its very style, is most clearly towards a more intellectual position in the later books, and a continued use of earlier expressions would thus be more strange than the modifications which do in fact exist. At the same time the previous marked preoccupation with simple scriptural ideas cannot reasonably be assumed to have disappeared from Rabelais's mind because or when it disappeared from his work. Here, as in almost every case to be studied, the pattern is of a synthesis, rejecting nothing once uttered and always striking roots deeper into the subsoil of philosophy. In the two definitions of God, in the two parallel texts about Christ, the *Tiers* and *Quart Livres* are exactly similar, and amplify in exactly the same way the more direct and scriptural texts of the first two books, and the contemporary minor works. There is not one instance in any of the four books where one text concerning God conflicts with another, not one where haphazard composition betrays itself, and on these grounds alone it can be claimed that Rabelais's thought was complete, coherent and consistent throughout the years of his literary activity. In the absence of any contrary evidence, it may be said that Rabelais's views on the Godhead as seen in his work are based on his Franciscan training and represent no important departure from it.

APPENDIX

THE NAMES OF GOD IN RABELAIS

	Garg.	Pant.	TL	QL	Total
bon	2		5	4	11
eternel	2			1	3
saulveur	2				2
servateur		1	4	7	12
conservateur		1		1	2
protecteur		2	1		3
seigneur	1	4	1	3	9
roy			1		1
souverain	1	1			2
createur ⎱ plasmateur ⎰	2	3	2	1	8
grand	1		2	2	5
tout puissant ⎱ omnipotent ⎰		3			3
juste	2		1		3

No account is taken of the differences between editions, nor do the figures claim to be infallibly accurate, but they show the basis for our conclusions in the chapter 'God'.

10 : THE SPIRIT WORLD

NATURE could never abhor a vacuum more than did the philosophers of the ancient world. The detailed and complex hierarchy of beings which they set up between God and man was no fruit of idle speculation, but the expression of a fundamental law governing their mental operations. When the more precise doctrines of Christianity replaced the hospitable syntheses of paganism, this law continued to operate and in the main the only development is one of terminology. With the curious atmosphere of the Renaissance, the law still obtained and only a fresh confusion of terminology marked the new fashion for things antique, practised by those whose closer heritage was more persistently in their minds than their protests of disavowal suggest. A priori it can be asserted that all Rabelais could learn in addition to normal Scholastic teaching on spirits would be detail, either historical or verbal, and no new principles whatever needed to be postulated. To a classical scholar coming upon Scholasticism, the problem is quite different, but the case must be rare and is not that of Rabelais. As far as the work, though most probably not the personal philosophy, of Rabelais is concerned, the first two books show a conception of the spirit world in line with popular beliefs of the time and with only infrequent hints of a systematic philosophy underlying it. Not unnaturally, the evil spirits play a more prominent part than the good; contemporary speech too quoted devils at least as often as God.

Typical of purely popular, even farcical (in a dramatic sense) notions are the references in the last chapter of *Pantagruel*, announcing the forthcoming attractions (XXXIV, 333): 'comment Pantagruel . . . combatit contre les diables et fist brusler cinq chambres d'enfer . . . et getta Proserpine au feu, et rompit quatre dentz à Lucifer et une corne au cul.' The mixture of classical and biblical mythology was an old medieval popular tradition. In similarly popular vein, though nearer realism than romance, is the chapter in *Gargantua* where Gymnaste is challenged by the enemy captain (XXXV, 126): 'Agios ho Theos. Si tu es de Dieu, sy parle! Si tu es de l'Aultre, sy t'en va!' and having thrown the enemy into confusion, he makes them flee crying: 'c'est un lutin ou un diable ainsi desguisé. Ab hoste maligno libera nos, Domine!' Panurge uses the same formula of exorcism with more success (*Pant.*/xiv, 251): 'Mais je fis le signe de la croix criant: "Agios athanatos, ho Theos!" Et nul ne venoit.' These amateur attempts at exorcism need not be taken as exaggerated for literary purposes; the evil eye is still a potent enough fear in many places to this day. The incidents are entertaining illustrations of contemporary superstition, but no more than that on the intellectual plane.

Still popular, but now quite serious, are the words of Grandgousier to the pilgrims returning from their journey to placate St. Sebastian. He attacks those who attribute evil powers (in this case plagues) to particular saints (*Garg.*/xlv, 153), saying: 'Blasphèment-ilz . . . les justes et sainctz de Dieu qu'ilz les font semblables aux diables qui ne font que mal entre les humains, comme Homère escript que la peste fust mise en l'oust des Gregoys par Apollo, et comme les poètes faignent un grand tas de Vejoves et Dieux malfaisans?' Here something like a thought can be seen behind the words; the appeal to pagan authors for confirmation of a purely Christian argument is not fortuitous, and will form the basis for much of the theory in the later books.

Several other references[1] to devils belong to popular tradition and add nothing to this study. Of a more erudite nature are such statements as this quotation from Ficino (*Garg.*/x, 57): 'Plus dict que en forme leonine ont esté diables souvent veuz, lesquelz à la presence d'un coq blanc soubdainement sont disparuz.'[2] Another of Scholastic inspiration is when Panurge asks (*Pant.*/xviii, 274): 'Y-a-t-il homme tant sçavant que sont les diables?—Non, vrayement (dist Pantagruel), sans grace divine especiale.'[3] This last is the most interesting so far, partly because Pantagruel is normally the mouthpiece for Rabelais's own views, and partly because of

---

[1] Cf. p. 130: 'Les diables ont passé pour en emporter les âmes damnées.'

[2] Boulenger's note attributes this to *Procli de Sacrificio*.

[3] The belief that daemons possessed superior knowledge was classical, and discussed with many similar topics by St. Augustine. Isidore collected an impressive number of facts about demonology which medieval writers in their turn frequently quote, sometimes ascribing them to him and sometimes to his original authorities. Isidore has this to say about daemons' knowledge: 'Daemonas a Graecis dictos aiunt, quasi δαήμονας, id est peritos ac rerum scios. Praesciunt enim futura multa, unde et solent responsa aliqua dare. Inest enim illis cognitio rerum plus quam infirmitati humanae, partim subtilioris sensus acumine, partim experientia longissimae vitae, partim per Dei jussum angelica revelatione. Hi corporum, aeriorum natura vigent.' *Etymol.* lib. viii, cap. xi. 15–16.

the systematic thought it presupposes. The ministers of evil, as spirits, are higher in the plane of knowledge than men, who can, however, on occasion draw on help from God to overcome them. Two more references from *Gargantua* are equally promising. In the very first chapter a theme is stated which Rabelais was still embroidering twenty years later (I, 30): 'les diables, (ce sont les calumniateurs et caffars)'. This parenthesis, prompted originally on philological grounds, must have appealed to him, and may eventually have coloured his thought on the subject of evil. In this instance, the inclusion of 'caffars' indicates the *jeu de mots*, and the context is not really diabological. Deeply embedded in his philosophy, though, is Rabelais's next mention of the idea. Ulrich Gallet concludes his Ciceronian harangue to Picrochole by enumerating the possible motives for his aggression, of which the last is (XXXI, 116): 'Si l'esperit calumniateur tentant à mal te tirer, eust par fallaces espèces et phantasmes ludificatoyres mis en ton entendement que envers toy eussions faict choses non dignes de nostre ancienne amitié . . .' The mechanics of this deception have been fully explained by Gilson,[1] and there is no need to dwell further here on the very technical Scholastic doctrines represented. The idea which recurs is that of the devil, 'l'esprit calumniateur', deceiving, not compelling man against his will, but falsifying the evidence presented to the will by the understanding.

The information about angels in the first two books is much more sketchy, and amounts to little more than passing mentions. Pantagruel in his prayer before battle calls on God (*Pant.*/XXIX, 313): 'qui as mille milliers de centaines de millions de legions d'anges, duquel le moindre peut occire tous les humains et tourner le ciel et la terre à son plaisir, comme jadis bien apparust en l'armée de Sennaccherib.' With allowances for gigantic arithmetic, the words are substantially those of the Bible.[2] There is another Biblical reference in *Gargantua* (X, 57), when Raphael's appearance before Tobias is quoted to illustrate a point quite irrelevant here. This particular book seems to have appealed to Rabelais, who quotes the same chapter again in the *Tiers Livre* (XLI, 407) and a little earlier, in the *Almanach* for 1533, had quoted ch. XII. Finally, for the sake of a complete record, these are Grandgousier's parting words to the pilgrims (*Garg.*/XLV, 154): 'Vous aurez la garde de Dieu, des anges, et des sainctz avecques vous.' As far as angels

---

[1] Gilson, *Idées et Lettres*, p. 207.   [2] 2 Chron. xxxii.

are concerned, Rabelais in his first period shows the most ordinary views, but is apparently not very interested in the intricate problems involved.

With the *Tiers Livre* a very much fuller picture begins to take shape. From the first words of the book, with the dedicatory poem to Marguerite de Navarre, 'A l'esprit de la Royne de Navarre', the unseen world plays a prominent part. Antique and Christian demonology appear side by side, until in the *Quart Livre* a whole group of chapters is given over to a synthesis at once complex and suggestive.

The hierarchy of evil spirits includes, not unnaturally, some of the popular elements from the earlier books. The lively episode of Papefigue introduces us to the medieval world of demon-king and imps apprentice, with certain topical accretions. (*QL*/XLVI, 684) Lucifer gives permission for his junior assistant to visit the island, a little later we read of his varied diet, of his 'plein chapitre' and other personal details. All this belongs to the world of medieval imagery, the picturesque details of stained glass, of sculpture, of manuscript illumination, as well as to the popular theatre. It would, however, be a mistake to dismiss it outright like the similar references at the end of *Pantagruel*. Not so very long before Luther's reputed encounter with the devil in person had not been generally treated as pure fantasy, and even when Lucifer was a figure of fun, his existence was not called in doubt.

More philosophical is an explanation of how things in themselves indifferent are right or wrong, Pantagrual says (*TL*/VII, 374): '—bien, si bonne est et par l'esprit munde reiglée l'affection; mal, si hors aequité par l'esprit maling est l'affection depravée'. A few chapters further on he uses a similar idea, disagreeing with Panurge's interpretation of the Sibylle's words (XIX, 416): 'L'esprit maling vous seduit, mais ecoutez . . .'

The idea of deception (intellectual and thence moral) is the most frequently found of those connected with the works of darkness. An interesting phrase comes at the end of Pantagruel's extremely erudite discourse on dreams (XIV, 402): 'souvent l'ange de Sathan se transfigure en ange de lumière . . . , l'ange maling et seducteur au commencement resjouist l'homme, enfin le laisse perturbé, fasché et perplex.'[1] Here the idea of seduction is linked with the notion of a Satanic hierarchy, practising deception by

[1] Cf. the similar experience of Simon Stylites in Menot, op. cit. p. 14.

assuming the guise of their angelic counterparts. As so often in Rabelais, the idea lingered, and the same Pauline text is quoted again, this time by Epistemon in connexion with the record of Bridoye (XLIV, 507): 'la fraulde du Calumniateur infernal, lequel souvent se transfigure en messagier de lumière.' The deception this time is attributed to the devil himself, and not just to one of his emissaries, but the idea is the same. Two verbal points may be noted from the comparison of these two texts: '*l'ange*' becomes '*messagier*', and '*Sathan*' '*Calumniateur*'. The difference is purely a verbal one, but in the case of the second marks so strong a personal predilection on the part of Rabelais that, as already suggested, it may eventually have coloured his thought.

We have seen already in *Gargantua* that the *jeu de mots* on '*diable*' was originally literary, and the *Quart Livre* gives two more examples of deliberate emphasis laid on the philological aspect. In the *Ancien Prologue* there is a long development which may explain this emphasis: (755)

Si . . . entendez les calumniateurs de mes escriptz, plus aptement les pourrez-vous nommer diables. Car en grec calumnie est dicte *diabole*. Voyez combien detestable est devant Dieu et les anges ce vice dict calumnie (c'est quand on impugne le bienfaict, quand on mesdict des choses bonnes) que par iceluy, non par autre, quoique plusieurs sembleroient plus enormes, sont les diables d'enfer nommez et appelez.

There follows much more about these personal enemies of Rabelais, now called '*diables*'. In an age when philology and religion were so closely linked, and equally dangerous for deviationists, there would be nothing strange in Rabelais taking the *calumnie-diabole* equation just as seriously as appears from this text. As one might expect, a second direct reference to the Greek origin of the word is to be found, in the dedicatory *Epitre* to Odet de Chatillon of some four years later, again in connexion with his enemies: (542) 'l'esprit calumniateur, c'est Διάβολος.'[1] The devil himself appears once more in the *Tiers Livre* during a discussion on dice. Pantagruel says (XI, 386): 'Le mauldict livre du *Passe-temps des dez* feut, long temps a, inventé par le Calumniateur ennemy: en Achaie . . . faisoit jadis, de present en plusieurs lieux

---

[1] Cf. the etymologies proposed by Menot and Messier, ch. 6 above. Isidore knew better.

faict maintes simples âmes errer et en ses lacz tomber.' Of the knuckle-bones he adds: 'Ce sont hamessons par lesquelz le Calumniateur tire les simples âmes à perdition eternelle.' A facetious reference by Panurge a moment later to the apocryphal *Liber de patria diabolorum* by Merlin Coccaie, brings out the difference between the serious and the comic. Pantagruel's Classical examples of the devil's wiles are, of course, perfectly consistent with Christian teaching: Satan has been the same through the ages, and no new devil came to take his place at the time of the Christian revelation.

All these texts concern calumny or deception, or both, and since they are not related in context nor concentrated in any one part of the work may reasonably be taken as the expression of Rabelais's mature thought on the subject of evil. The most striking fact is the absence of any idea of sin as such, and the emphasis on the intellectual process by which men are impelled to do wrong. Falsification of motives, representation of evil inspiration as good, exploitation of simple souls are so many ways in which the devil does his work. The responsibility for erring is thrown squarely on the shoulders of man, who by vigilance can always outwit the forces of evil. Any suggestion that sin is pre-destined or outside man's control is completely incompatible with what Rabelais says. He seems to be quite clear, however, that the powers of darkness are organized and that those who fall receive their due punishment, though not necessarily in the popular Hell of *Pantagruel*.

A rather specialized addition to the hierarchy of evil is Antichrist, whose appearance is only fleeting but not without interest. As they leave Her Trippa, Panurge rails at the (xxv, 444) 'sorcier au diable, enchanteur de l'Antichrist.' A whole litany of Frère Jan's virile attribute follows, and then Frère Jan himself says (xxvi, 447): 'Sçaiz-tu pas que la fin du monde approche? . . . L'Antichrist est desja né, ce m'a l'on dict. Vray est qu'il ne fait encores que esgratigner sa nourisse et ses gouvernantes, et ne monstre encores les thesaures, car il est encores petit.' It looks almost certainly as though Panurge's outburst had led Rabelais to add the second reference, which derives from Scholastic authority. The name was familiar enough as a term of abuse, but the more recondite doctrines concerning the coming of Antichrist were hardly common property. The acquaintance with occult writers demonstrated by the chapter on Her Trippa was no doubt the occasion of Rabelais's temporary interest in this odd apocalyptic figure, but he would not have to go outside his own order of Minors to find Roger Bacon[1] seriously speculating as to the direction of Antichrist's eventual coming.

Of the lesser ministers of the evil one, there are several mentions on a par with those of the earlier books, popular or farcical. To this category belongs the first part of Panurge's long protestation after Raminagrobis's dangerous words. All the old favourites are there, Proserpine, Lucifer, Demiourgon and much embroidery on well-known diabolical themes besides. One phrase is worth noting as an example of Rabelais's constant habit of repetition (XXIII, 430): 'Je les oy [diables] deja soy . . . entrebattans en diables à qui humera l'âme Raminagrobidicque et qui premier de broc en bouc la portera à messer Lucifer.' In the *Quart Livre* the Papefigue episode, already quoted, offers some more diabology of this kind, including this phrase (XLVI, 687): [Lucifer] promist double paye et notable appoinctement à quiconque luy en apporteroit une [âme de cafard] de broc en bouc.' No significance attaches to these repetitions as regards their contents, but the fact that they so frequently occur strongly suggests a static reservoir of ideas from which Rabelais drew over a period of years.

Panurge's discourse does not remain on this popular level, and towards the end he shows himself something of a connoisseur in diabology. To be exact, he speaks of the time when he studied at Toledo, where (*TL*/XXIII, 433): 'le Reverend Père en diable Picatris, recteur de la faculté diabolologique, nous disoit que naturellement les diables craignent la splendeur des espées aussi bien que la lueur du soleil.' Examples from the classics, from recent history, from 'les massoretz et caballistes', follow in support of this theory. Panurge goes on:

Car, parlant en vraye diabolologie de Tolète, je confesse que les diables vrayement ne peuvent par coups d'espée mourir, mais je maintiens scelon la dicte diabolologie qu'ilz peuvent patir solution de continuité, comme si tu couppois de travers avecques ton bragmard une flambe de feu ardent ou une grosse et obscure fumée. Et crient comme diables à ce sentement de solution, laquelle leurs est douloureuse en diable.

---

[1] R. Bacon, *Opus Tertium* (part), pp. 11–12.

He next describes the clamour and din of the battle-field:

Mais le grand effroy et vacarme principal provient du deuil et ulement des diables, qui, là guestans pellemelle les paouvres asmes des blessez, reçoivent coups d'espée à l'improviste et patissent solution en la continuité de leurs substances aerées et invisibles . . .

Another echo of this comes in the Papefigue story, which ends thus (*QL*/xlvii, 689): 'Le diable, voyant l'enorme solution de continuité en toutes dimensions, s'escria: "Mahon, Demiourgon, Megère, Alecto, Persephone, il ne me tient pas!" '

Apparently even when it is only anticipated, nothing is more frightening to devils than 'solution de continuité.' At all events, the verbal similarities between the two unrelated episodes are sufficiently close to suggest that Rabelais's Toledan authority was still in his mind half a dozen years later. Which particular authority he had before him for this chapter is not very important. The doctrines were by no means confined to students of the occult. In many Scholastic authors Rabelais would have found: 'Definitio daemonum . . . quod ait daemones esse genere animalia, animo passiva, mente rationalia, corpore aeria, tempore aeterno.'[1] The essential details of Toledan diabolology are all there: 'substances aerées et invisibles', immune from death by sword because 'tempore aeterno', and liable to 'solution de continuité' and pain because 'animo passiva'. There is no need to look beyond standard Scholastic doctrine for the original thought behind Rabelais's chapter, though the more recondite details no doubt came from later reading. Anyone trained in Scholastic ways would find no new ideas in Rabelais's exposition, and even if it is deliberately adapted for comic effect, the arguments and facts contained in it would have won general acceptance.

Far more involved than the nature of evil spirits is that of the good ones, and the change between the very cursory notices of the first two books and the others with their technically bewildering richness is at once obvious. In the case of angels only can continuity be dimly seen running through the work. Two mentions of angels have already been noted in connexion with Satan, where the deception of the devil clothing himself in the armour of light is exposed. The first of these contrasts the

---

[1] 'Daemons are animal by genus, passive in spirit, rational in mind, airy of body, in eternal time.' St. Augustine, *Civitas Dei* lib. ix, cap. viii, quoting Apuleius, and frequently quoted in his turn by, among others, SS. Bonaventura and Thomas.

respective effects of the good and evil spirits (*TL*/xiv, 402): 'l'ange bening et consolateur, apparoissant à l'homme, l'espovante au commencement, le console en la fin, le rend content et satisfaict.' The second (*TL*/xliv, 507) gives 'messagier de lumière' instead of 'ange' and thus points out once more Rabelais's fondness for achieving literary variations by changing between Greek, Latin and French synonyms. A third angelic reference comes from Pantagruel, who comments upon an anecdote about Alexander the Great refusing to hear an undistinguished adviser (*TL*/xvi, 407): 'Et peut-estre que celluy homme estoit ange, c'est à dire messagier de Dieu envoyé, comme feust Raphael à Thobie.' The philological parenthesis is typical, and the choice of an example is also interesting. The only other specific instance of angelic apparition to be found in the work has already been noted (in *Gargantua*) and is exactly the same as this. It is true that the book of *Tobit* was doctrinally not dangerous, and being of an attractive literary and dramatic quality was more appreciated in the Middle Ages and sixteenth century than other more edifying books of the Bible, but it is at least worthy of note that Gabriel, the angel of the Annunciation, and Michael, captain of the heavenly host, were certainly as well known as Raphael, and are yet not chosen for either of Rabelais's examples.

These three references are all perfectly straightforward, and all drawn from Scripture. Of a very different character are those which follow. From the *Tiers Livre* onwards Rabelais seems to delight in syntheses between ancient and modern, classical and Christian, at first sight quite haphazard, but on closer inspection revealing a definite intention. One should look not so much for clearcut, logical method in Rabelais, as for broad consistency. Introduced with the angels of darkness and light to fill the gap between God and man, come the figures of later classical demonology, *daemones*, heroes, *genii*. It is not likely that Rabelais went much further than Plutarch for his information, and that imprecise author's complexity does not help to produce those qualities of clarity without which demonology becomes mere fanciful invention instead of philosophy.

Typical of Rabelais's mature attitude is the first reference to the subject, from the first chapter of the *Tiers Livre* (i, 354): 'De faict Hesiode en sa Hierarchie colloque les bons daemons (appelez-les, si voulez, anges ou genies), comme moyens et mediateurs des dieux et homes, superieurs des homes, inferieurs des dieux. Et pource que par leurs mains nous adviennent les richesses et biens du ciel et sont continuellement envers nous bienfaisans, tousjours du mal nous praeservent, les dict estre en office de rois. . . .' The quotation is, in fact, at second-hand from Plutarch, who rather frequently invokes the authority of Hesiod. Most interesting for the light it throws on Rabelais's thought is the parenthesis 'appelez les, si voulez, anges ou genies'. Neither Hesiod nor Plutarch would, of course, have used the Christian (and Hebrew) notion of angels to explain their text, and the word *'genies'* supplies a Roman equivalent which adds nothing to the original but brings out the purpose of Rabelais's comment. For Rabelais the Christian truth is absolute, under no circumstances to be questioned, or modified, but that is no reason for rejecting pagan ideas which appear fundamentally the same, and need only appropriate philological notes before they can be included in a general synthesis of thought extending on both sides of the Incarnation. The parenthesis may have seemed to Rabelais necessary as well as a literary embellishment, because the Greek word *'daemon'* had taken on a standard meaning from New Testament days, perpetuated in Latin and still current in modern English and French. A single example of this usage is a remark by Gargantua in the *Tiers Livre*, speaking of the parents concerned in clandestine marriages (XLVIII, 519): 'Ilz, toutesfois, tant sont de crainte du Daemon et superstitiosité espris . . .' The epithet *'bon'* applied to a daemon would seem to all but the learned quite as paradoxical as, for instance, *'bon diable'*, but for Plutarch, as for Plato before him, the daemons were spirits good or bad according to their nature. Both *'ange'* and *'genie'* can be equally qualified as evil, but otherwise are terms as generic as *'daemon'*. The particular definition given here of daemons as intermediaries was basic for Plutarch, who seems to have been inspired by a text from the *Symposium*.[1] The last of the functions ('de mal nous praeservent') is similar to the Christian idea of guardian angels, who in effect obviate the necessity for direct divine intervention. One recalls the words of the Tempter in the wilderness: 'to give His angels charge over thee. . . .'[2]

The next text of this kind introduces a new element, the hardest of all to resolve satisfactorily. It comes in a very serious speech

---

[1] G. Soury, *la Démonologie de Plutarque*, p. 20.   [2] Luke iv. 10.

of Pantagruel concerning the gift of prophecy traditionally vouchsafed to dying men (*TL*/xxi, 424):

... aussi les anges, les heroes, les bons daemons (selon la doctrine des platoniques) voyans les humains prochains de mort comme de port très sceur et salutaire ... les saluent, les consolent, parlent avecques eulx et jà commencent leurs communiquer art de divination.

We know already that the office of the '*anges benings*' is to console and here they are shown revealing the secrets of future things to men. The list now adds '*heroes*' to the previous one. 'Les platoniques' seems once more to be Plutarch, or perhaps a modern Platonist commentator like Ficino, and '*anges*' is therefore an addition by Rabelais or another modern hand, made in the same sense as that of the previous text. The idea that dying men have the power to prophesy had been acknowledged by others than the Platonists and can be found in most Scholastic authorities.[1] Granted the earlier identification of '*anges*' and '*bons daemons*', the idea is normal enough, but the exact place of heroes is not easy to determine, and can only be surmised after comparing one or two other texts.

The third occasion when angels appear in unusual company is a crucial one for Rabelais's philosophy. Pantagruel and his companions have been having a long and serious discussion on immortality and kindred subjects, and the last words Pantagruel speaks before telling the great story of Pan and ending the discussion are these (*QL*/xxvii, 639): 'Je croy que toutes âmes intellectives sont exemptes des cizeaulx de Atropos. Toutes sont immortelles: anges, daemons, et humaines.' Coming as it does between two quotations from Plutarch, this phrase looks more like a personal profession of faith than most in Rabelais, and though the idea was naturally a common one, the exact choice of expression suggests that for once Rabelais was relying on no external authority as a screen for his own belief. For Scholastic philosophy, angels were, like men, endowed with an *anima intellectiva* as against the *animae vegetativae et sensitivae* of lower creatures. Similarly, *daemones* for the classical authors (and indeed demons for the Christians) shared the same nature. The brevity of this

---

[1] St. Thomas, for example, quotes Gregory for a view which he discusses and accepts: 'Anima quando appropinquat ad mortem praecognoscit quaedam futura subtilitate suae naturae ... Aut etiam cognoscit futura revelatione angelica. Non autem propria virtute.' *Summa Theologica*, 2.2 q. 172 ad I.

particular text makes it problematic whether '*daemons*' is here meant generically to cover good and evil alike, or whether for once Rabelais is using the word in its more usual Scholastic sense. The preceding chapters give every indication that the first is the case, and that the phrase means in effect 'spirits, Christian or pagan, and human beings.' Though Rabelais's mind was anything but tidy, it must have seemed illogical to him that at least the good spirits of the pre-Christian world, neither denied nor even discussed by most Scholastic writers, should have any different sort of existence from the immortal angels of Christianity. From a purely philosophical point of view, Platonic or Aristotelian spirits could be defined like any other part of creation and theological complications are only secondary to intellectual unity.

This latter point is borne out by another passage, from a purely pagan context. Panurge's famous praise of debt is to be taken no more seriously than anything else Panurge says, but it bears witness to Rabelais's apparently considerable erudition. With the cessation of debts, says Panurge (*TL*/III, 363): 'Juppiter . . . suspendera toutes les intelligences, dieux, cieulx, daemons, genies, heroes, diables, terre, mer, tous elemens.' Though the devils are a little unexpected in this company, the angels are this time absent, and also, rather oddly, men. Just what heroes are meant to be is still not clear.

The Macraeon chapters bring a solution a little nearer, but not without adding their own complications. When Pantagruel discusses with the Macrobe about the island to which they have come, he hears (*QL*/XXVI, 634): 'En ceste obscure forest que voyez . . . est l'habitation des Daemons et Heroes, lesquelz sont devenuz vieulx, et croyons . . . que hier en soit mort quelqu'un.' Pantagruel pursues the topic, using the same simile of the candle as Plutarch, from whom the whole episode is taken, and gives as his own view: 'Tout le temps qu'elles habitent leurs corps [les âmes nobles et insignes], est leur demeure pacificque . . . sus l'heure de leur discession . . .' There follows an account of the troubles noted abroad at that time. Pantagruel's words already help to clear up the confusion about heroes, and his precise choice of the word '*discession*' in place of the Macrobe's '*mort*' and '*trespas*' is a variation not solely due to literary considerations. Still more helpful is the title of the chapter, 'le Manoir et Discession des Heroes.' If the '*daemons*' are not mentioned in the

title it is extremely probable that it is because Rabelais (though
not his source, Plutarch) identified them here with 'heroes', and used
the two words together without intending to describe two different classes of beings. However that may be, it is quite certain that
daemons as such were not Rabelais's concern in this, the most
considerable group of chapters in the whole work, where he sets
forth what are unmistakably his own views on the subject of
heroes. The titles of the following chapters demonstrate this at
once (ch. xxvii): 'Comment Pantagruel raisonne sus la discession
des âmes heroiques,' (ch. xxviii) 'Comment Pantagruel raconte
une pitoyable histoire touchant le trespas des heroes.' This shows
the clear difference between Rabelais's somewhat uncritical cita-
tion of classical authorities and his definitive personal philosophy.
In the case of 'les bons daemons' he supplied his own interpretation ('anges et genies'), here in the case of heroes he gives
two examples as well as an explanation: Guillaume du Bellay
and Pan.

After several inconclusive instances of Rabelais's use of the
word 'heroes', these chapters show that he finally had a perfectly
clear conception of what he meant. The essential point is that
Pantagruel (and by implication Rabelais) conceived heroes as
having bodies plus souls of unusual excellence, which at some
given moment are separated from the body, and in the words of
Pantagruel (xxvii, 637): 'telles venerables âmes laisseront leurs
corps et la terre.' Their future destination is also known: 'les
cieulx benevoles comme joyeulx de la nouvelle reception de ces
beates âmes.' Not only is this doctrine no longer vague, but it is
not even strikingly novel. From it emerges a distinction which
the Macrobe's words do not necessarily belie: the daemons, like
angels and *genii*, are pure spirits, while the heroes are at least
temporarily endowed with a body. At last the synthesis begins
to take on some recognizable shape, though it can hardly be
pretended that the simplification is complete. One last example
from this section illustrates very well the difference between
Rabelais's attitude to quoted authority and his personal belief.
Questioned by Frère Jan on the subject of immortality, Pantagruel
quotes (or rather, paraphrases) Plutarch again, who in his turn
quotes Pindar, Hesiod and the Stoics. One of the sentences begins (xxvii, 639): 'Quant aux semi-dieux, Panes, Satyres, Sylvains,
Folletz, Aegipanes, Nymphes, Heroes et Daemons . . .' and says

their age is 9,720 years. Frère Jan very reasonably exclaims: 'Cela n'est point matière de breviaire. Je n'en croy sinon ce que vous plaira.' To this Pantagruel answers with his opinion already quoted: 'Je croy que toutes âmes intellectives . . . sont immortelles . . .' The list of demi-gods and so on, enlarged from the original which only spoke of Naiads, is not taken seriously even by Frère Jan, and it would be a waste of time to seek in it any personal beliefs of Rabelais. It is a pity that other remarks are not provided with an equally reliable touchstone.

This disposes moderately well of the heroes, and the *genii* present rather less difficulty. The equation of *genii* with angels and '*bons daemons*' has already been quoted, and with that in mind it is reasonable to make further identifications. The learned Epistemon gives the key in a remark to Panurge about prophecy (*TL*/xxiv, 437): 'Aulcuns Platonicques disent que qui peut veoir son Genius peut entendre ses destinées. Je ne comprens pas bien leur discipline, et ne suys d'advis que y adhaerez.' Jamblichus and Servius apparently advance this theory, but it is clearly enough in the tradition of Plutarch, with his famous accounts of *genii* in the *Lives*, so extensively used in the sixteenth century literature.[1] The *Genius* is in this instance the personal spirit or daemon, not a general intermediary between God and man.

The same idea comes again in a special and celebrated connexion: the daemon of Socrates. Mentioned by Plato, this daemon inspired Plutarch to write a treatise with that title, *De Genio Socratis*. In Rabelais's day it must have been the best known of all classical examples, as the prestige of Socrates, never wholly dimmed during the Middle Ages, had reached new brilliance at the time of the Renaissance. Rabelais twice refers to it, using the Greek '*daemon*' instead of the Latin '*genius*', but without doubt intending no distinction of meaning between the two. The first text is a passing reference in a comic context. Nazdecabre, the deaf mute called in for consultation on Panurge's problem, has just sneezed, and Pantagruel says (*TL*/xx, 421): 'Cestuy esternuement (selon la doctrine de Terpsion) est le daemon socratique.' The authority of Terpsion is misleading, as the whole sentence, including his name, is a literal translation from the dialogue of Plutarch just mentioned. It would be a break with his usual

---

[1] 'My genius is rebuked, as it is said Mark Antony's was by Caesar.' *Macbeth*, iii, i.

habits of mind had Rabelais not subsequently recalled this interesting theory, and in the *Quart Livre* we find it again. This time the companions are debating whether to land on the island of Ganabin, when Pantagruel says (LXVI, 746):

Je sens en mon âme retraction urgente, comme si feust une voix de loing ouye, laquelle me dict que ne y doibvons descendre. Toutes et quantes foys qu'en mon esprit j'ay tel mouvement senty, je me suis trouvé en heur, refusant et laissant la part dont il me retiroit; au contraire en heur pareil me suys trouvé, suyvant la part qu'il me poulsoit, et jamais ne m'en repenty. C'est (dist Epistemon) comme le Daemon de Socrates, tant celébré entre les Academiques.

The mechanics of this inner voice attributed to Socrates and attested by several witnesses are thus explained by Pantagruel (and Plutarch), but it is perhaps significant that not he but Epistemon makes the comparison, the more so as the *Tiers Livre* shows Pantagruel perfectly well aware of Socrates's reputed voice. Maybe Pantagruel took his inner prompting to be divine, directly or indirectly, but as the conversation stands, one can only speculate.

So far the examples given of *genii* are more or less direct borrowings from the classics, with no specially personal gloss by Rabelais, and but for a fortunate coincidence we should have to be satisfied with that. However, in the *Sciomachie*, a very official and formal piece of writing which barely goes beyond description of events, one very helpful phrase occurs. The Sciomachie was part of the official celebrations held in Rome by Cardinal du Bellay on the occasion of the birth of a son to Henri II in 1550. Rabelais begins his account by speaking of the exact and circumstantial rumour of the birth, which apparently without any rational explanation circulated in Rome on the very same day, though it was seven days before official news reached the city from France. Rabelais comments (935): 'Est un poinct sus lequel les Platonicques ont fondé la participation de divinité ès dieux tutelaires, lesquelz nos theologiens appellent anges gardians.' the 'dieux tutelaires' include almost certainly the *genii* and Socratic daemon mentioned elsewhere, and the typical parenthesis of 'nos *theologiens*' supplies the final link in the chain. From the first text in the *Tiers Livre* we know that *genii* are the same as angels and '*bons daemons*', and from this we now learn that they perform the particular function of looking after one individual or group, which Christian theologians attribute to guardian angels.[1]

The ideas of Rabelais are admittedly not clearcut, but an investigation into his demonology reveals once more the basic consistency of all his thought, and shows too his constant preoccupation in the later books: to achieve some viable synthesis between classical and Christian authorities. In every case Rabelais somewhere gives an indication of his own views, either by direct comment (as in the equation of angels and 'bons daemons') or by implicit comparison (as in the case of du Bellay and the heroes). As it stands Rabelais's interpretation of the spirit world seems to be as follows: first come the angels, pure spirits and messengers of God on specific occasions, normally understood in a Christian context. To these correspond in the non-Christian world the daemons, distinguishable like angels as good or evil, but always (or with a single exception) taken by Rabelais to be good. Strictly speaking, both angels and daemons are generic terms for *all* the inhabitants of the spirit world, but generally Rabelais seems to treat angels at least as ranking higher than the next in the hierarchy, the *genii*, the *daemons socratiques*, or the *dieux tutelaires* of the *Sciomachie*. The distinction between Latin '*genius*' and Greek '*daemon*' corresponds to a limitation in function of the *genii*, which is philologically quite inexact but which Rabelais finds convenient. These special functions do not affect the nature of *genii*, Socratic daemons and the rest, who are equally pure spirits. It does, though, allow the purely pagan conception of a personal spirit to be correlated with the Christian idea of guardian angels without bringing in the uneasy question of divine (in a Christian sense) intervention which the associations of the word '*ange*' might suggest.

Next come the heroes, who after some vague and general references are defined firmly enough as human souls of exceptional merit.[2] Rabelais's cautious treatment of the Macrobe's speech (from Plutarch) compared with the eloquent account of

---

[1] Pseudo-Dionysius was the great authority on the celestial hierarchy, to which he devoted a treatise setting out in minute detail the tasks of protection assigned to the nine choirs of angels. It is odd that Rabelais never refers to him, but Bonaventura, Thomas and Scotus quote him extensively.

[2] Cf. Isidore's entry: 'Heroas . . . quo nomine appellant alicujus meriti animas defunctorum, quasi ἀηρωας, id est viros aerios, et caelo dignos propter sapientiam et fortitudinem.' op. cit. lib. viii, cap. xi, 98.

du Bellay's death shows that in this case experience weighed more with him than classical authority. It would be asking too much to look for explanatory notes by Rabelais on each of the many problems raised by his scattered philosophy, and here we can only hazard a guess at a rapprochement which might have been made. In an early text Grandgousier speaks of 'les justes et sainctz de Dieu' as opposed to 'les diables', and it could be that if Rabelais had ever thought out seriously his attitude to the saints of Christian teaching, he would have found it similar to his notions about heroes in general and du Bellay in particular.

This philosophy may be compared with that of Hesiod as quoted by Plutarch: 'Primum Deos, mox Daemones, multos et bonos, deinde Heroas, postremo homines . . .'[1] The hierarchy is plainly the same as in Rabelais, and the only difference is that monotheism is replaced by polytheism in the Greek. The ideas which come next in Plutarch's text, however, diverge widely from those of Rabelais: 'ex hominibus in heroas praestantiores animi, ex heroibus in Daemones mutantur: ex Daemonibus autem animi perquam pauci . . . divinitatem consequuntur.'[2] There is no doubt that Rabelais found this thoroughgoing metempsychosis quite unacceptable, except only for the first transition. In quoting from his many sources Rabelais at first gives the impression of offering the widest variety of doctrines in a quite undiscriminating way, but those passages in which his personal comments appear are sufficiently numerous to offset this impression. The process of assimilating as much classical thought as possible into a mind already well-versed in Scholastic ways produces its own characteristic results.

An analysis of Ronsard's *Hymne des Daimons*[3] brings out the sharp distinction between Rabelais's treatment of demonology and that of a man thoroughly grounded in the classics but with no more than amateur status in theology. The poem is a comprehensive catalogue of everything Ronsard could remember about spirits, good and bad, arranged in fairly logical sequence by effects, native elements and so on, but without the slightest attempt at synthesis. His personal experience, for instance in

[1] Turnèbe, trans. of *De Defectu*, p. 79. On the same page occurs the parenthesis 'Daemones (Latini Lares aut Genii dicuntur).'
[2] 'The more outstanding souls are transformed from men into heroes, from heroes into daemons, and from daemons some few . . . pass on to divinity.'
[3] P. Ronsard, *Œuvres*, vol. ii, p. 167.

fighting off daemons with a sword, is given no more emphasis than improbable stories from Norway. Though Ronsard quotes more from contemporary sources or popular mythology than from the classics, his tone is only occasionally Christian, and he leaves a much less coherent impression than Rabelais. It is particularly striking that the naive animism of the people, who saw devils or spirits in many natural features or phenomena, should be treated so extensively by Ronsard and almost ignored by Rabelais, despite the fact that the original Pantagruel was a Celtic imp supposed to cause thirst in his victims. The reason for the contrast between the two men is not far to seek: Rabelais's deeply rooted Franciscan training provided him with a touchstone which enabled him to use discrimination in dealing with theories of whatever provenance, and this Ronsard was quite unable to do. Similar comparisons could be made with other contemporaries of Rabelais, but the conclusion would be the same:[1] Scholastic training leaves an indelible mark.

---

[1] For example Amaury Bouchard, who in a charming and elegant manuscript dedicated to François I, *De l'Excellence et Immortalité de l'Âme* shows an eclecticism reminiscent of Ficino. Zoroaster is frequently quoted (in Greek) as are all the classical neo-Platonists, and Pico, Ficino and Cusa, but also SS. Augustine, Jerome and Thomas. He writes, p. 26: 'les aultres platoniques qui disent que scelon les meurs et condicions les ames prenent leurs anges lesquelz aulcuns deulx appellent genies,' and just before 'aultant de legions de ses anges qu'ils appellent daemones.' Apart from these and other verbal similarities the whole tone of the work recalls the classical side of Rabelais's synthesis, and the daemon of Socrates is amply discussed (p. 80), but Bouchard leaves medieval diabology alone. Mutual influence is reasonably certain between friends of such long standing, but still accounts for only a part of Rabelais's system. The work dates probably from c. 1530, but deals with a subject they must have discussed long before. See also H. Busson, *Sources du Rationalisme*, pp. 174–8.

11 : PAN

THE group of chapters in the *Quart Livre* immediately following the end of the partial edition has an exceptional interest for the study of Rabelais's thought. As a body of text, this section is as substantial as the Pantagruelion or Gaster chapters, which are equally homogenous, or as the central consultations in the *Tiers Livre*; the chapters deal with questions of fundamental importance (which the others do not); they represent the latest known state of Rabelais's mind on these problems, and even if the *Cinquiesme Livre* is accepted as authentic it could be only a little later in composition; above all the sources for these chapters are comparatively easy to determine, or at least discuss, because the greater part is a close imitation of Plutarch and the comments interspersed throughout can be more satisfactorily accepted as Rabelais's own than is usually the case. The main questions at issue are closely related, and in discussing them it is impossible not to repeat some of what has been said elsewhere. Immortality, the meaning of comets and such portents, the connexion between this world and the next and finally a personal interpretation of the basic truth of Christianity are the ideas treated in these chapters, and it need hardly be stressed that the latter alone demands the most rigorous examination if any convincing statement of Rabelais's religious views is to be made. The final chapter, on Pan, cannot be properly understood out of its context, and it is first necessary to trace the signs which ultimately lead to it.

A literary analysis provides some serious reason for thinking that these particular problems of the *Quart Livre* had been in Rabelais's mind at the time he wrote the *Tiers Livre*, and that he sketched a tentative approach there which bears some striking resemblance to the final version of the *Quart Livre*. To what extent the *Tiers* anticipates the *Quart Livre*, or the *Quart* remembers the *Tiers Livre*, it is impossible to say, but a common pattern can be established. In ch. xxi of the *Tiers Livre*, in the series of consultations discussed by Pantagruel and tried by Panurge, the suggestion is made that Panurge should seek advice from a dying man, and better still, a dying poet. Pantagruel quotes the legend of the

swan's song, and then the theory that poets, like swans under the
special protection of Apollo, are also endowed in their last hours
with the gift of prophecy. Leaving the realm of mythology,
Pantagruel says (xxi, 424): 'J'ay dadventaige souvent ouy dire
que tout homme vieulx, decrepit et près de sa fin facilement divine
des cas advenir.' The reason for this is no longer fanciful but
philosophical. Using the graphic simile of the mariners at sea
watched by those on shore, Pantagruel continues:

. . . aussi les anges, les heroes, les bons daemons (scelon la doctrine
des platonicques) voyans les humains prochains de mort comme de
port très sceur et salutaire, port de repous et de tranquillité hors les
troubles et sollicitudes terriennes, les saluent, les consolent, parlent
avecques eulx et jà commencent leurs communiquer art de divination.

Most critics seem to think that the 'platonicques' refers to the
Phaedo, but Plutarch in *De Genio* (ch. xxiv) has a very similar
passage and Rabelais may equally well have been thinking of this,
though the whole chapter has reminiscences of the *Phaedo*.
Wherever Rabelais took his text, the idea is common to all
Platonists, and as an explanation of one form of prophecy may
be compared with Rabelais's equally Platonic theory of dreams,
where direct participation in God's wisdom rather than the mediation of spirits is made the cause of prophecy. The fact, and to
some extent the explanation, stated by Rabelais is not in this
instance a marked break with Scholastic tradition.[1] The spirits,
angels and even demons for the Scholastics, daemons and heroes
for the pagans, and all of them for Rabelais, were generally admitted to know future contingents, and therefore their communication of this knowledge to those souls so shortly to become
pure spirits presented no serious doctrinal difficulty.

The following paragraph is already a strong indication that
something more than abstract philosophical speculation is at
stake. Pantagruel quotes some biblical and classical examples of
his thesis, and then:

seulement vous veux ramentevoir le docte et preux chevalier Guillaume
du Bellay, seigneur jadis de Langey, lequel mourut le 10 de janvier . . .
1543 . . . Les troys et quatre heures avant son decès il employa en parolles
vigoureuses, en sens tranquil et serain, nous praedisant ce que depuys
part avons veu, part attendons advenir . . .

---

[1] See previous chapter, p. 117, n. 1.

The confident expectation that Langey's prophecy would be ful-filled was all the more remarkable for the absence of any hint or sign at the time which might have led them to expect the events predicted. We know that du Bellay made a deep impression on those with whom he came into contact, and contemporary historians like Sleidan,[1] as well as his more recent biographer Bourilly, agree about his outstanding qualities. Rabelais as Langey's physician was intimately concerned with his patron's last hours, and was with his fellow-doctor Taphenon responsible for the preparation of the body for burial. The provision made for Rabelais in Langey's will and his continued service with Cardinal Jean du Bellay, Guillaume's brother, explain the appar-ently gratuitous reference only in part. A man's death is not the most suitable subject for eulogy prompted by motives of self interest, and the opening chapters of the *Tiers Livre* would have offered a far better occasion for this sort of ingratiation. Every piece of evidence supports the belief that Rabelais was genuinely affected by this incident, that he took it very seriously and that he expected his readers to take it seriously. It is one of the rare moments in the work when Rabelais allows his personal (as distinct from polemical) feelings to come to light, and would be notable for that reason if for no other.

The final section of this chapter is the death-bed scene of Raminagrobis, the old poet. This may have some foundation in fact but is written with an obvious bias. The scene begins with a direct reference to the *Phaedo* (the white cock promised to Aesculapius by Socrates in his dying words) and ends with a reminiscence of two of Erasmus's *Colloquia*.[2] The tone is pointedly Evangelical, but besides the partisan note, Raminagrobis's death is that of a perfectly devout Christian, who happens to resent the intrusions of the rival Mendicants.

The pattern of the whole chapter is thus triple; beginning with the enunciation of a philosophical, in fact Platonic theory, going on with the first-hand example of du Bellay and finishing with the model of a Christian death. The link between the sections is the gift of prophecy vouchsafed to dying men from the spirits in the other world.

A second text in the *Tiers Livre* is no more than a brief reference,

[1] J. Sleidan, *Commentaires*, lib. xv, p. 552 (French trans. 1555).
[2] Erasmus, 'Funus' and 'Charon' in *Colloquia*.

but is so apposite to the similarity noted between the two books
that it must be mentioned. On the way back from Raminagrobis,
Panurge seeks the advice of Epistemon. This learned scholar
makes two suggestions in a halfhearted way. The first is that
(xxiv, 437): 'aulcuns Platoniques disent que qui peut veoir son
Genius peut entendre ses destinées,' which looks like another echo
of Plutarch's *De Genio*, and the second is that Panurge should visit
some oracle, of which a long list is then given. Epistemon ends:
'Mais vous sçavez que tous sont devenuz plus mutz que poissons
depuys la venue de celluy roy servateur, onquel ont prins fin tous
oracles et toutes propheties.' Panurge caps this with the suggestion
that they should visit 'les iles Ogygies', where a race of prophets
lives and where Saturn lies bound. This last reference is, from its
form, taken from Plutarch's *De Facie*, but in slightly altered terms
appears also in *De Defectu*. Presented with a purely pagan problem
Rabelais characteristically gives it a Christian interpretation. The
evidence is too slight to conclude whether Rabelais's comment is
meant to be personal or follows consciously the long and respectable line of authorities beginning with Eusebius's *Praeparatio
Evangelica*, who linked the prophecies of the pagan world with
Christian doctrine. The idea was a commonplace in the Middle
Ages, when the Sibyls took their place in Church art beside the
Jewish Prophets and when Virgil's Messianic Eclogue won him
near membership of the Church;[1] Rabelais and his readers would
take it for granted, but it is a little unexpected to find the flood
of classical erudition in the chapter concerned thus interrupted.

In the *Quart Livre* all these elements are blended into the
Macraeon episode, and a textual comparison is revealing both for
the light it throws on Rabelais's methods of composition and for
the mental habits it suggests. The partial edition finishes with the
great storm, with no hint of what is to follow, and it has been
shown that the 1552 edition gives an account of the tempest even
more closely similar to that of Erasmus's *Naufragium*. This is not,
however, its only literary parallel; at the end of the tempest
Epistemon cries (xxii, 625): 'je voy terre, je voy port, je voy
grand nombre de gens sus le le havre!' When they land, Pantagruel
(xxv, 632) 'ne voulut partir du mole que tous ses gens feussent en

[1] E. Langlois, *Connaissance de la Nature au Moyen Âge*, p. 71, quotes the tradition
that St. Paul regretted that Virgil was dead for 'Quem te', inquit, 'reddidissem/Si
te vivum invenissem '.

terre.' The subsequent details given by the Macrobe show that this is indeed 'port très sceur, hors les troubles et sollicitudes terriennes.' and if they are not actually there to greet the travellers, 'Daemons et heroes' are not far away in the forest. Except for the angels (hardly suitable company in this context), there is no detail of the nautical simile in the *Tiers Livre* omitted from this description. The coincidence, if it is no more than that, is certainly striking, and not very easily explained. What follows makes it seem more unlikely that the resemblance to the *Tiers Livre* is purely fortuitous. The theme of the *Tiers Livre* passage is the communication between the spirit and human worlds which accounts for the power of dying men to prophecy, the theme of the *Quart Livre* is the communication between the two worlds, again effected on the occasion of death, but this time through natural phenomena, storms, comets and so on. After the Macrobe has described the island and his opinions concerning the death of heroes, Pantagruel elaborates the argument with the simile of the candle, and then Epistemon refers briefly to the death of Guillaume du Bellay. The mention of this incident is enough to attract our attention, but this time it is no more than a footnote to Pantagruel's words 'eversions des republiques', which result from the death of these 'âmes nobles et insignes'. Pantagruel proceeds to give a catalogue of classical examples before reverting to the main theme in the next chapter. There, he says (xxvii, 636): 'aulcunes telles âmes tant sont nobles, precieuses et heroiques, que de leur deslogement et trespas nous est certains jours davant donnée signification des cieulx.' These signs are then described as 'comètes et apparitions meteores.' It is, he says, as if a last chance were being offered to men on earth to take counsel of these great souls. Pantagruel concludes:

C'est que, pour declairer la terre et gens terriens n'estre dignes de la presence, compaignie et fruition de telles insignes âmes [les cieulx] l'estonnent et espovantent par prodiges, portentes, monstres et aultres precedens signes formez contre tout ordre de nature. Ce que veismes plusieurs jours avant le departement de celle tant illustre, genereuse et heroique âme du docte et preux chevalier de Langey, duquel vous avez parlé.

The tale is taken up by Epistemon, who recalls the portents seen before Langey's death, lists the witnesses, including Rabelais himself, and ends: 'tous pensans . . . que les cieulx le repetoient comme à eulx deu par proprieté naturelle.' Just as in the *Tiers Livre*, the recent example of Langey's death is cited in support of a general philosophical theory, this time the personal touch underlined by Rabelais's own signature as a present witness.

The reference in the *Tiers Livre* and the first brief reference in the *Quart Livre* are capable of a rational interpretation, and could conceivably be attributed to a sincere or interested desire of Rabelais to flatter the family of his late patron. We know from various sources[1] that the du Bellays had an extremely efficient intelligence service, mainly in Germany, of which Rabelais must have been aware, and in which he may even have served while at Metz, and this would explain in large measure the apparently inspired prophecies which came to be fulfilled. Again, the situation in Piedmont was so very delicate (and so mismanaged by Langey's predecessor, Montjehan) that the sudden death of the only man who seems really to have controlled it would naturally account for the reversal of French fortunes in that theatre, and to some extent elsewhere. Knowing these political facts, not familiar to the general public, Rabelais may be imagined as colouring them slightly with hints of supernatural influence in order to impress his readers. There would be no compelling answer to this rationalist explanation but for the third and last reference to Langey's death. In every way this outweighs the other two in importance and authority. Unfortunately there seems to be no contemporary confirmation of Rabelais's report, but it is hardly credible that he would list so many independent witnesses if his account of the portents were untrue. Indeed, if it were untrue, far from winning the favour of the du Bellay family, Rabelais would be offering them a grave affront. Failing historical corroboration, it seems reasonable to accept the fact of the portents, whatever they may have been. This being so, the deep impression produced on Rabelais by the event at once appears in its true light. The facts of prophecy and French reverses are open to rational explanation, as has just been shown, but the portents are emphatically not to be interpreted in these terms. The belief in portents of this kind and their significance was so universal[2] that no special explanation

---

[1] V. L. Bourrilly, *Guillaume du Bellay* deals at length with this question, giving the main sources.

[2] Cf. Sleidan, op. cit. pp. 566 and 749.

need be looked for in Rabelais's case. Having linked the 'prodiges horrificques' with the death of Langey, Rabelais drew the natural conclusion from the philosophical theory with which he begins this section. What must have seemed to Rabelais a direct confirmation of the theory quoted from Plutarch gave that theory a quite unique value in his system.

The serious tone of the debate is enhanced by the memory of Langey, but the last speech of Pantagruel overshadows everything else for its direct and unequivocal answer to two fundamental questions—the immortality of the soul and the relationship of Christianity to paganism. Even to approach such problems was risky and to expound unusual views could be fatal. To give unusual views for any other motive than personal conviction would have been foolishly provocative, and it can be quite safely assumed that Rabelais is speaking for himself in these striking lines.

Leaving for a moment the question of signs and portents, Pantagruel, at Frère Jan's request, gives the views on immortality, first of various classical authorities, as quoted by Plutarch, and then his own: 'Je croy que toutes âmes intellectives sont exemptes des cizeaulx de Atropos. Toutes sont immortelles; anges, daemons et humaines. Je vous diray toutesfoys une histoire bien estrange mais escripte et asceurée par plusieurs doctes et sçavans historiographes à ce propos.' The story is, of course, that of Pan's death, which Rabelais interprets as relating to Christ.

This is the final point of similarity with the *Tiers Livre*: a Platonic (or neo-Platonic) theory in each case concerning death and its attendant phenomena, the case of Langey's death used in each as a particular example, in the *Tiers Livre* a Christian death, in the *Quart Livre the* Christian death. The associated details of the storm and so on bring out still more forcibly what may have begun as a literary, but seems to have ended as a philosophical reminiscence. The second passage quoted from the *Tiers Livre* is equally reminiscent of the corresponding passage, the Pan chapter, in the *Quart Livre*. 'Celluy roy servateur' becomes 'celluy grand servateur des fidèles', the theme of silent oracles in the *Tiers Livre* is balanced by the whole chapter of Plutarch's *De Defectu* quoted here, and, most strange, Panurge's remark about Saturn and the 'Iles Ogygies' with which the *Tiers Livre* chapter ends is the passage immediately following (in slightly different form) the Pan legend in *De Defectu*. Its total omission from the Macraeon group of chapters, in which the smallest details of Plutarch's accounts appear, could be explained by the assumption that Rabelais only knew the relevant passage of Plutarch at second hand, which is almost certainly not the case, in view of his known enthusiasm for Plutarch and other quotations from this dialogue. It has been suggested elsewhere[1] that the immediate source for these chapters is Postel, who equally omits the Saturn reference, but at the same time the possibility must not be overlooked that Rabelais deliberately left out the passage to avoid repeating what he had already said in a very similar context in the *Tiers Livre*.

This literary parallel has been studied in some detail, because if it is accepted as valid it proves a preoccupation of some duration on Rabelais's part with the particular problems enumerated, and suggests a link between his classical erudition, his personal experience with Langey and his Christian (not to say Scholastic) upbringing. As a pattern of the synthesis which as far as can be ascertained from the work represents Rabelais's thought, this is of the greatest value. The relative importance of the three factors is the central point of our inquiry, and therefore the place of the Pan chapter in the development of these themes is of capital importance for any attempt at evaluation. Failure to admit anything like a coherent system of thought in Rabelais over a period of years invalidates this contention, but all evidence does point to the existence of such a system. Rabelais's treatment of texts from *De Defectu* is illuminating in itself. His ch. xxv, with the description of the island, is a close paraphrase of Plutarch's ch. xvii, altered only in that the traveller in Plutarch lands before the storm; Rabelais's ch. xxvi continues Plutarch's ch. xviii, with the explanation of the storm and the simile of the candle. The final sentence of Plutarch about Saturn is omitted. At the end of ch. xxvii Rabelais returns to Plutarch, quoting his ch. xix on the Stoics. So far Rabelais has not altered Plutarch's order, but his next words refer back (quoting Plutarch by name) to ch. xi, whence he quotes the views of Pindar and Hesiod, considerably elaborated by him with gratuitous classical erudition. Postel, or some other author, could have provided Rabelais with the requisite quotations, and Postel actually gives them in the same order, but this does not explain the situation of the Pan story,

---

[1] Krailsheimer, 'Rabelais et Postel' in *BHR* 1951.

last in Rabelais's arrangement and ch. XVII in Plutarch. All the other authors who use Plutarch maintain his arrangement, yet here we have Rabelais deliberately changing this order for reasons of his own. The most obvious explanation is that Rabelais wished to grade the subjects of his text in ascending order of importance; first the classical author beloved of the sixteenth century, then the recent and celebrated Langey, finally Christ. The common theme is the effect on nature of the death of great men, supported in turn by Plutarch, by living witnesses and by the New Testament. Plutarch's theme, on the other hand, is (in this part of the dialogue) the immortality of daemons, which becomes a purely secondary one for Rabelais, who naturally could not have expressed an open mind on the subject like Plutarch, and who anyhow had long since decided his belief. The composition of these chapters, so homogenous in their thought and expression, shows the greatest care in selecting and arranging material of a varied nature.

The Pan story is introduced by a 'toutesfoys' which poses a minor problem. On the face of it, the word seems to indicate an exception to the rule of immortality just stated by Rabelais through Pantagruel, and if so apparently implies that Pan-Christ was mortal. There is something similar in Plutarch, where the story is used to attack a previous speaker, who claims immortality for daemons, but this does not altogether satisfactorily explain Rabelais's text. Since signs in nature and not immortality provide the theme which Rabelais wishes to state, he does not bother to explain the apparent contradiction. All the other cases ever observed of these portents concerned the passing of a great man's soul from the world of matter to the world of spirits, a transition from one part of the *created* universe to another. In the case of Christ alone, the transition was from the world of matter to the infinite, eternal dwelling-place whence He had come; the created universe no longer included Him as a part who is its own whole. If something like this were in Rabelais's mind, it would explain the 'toutesfoys' as introducing an exception to the rule, but one which Rabelais knew to be unique and which thus does not disprove the rule.

In the actual relation of the story, Rabelais makes one small alteration which is in fact decisive for his interpretation. To the original '*Πάν μέγας*' he adds the one word 'Dieu', 'Pan le grand

Dieu', and at a stroke makes his presentation of the story different from the normal tradition. His comments at the end of the tale follow more naturally after this simple addition. First he offers his interpretation of Pan as 'celluy grand servateur des fidèles,' with a barely veiled gibe at his enemies 'les pontifes, docteurs, presbtres, et moines de la loy mosaicque.' Then he shows how the word 'πᾶν' applies particularly well to Christ 'veu qu'il est le nostre tout, tout ce que sommes, tout ce que vivons, tout ce qu'esperons est luy, en luy, de luy, par luy.'[1] Postel before him had already made the philological point in his interpretation of Pan as Christ, and it is sufficiently obvious to have occurred to others, though not often in this particular context.

As well as the word's philological significance, Pan was also the name of the shepherd god, more exactly demi-god, and this is the next variation on Rabelais's main theme. 'Le bon Pan, le grand pasteur, qui, comme atteste le bergier passioné Corydon, non seulement a en amour et affection ses brebis, mais aussi ses bergiers.' The references to Virgil and St. John fit in well with this Christian treatment of pagan legend. It is curious that 'Panes' are listed as demi-gods in the chapter preceding this, and the confusion of the All and the shepherd god is less admissible on that account. Another curious coincidence, noted earlier, is that one of the medieval meanings for 'servator' (whence servateur) given by du Cange is 'pastor gregarius', which gives a double link with the idea of the good shepherd. The third sentence brings back the central theme of the whole section: 'A la mort duquel feurent plaincts, souspirs, effroys et lamentations en toute la machine de l'univers, cieulx, terre, mer, enfers.' The real point of the chapter is thus made clear, and the Pan story becomes the final, crowning illustration of the theory of portents. The exceptional nature of Christ's death is shown by the universal mourning, including even the heavens, which in other cases are described

[1] A special acknowledgement is due to M. A. Screech, 'The Death of Pan and Heroes in Rabelais', in *BHR* 1955, to whom we are indebted for an admirable analysis of the classical and humanist affinities of Rabelais's version of the tale. Working quite independently he arrives at similar, and complementary, conclusions to those presented here. In particular, by discovering the reference in Paul Marsus's Commentary on Ovid's *Fasti*, so far the earliest known, and by pointing out contemporary identifications of Pan with Christ, the Good Shepherd, he has added considerably to our understanding of this extremely important Renaissance theme. His wider conclusions concerning Stoic and Evangelical influences on Rabelais are too far-reaching to be discussed here, but with reservations which will be apparent we accept them.

as 'joyeulx à la reception de ces beates âmes.' They too were losing
the greatest soul ever to be parted from its body. Pantagruel ends
with a chronological justification of his theory: 'A ceste miene
interpretation compète le temps, car cestuy très bon, très grand
Pan, nostre unique Servateur, mourut lèz Hierusalem, regnant en
Rome Tibère Cesar.' The authority for the natural phenomena
(eclipses, &c.) at the time of the Passion was scriptural, and quite
unimpeachable, and had long been one of the favourite *points de
départ* for Christian apologists. The historical identity of these
phenomena with similar ones reported by more or less contemporary pagan writers had an obvious propaganda value which had
been fully exploited.

The four features of Rabelais's interpretation—All, shepherd,
universal mourning, chronology—are all to be found in other
authors in similar connexions, but seldom if ever combined in
just this way. The first assumption, that Pan for the Greeks could
bear a monotheistic interpretation, was a typical product of the
enthusiastic philology of the Renaissance and continued for a
century or two to inspire similar comments. One of the great
drawbacks for those who wished to reinstate the philosophers of
Greece and Rome in the honourable position from which their
paganism debarred them was their obvious and notorious polytheism. If Plato was 'divine' for the Middle Ages it was because
a vague sort of monotheism could be read into his then known
works, and more particularly because the neo-Platonists with their
trinity, The One, the Word, the World Soul, came so near Christian
theology. Rediscovery of the Platonic corpus led to a new attempt
to Christianize Plato, not in the same sense or with the same object
as St. Thomas's baptism of Aristotle, but in the spirit of comparative religion. By the end of the seventeenth century, Ralph
Cudworth,[1] following Rabelais's interpretation of Pan as Christ,
actually quotes the end of the *Phaedrus*, where Socrates prays to
Pan, as proof of the monotheism of the Greeks, or at least of
Socrates. Though the context of this dialogue makes it indisput-
ably clear that a local woodland deity is concerned, the uncritical
humanists of the sixteenth century would have been even more
easily misled than Cudworth. Such a misconception of Greek
religion was also assisted by late classical writers whose authority
in the sixteenth century was quite disproportionate to their real

[1] R. Cudworth, *Intellectual System of the Universe*, vol. i, p. 585, n. 1 (1678).

importance. Thus Macrobius (a specially appropriate author for this dialogue with 'le bon Macrobe') writes: 'Hunc deum [Pana] Arcades colunt appellantes τὸν τῆς ὕλης κυριον, non silvarum dominum sed universae substantiae materialis dominatorem significari volentes, cuius materiae vis universorum corporum, seu illa divina sive terrena, componit essentiam.'[1] Following Macrobius, the early encyclopaedist Isidore[2] of Seville, who was copied throughout the Middle Ages, writes:

Pan dicunt Graeci, Latini Silvanum, deum rusticorum, quem in naturae similitudinem formaverunt: unde et Pan dictus est, id est omne. Fingunt enim eum ex universali elementorum specie . . . caprinas ungulas habet, ut soliditatem terrae ostendat quem volunt rerum et totius naturae deum: unde Pan quasi omnia dicunt.

This is far from the lofty monotheism later ascribed to Socrates, but contains the germ of an idea which could be quite easily developed into something like Rabelais's 'nostre tout'. The true significance of Pan for the Greeks is quite irrelevant, as Rabelais and his contemporaries completely lacked the critical apparatus necessary for deciding the question, and these quotations show that the standard late Classical and thence mediaeval conception of Pan included the philological interpretation as well as the pastoral.

The next point, the idea of the good shepherd, was naturally a commonplace, made familiar in poetry through Virgil and applied freely in a metaphorical sense. Marguerite of Navarre[3] calls her dead brother 'le grand Pan' and shows him mourned by his shepherds; the author of the *Cinquiesme Livre*, paraphrasing on his original (probably Lucian) describes Pan (XXXIX, 889) as 'homme horrificque et monstrueulx' with his animal-members 'homme hardi, courageux, hasardeux et facile à entrer en courroux.' Thus the purely pagan traditions of the satyr-like Pan existed in literature side by side with the sublimated good shepherd based on Christian tradition.

The lamentations of the story have been variously explained, depending on an author's general interpretation. Thus Ficino[4] does not diverge very far from Plutarch: 'testantur enim ex multis

---

[1] Macrobius, *Saturnalia*, I. xxii. 2 (ed. Teubner).
[2] Isidore, *Etymologiarum*, lib. VIII, xi, 81.
[3] Marguerite de Navarre, *Comédie sur le Trespas du Roy*. (1547).
[4] M. Ficino, *Theologia Platonica*, lib. x, cap. ii, pp. 147–8.

prodigiis quae suis temporibus contigerunt, Pana magnum dae-
monem, aliosque multos daemones eiulasse primum, deinde etiam
obiisse.' Agrippa[1] quotes this verbatim in his turn. Those writers
who were primarily interested in the nature of demons naturally
tended to emphasize this classical evidence of demons' mortality.
An extension of this principle led to the use made by Christian
apologists of the same story. For Eusebius,[2] the pagans themselves provided unwitting but adequate testimony to the false-
ness of their own religion and the truth of the Christian revelation.
For him, Pan was a well-known pagan god whose death as related
by Plutarch coincided with the work of Christ in ridding the world
of evil spirits. He writes:

> So far Plutarch. But is is important to note the time at which he
> says the death of the daemon took place. For it was the time of Tiberius
> in which our Saviour, making his sojourn among men, is recorded to
> have been ridding human life from daemons of every kind: so that there
> were some of them now kneeling before him and beseeching him not
> to deliver them over to the Tartarus that awaited them. You have
> therefore the date of the overthrow of the daemons, of which there
> was no record at any other time.

This became the traditional interpretation and one which
Rabelais had every opportunity of knowing.[3] The translation
made by George of Trebizond in 1470 was widely read, and a
Greek edition was published shortly before the *Quart Livre* by
Henri Estienne. Petrus Crinitus[4] was one of the authors who
quoted the story from Eusebius and gave Eusebius's comment at
the end. From a Christian point of view, the confirmation of a
known feature of Christ's ministry, the expulsion of demons, by
external sources was valuable in itself, when so few external witnesses were to hand. It is still not certain who first proposed the
identification of Pan with Christ, but whether it was Marsus, as
now seems very likely, or someone else the reason for the shift of
emphasis must be sought in a slightly different interpretation of
the lamentations combined with the historical event in Tiberius's
reign.

---

[1] H. C. Agrippa, *De Occulta Philosophia*, lib. III, cap. xvi, p. 241.
[2] Eusebius, *Praep. Evangelica*, lib. v, cap. xvii, p. 206 (tr. Gifford).
[3] Despite the often quoted but quite false view of S. Reinach, *Cultes, Mythes,
Religions*, vol. iii, pp. 1–15 (1913).
[4] P. Crinitus, *De Honesta Disciplina*, lib. XIV, cap. iii, p. 213.

Nearest and yet quite contrary to Rabelais's interpretation comes that of Mexia,[1] who gives more data than Rabelais for concluding the same thing and then offers a completely opposite explanation. He is concerned, like Eusebius, to show that pagan gods and oracles all failed at Christ's coming, and he gives an interesting and rather free version of the Pan story to prove his point. For him, as for Eusebius, but more explicitly, Pan is 'el grande demonio, el Dios Pan' and 'el gran diablo Pan', while a final comment explains: 'Porque Pan llamaban ellos al dios de los pastores.' What gives Mexia's version a special interest is his next passage. Continuing the exposition of his main theory, the testimony of pagans to Christ's presence on earth, he speaks of the heavenly portents, eclipses, earthquakes and the rest observed at Christ's death both by the Evangelists and by pagans. He quotes Josephus and then gives the famous story of Dionysius (Denis) the Areopagite, who is described as a learned astrologer commenting on the phenomena: 'Either the frame of the world shall be dissolved, either the God of nature presently suffereth . . . for which cause . . . the sages of Athens strangely disturbed did to be built incontinently an altar to the God unknown [Acts xvii. 22-23]'. This clue to Rabelais's text is made more helpful still by an editorial comment of Juan Cromberger, giving the authority of Petrus Comestor (*Scol. Hist.* cap. xvii), Jacques Lefèvre at the end of his commentary on Sacrobosco's *De Sphaera* and also Erasmus's commentary on Matt. xvii, Origen, Bede and Augustine. Earlier in the chapter Paulus Orosius, Eutropius, Eusebius and St. Jerome are all cited as well.

This precious list of sources enables us at once to reconstruct Rabelais's most probable scheme of composition. An additional comparison makes this even clearer. The only authors at present known to have proposed Rabelais's interpretation before him are Marsus, Postel and Bigot. Postel's[2] chapter heading tells us what to expect: 'De substantiis separatis, sive daemonibus, geniis, &c.' and his whole chapter is on these lines. After telling the story he writes:

Haec Plutarchus: quae multiplicem daemonum experientiam, substantiarumque separatarum demonstrant; tum vero manifesto

---

[1] P. Mexia, *Silva de Varia Leccion*, Pt. ii, cap. xxxiii, p. 455 and English trans. by T. Fortescue (1571).
[2] G. Postel, *De Orbis Concordia*, lib. i, cap. vii, p. 51; cf. also lib. i, cap. xii.

fidem faciunt de morte Jesu Christi, qua tum contremerunt infernus, ubique daemones sunt profligati et afflicti. Sed non est admittendum, quod hac infert ex eo, mortales daemones esse.

It is this latter idea which leads him to his conclusion:

sed quia corpore magnus ille Πάν universi arbiter moriebatur, sentiebant suam profligationem futuram—Itaque nec poterant validiora testimonia de tempore mortis Christi, nec de substantiis separatis adferri. Nulli alii quam Christo certe omnium rerum moderatori, instauratori et arbitro τοῦ παντός vocabulum competit.

What brings Postel to his interpretation is his desire to prove, like Rabelais, that 'toutes âmes intellectives . . . sont immortelles: anges, demons et humaines', and in explaining away the apparent exception (cf. Rabelais's 'toutesfoys') he uses the identification of Pan and Christ based on philological grounds. Once having made the identification, he uses it again, in De Orbis and also in De Etruriae,[1] as one of the 'externa testimonia de morte Jesu Christi'. Exactly the same approach is used by Bigot,[2] who quotes the Pan story to illustrate the theme of oracles and spirits foretelling the future and gives the same philological explanation of 'Pan'. Referring back to his text, he speaks later of 'afflictiones lamentaque daemonum Thami,' showing his affinity with the traditional theory of Eusebius, Ficino and the others. In Bigot's case, the 'externa testimonia' are quite secondary to the idea of demons' immortality.[3]

This comparison brings out very well the particular bias Rabelais gives to the story; in his context intellective immortality is a subsidiary issue, and though the Pan story has a direct and obvious bearing on this theme, Rabelais's complete silence regarding the nature of Thamous's voice, the identity of the mourners on shore and their relationship to Pan, makes the chapter relatively insignificant as a contribution to demonology. As a further example of the cause and effect observed at the tempest and at Langey's death it follows quite naturally, and needs no more

---

[1] Id. De Etruriae, p. 57.

[2] G. Bigot, Christianae Phil. Praeludium, lib. ix, p. 442. This rare work is quoted for the passage in question by Screech, art. cit, who reproduces it in extenso, with emendations to the defective text.

[3] Bigot seems to find himself in some embarrassment as a result of his quotation, and goes to some pains in his Epilogue to the reader, p. 535, to justify his excessive use of demonology.

comment than Rabelais has given it. What Rabelais has done in effect is to combine Postel's (rather than Bigot's) philological identification of Pan-Christ with the historical evidence of the Passion as given in Mexia, though not necessarily from that author. The link is the remark attributed to Dionysius, and as soon as one sees this and the philological interpretation side by side the solution to the whole problem becomes evident.[1] Checking the sources given in Mexia, we find that Petrus Comestor[2] writing of the earthquakes, &c. which followed the Passion says: 'Dionysius dixit quod Deus naturae patiebatur': Sacrobosco[3] (John of Holywood) adds to this the story of the altar to the unknown God: Lefèvre in his commentary on Sacrobosco uses the same words:[4] the French translation of Sacrobosco by Jehan Loys (1546) gives 'ou le Dieu de Nature souffre . . .' Besides these, Vincent de Beauvais,[5] perhaps the greatest of medieval encyclopaedists, gives the whole story, together with the unknown God; in his chapter on eclipses, Pierre d'Ailly[6] writes: 'aut deus naturae patitur, aut totius mundi machina destruitur', and most interesting of all, Michael Scot[7] in his commentary on Sacrobosco adds at the end: 'Dicebant [Athenienses] enim quod creatum compatiebatur suo creatori dedicantes eos aras deo dubioso suo ignoto.' It is worth adding that in Sacrobosco and all the commentaries on his work, this text comes in a very conspicuous place at the very end of the book, as a crowning example of previous theories.

This impressive list of Scholastic authorities could certainly be much enlarged, and the origin of the story in the hagiology of St. Denis in the *Golden Legend* undoubtedly explains its wide diffusion. An early Franciscan book of exempla, of Irish provenance, quotes the story[8] and an even more convincing testimony to its universal

---

[1] L. Karl, 'Sur la Mort de Pan dans Rabelais' in *Mélanges Picot* (1913), seems to have realized that there was a connexion, but without developing his theory.

[2] P. Comestor, *Historia Scol.* cap. clxxv.

[3] J. de Sacrobosco, *De Sphaera*, lib. iv, at end. In the same volume as this work (ed. Venice 1518) are the commentaries of Lefèvre, P. D'Ailly and M. Scot, referred to below.

[4] J. Lefèvre d'Etaples, *Comm. de Sphaera*, lib. iv, cap. xix at end.

[5] Vincent de Beauvais, *Speculum Naturale*, lib. iii, cap. vii (on eclipses).

[6] P. d'Ailly, *Comm. De Sphaera*, qu. 14 ad 2. corr.

[7] M. Scot, *Comm. de Sacrobosco*, last words.

[8] *Liber Exemplorum*, p. 3 (Brit. Soc. Fran. Studies, vol. i).

familiarity is the fact that Maillard and Menot[1] quote precisely the same words of Dionysius in each of their Passions. The special honour paid in France to St. Denis, identified in the Middle Ages with the Dionysius of the legend, perhaps increased still more the general use of his words in sermons for the people as well as in treatises for the learned. It can therefore be stated without any hesitation that Rabelais could not possibly have been ignorant of these words or, indeed, have forgotten them, so constant is their repetition. In every version of the story Dionysius's words include the phrase 'Deus Naturae' and in French 'Dieu de nature'. Now this, as we have seen from Isidore's 'totius naturae deus', was a standard definition of Pan, and would quite easily evoke the name of Pan in a man who was currently interested in Plutarch's story. The substitution in Dionysius's exclamation of 'Pan' for 'deus naturae' is simple, and at once gives the identification Pan-Christ, supported by both philological and meteorological arguments. The second part of Dionysius's exclamation is equally conclusive; for him and for all those who quoted him; 'totius mundi machina destruitur' is the only other explanation of the phenomena they observe, and exactly this phrase, 'toute la machine de l'univers', comes in Rabelais, when Postel and Bigot had dwelt on the demons' lamentations.

Another point is equally relevant. Rabelais's *point de départ* for these chapters was the effect on nature, the signs and portents, connected with the passing of great souls, and from this point of view he would have been led to the Dionysius story by almost any medieval treatise on astronomy or meteorology. He could equally well have been led to the same result by starting from a study of 'externa testimonia'. Petrus Comestor brings in the portents following the Passion in just this way, and this was the regular Scholastic approach to the historicity of the gospels. Eusebius, whose *Praeparatio Evangelica* has already been mentioned, was even better known as an ecclesiastical historian, and most of the authors quoted above refer to him by name. In his great chronological survey *Chronicorum Canonum*, translated by St. Jerome, the following entry comes under A.D. 32:

Jesus-Christus secundum Prophetias, quae de eo fuerunt prolocutae, ad passionem venit anno Tiberii XVIII: quo tempore etiam in aliis Ethnicorum commentariis haec ad verbum scripta reperimus: 'Solis

[1] Maillard in his Passion at Paris, Menot at Tours and Paris.

facta defectio: Bithynia terraemotu concussa, et in urbe Nicaea aedes plurimae corruerunt.' Quae omnia his congruunt, quae in passione Salvatoris acciderunt.[1]

Further similar references follow, from Phlegon, Josephus and others. Thus from the earliest times the main proof that Christ's death did happen under Tiberius was directly associated with the gospel account of the portents seen at the time of the Passion. History and meteorology are inseparable in this matter, and no one with the slightest interest in either subject could fail sooner or later to be reminded of Dionysius's words.

Seen in this light, Rabelais's presentation of the story can be more adequately judged. The probability is overwhelming that he knew from Marsus, Postel, Bigot or another so far unidentified author that Pan could be identified with Christ; it is very likely that he knew also the older interpretation of Eusebius, again either directly or through some intermediary like Crinitus, and preferred the other, no doubt attracted by the philological approach. At the same time, the theme of meteorological phenomena would make him more attentive to that aspect of the Passion than to the vaguer theme of demonology, and any reflection on these lines could not fail to remind him of Dionysius's words. The very appropriate definition of Pan as the god of *nature* fits in even better with Rabelais's context than the more general idea of the All, and gives him a direct link with the historical events under Tiberius. Though Rabelais goes against the traditional interpretation of Eusebius in the identification of Pan, in other respects he is closer to the Scholastic tradition than any of his predecessors. Mexia's mention of Dionysius (which may not have been originally his own) shows that the connexion was one that came naturally to a writer of wide interests, and it is indeed difficult to find a really satisfactory explanation of Rabelais's text which excludes the hypothesis expounded above.

The constant pattern of Rabelais's thought, which starting from a Christian education seeks to incorporate as much as possible of classical philosophy, is nowhere more clearly seen than here. It comes as something of a shock to preconceived notions of the Renaissance attitude to find that the Middle Ages had never ceased to follow Eusebius in making use of every pagan author

---

[1]Eusebius, *Chron. Canonum*, lib. post. (Basle 1529).

who could further the cause of Christian apologetics. To the Greeks, that is to Dionysius, a monotheistic idea is attributed before there can be any question of direct contact with the apostles, and by extension it is easy to see how the idea of grace, coming as readily upon Ethnic as Hebrew prophets, could develop. The importance of pagan historians is often pointed out by Rabelais (cf. Gargantua's letter) in a humanist sense, but here he uses Plutarch just as the Scholastics would have done. If he uses philology to support his interpretation, he is only following directly on the line deriving from Isidore and his *Etymologies*; in citing the phenomena of the Passion he is quoting the example best known in all Scholastic treatises on meteorology and kindred subjects. Even the juxtaposition of Virgil and St. John is the sign of a humanism which did not wait for the sixteenth century to come to full maturity. While it would be absurd to deny that this chapter, like those preceding it, is typical of the Renaissance outlook, it is no less absurd to forget that in not a few respects the 'Renaissance outlook' had already existed for some centuries. One may go even further and say that the eulogy of Langey and his death are no more the signs of man's reawakening interest in man than the Pan chapter, and that this too would have aroused no flicker of surprise in the medieval reader. Rabelais's emancipation from the habits of medieval and Scholastic thought must be sought elsewhere than in these chapters on such fundamental subjects.[1]

---

[1] This fascinating legend has been the subject for a great deal of research from the earliest times. A Danish folklore specialist has examined the recurrence of the legend in its many forms in European, and specially Scandinavian, folklore, and her conclusions are very interesting. She finds that Plutarch's version shows:

> germansk sagnoverlevering i hvert fald i dette tilfaelde er kommet ind i romerriget og har forbundet sig med antike overlevering om guden Pan, der før øvrigt ikke har anden tilknytning til dødsbudskabsagnet end den, at han er en naturmystisk gud ligesom de vaetter, sagnet overalt i den germanske overlevering er knyttet til.

In other words, the Pan legend as Rabelais knew it really belonged to the same old Celtic mythology as the original imp Pantagruel, and only became absorbed into late classical mythology because Pan, the nature-god, came nearer than any other classical deity to the nature-spirit of the Celtic-Germanic version. This is another refutation of Reinach's theory of the story's Levantine origin, and does not really affect our study, except to show how a genuinely popular myth only came into what had started out to be a popular book when its humble origin was decently obscured in borrowed Greek form. See I. Boberg, *Sagnet om den store Pans Død.*

12 : MAN

SOMEWHERE between the Lord of Creation of modern thought and the *'roseau pensant'* of Pascal comes man as Rabelais conceived him. Since 'humanism' is one of the words automatically associated with Rabelais, it can do no harm to look for more precise definitions before giving the word yet another connotation. If it is true that *'animal rationale'* remained the standard definition of man from Greek times to Descartes and later, it is equally true that no medieval thinker would have hesitated to give the essential definition of man as a being endowed with an immortal soul. *'Animal rationale'* accounts for this life, immortal soul for the other. It requires a conscious and constant effort of will to realize that, for the medieval, and largely for the Renaissance, thinker, the other world was not merely more important than this *sub specie aeternitatis*, but at least as real, and for not a few philosophers, more real. It is therefore logical and even inescapable to begin looking at Rabelais's idea of man where he himself would have begun: with his soul.

Rare to the point of freakishness were those who in Rabelais's day genuinely held a materialist view of the soul. Its immortality, though understood in various ways, was not a truth seriously denied by any considerable body of people. Even such a man as Dolet, condemned technically for casting doubt on the souls' immortality,[1] was actually innocent of that crime, whatever his private thoughts may have been. In Rabelais the life to come is certainly not jumped, and glimpses of it vary from the purely popular to the profoundly philosophical.

Traditional and typical of ordinary beliefs is the speech of Gargantua when he has lost his wife in childbirth (*Pant.*/III, 204): 'Ma femme est morte . . . elle est bien, elle est en paradis pour le moins, si mieulx ne est: elle prie Dieu pour nous . . .' The average sixteenth-century reader would recognize his own conception of an afterlife in these words, naive and anthropomorphic. The *reductio ad absurdum* of this approach to the afterlife is to be found in Epistemon's visit to the underworld (*Pant.*/xxx). Some critics

---

[1] In his translation of the *Axiochus*.

have insisted on the sinister meaning of this episode, allegedly ridiculing the doctrine of immortality, Lazarus's resuscitation and much besides, but to do so is to condemn much of the medieval drama which the Church quite willingly sponsored.

It is not difficult to detect the changed tone in Gargantua's famous letter to his son. To the reader who had smiled at Epistemon's account, it would never occur that this letter could be anything but serious. It is not possible, or even relevant, to know Rabelais's personal motives in setting out these views, but there can be no doubt as to the impression they made. M. Gilson[1] has easily shown the perfectly orthodox nature of these ideas. Gargantua's concern is with the world below, but the whole tenor of his letter shows that the guaranteed immortality of the soul is the background to these reflections on human life. Greatest of God's gifts is immortality, promised for the soul and possible even in this transitory life in one sense (*Pant.*/viii, 224), 'perpetuer son nom et sa semence.' Our first parents suffered pain of death for their sin, but death only of their bodies, and Gargantua is splendidly eloquent on the mitigation which even this punishment has undergone: 'Quand mon âme laissera ceste habitation humaine, je ne me reputeray totallement mourir, ains passer d'un lieu en aultre, attendu que en toy et par toy je demeure en mon image visible en ce monde . . .' It is the last words which are operative. Only a man firmly convinced of the prize of immortality awaiting him in the other world would derive comfort from the thought of his image persisting 'en ce monde'. In his closing words he reminds his son again 'ceste vie est transitoyre': to stress the fleeting nature of this life unless there is hope of a life to come is absurd in such an enthusiastic exhortation to study; to deny to all but legitimate fathers a taste of immortality quite inconsistent with the fervent submission to God and his word. That individual survival, rather than the collective soul of Averroes, is in Rabelais's mind can hardly be doubted. The insistence on family continuity, several times repeated in the work, is evidence in itself that any surrender of personality was abhorrent to Rabelais.

The theme of immortality (and of Judgement Day) was evidently linked in Rabelais's mind at the time with particular biblical texts. To the Pauline references of Gargantua's letter we may add another from the roughly contemporaneous *Almanach*

---

[1] In the article 'Rabelais Franciscain' in *Idées et Lettres*.

for 1535 (930): 'Vous convient souhaiter (comme S. Pol disoit
Phillip. I . . .) que vos âmes soient hors mises ceste chartre tenebreuse du corps terrien et joinctes à Jesus le Christ. Lors cesseront
toutes passions, affections et imperfections humaines. . . .'
The theme is not confined to the earlier period, where there is
every indication of unusual religious preoccupation, and less
closely scriptural but more detailed references to the same subject
come in the later books. Raminagrobis on his deathbed, for all his
dislike of the friars, is no impious mocker. He looks forward to
(*TL*/xxi, 426) 'le bien et felicité que le bon Dieu a praeparé à ses
fidèles et esleuz en l'aultre vie et estat de immortalité.' These
sober words can be compared with Panurge's long variations on
the diabological theme, where the intention to parody is unmistakable.

In the *Quart Livre* the question is debated at greater length, this
time without nominal references to Christian teaching, and the
conclusions are stated unequivocally in philosophical terms. The
discussion with the Macrobe has already been treated in some
detail, but two quotations may appropriately be repeated here.
Speaking of Langley's death, Epistemon describes the attendant
signs and concludes (xxvii, 638): 'Tous pensans . . . que de brief
seroit France privée d'un tant perfaict . . . chevalier . . . et que
les cieulx le repetoient comme à eulx deu par proprieté naturelle.'
The phraseology is classical, and the context quite general, but
there is no mistaking the assertion that du Bellay at least was to
enjoy individual survival. The second remark has already been
mentioned, and is admittedly being made to carry a heavy load
of argument, but for reasons stated earlier it appears to have
exceptional authority (xxvii, 639): 'Je croy (dist Pantagruel) que
toutes âmes intellectives sont exemptes des cizeaulx de Atropos.
Toutes sont immortelles: anges, demons et humaines.' This formal
affirmation of belief in immortality remains Rabelais's last word
on the subject, unless the authenticity of the whole *Cinquiesme
Livre* is ever established. Whatever his religious views at this time
it is impossible to overlook his acceptance of this doctrine from
a philosophical point of view. From his first book to his last, the
immortality, indeed the personal immortality, of the soul remains
a cardinal tenet of Rabelais's philosophy.

The nature of this immortal soul is of some importance and
fortunately a long and closely reasoned passage gives some clues

as to Rabelais's ideas about this. By no more than a literary coincidence, this passage is anticipated in an absolutely casual remark
by Grandgousier about his growing son (*Garg.*/xiv, 69): 'son
entendement participe en quelque divinité.' Expanded, this phrase
recurs in Pantagruel's discussion on dreams in the *Tiers Livre*. The
Platonism of this speech is much embroidered by the classical
references which follow it, but its spirit is not affected (xiii, 393):

Nostre âme, lorsque le corps dort . . . s'esbat et reveoit sa patrie qui
est le ciel. De là receoit participation insigne de sa prime et divine
origine, et en contemplation de ceste infinie et intellectuale sphaere
. . . (c'est Dieu . . .) . . . note non seulement les choses passées en
mouvemens inferieurs, mais aussi les futures, et les raportent à son
corps et par les sens et organes d'icelluy les exposant aux amis, est
dicte vaticinatrice et prophète. Vray est qu'elle ne les raporte en telle
syncerité comme les avoit veues, obstant l'imperfection et fragilité des
sens corporelz . . .

The essential elements of Platonic psychology are all there; the
divine origin of the soul, its temporary attachment to the body
and its dependence on the imperfect body for communicating with
others. A moment later Pantagruel ends his speech: 'aussi ne peult
l'homme recepvoir divinité et art de vaticiner, sinon lorsque la
partie qui en luy plus est divine (c'est Νοῦς et Mens) soit coye,
tranquille, paisible, non occupée ne distraicte par passions et
affections foraines.' There is a confusion, apparently conscious,
between the meaning given to 'divine' at the beginning and end
respectively of this passage. 'Sa divine origine' means 'divine' in
the usual sense of 'connected with God', as the parenthesis 'c'est
Dieu' makes clear, but in the other phrase 'divinité' is used in the
sense of 'divination' to equal 'art de vaticiner', while 'la partie . . .
divine' must be taken to include both these senses. In fact the
single word 'divin', with its philological development, is a résumé
of Pantagruel's theory of prophecy. For him, the divine spark of
Plato's psychology confers on each soul the potential gift of
temporary participation in the divine omniscience and thus of
prophecy. The spiritual vision may suffer in relying on the fallible
organs of the body for expression, but such distortion results
from the mixed nature of earthly life, not from any defect in the
soul. As for the typically bilingual parenthesis 'c'est Νους et
Mens', the complex distinctions between νοῦς-ψυχή-πνεῦμα were
a feature of later Platonists like Plutarch, and were, in the

sixteenth century, the subject of dispute between Averroists and orthodox.[1] Continuing his instructions to Panurge, Pantagruel dwells on the importance of suitable nourishment before one tries to dream prophetically. If one is too hungry 'les vènes . . . retirent en bas cestuy esprit vaguabond, negligent du traictement de son nourisson et hoste naturel, qui est le corps.' This could, as Gilson suggests,[2] be a precise medical reference to one of the three 'spiritus vagi', but it might equally well be a more vague allusion, like 'animula vagula blandula, hospes comesque corporis.' In any case, the meaning is clearly that bodily discomfort brings the soul back from 'contemplation des choses celestes'. The next paragraph seems to support the second interpretation: 'l'esprit ne receoit les formes de divination par songes si le corps est inquieté et troublé par les vapeurs et fumées des viandes praecedentes, à cause de la sympathie, laquelle est entre eulx deux indissoluble.' The next words resume the argument of the preceding paragraph and define the relationship between body and soul. The frequent changes in terminology, varying according to the author being quoted, make the distinction between *âme-νους* and *mens-esprit* far from clear, but the continuity of the passage encourages a broad rather than a precise interpretation.

Elsewhere, on the subject of folly, Pantagruel says (*TL*/XXXVII, 484):

aussi faut-il, pour davant icelles [Intelligences motrices] saige estre: je diz sage et praesage par aspiration divine et apte à recepvoir benefice de divination, se oublier soy-mesmes, issir hors de soy-mesmes, vuider ses sens de toute terrienne affection, purger son esprit de toute humaine sollicitude et mettre tout en nonchaloir.

The play on 'divine-divination' reappears, and the injunctions to clear 'l'esprit' are exactly parallel with the sentence quoted above 'non occupée ne distraite par affections foraines.' For all the confusion of his language, Rabelais's thought is consistent and even, if one looks at it closely enough, reasonably clear.

The connexion between body and soul is mentioned in quite

---

[1] The Isle de Ruach in the *Quart Livre* may be an allusion to this. The Averroists of the Renaissance made much of the fact that Hebrew 'ruach' is Greek 'πνεῦμα', and Rabelais may have been thinking of this when he wrote: 'Ilz ne vivent que de vent.'

[2] Gilson; 'Notes médiévales sur le *Tiers Livre*;' in *RHF* II, p. 83 n. 14.

a different context in the *Quart Livre*. Writing to his father, Pantagruel says (IV, 570): 'comme à tous accidens en ceste vie transitoyre non doubtez ne soubsonnez, nos sens et facultez animales pâtissent plus enormes et impotentes perturbations (voyre jusques à en estre souvent l'asme desemparée du corps ...).' 'La sympathie indissoluble' between body and soul was a fact of which Rabelais was always aware.

Besides the immortal soul and its powers of divination, there are other mental processes of a more practical nature with which Rabelais shows himself familiar. The letter just quoted goes on to state the mechanics of memory: 'et facilement acquiesçoys en la doulce recordation de vostre auguste majesté, escripte ... on posterieur ventricule de mon cerveau, souvent au vif me la representant en sa propre et naïfve figure.' More technical and extended is the discourse of Rondibilis on (*TL*/XXXI, 464) 'la forme d'un homme attentif à quelque estude.' The operation of 'sens commun, de l'imagination et apprehension, de la ratiocination et resolution, de la memoire et recordation' assured by the supply of 'espritz' coming from 'le retz admirable', and ultimately from the heart, where 'esprits vitaulx' have become 'animaulx', is all explained in the language of contemporary medicine.[1]

This technical language, being that of his chosen profession, Rabelais uses throughout the book with obvious pleasure. In *Gargantua*, Picrochole's illusions are supposed due to (XXXI, 116) 'fallaces espèces et phantasmes ludificatoyres mis en ton entendement'. In the chapter on dreams in the *Tiers Livre* Pantagruel concludes by referring to the two gates of dreams, of which the ivory one (XIII, 398) 'empesche la penetration des espritz visifz et reception des espèces visibles,'[2] and numerous other examples could be produced in the same sense. When he was writing of the mind and its operations, Rabelais was giving professional judgements and had no need of speculation or reference to other authors.

The borderline of metaphysics once crossed, the same knowledge and the same language applied equally to the brain and its processes as to the body. The inferior nature of the body, material and corruptible, is never called in question. Gargantua in his letter sounds the note which echoes through the work (*Pant.*/VIII, 225): 'la moindre partie de moy, qui est le corps ... et la meilleure, qui

[1] Ibid., p. 83, n.15, and in *Idées et Lettres*.   [2] Ibid., p. 86, nn.22, 23.

est l'âme.' The effects of corporeal bonds on the soul have already
been seen in the chapter on dreams, and in no single passage is
there a serious example of the body being exalted to equal, let
alone rival, the mind (or soul). For Rabelais, as for the Scholastics,
'Anima intellectiva est forma specifica hominis.'[1] This was no
abstract philosophical axiom, but a fundamental belief governing
the affairs of everyday life. Granted the natural inferiority of the
body, Rabelais, as a doctor, if for no other reason, did not despise
it, and indeed saw in its mechanism a source of wonder.

His knowledge of physiology and kindred subjects has been
amply discussed by other critics, and it would serve no useful
purpose to repeat their findings here. From the comparatively
simple details of Gargantua's birth to the intricacies of Panurge's
praise of debt, the work abounds in physiological and anatomical
references. The microcosm as espounded by Panurge is described
by Gilson as 'un résumé incroyablement dense, et toutefois d'un
mouvement admirable, de toute la physiologie médiévale: leur
commentaire intégral formerait un "De usu partium corporis
humani" au complet.'[2] Such a judgement needs no elaboration
here.

As for the preservation of health, Rabelais as doctor joins with
Rabelais as author to claim the therapeutic properties of his book.
In several of the Prologues, and in the Dedication to Cardinal de
Chastillon he refers to these properties, in the latter case actually
giving a philosophical explanation (541): 'par transfusion des
esperitz serains ou tenebreux, aerez et terrestres, joyeulx ou
melancholiques du medecin en la personne du malade.' Since it is
our task to make the most of this transitory life, bodily health is a
duty no less than spiritual welfare, and the balance between the
two is brought out through all the work. Rabelais's Platonism
does not reach the extremes of mysticism which ignores earthly
things, but his cult of health equally rejects the debased Epicure-
anism with which his name is so often linked in the popular
imagination. Rabelais's conception of man firmly welds his
immortal soul and his mortal body in exactly the same relationship as the Scholastics had taught.

The place of man in the universal hierarchy is central and in the
higher section of intellective beings subordinate. The details of
Rabelais's demonology show how many and of what kind were

[1] Scotus, *In Sententias*, 4 d. 43. qu. 2. nn. 4, 5.   [2] Op. cit. p. 79., n. 13.

the beings which linked man with God, the supreme spiritual essence. The other aspect, which shows man lord of finite creation is best seen in Panurge's praise of the *braguette*, an unexpected treasury of ideas. (*TL./*VIII, 377) 'Nature créa l'homme nud, tendre, fragile, sans armes ne offensives, ne defensives . . . comme animant . . . né à jouissance mirificque de tous fruictz et plantes vegetables, animant né à domination pacificque sus toutes bestes.'[1] The end of the 'premier aage d'or' broke up this idyll, and man 'voulent sa première jouissance maintenir et sa première domination continuer . . . eut necessité soy armer de nouveau.' The ability of man to profit from created things is the theme of the last two chapters of the *Tiers Livre*, extolling the inestimable benefits of Pantagruelion. This dream of progress can be, has been, exaggerated, but serves none the less as a reminder that Rabelais's was a universal outlook in a very real sense, more so than our own, since eternity and heaven marked the upper limits of his system where cautious theories of relativity mark ours. Whether or not Rabelais believed that man could ever become 'maître et possesseur de la nature', he certainly did not believe this to be the most desirable aim of human endeavour, if the evidence of his work has any validity. The supernatural world is far too important for Rabelais to be content with easier but more limited conquests here below.

A final detail of Rabelais's attitude to man is probably more psychological than philosophical, but may be mentioned. In marked contrast to his treatment of mothers, Rabelais goes out of his way to stress the joys of fatherhood, more exactly of legitimate fatherhood. Gargantua's letter is an early and typical example of this, but many others can be found throughout the book. Even the ignoble Panurge finds this a cogent reason for marrying, seeing Gargantua's attitude to Pantagruel (*TL/*IX, 382). Relations between the giants themselves show exceptional, perhaps exaggerated, affection between father and son, and our knowledge of Rabelais's family history tends to confirm that he had an equal dynastic consciousness in real life. As a priest, albeit irregular, he was denied this joy for himself, and his work quite possibly reflects some of his frustration as well as his filial affection for his own father. With these directly psychological factors goes what seems to be a philosophical belief, that continuity of genera-

[1] See below, chapter 22, for Maillard's account of the Fall.

tions is the sort of immortality on earth mentioned by Gargantua, and that this continuity is the special responsibility of the father. For Rabelais as for the Scholastics (who, it is relevant to note, were also celibates) man meant 'vir' rather than 'homo', and it is not only the question of perpetuating a family which explains this outlook. The feeling that woman was an afterthought in the scheme of things was, of course, encouraged by theology, but apart from anti-feminism, a completely self-sufficient attitude in men existed as a matter of course at a time when men had held for centuries a virtual monopoly of intellectual activity.

Various aspects of man's activities, in society, religion and so on, belong to other chapters. In this one an attempt has been made to collect such information on the nature of man as Rabelais offers. From this point of view, even admitting the emphasis on Platonism, one can detect little sign of innovation. Soul, mind, body receive their appropriate treatment, and the resultant conception of man shows a balanced, and on the whole detailed, interpretation of medieval doctrines.

13 : WOMAN

W HILE most of the general remarks made about man in the previous chapter apply also to woman, it would be wrong to suppose that Rabelais regarded the two halves of the human race as being in all respects equally human. What he has to say about woman as such is not very much, but even in his silence an attitude is to be discerned.[1] Most critics have remarked on the virtual absence of female characters from Rabelais's work, even from the *Tiers Livre*, where for much of the book the nominal theme is marriage, and though such persons as the victim of Panurge's Parisian pranks, the Sibyl of Panzoult or the wife of the Papefigue peasant hold the stage for a few moments, it could hardly be claimed that they represent womanhood. This literary omission is probably more significant than some of the more positive arguments concerning the status of woman. Certainly a reader's first impression is that Rabelais is just not interested until the discussions of the *Tiers Livre*, and that he shows no interest thereafter.

The first books provide an opportunity for confirming this initial impression. As mentioned in the previous chapter, Rabelais constantly refers to paternity, to the joys of having legitimate off-spring and to the special relationship between father and son. One needs no erudition to infer from this that he is in favour of marriage, and of wives inasmuch as children have to have mothers. However, what Rabelais has to say of mothers is something less than enthusiastic. A facetious remark in *Gargantua* may well summarize Rabelais's abiding views on the whole subject: on the young giant's return to his home (xxxvii, 131): '*Suppl. Suppl. Chron.* dict que Gargamelle y mourut de joie. Je n'en sçay rien de ma part, et bien peu m'en soucie, ny d'elle ny d'aultre.' In

---

[1] In a recent book, *The Rabelaisian Marriage*, M. A. Screech treats Rabelais's view on marriage in general and women in particular in great detail. He throws much light on Rabelais's sources and affinities, and insists that the legend of his anti-feminism will not stand up to scrutiny. It is quite beyond the scope of the present chapter to challenge, or even discuss, Dr. Screech's scholarly work, but it should be said that while no one could deny the value of the evidence he adduces, his conclusions are highly controversial, and in some cases quite unacceptable. See also his article 'Rabelais, de Billon and Erasmus' in *BHR*, 1951.

fact Gargamelle plays virtually no part in the book once she has given birth somewhat unconventionally to her (presumably) only child, and the words just quoted are an afterthought, for she had long since been forgotten.

Her summary disposal may be compared with that of Badebec, Pantagruel's mother, who in composition, though not in chronology, was created first. She gives birth to her first child and promptly dies, and though her husband alternates between grief at losing her, and joy at having a son and heir, her memory is not long kept alive once she has been laid to rest. After only a few minutes Gargantua cries (*Pant.*/III, 204): 'Seigneur Dieu, faut-il que je me contriste encores?' Having mourned for a little while, he has soon had enough of tears and concludes: 'Il me fault penser d'en trouver une aultre.' No doubt the last phrase could be interpreted as marriage propaganda (though in fact he does not remarry), but it is surely more sensible to see in both incidents a casual, offhand attitude to women, amounting to benevolent neutrality at best. In each case the mother's only role is to produce a son, after that she is expendable. A widower who is a father, Rabelais seems to say, has nothing to complain about.

These references are lighthearted and popular in tone, but it would be a grave error of method to dismiss them for that reason. On the contrary, the attitude they represent will be clearly understood and not easily forgotten by even the most inattentive reader. Perhaps Rabelais's indifference to mothers and motherhood is a consequence of his own childhood, perhaps it has something to do with the embarrassing products of his adult indiscretions, perhaps other factors are at work, but the result can hardly be ignored.

It may be that his Franciscan training inspired one or two details in this connexion. The prodigious birth of Gargantua may well be a passing reference to the interminable controversies in which the Franciscans had long been engaged against the Dominicans in defence of their doctrine of the Immaculate Conception, or to other theological debates involving physiology. The theory that the conception of Christ (as the Word) was effected through the Virgin's ear was widespread, and held by Bonaventura among others,[1] and Rabelais may be deliberately

---

[1] See V. L. Saulnier, 'Dix Années sur Rabelais' in *BHR*, 1949, quoting F. Rémigereau.

offering auricular birth as a farcical alternative to auricular conception. It is more likely that he had in mind some of the more extraordinary explanations of how the Virgin was herself conceived without sin (i.e. the Immaculate Conception of the controversy, which is not to be confused with the conception of Christ). The preacher Guillaume Pépin had, for example, devoted part of a sermon to rejecting the theory that Mary was not only conceived immaculately but born uniquely, like a sunbeam proceeding from the navel of St. Anne.[1] Some support for the idea that Rabelais had this controversy in mind derives from some remarks in the following chapter (*Garg.*/VII) where he discusses the baby's feeding: 'Combien que aulcuns docteurs scotistes ayent affermé que sa mère l'alaicta', being able to supply sufficiently copious draughts, 'ce que n'est vraysemblable et a esté la proposition declairée mammalement scandaleuse, des pitoyables aureilles offensive, et sentent de loing heresie.' The explicit mention of Scotists and the parody of the Sorbonne's formula of condemnation strongly suggests an echo of some Scholastic controversy about the Virgin and her qualities, such as were all too frequent at the time.

If, as is surely the case, the giants are representative in word and deed of Rabelais's own views, their relations with women other than their wives might be expected to give a hint of what Rabelais thought desirable. In fact there is very little to report. Before marriage Gargantua had an indeterminate period sowing wild oats, and under his sophist masters would, with his friends (*Garg.*/XXII, 90): 'après soupper . . . alloient voir les garses d'entour, et petitz bancquetz parmy, collations et arrière collations,' but innocuous as this sounds, it was all changed under the new regime: 'quelquefois alloient visiter les compaignies des gens lettrez, ou des gens qui eussent veu pays estranges.' Pantagruel, child of the New Learning, had not the excuse of bad masters for bad conduct, and his only recorded escapade sounds perfectly decorous (*Pant.*/XXIII, 291): 'Pantagruel receut d'une dame de Paris (laquelle il avait entretenue bonne espace de temps) unes lettres.' Having deciphered its reproachful message: 'luy souvint comment à son despartir n'avoit dict adieu à la dame, et s'en contristoit, et voluntiers feust retourné à Paris pour faire sa paix

---

[1] 'Ad instar radium solis procedentis ex umbilico B. Annae,' in *Opus de Adventu*, quoted by Méray, *La Vie au Temps des Libres Prêcheurs*, vol. ii, p. 160.

avecques elle,' but Epistemon briskly recalls him to the task in hand, and they set sail to defend their homeland.

This casual concession to the courtly tradition in the case of Pantagruel, and the inferred slight on sophists' morals in Gargantua's, is all that Rabelais permits his heroes by way of feminine diversion in all four books. Considering the insignificant role of their wives, one can hardly claim that the giants are shown to take an interest in women. As for the lecherous antics of Panurge, the bawdy comments of Frère Jan on monks and nuns and the other odd sexual references scattered through the work, one can only say that Rabelais is there courting popularity quite blatantly, and is certainly doing nothing to enhance the dignity of women.

Trivial as they may seem, these references add up to a recognizably consistent whole, and quantitatively far outnumber those in which women are treated with even marginal respect. In the first two books there is only one sustained discussion which is wholly favourable to women as such, that is as distinct from women as members of the family unit. Already in Gargantua's letter there is a passing reference to learned women, but in the Thélème episode Rabelais presents a detailed picture of feminine emancipation which contrasts strangely with his remarks elsewhere. The prominent position of this episode at the end of the book, its length and internal consistency and above all its serious tone have earned for it a respect and fame really disproportionate to its true importance in Rabelais's work as a whole. None the less, it was meant to catch the eye and cannot be ignored.

The idea of men and women living together in harmony without cohabiting is not one which fits in easily at first sight with the rest of the book, but then the motto 'Fay ce que voudras' is not meant to apply to the ordinary people who inhabit the previous chapters. The careful provisos about heredity, education, environment and so on which qualify the Thelemites' unique rule are aristocratic, not to say Utopian, in conception. In this ideal community the men take their cue from the women in matters of dress, daily occupation and general conduct. The purpose of the whole enterprise, so we are told, is that the community should represent for those who remain in it a sanctuary of culture and godly life (for Evangelical Christianity is an integral part of the programme) and, for those who leave, the best possible preparation for perfect marriage with a mate already selected under ideal conditions. Several observations suggest themselves; Lefranc made much of the absence of a central chapel in the abbey, and wrote off the individual oratories as 'paratonnerres', and Febvre had no difficulty in exposing this for the nonsense it is.[1] A much more notable omission is sexual intercourse, for while promiscuity understandably has no place in an ideal community, one might have expected some form of matrimonial probation for those who are to spend the rest of their lives together. Rabelais is not writing about the facts of life as they exist, but as he thinks they ought ideally to exist, and in Utopia biology has no place; they must leave to marry. Besides, however one may interpret the rather ambiguous regulations, it is clear that the Thelemites enter very young, and are perhaps also meant to leave young, though this is obscure. Rabelais's argument seems to be that co-education at an undergraduate age can still lay enough stress on piety, culture and courtesy to render carnal impulses harmless.

All this is clearly wishful thinking, and a prospectus for a brave new world rather than a survey of one already existing. An abbey without rules, co-education without sexuality, marriage without tears; on such a platform any candidate would win the idealist vote, and Rabelais is here running on the Platonist ticket as already popularized in Renaissance Italy. To call this propaganda for women is simply unrealistic.

As a footnote to Thélème it may be said that Rabelais's idea of an abbey of men and women, with women enjoying equal rights, was not so revolutionary as some scholars seem to think. Fontrevault, which he knew from his earliest years, had been founded in the twelfth century for just such a community of high-born men and women, presided over by an abbess who was often of royal blood. In England, which had its native Gilbertines on the same pattern, the Swedish order of Brigittines (founded by St. Bridget) had at Syon, near Richmond, a house of international fame and exceptional devotion, where Thomas More was a frequent visitor.[2] Though Fontrevault had in Rabelais's day lost some of its former glory, Syon remained a place of learning, culture and piety to the tragic end, and its mother house at Vadstena in Sweden enjoyed such prestige that it lasted many years after the whole of Sweden had become Protestant. There can be no doubt

---

[1] Febvre, op. cit., p. 112.
[2] See M. D. Knowles, *Religious Orders in England*, vol. iii, esp. p. 212 seq.

that the discussions begun at Fontenay with Bouchard, Tiraqueau and others, as well as the influence of Castiglione and similar Italian and French writers, inspired much of the detail of Thélème, but Syon Abbey, where both Erasmus and More had an intimate friend and of which they spoke so highly, deserves more than a passing thought.

With the *Tiers Livre* the whole picture changes. The problem of Panurge occupies a good many of the chapters, and Rabelais fully exploits the situation in order to discuss the questions of women and marriage from as many angles as possible. Throughout this book, and the next, Pantagruel is much more obviously 'l'idée et exemplaire de toute joyeuse perfection' than before, and all he says is authoritative. An early remark sets the tone; answering Panurge's query about the instruction in Deuteronomy that newly wed husbands should be exempt from military service for a year, Pantagruel gives his opinion and ends by supposing the husbands killed and the widows marrying again (*TL*/vi, 371): 'les fecondes à ceulx qui voudroient multiplier en enfans; les brehaignes à ceulx qui n'en appeteroient, et les prendroient pour leurs vertuz, sçavoir, bonnes graces, seulement en consolation domesticque et entretenement de mesnaige.' Such a balanced view of wifely functions is considerably more realistic than the pipe-dreams of Thélème. Panurge's references to 'les prescheurs de Varennes' and Frère Enguainnant, who condemn second marriages, remind us that from now on he is to be the mouthpiece of reactionary orthodoxy.[1]

The various consultations which occupy the major part of the *Tiers Livre* tell us more about divination than women, until we come to the central section in which Hippothaddée and Rondibilis deliver their opinions. The Pauline ring of Hippothaddée's speeches is unmistakable, and though he says nothing out of the ordinary, he may fairly be described as typical of the old school of Evangelicals. For him the most worthy woman is (xxx, 461): 'celle qui plus s'efforce avecques Dieu soy former en bonne grace et conformer aux meurs de son mary.' Comparing a wife to the moon, whose only light is that reflected by the sun, he tells Panurge: 'Ainsi serez-vous à vostre femme en patron et exemplaire de vertus et honesteté.' After hearing part of Trouillogan's

---

[1] Cf. Menot on the relative merits of virginity, wedlock and widowhood, p. 54 above.

advice, Hippothaddée compares it with St. Paul's words (xxxv, 478): 'ceulx qui sont mariez soient comme non mariez,' and Pantagruel interprets this 'femme avoir est l'avoir à usaige tel que Nature la créa, qui est pour l'ayde, esbatement et societé de l'homme.' This reasoned answer, like the preceding remarks, takes for granted that woman is inferior to man in the natural and moral order, but in no way blames her for it.

The whole debate reaches its climax with the speech of Rondibilis who, as a doctor, inevitably stands closer to his author than the other speakers, but who still falls short of Pantagruel's perfect wisdom. His judgement is undoubtedly meant to carry particular weight, and though it is reinforced by technical medical details it remains substantially the same as that of the theologian. Rondibilis disposes easily enough of Panurge's first question, by considering all the alternatives to marriage and then convincing him that he has no other choice. He then goes on to the second question, 'seray-je point cocu?', and launches into a long discourse on the nature of women, embellished by references to various classical authors and finally Plato (xxxii, 467):

Quand je diz femme, je diz un sexe tant fragil, tant variable, tant muable, tant inconstant et imperfcict, que Nature me semble (parlant en tout honneur et reverence) s'estre esguarée de ce bon sens par lequel elle avoit créé et formé toutes choses quand elle a basty la femme . . . Et, y ayant pensé cent et cinq cens foys, ne sçay à quoy m'en resouldre, sinon que, forgeant la femme, elle a eu esguard à la sociale delectation de l'homme et à la perpetuité de l'espèce humaine, plus qu'à la perfection de l'individuale muliebrité. Certes Platon ne sçait en quel ranc il les doibve colloquer, ou des animaus raisonnables, ou des bestes brutes. Car Nature leurs a dedans le corps posé en lieu secret et intestin un animal, un membre, lequel n'est ès hommes . . .

Under the influence of this animal (the womb), he goes on, all rational faculties are liable to be suspended and the whole of a woman's personality may come under its domination. A long medical discussion follows, concluded by a word of praise for the rare 'preudes femmes, lesquelles ont vescu pudicquement et sans blasme, et ont eu la vertus de ranger cestuy effrené animal à l'obeissance de raison.'

The technical details are not relevant here; what matters is the damning distinction made between the two halves of the human race in terms which anyone could understand. Since the distinctive

feature of man, by which he differs from the animals, is the use of
reason, and since women are constitutionally subject to the
domination of their inner, autonomous animal, they are not fully
to be accounted rational, and therefore human. The praise of the
exceptional 'preudes femmes' does nothing to attenuate the attack
on the sex as a whole. Whatever Plato, Galen, Tiraqueau or others
may or may not have said, the speech of Rondibilis as it stands is
the climax to all the others and offers no grounds for thinking that
Rabelais's medical training had caused him in any way to reject
the traditional medieval belief in woman's inferiority. It is ironic
that Plato should be chosen to fire the fatal shot against women,
and significant that the *Timaeus*, the only one of his dialogues
universally known in the Middle Ages, should be the weapon.

No other comment on women in the *Tiers Livre*, or elsewhere
in Rabelais, can compare in vigour or detail with that of Rondibilis, but the last word must go to the giants (now reduced to
human stature). It must be remembered that Pantagruel too is
single, and that much of the advice received by Panurge and most
of the discussion on marriage applies to some extent to him as
well. Towards the end of the book father and son appear together
for an interview on Pantagruel's future. After all the time and
trouble given to resolve Panurge's problem, Pantagruel's words
to his father are rather remarkable (XLVIII, 516): 'Père (dist
Pantagruel) n'y avois-je pensé; de tout ce negoce je m'en deportoys
sus vostre bonne volonté et paternel commendement.' Never
having known his mother Pantagruel seems in no hurry to know
a wife, and it is he, not Rondibilis, who is held up as the model of
perfection. For dynastic reasons he must, of course, marry, and
he says that he is happy enough to do so, but this leaves the status
of women exactly where it was in the early books.

Gargantua adds a little to the final picture in his long tirade
against clandestine marriages, for this is the only passage in any
of the books where both parents are associated, if not in equality,
at least in common distress. The vehement and emotional account
of how the parents mourn the loss of their daughter, tricked into
a fate worse than death by an unscrupulous adventurer, abetted
by corrupt priests, is unusual for its passion and sustained invective. One of the most poignant sentences is towards the end
(XLVIII, 519): 'Et restent en leurs maisons privez de leurs filles
tant aimées, le père mauldissant le jour et heure de ses noces, la

mère regrettant que n'estoit avortée en tel tant triste et malheureux
enfantement; et en pleurs et lamentations finent leurs vie, laquelle
estoit de raison finir en joye et bon tractement de icelles.' The
chief joy of which the parents have been robbed is the opportunity
of having grandchildren to cause them pride and solace in old age.
From first to last the role of woman, whether mother, wife, or
daughter is seen in terms of 'la perpetuité de l'espèce humaine
plus que la perfection de l'individuale muliebrité,' or, in simpler
terms, women are always seen as members of the family, not as
persons in their own right.

This insistence on the function which women are by nature
intended to perform stresses that her distinguishing characteristic
is physiological, and thus confirms her inferiority compared with
man, the noblest because the only rational animal. It is interesting
in the context of the sixteenth century 'Querelle des femmes' to
assign Rabelais to one camp or the other, but it is not really very
helpful to a broader appreciation of his thought. He was not an
extreme anti-feminist, but was solidly traditional in regarding
woman as naturally inferior to man, less interesting and much
less rational. It goes without saying that he is in favour of
marriage, because he lays so much store by the family, but his
heroes and models of perfection are more concerned with their
children than their wives. By a circuitous route Rabelais rejoins
the preachers,[1] for they had denounced women as sinful and
inciting man to sin (that is to sex), while Rabelais uses their
sexuality to condemn them as irrational and inciting rational man
to lower pastimes than those for which his intelligence fitted him.
One and all agree that this is a man's world.

---

[1] Cf. Menot's argument against adultery 'propter fragilitatem sexus, sic gravius
est in viro qui debet se ostendere fortiorem et virtuosiorem quam mulier.' (P/415).

14 : NATURE

BEHIND creatures and the larger world of matter with its physical laws stands a conception of Nature herself, in her relationship to the created world, to man and to God. It is a truism that every age has its own conception of Nature, but it is still only too easy to read into Rabelais, and the Renaissance in general, such sentiments as our own intellectual climate would produce. Religion on the one hand and science on the other are probably always the most potent factors in determining an attitude to Nature, and in Rabelais's case they are decisive. Various texts scattered throughout the work bear on the subject of Nature, and failing a clear definition, which it would be hardly reasonable to expect, one can only look for answers to specific questions; what Nature permits or forbids, what she can and what she cannot do. By selecting the widest possible variety of Rabelais's use of the words 'Nature' or 'naturel' it is possible to reconstruct some of their main associations in his mind.

The natural function on which Rabelais has most to say is generation. A number of texts from the *Tiers Livre* deal with this subject from various points of view, and while the nominal theme of Panurge's marriage explains Rabelais's particular interest here, his emphasis on fertility seems to be due to more than this literary context. The very first page of the *Tiers Livre* contains an enthusiastic description of the fertility of the Utopians such that: 'au bout de chascun neuviesme mois sept enfans pour le moins, que masles que femelles, naissoient par chascun mariage . . .'. The first mention of marriage, just before Panurge gets the flea in his ear, is in the question (*TL*/vi, 371): 'pourquoi les nouveaulx mariés estoient exempts d'aller en guerrc [pour la premiere année]', to which Pantagruel replies: 'Scelon mon jugement c'estoit affin que pour la premiere année ilz jouissent de leurs amours à plaisir, vacassent à production de lignaige et feissent provision de heritiers. Ainsi pour le moins si l'année seconde estoient en guerre occis, leur nom et armes restast en leurs enfans.' This principle is expanded in Panurge's praise of the braguette (viii, 376):

Voyez comment nature, voulent les plantes et arbres, arbrisseaulx,

herbes et zoophytes, une fois par elle créez, perpetuer et durer en toute
succession de temps sans jamais deperir les espèces, encores que les
individuz perissent, curieusement arma leurs germes et semences, ès
quelles consiste icelle perpetuité.

Nature here appears as fertile mother of the created world, pro-
ducing and conserving. Man too falls within her kingdom:

Ainsi ne pourveut nature à la perpetuite de l'humain genre, ains créa
l'homme nud, tendre, fragile—but later comes to his rescue: Con-
siderez comment nature l'inspira soy armer, et quelle partie de son
corps il commença premier armer. Ce feut la couille.

The necessity for this is stated a little later:

La teste perdue, ne perist que la personne; les couilles perdues periroit
toute humaine nature. C'est ce que meut le guallant Cl. Galen, lib. I *de
spermate*, à bravement conclure que mieulx (c'est à dire moindre mal)
seroit poinct de coeur n'avoir, que point n'avoir de genitoires. Car là
consiste, comme en un sacre repositoire, le germe conservatif de
l'humain lignaige.

This whole chapter with its extreme materialism is a little
suspect as coming from Panurge, not normally a character to be
taken too seriously. However such an eulogy of the genitalia need
not be regarded as either unusual or absurd for its day. The only
point to remember is that Panurge at the beginning of the *Tiers
Livre* constitutes himself something of an authority on Scholastic
philosophy and any bias his ideas may have is more likely to be
medieval than Renaissance. In this instance he is echoing a recurrent strain of medieval profane literature, which is, however, based
directly on the teaching of the Schools. Père G. Paré, O.P. has
shown in his study on the *Roman de la Rose* how close are the ties
between Jean de Meung and the Schools in this matter where one
might expect to find their greatest divergence. Jean de Meung
extols the organs with 'force de generacion', he too dwells on the
preservation of human continuity through children replacing their
parents, in his book the Aristotelian principle 'generatio unius
corruptio alterius' is much in evidence. The attitude of the *Roman
de la Rose* towards the organs of reproduction, 'les oeuvres mon
père [Dieu]', is compared by Paré[1] with that of SS. Thomas and
Albert, both of whom taught that sexual intercourse is essentially

---

[1] Paré, *Le Roman de la Rose et la Scolastique Courtoise*, p. 151 seq.

good insofar as it fulfils a divine intention and that if they help
to ensure the perpetuation of the species even the carnal pleasures
of sex are not necessarily reprehensible. If one is inclined to think
of medieval figures like Jean de Meung (or the wife of Bath) as
glorying in man's lower nature in opposition to ecclesiastical
doctrine, it is only their extreme conclusions, not their fundamental premisses, which make them so appear. From a finalistic
point of view Panurge's sentiments are orthodox enough, and
even if their presentation is burlesque in part, his words are more
effectively counterbalanced elsewhere than is the case with Jean
de Meung.

The idea of generation succeeding generation is not for long
forgotten. After the dialogue which follows the braguette chapter,
the last reason for marrying put forward by Panurge has a
familiar ring (IX, 382): 'Je n'aurois jamais autrement filz ne filles
legitimes èsquelz j'eusse espoir mon nom et armes perpetuer;
èsquelz je puisse laisser mes heritaiges et acquestz.' A picturesque
repetition of the same theme ends Panurge's lengthy apostrophe
to Frère Jan (XXVI, 447):

Et suys d'advis que dorenavant en tout mon Salmigondoys, quand on
vouldra par justice executer quelque malfaicteur, un jour ou deux
davant on le fasse brisgoutter en onocrotale, si bien que en tous ses
vases spermaticques ne reste de quoy protraire un Y gregoys. Chose si
precieuse ne doibt estre follement perdue! Par adventure engendrera-il
un homme. Ainsi mourra-il sans regret, laissant homme pour homme.

Even for Panurge, *paillardise*, of which Rabelais has been so freely
accused, has a teleological justification (one cannot say a moral
one) which lifts it out of the category of mere indulgence. The
natural dynastic instinct of the previous quotation is rather a
counsel of perfection; failing legitimate offspring, man can still
find justification and consolation in 'laissant homme pour
homme'. It is hard not to recall Rabelais's personal experience in
this matter and wonder how much consolation he derived from
his three (or more) children. This seems to be a case where
philosophical conviction is stronger than psychological inclination.

Rondibilis sounds a scientific note in the discussion on Nature's
fertility. The third of his remedies against the sting of concupiscence is (XXXI, 463):

par labeur assidu. Car en icelluy est faicte si grande dissolution du corps que le sang n'a temps ne loisir ne faculté de rendre celle resudation seminale et superfluité de la tierce concoction. Nature particulierement se la reserve comme trop plus necessaire à la conservation de son individu, qu'à la multiplication de l'espèce et genre humain.

Desirable as may be the conservation of the individual, the continuity of the human species must always take first place. Rondibilis gives point to this at the end of the same chapter: 'si [Panurge] rencontre femme de semblable temperature ilz engendreront ensemble enfans dignes de quelque monarchie transpontine. Le plus toust sera le meilleur, s'il veut voir ses enfans pourveuz.'

To the views of Pantagruel, Panurge and Rondibilis may be added those of Gargantua in the same book. Speaking to his son about clandestine marriages, the old king attacks the abuse in Erasmian terms. For him these criminals deprive their victims, the parents, of (xlviii, 518): 'ceste felicité de mariage, que d'eulx ilz veissent naistre lignaige raportant et haereditant, non moins aux meurs de leurs pères et mères que à leurs biens, meubles et hæritaiges.' These words recall those of a dozen years before (*Pant.*/viii, 224):

Entre les dons, grâces et prerogatives desquelles ... Dieu a endouayré et aorné l'humaine nature à son commencement, celle me semble singulière et excellente par laquelle elle peut en estat mortel acquerir espèce d'immortalité et, en decours de vie transitoire, perpetuer son nom et sa semence; ce que est faict par lignée yssue de nous en mariage legitime.

Even after so long a time, Gargantua and his author are consistent with themselves. These two remarks of Gargantua are the most effective counterblast to the more extreme theories of Panurge. Given the difference between the characters of Panurge and the giants, their respective views on the subject are more similar than one might expect. Between Panurge's purely materialistic finalism and Gargantua's religious patriarchalism there is no contradiction; one is the complement of the other; both insist on the fertility principle on which human and all other life depends.

If the idea of continuity is best seen in human beings, Nature's creative work in the lower orders of animals, plants and so on is not neglected and gives some useful indications of Rabelais's views. An early remark by Panurge illustrates Nature's powers; addressing the dame de Paris he says (*Pant.*/xxi, 283): 'La vostre [beauté] est tant excellente, tant singulière, tant celeste, que je crois que Nature l'a mise en vous comme un parragon pour nous donner entendre combien elle peut faire quand elle veut employer toute sa puissance et tout son sçavoir.' Equally trite is Panurge's exclamation in his praise of debt (*TL*/IV, 365): 'O comment Nature se y delectera en ses oeuvres et productions.' These two texts remind us as far as they go that Nature is conceived as a productive force on her own account. Nature, too, decides the form and utility of her works. Pantagruel says (*TL*/XVI, 407): 'Nature me semble non sans cause nous avoir formé aureilles ouvertes, n'y appousant porte ne clousture aulcune, comme a faict ès oeilz, langue et aultres issues du corps.' More explicit is Rondibilis's remark (*TL*/XXXII, 467): 'Nature me semble (parlant en tout honneur et reverence) s'estre esguarée de ce bon sens par lequel elle avoit créé et formé toutes choses, quand elle a basty la femme.' He can only conclude that this is because: 'elle a eu esguard à la sociale delectation de l'homme et à la perpetuité de l'espèce humaine, plus qu'à la perfection de l'individuale muliebrité.' Pantagruel expresses a similar idea, already quoted (*TL*/XXXV, 478): 'femme avoir est l'avoir à usaige tel que Nature la créa, qui est pour l'ayde, esbatement et societé de l'homme.' From these two speakers Nature appears as responsible for the form and existence of all created things, and the previous themes of finalism and fertility are reasserted.

Nature's activity among the humbler things can be judged from two examples (*TL*/XLIX, 522): 'Tant l'a cherie [Pantagruelion] Nature, qu'elle l'a douée en ses feuilles de ces deux nombres impars [5 et 7] tant divins et mysterieux.' and (*QL*/LIX, 721): 'l'industrie de Nature appert merveilleuse en l'esbatement qu'elle semble avoir prins formant les coquilles de mer.' These, and many other, texts could be misleading if taken by themselves. The autonomy of Nature is not discussed in them, but it cannot be assumed that Rabelais's evident consciousness of her wonderful works led him to forget her supreme master. Her industry, ingenuity, fecundity are the principles which explain the shape of things, including ourselves, but to stop at that and credit Rabelais with a sort of Rousseau-esque naturalism before his time is to put the Middle Ages in the same category. The place of Nature was so much taken for granted that no medieval person could seriously regard her as a possible rival of the spiritual powers, let alone of

God. To quote Paré again: 'Nature est vicaire de Dieu,'[1] and though subordinate to him her laws must be obeyed: 'déroger aux lois de la Nature ce sera désobeir à Dieu lui-même.'

The so-called 'laws of nature' (as distinct from natural laws) explain the principles governing her creative and formative activity. The Aristotelian concept of the 'natures' of things and the conception implied in the modern 'unnatural' are fundamental parts of medieval as of Renaissance thought. In an *a priori* system which admitted of innumerable exceptions, miracles and monsters represented one way of trying to save both theory and phenomena. It was useless to pretend that Nature's laws were never to be broken when hagiology on the one hand and observation on the other proved the contrary. The references to this natural order vary from the merely facetious to the technical and are very numerous. Typical of the facetious sort is this parody of Scholasticism (*Garg.*/VIII, 49): 'Lors commença le monde attacher les chausses au pourpoinct, et non le pourpoinct aux chausses; car c'est chose contre nature, comme amplement a declaré Olkam sus les *Exponibles* de M. Haultechaussade.' Serious, to the point that the most extreme philosophical beliefs have been read into it, is the comment on the rule of Thélème (*Garg.*/LVII, 181): 'gens libères, bien nez, bien instruictz, conversans en compaignies honnestes, ont par nature un instinct et aguillon, qui tousjours les poulse à faictz vertueux et retire de vice, lequel ilz nommoient honneur.' Even if these words are taken at their face value, and much of the Thélème episode is of highly controversial significance, they cannot be explained by naturalism in the usual modern sense. Nothing could be more explicitly contrary to the idea of the noble savage, or even to an overwhelming optimism regarding human nature, than these detailed conditions: free estate, good family, with the best environment not only in childhood but throughout adult life. If men and women under such Utopian conditions did not manifest 'un instinct et aguillon' there would be no hope for mankind. The ethical implications of these chapters do not affect the present issue; it is enough to realize that 'nature' as read in this context is far from indicating 'human nature' in a general sense.

Panurge in his praise of debt uses the natural order to reinforce his argument (*TL*/III, 364): 'Si que chose plus facile en nature

[1] Ibid., p. 198.

seroit nourrir en l'aer les poissons, paistre les cerfz on fond de
l'Ocean, que supporter ceste truandaille de monde qui rien ne
preste.' The maintenance of each creature in its appropriate, its
'natural', sphere is one of Nature's chief functions. The operation
of a normal process of organic chemistry is equally a function of
Nature (TL/xiii, 397): 'Car ceste ferveur naturelle, laquelle abonde
ès fruictz nouveaulx et laquelle par son ebullition facillement
evapore ès parties animales. . . .' The daily rhythm of our lives is
dictated too by the ordinances of Nature (TL/xv, 403): 'Nature a
faict le jour pour soy exercer, pour travailler et vacquer chascun
en sa neguociation; et pour ce plus aptement faire, elle nous
fournit de chandelle, c'est la claire et joyeuse lumière du soleil.
Au soir elle commence nous la tollir . . .' Our bodies function in a
regular fashion according to the intentions of Nature, ever mindful of her duty to perpetuate the species. Rondibilis describes the
effect of anti-aphrodisiac drugs (TL/xxxi, 462): '[ilz] glassent et
mortifient le germe prolifique, ou dissipent les espritz qui le
doibvoient conduire aux lieux destinez par nature. . . .' In this
instance, the *natural* effects of the drugs act against the *natural*
processes of the body, and it is man who reverses the usual natural
order by bringing the two opposites together. As in the text from
Thélème, Nature's activity is not exclusively physical, or at least
has moral repercussions. Rondibilis again, inveighing against the
feminine character, says (xxxii, 468): 'Si Nature ne leurs eust
arrousé le front d'un peu de honte, vous les voyriez comme
forcenéez courir l'aiguillette.' In this sense, as in Thélème, natural
impulses are not animal impulses, or even 'natural' in the modern
usage. A good example of real animal instinct is to be seen in the
gozal's description (QL/iii, 568): 'Vous sçavez qu'il n'est vol que
de pigeon, quand il a oeufz ou petitz, pour l'obstinée sollicitude en
luy par nature posée de recourir et secourir ses pigeonneaulx.'
The preservation of the species lies once more behind a fact of
natural history.

   On the universal scale Nature is no less active. One of the
wonderful properties of Pantagruelion is to facilitate travel (TL/
li, 531): 'Icelle moyennant, sont les nations que Nature sembloit
tenir absconses, impermeables et incogneues, à nous venues, nous
à elles.' Higher still in the scale are the effects produced at the
death of heroes (QL/xxvii, 637): '[les cielz] espovantent par
prodiges, portentes, monstres et aultres precedens signes formez

contre tout ordre de nature,' but the heavens too have their nature, superior to that which rules our world: 'les cieulx le [Langey] repetoient comme à eulx deu par proprieté naturelle.' Here we are almost in the realm of miracles, seeing the intervention of a power greater than any we can understand, but one ruled nevertheless as part of the cosmic order in just the same way as earthly Nature. The universe is not haphazard, and apparent exceptions can be explained by reference to the supreme purpose governing all creation. *Sub specie aeternitatis* even Antiphysie has a place. In his apologue of Physis and Antiphysie, Rabelais gives a description of Nature which, though not his own, represents all that he seems to have thought about her (*QL*/xxxii, 650): 'Physis (c'est Nature) en sa premiere portée enfanta Beaulté et Harmonie sans copulation charnelle, comme de soy-mesmes est grandement feconde et fertile.' As we have seen the main themes of fecundity and harmony recur constantly in Rabelais's work.

Most of the laws of Nature mentioned by Rabelais belong to the scientific side of his thought omitted from this study, but two in which Nature is specifically named bring out the idea of harmony just quoted (*Garg.*/xxiii, 90): 'Nature ne endure mutations soubdaines sans grande violence,' and the famous (*QL*/lxii, 733): 'Vacuité n'est tolerée en Nature.' There is almost an idea of permission implied in the formulation of these laws which suggests a personification of Nature, 'Dame Nature' of the Middle Ages. These last two laws are a reminder that the powers of Nature are not unlimited, and that though supreme in her own sphere, she is only 'vicaire de Dieu', to use Paré's phrase. God comes first from all eternity and his primacy is absolute (*Garg.*/xx, 83): 'Les articles de Paris chantent que Dieu seul peult faire choses infinies, Nature rien ne faict immortel, car elle mect fin et periode à toutes choses par elle produictes, car omnia orta cadunt.' The mocking tone of the reference is directed at the doctors, not at the doctrine; no other could have been advanced without mortal danger, even if a serious alternative had existed. The eternity of the world, it is true, was currently held by some Averroists, but unless Rabelais's personal beliefs were utterly at variance with those expressed in his book, there is no trace of such a philosophy in him.

Besides the ultimate power of God, other limitations are imposed on Nature, who unlike her Lord and Creator is not perfect.

We have seen already that Rondibilis considers the production of woman to have been one of Nature's rare mistakes, and Bridoye refers to a legal codification of natural error (*TL*/xxxix, 490): 'par disposition de droict, les imperfections de Nature ne doibvent estre imputées à crime . . . Et qui aultrement feroit non l'homme accuseroit mais Nature.' The whole episode of Pantagruelion is concerned with Nature's limitations, this time in comparison with the ingenuity of man. Arts and sciences, material progress of every kind depend in the last analysis on the raw materials supplied by Nature, but can only be developed by man and his reason. In the *Quart Livre* the Gaster episode tells much the same story, but ranging even more widely (LVII, 718): 'Gaster mesmes ès animans brutaulx apprent ars desniées de Nature': lacking reason, the lower creatures can yet devise expedients to supplement what Nature has given them. Gaster is described as (LXI, 730) 'noble maistre des arts' and his way of life thus: 'par institution de Nature pain avecques ses appenaiges luy a esté pour provision adjugé et aliment, adjoincte cette benediction du ciel que pour pain trouver et guarder rien ne luy defauldroit.' This division of activity between Nature and heaven is very interesting and corresponds with Aristotelian and medieval views on art (in the widest sense) and Nature.[1] The end of the same chapter gives another example of this same idea; of artillery Rabelais writes: 'Nature mesmes s'est esbahie et s'est confessée vaincue par art.' The conquest of Nature by art is the main lesson of both the Pantagruelion and Gaster episodes; it is the proper and necessary complement to the eulogies of Nature as creator and ruler of things. God is tacitly recognized in the background all the time, but these two episodes put man too explicitly in his proper place vis-à-vis Nature.

While the two episodes in question implicitly point the distinction between reason and Nature, it is practical rather than pure reason which is exemplified. The more abstract distinction is, however, made in an interesting text which comes just before the Pantagruelion chapters, and though an allusion rather than a definition conveys a perfectly clear meaning. Gargantua ends his diatribe against clandestine marriages by exculpating those who avenge themselves on the conniving priests. The *point de départ*

---

[1] Besides Paré's references, there is a whole chapter on the subject in Vincent de Beauvais's *Speculum Naturale*.

is legal; the avengers have found themselves brought to justice by the other priests (*TL*/xlviii, 519):

Mais ne en aequité naturelle, ne en droict des gens, ne en loy imperiale quelconques, n'a esté trouvée rubricque, paragraphe, poinct ne tiltre par lequel fut poine ou torture à tel faict interminée, raison obsistante, nature repugnante. Car homme vertueux on monde n'est, qui naturelle-ment et par raison plus ne soit en son sens perturbé, oyant les nouvelles du rapt, diffame et deshonneur de sa fille, que de sa mort. Ores est qu'un chascun trouvant le meurtrier sus le faict de homicide ... le peut par raison, le doibt par nature occire sus l'instant ...

Even for Rabelais, the triple repetition of 'nature et raison' is unusual, and emphasizes the importance of the point he is making. The *jus naturale* referred to in the first sentence belongs properly to ethics, but the three other mentions suggest the respective functions of Nature and reason in human behaviour. The prompt-ings of Nature are ratified in this case by reason, but in other instances reason can and must check Nature, to prevent murder, for example, committed in a fit of anger. As this is the only occurrence in Rabelais of this particular idea, it is unfortunately not possible to make any comparisons, but the force of Gargan-tua's words is such that they must be taken seriously. The limitation of Nature implied in them is in fact more important than that put forth at greater length in the Pantagruelion and Gaster episodes.

Two texts from the *Cinquiesme Livre* conveniently resume these limitations of the power of Nature, and whether authentic or not they are worth quoting for the remarkably concise manner in which they cover what has just been said. On the method of dividing heritages, Editus says (iv, 780): 'comme raison le veult, nature l'ordonne et Dieu le commande.' The distinction between the three is precise and formal. A little further on comes this note (ix, 795): 'Vray est comme en toutes choses (Dieu excepté) advient quelquefois erreur. Nature mesmes n'en est exempte, quand elle produit choses monstrueuses et animaulx difformes.' Rabelais's philosophy of Nature is in line with medieval tradition both in praising the wonders of Nature and in setting very firm limits to her power. It may be doubtful whether he wrote the two texts just quoted but there can be no doubt that he agreed with their sentiments.

It is interesting to compare the remarks of Rabelais, mostly disconnected and scattered through the four books, with the detailed theories of the *Roman de la Rose* as Paré has analysed them: 'Ordonnées à la fécondité, les lois de la nature revêtent un caractère de nécessité . . . Il y a un ordre de causes secondes; il y a une *Nature* constituée de l'ensemble organisée des natures.'[1]

On Nature's limitations, Jean de Meung is as clear as Rabelais:

Nature est puissante et féconde sans doute. Elle est la source de toute vie et de toute beauté. L'homme a reçu d'elle toutes les ressources dont il dispose. Et pourtant sa vertu n'est pas si grande qu'elle puisse lui donner la raison . . . Il est difficile d'affirmer plus clairement la dépendance de l'homme à l'égard de Dieu tout en reconnaissant ses droits de nature. C'est l'homme tel qu'il apparaît dans les œuvres des grands scolastiques du moyen âge, l'homme en possession de tous ses moyens de nature et cependant orienté vers Dieu.[2]

Paré's comments on his text are so appropriate to Rabelais that it is hard to stop quoting him. Perhaps even more effective than textual rapprochements between Rabelais and Scholastic authors are these views expressed on a work of literature whose Scholastic sources cannot be doubted. Most of Paré's remarks need no modification to be applied to Rabelais; this in itself is a striking testimony to the wealth of doctrine to be quarried in his work and to the persistence in him of Scholastic ideas over so long a period.

[1] Paré, op. cit., p. 154.   [2] Ibid., p. 201.

15 : RELIGION

THE nature of Rabelais's religion remains the most controversial problem among so many others which prevent a full understanding of his true significance. Evidence from his personal life, evidence from his work, attacks from Rome, attacks from Geneva, the personal protection of two cardinals, the personal enmity of a third; there is at once too much and too little material to provide a solution both convincing and impartial. Even the great contribution of M. Febvre has only cleared some of the ground; the theories of Lefranc which he so effectively refutes are not worthy of so painstaking an examination. Political and personal repercussions intervene to prevent us forming even a general opinion of what Rabelais's contemporaries thought about his religion. Comparison with other authors tends often to confuse the issue; their credentials too must be examined. Besides, as Febvre so rightly says, what Rabelais throws out in passing can hardly be expected to provide an unequivocal confession of faith in an age when professional theologians saw their own reasoned arguments subjected to endless debate. Whether Rabelais was ever in the Protestant camp, and if so, for how long, whether his work is a truthful expression of his feelings, what the ordinary sixteenth-century reader (if there was one) really thought of passages which puzzle us, are not questions to be answered here. In trying to collate Rabelais's views on religion one should look specially for any shift of emphasis between the first two and last two books. Here more than anywhere else it is of vital importance to note the mouth into which remarks are put; for the sixteenth-century reader this point was probably decisive.

Fundamental in any religious discussion of the day was the attitude to faith and works respectively. On the matter of faith Rabelais says little enough, and at that extremely tenuous. In the first editions of *Gargantua* Rabelais calls upon his readers to believe in the giant's marvellous nativity (VI, 45 n.): 'Pour ce qu'il y a nulle apparence . . . Car les Sorbonistes disent que foy est argument des choses de nulle apparence.' This definition,

Pauline in origin,[1] was used too by Erasmus, but was not one generally accepted by theologians because of its context and was thus withdrawn from later editions, presumably for reasons of prudence. Far more significant, and the subject of continued debate, is the phrase in Gargantua's letter to his son (*Pant.*/VIII, 228): 'foy formée de charité.' Whatever the precise inspiration of these words, it has been shown[2] conclusively that idea and expression alike are Scholastic, and Rabelais at least can have had no doubt about its meaning. Among the prayers recited each night by Gargantua comes an act of faith (*Garg.*/XXIII, 97): 'ratifiant leur foy envers luy [Dieu]'. Just before the battle with the Dipsodes Pantagruel affirms his faith (*Pant.*/XXVIII, 306): 'metz tout ton espoir en Dieu, et il ne te delaissera point; car de moy . . . je n'espère en ma force ny en mon industrie, mais toute ma fiance est en Dieu, mon protecteur, lequel jamais ne delaisse ceux qui en luy ont mis leur espoir et pensée.' There are commonplace remarks, and will certainly not support much theological scrutiny, but they show the explicit and to all appearances serious faith of the giants in the first two books.

The absence of such references in the later books proves nothing by itself, as other indications are not lacking to show that the giants have had no change of heart. One text in the *Tiers Livre* mentions faith in a slightly different sense but is very relevant. Pantagruel says (XXIX, 457): 'l'occupation principalle voyre unicque et totalle des bons theologiens estre emploictée . . . à extirper les erreurs et heresies . . . et planter profundement ès cueurs humains la vraye et vive foy catholicque.' Lest any suspicion of irony should attach to the last word, we have the extremely orthodox, if mildly Evangelical, utterances of Hippothaddée to reassure us. 'Catholique' had not the paradoxically restrictive sense it has today, but it is interesting to compare the use of the word above with Pantagruel's speech of many years before (*Pant.*/XXIX, 312): 'Ton [Dieu] negoce propre qui est la foy . . . car en tel affaire tu ne veulx coadjuteur sinon de confession catholique et service de

---

[1] Heb. XI. i. For a full discussion of this, and other texts in Rabelais concerning faith and works, see Screech, *l'Evangélisme de Rabelais*, especially ch. i. He goes into greater detail, and examines more texts, than has been possible here, but comes to generally similar conclusions.

[2] Gilson, *Idées et Lettres*, p. 214. Cf. Maillard's opening sermon *De Stipendio Peccati*, f. 87: 'Domini an plures invenientur de vobis qui habent gratiam et fidem formatam caritate.'

ta parolle . . .' and his final vow: 'je feray prescher ton sainct evangile purement.' Rabelais's (and Hippothaddée's) Evangelical sympathies must be reconciled with his claim for the universality of the true faith. The exclusiveness of Geneva, uncompromising and clearly permanent, may well have been the final disillusionment which led Rabelais to pick on 'imposteur de Genève' as Calvin's damning qualification.

Except for the single phrase 'foy formée de charité', there is no statement about the relationship between faith and works. The superstitious abuses condemned in *Pantagruel* and *Gargantua* are those condemned by Erasmus, Luther and Calvin, but no less by the more progressive leaders of the Counter-Reformation. Gargantua's devotional life under the old régime is rightly mocked for its failure to match quantity with quality (*Garg.*/XXI, 85): 'Là [à l'eglise] oyoit vingt et six ou trente messes . . . Au partir de l'eglise, on luy amenoit sur une traine à beufz un faratz de patenostres de Sainte-Claude . . . en disoit plus que seze hermites.' Panurge's advances on the lady of Paris include the filching of her beads and liberal use of holy water. The same Panurge (*Pant.*/XXI, 284) 'à tous les troncs baisoit les relicques' and obtained profit both financial and spiritual (in indulgences). Pilgrimages are the object of special attention and Grandgousier condemns them (*Garg.*/XLV, 154) as 'odieux et inutilles voyages', but it is remarkable that the reason for his anger is the superstitious abuse by which saints were made responsible for evils. On the broader subject of devotional pilgrimages Rabelais is silent; more silent than his master Erasmus who poured some of his most acid scorn on the shrines of Canterbury and Walsingham. By implication Rabelais may be supposed to have disapproved of all pilgrimages, but in fact he picks the point of his attack so carefully that the most orthodox could only admit him to be in the right.

Similarly when Rabelais attacks monks and friars he chooses particular abuses, condemned too by the unimpeachably orthodox; their ignorance, their idleness, their gluttony, their mumbling of prayers, their lechery, venality and social uselessness. Rabelais knew well enough that the prescriptions of St. Benedict's and St. Francis's Rules are formal in attacking and trying to prevent just such abuses. He knew, too, that his former Abbey of Maillezais had contributed decisively to the drainage and protection of the surrounding land; that the whole face of Europe had been changed by the immense labours of Cistercians and Benedictines turning wildernesses into fertile pastures; that the very existence of his beloved ancient manuscripts had been assured by the unremitting industry of monastic scribes and librarians. Even the Friars, whom he seems to detest most of all, had made possible the growth of many of the greatest universities of Europe. The sixteenth-century picture of the regular orders was not a bright one, though in France it did not lack important exceptions, but the spirit of all monasticism lies in its ideals as set out in the Rules, not in their malpractices, however widespread at any given time. Former Franciscan and former Benedictine, secular canon and, till his death, beneficed priest, Rabelais may have had personal reasons for knowing and hating the religious life, but a *reasoned* attack on monastic principles as distinct from practice is not to be found in his works. There is, of course, Thélème with its parody of monastic vows and institutions, but one can no more imagine Rabelais being content with such a life than Frère Jan, the nominal founder. A comparison with Erasmus's famous dialogue *Militi et Carthusiani* shows how far Rabelais is from presenting a real picture of monastic life. Fasting is another of the monastic, and general, practices which Rabelais seems to have disliked, in the same way that he hated the incessant bell-ringing but his attacks are not sensational (*Pant.*/xxi, 282): 'ces dolents contemplatifs, amoureux de karesme, lesquelz point à la chair ne touchent,' is typical. Antipathy to the Church's rule of fasting, indeed to any inconvenient discipline, is as old as the rule but is hardly a serious argument. All these points, pilgrimages, pardons, monastic vows and vices, fasting, mechanical devotions have an obvious propaganda value, and in the explosive atmosphere of the 1530's were something of a manifesto, but they do not touch the essentials of doctrine, nor, on the whole, of the individual questions involved. 'Jusques au feu exclusivement' is very much the motto of this first Rabelais.

The later books mark in every way an evolution from the earlier ones, but critics have perhaps been too anxious to see a break in thought. There are fewer direct battle-cries, it is true, but those that there are seem familiar. Pantagruel speaks of (*TL*/xiii, 395): 'les escriptz de ces hermites jeusneurs . . . estre fades, jejunes et de maulvaise salive comme estoient leurs corps lorsqu'ilz composoient.' Quaresmeprenant is the personification of certain works, the incarnation of fasting (*QL*/xxix, 642): 'foisonnant en pardons, indulgences et stations, homme de bien, bon catholic et de grande devotion.' Homenaz, Bishop of Papimanie, tells the travellers that if they wish to see the sacred book (*QL*/xlix, 694): 'il vous conviendra, par avant, trois jours jeusner et regulierement confesser.' These attacks or merely gibes directed at fasting have gone a long way to make Rabelais's reputation as a self-indulgent glutton. The chapters on the Gastrolatres, detailed and explicit and introduced with the scathing quotation from St. Paul, are conveniently forgotten for the purpose of such theories. Fasting or over-eating in such contexts as these are much more matters of taste than belief, the natural reactions of a man who holds that: 'mediocrité est en toutes choses louable'.

Panurge in the later books is the champion of an orthodoxy which even the Sorbonne would have found embarassing. On the way back from Raminagrobis it is Panurge, not Frère Jan, who talks of heresy and charity (*TL*/xxiii, 430): 'Rctournons l'admonester de son salut . . . Ce sera oeuvre charitable à nous faicte.' When the ship laden with religious going to the Council of Chesil passes them, it is Panurge who sends them gifts of food and (*QL*/xviii, 613) 'deux mille beaulx angelots pour les asmes des trespassés.' This is perhaps a mild satire on almsgiving, particularly for the souls of the faithful departed, but how then are we to explain the same action by Pantagruel not only at Papefiguière but also at Papimanie? At the first (*QL*/xlvii, 689): 'Pantagruel donna au tronc de la fabricque de l'Ecclise dix huit mille royaulx d'or, en contemplation de la pauvreté du peuple et calamité du lieu,' at the other he gives (liv, 711): 'neuf pièces de drap d'or frizé sus frize pour estre appousées au davant de la fenestre ferrée, feist emplir le tronc de la reparation et fabricque tout de doubles escuz au sabot,' and leaves a marriage gift for the attendants. The impartiality of Pantagruel's generosity is in accord with his character, but we note that his gifts, even to the poverty-stricken Papefigues, are for the Church. If the Papefigues are meant, as some critics seem to believe, to portray the unfortunate Vaudois, the liberality is rather restrained. It is surely wisest to look for no hidden meaning either in the actions of Panurge or of Pantagruel; almsgiving in itself is taken for granted, the motives depend on the giver.

One small theological reference would not have escaped

Rabelais's contemporaries: Homenaz prays to his 'Dieu decretali-arche' (LIII, 709): 'Donne ordre que ces precieux oeuvres de supererogation, ces beaulx pardons au besoing ne nous faillent—' The works of supererogation, and the theology connected with them, may not have been dear to Rabelais, but the mere fact that Homenaz, a caricature of ultramontane orthodoxy, speaks of them is not enough to constitute an attack. The difficulty is always the same; Rabelais says just enough for us to guess at his real meaning, but never—or hardly ever—enough to commit himself outright. The extremists on both sides knew very well what the current shibboleths were, but a man could be a perfectly sincere Catholic and still not be offended, for instance, by the character of Homenaz and his exaggerated words. The best and surest guide to the thought of the later books where controversial matters are concerned is the attitude of Pantagruel. Often absent, as for instance from the Raminagrobis episode, more often than not silent, he is the author of the very few remarks and deeds to which we can pin Rabelais; for the rest it is always 'jusques au feu exclusivement.'

Of all the works necessary for salvation the sacraments naturally come first for an orthodox believer, and Rabelais's views on this subject would be carefully noted by his enemies on either side.[1] Once again the harvest is meagre and much less significant than some critics would have us think. Baptism is taken for granted, but Rabelais's comment shows more than social conventionality (*Garg.*/VII, 47): 'Gargantua feut porté sus les fonts et là baptisé, comme est la coustume des bons christiens.' The sacrament of penance has certain associations which make it particularly vulnerable to satire, and Rabelais does not hesitate to exploit these. The victims of Frère Jan's defence of the Abbey vineyard cried (*Garg.*/XXVII, 109): 'Confession! Confession! Confiteor! Miserere! In manus!' The prior and his monks attracted by the cries come out and: 'en confessèrent quelques uns. Mais, cependant que les presbtres se amusoient à confesser, les petitz moinetons coururent au lieu où estoit Frère Jan. . . .' The whole scene is one of high fantasy and as a satire even of confession is mild enough. When the shriven try to escape Frère Jan: 'les assommoit de coups, disant: 'ceulx-cy sont confès et repentans, et ont guaigné les

---

[1] Many comparisons suggest themselves between Rabelais's views both on the sacraments and monastic or clerical abuses and those of the preachers examined in chapters 3 and 4 above.

pardons; ilz s'en vont en Paradis, aussy droict comme une faucille . . .' Frivolous, even irreverent, this may be, but neither the speaker nor the context allows a serious interpretation. It is Frère Jan again who misinterprets a canonical injunction (*Garg.*/ XLII, 145):

Vous me semblez les prescheurs decretalistes, qui disent que quiconques voyra son prochain en dangier de mort, il le doibt, sus peine d'excommunication trisulce, plustoust admonnester de soy confesser et mettre en estat de grace que de luy ayder. Quand doncques je les voiray tombez en la rivière et prestz d'estre noyez, en lieu de les aller querir et bailler la main, je leur feray un beau et long sermon de contemptu mundi et fuga saeculi . . .

In the *Quart Livre* this chance remark of the monk comes unexpectely to life. Panurge, the superstitiously orthodox Panurge of the later books, has just succeeded in drowning the sheep and the merchants after them (VIII, 582): 'les preschoit eloquentement, comme si feust un petit frère Olivier Maillard ou un second frère Jan Bourgeoys; leurs remonstrant par lieux de rhetoricque les misères de ce monde, le bien et l'heur de l'autre vie. . . .'

The only other sacrament of which there is any mention in the first two books is the Mass, and strictly speaking that is not mentioned as a sacrament, but simply as a service. The Communion is quite neglected in Rabelais's satire, just as we know it played a very secondary part in contemporary devotional life. The Mass was a social occasion obligatory for all to attend, for the clergy a duty to perform, demanding of the laity no more than their physical presence. Gargantua hears twenty-six or thirty Masses under the old régime of his Scholastic tutors because the ordinary (in size) nobleman or prince would hear one or two; Frère Jan is 'un beau desbrideur de messes' because a Mass for him is like a parade for a soldier, so much time to be passed as swiftly as possible; Panurge plays his practical joke (*Pant.*/XVI) on the Cordelier during Mass because it is there (*la messe des Messieurs*) that the greatest number will see him; he waylays his prospective victim, the lady of Paris, at Mass because highborn ladies attended daily. The familiarity of the service had not in the first half of the sixteenth century been tempered with the mystery and devotion which a later age has brought, and in the contexts in which these references occur few would see grave cause for scandal.

As for other services, canonical hours figure largely in all four books in one form or another, never very serious. They were for Rabelais, as for all priests regular or secular, a daily task whose performance became more perfunctory and tedious as personal piety decreased. At the best of times such exercises can easily degenerate into mechanical repetition, 'moquedieu, non oraison', and Rabelais had good reason to know how meaningless the Divine Office can be. The burial service is another, like Baptism, which was as automatic then as a certificate today. Gargantua is quite content to have his wife put to rest in the old traditional way (*Pant.*/III, 204) 'ouyt la letanie et les Mementos des presbtres qui portoient sa femme en terre.' In all this Rabelais shows himself typical of an age which was familiar with the Church and its ceremonies to a degree we can hardly realize and able to bring sacred things into the most scabrous contexts. He was certainly not writing a work of piety, either for Rome or (before the event) for Geneva, but nor was he in this at any rate glorifying impiety.

With the later books the considerable toning-down of the popular element entails automatically a reduction in the references to everyday life. Besides, the academic setting of much of the *Tiers Livre* and the exotic atmosphere of the *Quart Livre* are more remote than Paris or the countryside round Chinon. There are the usual references to canonical hours, 'soupe de primes', 'la caballe monastique' at Matins, but on the whole the sacraments and services of the Church are less in evidence. Panurge's tale of Soeur Fessue makes fun of the seal of the confessional (*TL*/XIX, 419): 'Trop enorme eust esté le pesché reveler sa confession et trop detestable devant Dieu et les anges', but Pantagruel's impatient comment does not, as it stands, apply to this at all. Besides, the secrecy of confession must be admitted as desirable even by those who disapprove of the practice. In Panurge's suggestion that they should return to Raminagrobis, confession is not mentioned as such (though Frère Jan is there in case of need), but the expression (XXIII, 430): 'Nous le induirons à contrition de son peché, à requerir pardon ès dictz tant beats pères . . .' hints at the idea. Later, in the *Quart Livre*, it is Panurge who finds himself before Frère Jan in the position of the victims of Seuillé. During the storm it is Panurge alone who cries (XIX, 617): 'Frère Jan, mon père, mon amy, confession! Me voyez-cy à genoulx! Confiteor! Vostre saincte benediction!' and repeats his plea for confession several times, while the monk curses and swears as vehemently as he labours to help the crew. Homenaz, as we have seen, prescribes fasting and the most detailed confession before the sacred books can be displayed, but in the neighbouring island of Papefiguière, hereditary enemy of Papimanie, they seem to follow a familiar ritual (XLVII, 688): 'A bonne heure du matin le laboureur s'estoit très bien confessé, avoit communié comme bon catholicque, et par le conseil du curé, s'estoit au plonge caché dedans le benoistier....' This seems to be the only direct reference to Communion in any of the books, and tells us very little. No doubt 'bon catholicque' is as ironic as the similar description of Quaresmeprenant, no doubt the elaborate precautions of the peasant, following the advice of his *curé*, are meant to contrast comically with the crude but effective expedient of his wife, no doubt their years of being 'esclaves et tributaires' to the Papimanes had left them no choice in their form of worship, but the whole anecdote is so exactly in the medieval and popular tradition that it seems over-ingenious to seek for more than passing topical allusions. *Perhaps* Rabelais was thinking of the Vaudois, but not for very long. Beyond the desolation of the country, resulting from defiance of the Pope, there is nothing concrete to seize upon in this episode, certainly nothing doctrinal. Lastly, when they land in Papimanie, the travellers are at once conducted to the church where Homenaz says a Mass (XLIX, 695) 'basse et seiche' as it is past noon, but the only comments are facetious ones from Panurge and Frère Jan; Pantagruel with the rest of the party seems to accept the arrangement quite as a matter of course.

Baptism, Penance, Communion, the few references in the first two and last two books are not very informative nor essentially very different. Only one other sacrament is discussed specifically: Matrimony. In Gargantua's harangue to his son at the end of the *Tiers Livre*, he strongly condemns clandestine marriages, and blames the conniving priests more than the two parties concerned. This, though, is no attack on the sanctity of marriage as an institution, on the contrary, and if Gargantua condemns the priests who permit this abuse, it is quite certain that he would not regard a marriage as regular unless performed by a priest. There was, indeed, no alternative, and the Basché story gives a good idea of the form and character of the ceremony (*QL*/XII, 595): 'Vous, messire Oudart, ne faillez y comparoistre en vostre beau supellis et estolle, avecques l'eau benite, comme pour les fianser.'

The second time the ceremony is described (xiv, 601): 'Par Oudart feurent sus les fiancez dictz motz mysterieux, touchées les mains, la mariée baisée, tous aspersez d'eau benite', and the third time as well: 'Oudart, revestu sacerdotallement, les prend par les mains, les interroge de leurs vouloirs, leur donne sa benediction sans espargne d'eaue beniste.' Rabelais's readers would recognize all the details of a wedding at the local château, religious and profane details alike, but the solemnity of the marriage service is not what is mocked. It is not even a church wedding, not even a nuptial Mass, and as a presentation of the service is as factual and taken for granted as those of Baptism and Burial in *Pantagruel*. Extreme Unction may be considered mentioned by default in the episode of Raminagrobis, who sends off the friars obviously without receiving any sacrament from them, but he could well have received the last consolations from his parish priest, like his prototype in the 'Funus' of Erasmus. In any case there is too little to build up any convincing theories. Neither Confirmation nor Ordination is mentioned at all, but they are not likely to figure largely in literature at any time.

One remark from the *Cinquiesme Livre*, which has an authentic ring about it, seems to resume Rabelais's ideas about the functions of a priest. Protesting at Panurge's cowardice and the general refusal to land and attack the Chatz Fourrez, Frère Jan exclaims (xv, 807): 'Donques vous m'avez compagnon pris pour en cestuy voyage messe chanter et confesser? Pasques de soles! le premier qui m'y viendra aura en penitence soy comme lasche et meschant jecter au plus parfond de la mer en deduction des poines de purgatoire.' There is never any mention of another priest aboard (Rabelais himself is M. l'abstracteur, a doctor) and Frère Jan is the one to whom Panurge turns during the storm, so we may assume that the office of chaplain was not exercised very thoroughly during the voyage. All the same, Frère Jan as a priest, a monk who for his own reasons refused from the beginning to unfrock himself, knows that his profession can always be recalled 'pour messe chanter et confesser' whether he accepts or not. Priests, doctors, lawyers all have their own qualifications which permit them to practise their own calling, and Mass and confession had been for Rabelais professional duties no more and no less than judgement and healing. The casual familiarity of a professional, albeit retired, seems a more likely explanation of all the references to sacraments and services in all the books than the partisan, let alone atheist, intentions which have so often been attributed to Rabelais. As propaganda these texts are of minimal value, far too cautious to convince, as background they are entirely appropriate to the realistic picture of the whole work.

Except for a few general remarks about faith, most of this evidence about Rabelais's religion is more negative than positive. Quite different is his treatment of prayer, on which he has a good deal to say. Both the occasions and the form of these prayers are interesting. Gargantua in his new system of education learns to pray each morning and evening (*Garg.*/XXIII, 91): 'se adonnoit à reverer, adorer, prier et supplier le bon Dieu' on rising, and before retiring: 'Si prioient Dieu le createur, en l'adorant et ratifiant leur foy envers luy, et, le glorifiant de sa bonté immense et luy rendant grace de tout le temps passé, se recommendoient à sa divine clemence pour tout l'advenir.' Grandgousier prays too; when he hears the news of Picrochole's assault he calls on God (*Garg.*/ XXVIII, 111): 'Mon Dieu, mon Saulveur, ayde-moy, inspire-moy, conseille-moy à ce qu'est de faire . . . Bon Dieu tu cognois mon courage, car à toy rien ne peut estre celé. . . .' and follows up his prayer with genuine efforts towards a peaceful solution.[1] On his son's return, Grandgousier takes part in a discussion with Frère Jan and the rest on monks, and the subject of prayer comes up. Gargantua, apostle of the new order, condemns monks as useless, but his more conservative father mildly interposes (*Garg.*/XL, 140): 'Voyre, mais ilz prient Dieu pour nous.' Gargantua denies this, saying that the monks' mumbling is: 'moquedieu non oraison. Mais ainsy leur ayde Dieu s'ilz prient pour nous et non par peur de perdre leurs miches et souppes grasses. Tous vrays christians, de tous estatz, en tous lieux, en tous temps, prient Dieu et l'Esperit prie et interpelle pour iceulx, et Dieu les prent en grace.' This formal statement, of Pauline origin, about the nature of prayer is important not so much for the Evangelical sentiment as for the light it throws on subsequent incidents.

In his letter to Pantagruel (written in time though not in plot before these texts) Gargantua gives thanks to God for the gift of his son, and says (*Pant.*/VIII, 225): 'Continuellement requerons à Dieu qu'il efface nos pechés.' Thanksgiving and penitence are joined by supplication when Pantagruel in his turn prays before

---

[1] See Febvre, *La Religion de Rabelais*, p. 265 for other examples of prayer.

the battle (*Pant.*/xxix, 312): 's'il te plaist à ceste heure me estre en ayde, comme en toy seul est ma totale confiance et espoir, je te fais voeu.. . . .' The solemn and dignified tone of this prayer is striking but not so exaggerated that any suspicion of parody is aroused. These early habits of the giants persist in the later books, if anything more noticeably. Advising Panurge on his marriage, Pantagruel says (*TL*/x, 383): 'Il soy convient mettre à l'adventure, les oeilz bandez, baisant la terre et se recommendant à Dieu au demourant.' Hippothaddée repeats the same advice (*TL*/xxx, 461): 'Et continuellement implorerez la grace de Dieu à vostre protection.' Epistemon suggests that Bridoye's record may have been so good because (*TL*/xliv, 508): 'se recommenderoit humblement à Dieu le juste juge, invocqueroit à son ayde la grace celeste, se deporteroit en l'esprit sacro-saint du hazard et perplexité de sentence definitive.' The *Quart Livre* has even more examples, beginning with the Prologue (547): 'J'ay cestuy espoir en Dieu qu'il oyra nos prières, veue la ferme foy en laquelle nous les faisons, et accomplira nostre soubhayt, attendu qu'il est mediocre. . . .' The references to the Old and New Testaments which follow are, it is true, offset by the apologue of Couillatris, but the context is not by any means comic. The voyagers receive a pious send-off (1, 560): 'Pantagruel prenant congé du bon Gargantua, son père, icelluy bien priant (comme en l'Eglise primitive estoit louable coustume entre les saints christians) pour le prospère naviguaige de son filz et toute sa compaignie. . . .' On board Pantagruel exhorts his fellow-travellers: 'sus l'argument de navigation. Laquelle finie feut hault et clair faicte prière à Dieu . . . Après l'oraison feut melodieusement chanté le psaulme du saint roy David. . . .' The prayer and psalm were shared by the citizens of Thalasse, who also joined in the drinking afterwards. It has been pointed out by others that the proceedings are similar to those of an Evangelical meeting of those days, and the deliberate quotation of the setting by Marot of Ps. cxiv would not fail to attract attention when it was well known that the Sorbonne had condemned it. Nevertheless the form of service—address, public prayer, psalm in French—is not in itself reprehensible, and Rabelais risked no very serious repercussions in thus describing it. A clear sign of where his sympathies lay, this episode is still not one to 'épater le bourgeois' of the time. Another example of a public act of worship is towards the end of the *Quart Livre*,

when the wind finally springs up (LXIV, 741): 'Dont tous chan-
tèrent divers cantiques à la louange du très-haut Dieu des cielz.'
Perhaps, even probably, these were more vernacular hymns as
used by the Evangelicals, but the simple fact of the common
thanksgiving is all that can be noted with certainty. In his letter
home Pantagruel adopts the same tone as his father earlier (V, 572):
'Au reste, j'ay ceste confiance en la commiseration et ayde de
Nostre Seigneur . . . aydant Dieu Nostre Seigneur, lequel je prie
en sa sainte grace vous conserver.'
The crisis of the storm is inevitably the occasion for much
praying of various kinds. Panurge's plea for confession, his soon
forgotten vows and his appeal to God and the Virgin must be
judged in comparison with the behaviour of the others. Pantagruel
begins (XIX, 616): 'prealablement avoir imploré l'ayde du grand
Dieu Servateur et faicte oraison publicque en fervente devotion,
par l'advis du pilot tenoit l'arbre fort et ferme.' The order of his
actions is instructive; he does as much as anyone to save the ship
by his exertions, but first he prays and—presumably—leads the
'oraison publicque'. As the storm rises in violence Panurge's
frantic appeals continue, but Pantagruel himself cries (XX, 621):
'le bon Dieu Servateur nous soyt en ayde,' and the master pilot,
Jamet Brahier, who is a better judge of the situation than anyone
else, bids: 'Chascun pense de son asme et se mette en devotion,
n'esperans ayde que par miracle des cieulx!' When all hope seems
lost (XXI, 623): 'Alors feut ouye une piteuse exclamation de
Pantagruel, disant à haulte voix: "Seigneur Dieu, saulve-nous,
nous perissons! Non toutesfoys adviegne scelon nos affections,
mais ta saincte volunté soit faicte".' When land finally comes in
sight it is Pantagruel who thinks to say (XXII, 627): 'Il n'est céans
mort personne; Dieu Servateur en soit eternellement loué!'
Epistemon finds an opportunity before they land to give his
views on prayer (XXIII, 628): '[Dieu] fault incessamment implorer,
invoquer, prier, requerir, supplier. Mais là ne fault faire but et
bourne; de nostre part convient pareillement nous evertuer
et, comme dict le sainct Envoyé, estre cooperateurs avec luy.'
This, as we have seen, is exactly what everyone but Panurge
has done. Prayer comes first in any emergency, but action must
follow.
    Two other passages of the *Quart Livre* are a little unexpected.
Coming to the island of the Papefigues, the travellers do not want

to spend long there (XLV, 683): 'seulement pour prendre de l'eau beniste et à Dieu nous recommander, entrasmes dedans une petite chappelle près le havre ... En la chappelle entrez et prenans de l'eau beniste. ...' Granted that the French psalm in 1548 accords with Evangelical sympathies, to be consistent one is obliged to give equal weight to this unquestionably orthodox action. Pantagruel is there in person and the holy water is taken by the company as a whole, so the authority of this episode is hardly less than that of the other. An impartial picture must include both black and white. The other passage is so unexpected that at first sight one looks for a misprint, but it seems to be what Rabelais intended, however odd. After the meal and the end of the doldrums, Panurge of all people says (LXV, 743): 'Sans point de faute, nous doibvons bien louer le bon Dieu, nostre Createur, Servateur, Conservateur, qui par ce bon pain, par ce bon vin et frays, par ces bonnes viandes nous guerist de telles perturbations tant du corps comme de l'asme ...' The titles given to God and the tone, to all appearances perfectly reverent, come indeed strangely from the unworthy Panurge, but on the other hand his courteous salutation of the 'concilipètes' and his gift towards masses for the dead show that in externals he could conform to the accepted behaviour of the age.

All these texts concerning prayer in its various aspects give a vivid picture of a society in which prayer, whether of thanksgiving or supplication, is a constant practise. Gargantua, Pantagruel, Hippothaddée, Epistemon, Panurge, pray at different times, and it is only Frère Jan of the whole company who shows no inclination to pray except in oaths (and once, perhaps, as a soporific for Gargantua). The occasions of public prayer in the *Quart Livre*, the landfall to take holy water and commend themselves to God, the pilot's cry during the storm, when one has made every allowance for imitation (of Erasmus's *Naufragium* notably), for disguised satire, for partisan motives, all reveal an exceptional emphasis on prayer in all its forms. Febvre aptly turns Lefranc's expression 'paratonnerre' against him in connexion with the oratories at Thélème, but Thélème is a set piece, deliberately put out as a manifesto of progress and meant to catch the eye. It is quite otherwise with these texts from the *Quart Livre*, almost casual, mostly quite gratuitous. To explain them by motives of prudence is to overlook the flagrant imprudence of the attacks on Calvin, the caricature of Rome, the satire of Quaresmeprenant, which the enemies of Rabelais would notice and remember, while in all probability they would miss the passing references to piety. Whatever Rabelais's deeper motives may have been—and there seems no reason for not taking the facts at their face value—his readers were familiar with piety to a greater extent than we are today and without a definite lead from the author would have accepted it as part of Pantagruelism. In the light of what evidence there is, it seems most logical to conclude that the sentiments of the first two books, particularly Gargantua's remark 'tous christians prient Dieu', mean exactly what they say and are continued without a break into the *Tiers Livre* (where the context made them less obvious) and the *Quart Livre*. Such a theory has at least the merit of obeying the principle of parsimony.

Since the religious content of the first two books has been studied intensively by all critics, and the issues more or less clarified (if not agreed), it is perhaps useful to examine more carefully the later books, which are still considered by recent critics to mark a break-away into rationalism or worse. Febvre complains of the 'disette' of the *Tiers Livre* in religious references, and while this is not altogether just, it is true that the *Quart Livre* is much richer. As a point of method it is surely safe to assume that the views of the *Quart Livre* if consistent with those of the first two are likely to be equally consistent with those of the *Tiers Livre*, which for literary reasons apart from any others is not quite like the rest in form and therefore not in content. In the matter of scriptural studies the *Quart Livre* begins almost aggressively. The 1552 Prologue begins, like that of 1548, with 'Dieu en soit eternellement loué,' and goes on: 'Dieu, duquel je revère la sacrosaincte parolle de bonnes nouvelles; c'est l'Evangile . . .' A quotation from St. Luke is followed by a mention of Galen 'quoyque quelque sentiment il eust des sacres Bibles. . . .' The next page tells the readers: 'Discourez par les sacrées Bibles . . .' and quotes St. Luke again. Pantagruel's address on navigation in the first chapter is 'toute auctorisée des propos extraictz de la Sainte Escripture. . . .' The Bible comes up again in the Papefigue episode, when the peasant tells the devil (XLVI, 685): 'C'est pourquoy estez maudict en l'Evangile,' which annoys the devil, and in the next page we see why the gospel is a touchy subject: 'depuys certaines annees.

ilz [escholiers] ont avecques leurs estudes adjoint les saincts Bibles; pour ceste cause plus n'en pouvons au diable l'un tirer.' Actual quotations or paraphrases from Scripture are also frequent. In this matter at any rate, admittedly not the most important, the *Quart Livre* continues its predecessors.

More relevant to the charge of rationalism is the way in which relations between God and man are treated in the later books. The more mature attitude of Pantagruel is reflected early in his reverence for God, and his consequent disapproval of a certain type of humour. Panurge tells the story (probably borrowed from Erasmus) of Soeur Fessue, to which Pantagruel replies (*TL*/xix, 419): 'Vous jà ne m'en ferez rire. Je sçay assez que toute moinerie moins craint les commandements de Dieu transgresser que leurs statutz provinciaux.' The dry rebuke is a reminder that Pantagruel, like Rabelais, has grown older. A silence of particular significance is that of Pantagruel with regard to Raminagrobis. Having recommended the visit in the first place, he stays away and we never hear his views on the poet's supposed heresy or on Panurge's superstitious fears of damnation. One word from Pantagruel on this episode could well have been decisive, as Rabelais must have realized, and the hero is thus kept prudently in the background till the danger is past. Solemn and impressive are Pantagruel's words in the discussion on marriage (xxxv, 478): 'n'avoir femme est . . . pour elle ne contaminer celle unicque et supreme affection que doibt l'homme à Dieu.' This is unequivocal enough, the more so as the context is more serious than usual, Gargantua's presence lending dignity to the occasion. Pantagruel once more, pleading for Bridoye before the Court of Myrelingues, sounds a solemn note (xliii, 505): 'Et me semble qu'il y a je ne sçay quoy de Dieu . . . lequel, comme sçavez, veult souvent sa gloire apparoistre en l'hebetation des sages, en la depression des puissants et en l'erection des simples et humbles.' This echo of Magnificat fits in particularly well with the broad outline of Rabelais's religion, not so aristocratic as his philosophy.

The *Quart Livre* carries on these themes, and stresses them so much that it is impossible for them to be overlooked. Already in the 1548 Prologue there is the phrase (757): 'le plaisir et passetemps joyeux, sans offense de Dieu, du Roy ne d'autre . . . en la lecture de ces livres joyeux.' The Epistle to Cardinal de Chatillon takes up this idea again (541): 'le malade resjouir sans offense de Dieu,' and on the next page he protests that in his book there are: 'De folastreries joyeuses, hors l'offense de Dieu, et du Roy, prou.' The 1552 Prologue maintains the note of joyous reverence (545): 'tel est le vouloir du très bon, très grand Dieu, onquel je acquiesce, auquel je obtempère . . .' and ends in the same strain (559): 'Et de qui estez-vous apprins ainsi discourir et parler de la puissance et predestination de Dieu, paouvres gens? Paix! st, st, st! humiliez-vous davant sa sacrée face et recognoissez vos imperfections.' Joy and reverence are not incompatible, Rabelais would seem to say, but one must observe the conventions. Twice in the *Quart Livre* Pantagruel criticizes a story for transgressing his limits of propriety. After the Basché story, harmless enough at first sight, Pantagruel says (xvi, 606): 'ceste narration sembleroit joyeuse ne feust que davant nos oeilz faut la crainte de Dieu continuellement avoir.' Against a pleasantry of Frère Jan his reaction is much more violent (L, 696): 'Quand tels contes vous nous ferez, soyez records d'apporter un bassin, peu s'en faut que ne rende ma guorge. User ainsi du sacre nom de Dieu en choses tant ordes et abhominables! Fy! j'en diz fy! Si dedans vostre moinerie est tel abus de paroles en usage, laissez-le là, ne le transportez hors les cloistres.' It is interesting that in the very next chapter it is Epistemon who can no longer control his natural functions because (LI, 700): 'Ceste farce me a desbondé le boyau cullier,' while Pantagruel makes no protest at Homenaz's extravagances and says very little at all. As far as his own followers are concerned he tolerates no impiety, but as a guest of Homenaz he no doubt feels obliged to observe the traditional courtesies. Pantagruel's attitude is shown also in a remark he makes when the storm has ended (xxii, 626): 'Ores, si chose est en ceste vie à craindre après l'offense de Dieu, je ne veulx dire que soit la mort.' The phrase 'l'offense de Dieu' and the idea as well, returns so often to Rabelais's pen that it can hardly be accidental. The most likely explanation is that he was particularly sensitive to the charges of impiety levelled against him by his enemies, chief among whom he names 'les maniacles Pistoletz, les Demoniacles Calvins, les enraigez Putherbes.'

The 'paratonnerre' theory will always attract support among those who insist on Rabelais's atheism, but as a theory it suffers from the modest position of so many of the alleged 'paratonnerres'. The chapters which stand out, which leave the most lasting impression are those where one would expect to find Rabelais defending himself. The Prologues and the dedicatory Epistle to Chatillon can fairly be regarded as suitable places for exhibitions of prudence, but Pantagruel's brief censures of these three stories, his remarks about 'l'offense de Dieu' need a careful reader to notice them. A man whose watchword was prudence would not have risked the Pan story in such a book,[1] and would have avoided, for instance, Panurge's very risky devotions during and after the storm. If it was Rabelais's sensitivity, as we have suggested, it was the sensitivity of a man who feels himself innocent, a man who genuinely wished to escape the feeling of guilt which these attacks had engendered. One need not believe that Rabelais was devout, it would be perverse to try and prove such a thing, but there is justification for believing that he was serious in his intention of writing only 'joyeuses folastreries'.

With such a wealth of texts on various aspects of religion, faith, practise and the rest, it is interesting to see how very insignificant is the place of sin, in a doctrinal sense, and, almost as much, that of salvation. Odd references to sin occur, of course, when the devil or his ministers come on the scene (the Papefigue devil says (*QL*/XLV, 684): 'Je voys tenter du gaillard peché de luxure les nobles nonnains . . .') but the more serious characters have remarkably little to say about it. In his letter Gargantua writes (*Pant.*/VIII, 225): 'laquelle mienne conversation a esté moyennant l'ayde et grace divine, non sans peché (car nous pechons tous et continuellement requerons à Dieu qu'il efface nos pechés) mais sans reproche.' This follows what seems to be the only reference to original sin anywhere in the book, 'le peché de nos premiers parents' and the pain of death which resulted. For the rest, Gargantua and Pantagruel speak on various occasions of 'crainte de Dieu', 'offense de Dieu', confess their own weakness and need for divine guidance, but sin and salvation are not subjects which they discuss (immortality in the particular context of the *Quart Livre* is quite distinct from salvation). On the other hand, other characters in the later books have one or two observations of interest. In his story of Soeur Fessue Panurge makes the nun say (*TL*/XX, 419): 'craignant demourer en peché et estat de damnation, de paour que ne feusse de mort soubdainement praevenue,

---

[1] Compare Bigot's strange scruples in his Epilogue; he evidently found the story embarrassing, p. 139 n. 3 above.

je me confessay. . . .' Raminagrobis is sure that he is saved (*TL*/ xxi, 426): 'goustant le bien et felicité que le bon Dieu a praeparé à ses fidèles et esleuz en l'aultre vie et estat d'immortalité'; Panurge, though, is tormented by scruples (xxii, 427): 'est-il, Frère Jan, par ta foy, en estat de salvation? . . . il pèche vilainement, il blasphème contre la religion.' A little later Panurge says (xxiii, 430): 'Retournons l'admonnester de son salut . . . au moins, s'il perd le corps et la vie, qu'il ne damne son asme.' It is Panurge yet again in the *Quart Livre* who alone of the company goes out of his way to ingratiate himself with shiploads of monks (xviii, 613): 'ayant recommandé le salut de son asme à leurs devotes prières et menuz suffrages . . .'. Homenaz's attack on the heretics reminds Panurge of his experience with Raminagrobis. Homenaz becomes quite vindictive as he lists the penalties due to these wretches (l, 697): 'non seulement leurs corps et de leurs enfans et parents aultres occire, mais aussi leurs asmes damner au parfond de la plus ardente chauldière qui soit en Enfer.' About the only mention of salvation which is not suspect for one reason or another is that of Jamet Brahier during the tempest (xx, 621): 'Chascun pense de son asme et se mette en devotion. . . .' Even if one adds the references to Judgement Day in earlier works the total is still a meagre one considering the importance of the subject. Gargantua's letter refers to the Last Judgement, the *Almanach* for 1535 speaks of (929) 'vos asmes hors mises cette chartre tenebreuse du corps terrien et joinctes à Jesus le Christ,' otherwise there are no texts worth a mention.

With the burning problem of Faith and Works, that of Sin and Salvation was probably the most controversial of the day, and remembering how little Rabelais has to say about the first, his equal reticence about the second is not perhaps so surprising. Gargantua's letter remains the main source for most of the serious theology in either of the first two books, and try as one may Rabelais cannot be easily pinned down in any of the other passages. Febvre's[1] conclusion seems singularly appropriate: 'Ainsi chaque créature, debout devant Dieu son Créateur, répond de ses fautes et pour ses fautes, directement. Le salut, c'est oeuvre individuelle: affirmation d'accent tout moderne.' Whether or not the last words are justified, the rest seems to express very accurately the reasons for Rabelais's apparent indifference to salvation,

[1] Febvre, op. cit., p. 276.

as to confession and intercessory prayer. Panurge, the one character who consistently shirks every kind of responsibility, is precisely the one who shows himself most concerned with all these problems—and who makes least real effort. Because an idea is defended by an unworthy character it is not necessarily to be regarded as equally unworthy, and in some of the cases quoted in this chapter it is clearly not the deed but the motive of Panurge which is criticized. Before abuses one need not hesitate; superstitious pilgrimages, indulgences, invocation of saints and other similar practices are condemned outright by the author or the giants. The difficulty arises when, as with the sacraments, none of the texts gives any reliable statement of Rabelais's views. Confession was abused: Panurge alone is the champion of confession; the Last Sacrament was abused by predatory friars: Raminagrobis fulminates against the abuse; Matrimony was abused: Gargantua condemns the guilty priests. Communion has one single, very cautious mention, and yet whatever party Rabelais favoured he must have had definite views on this of all the sacraments. The more one goes into the question impartially of what Rabelais really meant his readers to think of his religion (to guess at his personal faith is pointless) the more evasive his answers seem to be.[1]

The nature of the difficulty appears very clearly from the *Sciomachie*. Describing a scene performed at Rome before numerous cardinals and Roman dignitaries, Rabelais tells how two clowns ran on to the mock battlefield, and went to the two corpses lying there (945): 'L'un les admonnestoit de leur salut, les confessoit et absolvoit comme gens morts pour la foy. . . .' When the spectators saw that the supposed corpses were only straw figures: 'Dont fut grande risée entre les spectateurs.' To be as orthodox as Rome—or as heretical as Geneva—mockery of the sacraments is hardly a valid criterion.

---

[1] Every religious nuance, from atheism to orthodoxy, has at one time or another been imputed to Rabelais, but opinion seems to be settling down in favour of some form of Erasmianism. Even here there is disagreement over definitions. M. Mann, *Erasme et les Débuts de la Réforme Française*, p. 185, writes of Rabelais: 'le Christianisme qui lui convient s'appelle la Philosophia Christi. C'est un évangélisme, fondé sur l'étude des textes, admettant le libre arbitre, s'exprimant surtout par une belle vie; un code moral, plutôt qu'une doctrine.' This seems an unduly narrow view, and a much fuller and more balanced account is given by Screech, op. cit., for whom Rabelais was a supporter of a Reform which never took place in France, but came closest perhaps to realization in England. For fuller evidence of what Rabelais's contemporaries found in him see M. De Grève, *l'Interprétation de Rabelais au XVI e siècle,* an indispensable work.

For the type of book he was writing, it was natural that abuses and superstitions should be ridiculed rather than that ordinary virtues should be depicted or extraordinary virtues extolled. It is only a trifling point, and may be no more than fortuitous, but throughout the work in all the disobliging references to the different monastic orders, the Carthusians are conspicuously absent. No order took a less active part in the life of the outside world, none carried fasting and asceticism to a greater extreme, and had Rabelais really wanted to make his point against monastic institutions he could have chosen no better example. In fact he is silent, and silent where Erasmus had been eloquent. Public unfamiliarity with the order cannot be the reason, the *Colloquia* alone dispose of that explanation, but simply the fact that where there is no abuse, the case with the Carthusians, there is no attack.

Striking a balance between the positive and negative aspects of Rabelais's religion as it appears from this inquiry, it seems that while he condemned every abuse a clear picture of his views on the sacraments and priesthood cannot be derived from the material at our disposal. In the matter of works, the less essential practises are satirized or condemned, on the principle that Pharisaism is not true religion even when sincere, but certain major works are prominent in his scheme: preaching, helping those in need, studying the Bible. Prayer plays an outstanding part in Rabelais's book, and is always the free and spontaneous communication between man and God, in public or private, whether for thanksgiving, supplication or acts of faith and contrition. There is no preoccupation with sin, and on the whole it seems fair to see behind Rabelais's caution a rejection of the principle of auricular confession, as making another man the channel for forgiveness, even if delegated by divine institution, and of the principle of intercessory prayer for similar reasons. Reverence, especially verbal, is emphasized; theological problems such as the nature of faith and conditions of salvation almost ignored. Nothing has been said here of the favourite questions of miracles, Hell, blasphemy and others, because none of the evidence adduced on those grounds to prove Rabelais's atheism or incredulity carries the slightest conviction, Febvre has dealt at length and in great detail with these secondary problems and at best they offer proof only of literary influences. Even if one admits with Febvre that there is enough in the text to justify talk of

Erasmian influence, this must remain only a partial answer to the question of Rabelais's religion, as Febvre himself admits in discussing the limits to which one can draw the parallel.

As a way of life, one may say that Rabelais's positive religion entailed a constant awareness of God and eternity, with all the stress laid (as Febvre says) on the individual's responsibility for his own salvation and for his personal relationship to God. Sacred things are not to be mocked, whatever one may think of Rabelais's fulfilment of his own precept, but no man-made doctrine or institution must ever be allowed to challenge the supremacy of God or His word. In the only text which is at all helpful, Rabelais seems to admit that theologians, at least 'les bons theologiens', have a definite place in his system; the question of authority for interpreting Scripture is not discussed anywhere else, though the falsehoods of the 'cafards, les massorètes et caballistes' is frequently denounced, and Calvin's 'imposture' less frequently but with equal vehemence. When all has been said, one cannot escape the fact that Rabelais's whole life was spent in one ecclesiastical circle after another, at Fontenay, at Maillezais, probably at the Hotel St. Denis in Paris, in Rome with Jean du Bellay; the intervals at Lyon, Metz, Turin are only intervals. This lifetime of religion at close quarters explains many of the later antipathies, but it is well to consider whether the habits of worship and thought inculcated from his youth may not have left positive traces as important in his religion of later life as the undeniable influence of Erasmus or Luther. As one says the two names, exactly the same reflection occurs concerning them as well: monastic training, even in the laxest of houses, does not pass away without leaving a trace. While fully subscribing to Febvre's contention that Rabelais was a Christian in the proper sense of the word, we should hesitate before denying him the name of Catholic, albeit wayward, as well.

16 : PROVIDENCE, FATE, AND FREE WILL

A SUBJECT in which Rabelais displayed constant interest in all his works, major and minor, is astrology. This particular subject is where religion and philosophy (in a broad sense) most often clash in his work, and his attitude to such problems as Grace, Free Will, Providence in the religious sphere inevitably decide his treatment of pseudo-scientific determinism in the philosophical sphere. Perhaps the most important single question in the study of Greek religious thought is that of Fate and for all their imperfect understanding of the ancient world, the sixteenth-century humanists could hardly fail to notice discrepancies between this pagan idea and the more commonly received doctrines concerning man's freedom and God's omniscience which theologians had been debating for centuries. By the latter part of Rabelais's literary life, Calvin had given the whole question an acutely topical importance, and it is interesting to see how Rabelais's ideas on astrology, as expressed in works written before Calvin's doctrine was yet generally known, compare with the few but significant opinions on Predestination of the later books. Any final judgement on Rabelais's optimism or pessimism, on the true nature of Pantagruelism must depend essentially on a proper appreciation of these factors.

Primacy in Rabelais's system goes to God's absolute power; his will cannot be modified in any way by creatures, and numerous texts stress this point. Directly linked with the supremacy of God's will is the idea that men have no right to try and read the secrets of this will. The most formal texts on this come, as might be expected, from the works on astrology. This sentence from the *Pantagrueline Prognostication* is of capital importance (920):

Et ne aura Saturne, ne Mars, ne Jupiter, ne aultre planète, certes non les anges, ny les saincts, ny les hommes, ny les diables, vertuz, efficace, ne influence aulcunes, si Dieu de son bon plaisir ne leur donne: comme dict Avicenne: que les causes secondes n'ont influence ne action aucune si la cause première n'y influe.

The authority of Avicenna is beside the point—Rabelais quotes all the Arabs he can think of in this particular work—but the philosophical justification for thus rejecting planetary influence is of great importance. The autonomy of second causes is the only basis on which astrology can claim any degree of infallibility, and this formal denial explains the substance of Rabelais's attacks. The fragment from the *Almanach* for 1533 emphasizes God's will still more (928): 'Mais ce sont secrets du Roy eternel, qui tout ce qui est et qui se fait modère à son franc arbitre et bon plaisir, lesquels vaut mieux taire et adorer en silence, comme est Tob. xii.' Quotations from the Psalms to the same effect are followed by a reference to the Lord's Prayer:

il nous convient humilier et le prier, ainsy que nous a enseigné Jesus-Christ Nostre Seigneur, que soit faict non ce que nous souhaitons et demandons, mais ce que luy plaist et qu'il a estably devant que les cieulx fussent formez . . . remettant le pardessus à ce qu'en est escrit ès ephemerides eternelles, lesquelles n'est licite à homme mortel traiter ou cognoistre . . .

The *Almanach* for 1535 repeats just the same ideas (930):

Reste donc que . . . nous deportons de ceste curieuse inquisition au gouvernement et decret invariable de Dieu tout-puissant, qui tout a créé et dispensé selon son sacre arbitre; supplions et requierons sa saincte volunté estre continuellement parfaicte tant au ciel comme en la terre.

The omnipotence of God, 'fiat voluntas tua', and the unseemliness of trying to pierce the divine secrets are the three basic notions of these texts. As evidence of Rabelais's thought they are of very qualified value; written against astrology, the form and nature of their attack is largely predetermined; appearing under the author's own name and destined for the wider public, their sincerity can be called in question, and these texts must be treated with reserve except when the opinions of the novel conform. There are, however, several indications in the four books of a state of mind remaining persistent in this respect.

From *Gargantua* come the words (VI, 42): 'Mais si le vouloir de Dieu tel eust esté, diriez-vous qu'il ne l'eust pu faire? . . . je vous diz que à Dieu rien n'est impossible.' The context, of strange births, is facetious but the idea certainly is not. In a different sense, God's will is invoked in Grandgousier's prayer when he hears of Picrochole's invasion (XVIII, 111): 'Donne-moy et pouvoir et sçavoir le rendre au joug de ton sainct vouloir par bonne discipline.' Grandgousier again speaks of God's will in answer to Frère Jan's question about noses (XL, 142): 'Parce que ainsi Dieu l'a voulu, lequel nous faict en telle forme et telle fin, selon son divin arbitre, que faict un potier ses vaisseaulx.' *Pantagruel* adds nothing to this, but with the *Tiers Livre* these ideas appear again. While Rabelais condemns astrology, which tries to make the will of God to an earthly measure and regulate it by the courses of the stars, he does not reject prophecy and foreknowledge of future events. There is no contradiction in this attitude, since the exposition on dreams completely safeguards God's omnipotence in this matter and at the same time explains Rabelais's conception of the future. The famous 'intellectuale sphère' is the text in question (*TL*/XIII, 394): 'A laquelle rien ne advient, rien ne passe, rien ne dechet, tous temps sont presens . . .' The last phrase is an exact description of God's relationship to time, of divine eternity, and explains that participation in divine knowledge by men in no way limits God's will,[1] being itself limited in any case by the imperfection of man's mixed nature.

A fuller treatment of foreknowledge occurs in Hippothaddée's advice to Panurge. Here the phrase 'si Dieu plaist' is admittedly exploited for its comic possibilities, but there is no parody of the thought behind it. The theologian tells Panurge that he will not be cocu (XXX, 459) 'si Dieu plaist', and replies to Panurge's sarcastic protests with an energetic defence of his words: 'Est-ce condition blasphème ou scandaleuse? . . . N'est-ce mettre exception canonique à toutes nos entreprinses, et tout ce que proposons remettre à ce que sera disposé par sa saincte volunté, tant ès cieulx comme en la terre.' He denies that this is a question of which the answer is hidden: 'en la chambre de ses très sainctz plaisirs. Le bon Dieu nous a faict ce bien qu'il nous les a revelez, annoncez, declarez et apertement descriptz par les sacres bibles.' The word of God, 'la Parolle', is His will, and while the Bible can obviously not provide for individual cases, it is the general expression of God's will concerning human behaviour and thus a reliable guide in all contingent events where a moral problem is involved. Rabelais is careful not to give as his own opinion that of a third

---

[1] Paré, op. cit., p. 110, quotes Boethius and St. Thomas to show how: 'les scolastiques voient dans la notion d'éternité l'application ultime de la prescience divine.' Compare this with Rabelais's own treatment of the question.

interesting text from the *Tiers Livre* where Epistemon puts forward his theory to explain the success of Bridoye's judgements by dice (XLIV, 508): 'comme disent les Talmudistes en sort n'estre mal aulcun contenu, seulement par sort estre, en anxieté et doubte des humains, manifestée la volunté divine.' This explanation, whatever Rabelais may have thought of it, preserves the supremacy of the first causes even in so trivial an instance as this.

The *Quart Livre* carries on the same thread. The first page of the Prologue has two references to God's will—speaking of his readers' health, Rabelais says: 'Dieu en soit loué et (si telle est sa sacre volunté) y soiez longuement maintenuz,' and the reason for his own is: 'tel est le vouloir du très bon, très grand Dieu—.' The end of the Prologue admonishes those who try to interpret God's will their own way (559): Et de qui estez-vous apprins ainsi discourir et parler de la puissance et praedestination de Dieu, paouvres gens?' The two themes of God's supreme will and man's inability to know it are those stressed in the minor works of nearly twenty years before. The tempest shows this attitude to God's will in action. At the worst moment Pantagruel cries out (XXI, 623): 'Non toutefoys adviegne scelon nos affections, mais ta saincte volunté soit faicte!' 'Fiat voluntas tua' from first to last seems to be the great prayer of Rabelais and his heroes. After the storm, Epistemon delivers a little homily on death, in which he combines this motif with appropriate classical allusions (XXIII, 628): 'Je consydère que si vrayement mourir est (comme est) de necessité fatale . . . en telle ou telle heure, en telle ou telle façon mourir est en la saincte volunté de Dieu.'

Even when He leaves the second causes to work out their effects by determining the moment of a man's death, God's supremacy is decisive to the last. Homenaz too, with his Papo-centric theology, has something to say of God's eternal purpose (LIII, 707): 'ceulx qui par divine prescience et eterne predestination, adonnez se sont à l'estude des sainctes Decretales.'

These quotations vary considerably in context and not all of them are serious, but they do show a quite striking conformity between three of the four books (there is not enough evidence to include *Pantagruel*) and the minor works first quoted. The constant emphasis on divine will and the temerity of men who take upon themselves to predict it extends further than the rather limited field of astrology. The persistence of the 'Fiat voluntas tua' theme can be linked with other ideas of Rabelais, and what Febvre has called 'cet étrange quiétisme',[1] so little in character with Rabelais's gospel of action, is probably not so very much out of place after all. How far Lutheran influences may be responsible is another question, and one whose answer had better await more complete information.

Though there is very little explicit information as to what Rabelais thought of the theological doctrine of predestination, there is no doubt from the few texts that do exist that Calvin's interpretation was abhorrent to him. The addition made in the 1542 edition to the Prologue of *Pantagruel* can hardly refer to anything else (196): 'prestinateurs et imposteurs' inserted between 'abuseurs et seducteurs'. The famous attack on Calvin in the *Quart Livre* as 'imposteur de Genève' seems to be an echo of this theme. Then there is the text already cited from the Prologue to the *Quart Livre*, seemingly written more in sorrow than in anger, condemning the temerity of those who presume to read God's predestination. The remark of Homenaz quoted above on 'divine prescience et eterne predestination' is a perfectly orthodox reference to two accepted notions whose interpretation alone caused dissension. On the one or two other occasions when Rabelais speaks of 'praedestiné' it is not at all in a theological connexion, and the adjective is used as an alternative to some other expression meaning just 'fated', though a gibe at Calvin would naturally occur to many readers for whom the word had become a shibboleth. Thus Panurge makes free use of the word on his discussion on marriage (*TL*/xxviii, 451): 'jamais homme n'eut en femme et en chevaulx heur tel que m'est predestiné'; again of his *cocuage* he says that all his advisers have told him so far: 'qu'il m'est ainsi praedestiné des cieulx'. Frère Jan takes him up on this and repeats the phrase before reciting his kyrielle which ends (xxviii, 454): 'puisqu'ainsi t'est praedestiné, vouldroys-tu faire retrograder les planètes . . .' with other celestial consequences, which in this context show clearly that 'praedestiné' is the work of the fates, planets or some other secondary power, not of God. Curiously enough it is Panurge again who uses the word (*QL*/xix, 618): 'Estoit-ce icy que de perir nous estoit praedestiné?' In these uses the word is quite independent of its current theological implications.

A cognate problem is that of Grace and Election, and though

---

[1] Febvre, op. cit., p. 321.

Rabelais has more to say on this than on predestination, the exceptionally technical nature of the problem no doubt accounts for the very general tone of his remarks. One of the most exact of all the references states the relationship between man's free will and divine grace, but it is probably relevant to note that Grandgousier, progressive but more cautious than his son, is the writer; of Picrochole's aggression he says (*Garg.*/xxxi, 112): 'Dont j'ay cogneu que Dieu eternel l'a laissé au gouvernail de son franc arbitre et propre sens, qui ne peult estre que meschant si par grace divine n'est continuellement guidé . . .' The same sentiment had already come from the pen of his son two years earlier (*Pant.*/viii, 225): 'laquelle miene conversation a esté, moyennant l'ayde et grace divine, non sans peché . . . mais sans reproche.' With Picrochole the withholding of grace was the cause of his error, with Gargantua its bestowal kept him in the path of righteousness. The same letter closes with a remark which Gargantua re-echoes more than once (viii, 228): 'les graces que Dieu te a données, icelles ne recepvez en vain. . . .' Mindful of his father's words, Pantagruel replies to Thaumaste's invitation to debate (xviii, 272): 'Seigneurs, des graces que Dieu m'a donné je ne vouldroys denier à personne en despartir à mon pouvoir, car tout bien vient de luy.'

Even to Panurge's facetious question (*Pant.*/xviii, 274): 'Y a-t-il homme tant savant que sont les diables?', Pantagruel replies quite seriously: 'Non vrayement, sans grace divine especiale.' These few remarks are far from indicating an obsession, but they all come from the giants and cannot therefore be ignored, and show moreover a remarkable degree of consistency one with another. The *Tiers Livre* adds a little more to the picture. On his death-bed Raminagrobis uses a word very seldom found in Rabelais, perhaps because of its disagreeable polemical associations: '*elu*'. He says (xxi, 426): 'le bien et felicité que le bon Dieu a preparé à ses fidèles et esleuz en l'aultre vie' is the object of his last meditations. The scene is brief, Panurge's comments absolutely farcical and Pantagruel is not there to give an authoritative opinion, so that it is quite impossible to say how far the old poet represents Rabelais's views and sympathies. The implied doctrine of election (and Raminagrobis's conviction that he is one of the elect) is not discussed, let alone approved, by anyone else and one can do no more than register its brief appearance.

The advice of Hippothaddée comes into a very different category, preceded as it is by Pantagruel's express defence of the
'bons theologiens', given in his presence and at his invitation, and
contested by no one save Panurge. Grace occurs frequently in
Hippothaddée's speeches, beginning with the Pauline charge
(xxx, 459): 'Avez-vous de Dieu le don et grace speciale de
continence?' he goes on in a most eloquent strain to explain his
cautious answer to Panurge's second question: 'N'est-ce nous
declairer tous dependre de sa benignité, rien sans luy n'estre, rien
ne valoir, rien ne povoir, si sa saincte grace n'est sus nous infuse?'
Later he says that the ideal wife should be: 'craignant l'offenser
et perdre sa grace par default de foy' and: 'qui s'efforce avec Dieu
soy former en bonne grace.' The whole speech ends with the
injunction: 'Et continuellement implorerez la grace de Dieu à
vostre protection.' From a theologian, and one of evidently
Pauline inspiration, this insistence on grace is not really surprising, but its concentration into a relatively short chapter enhances
its effect. Two references in the Bridoye episode carry on the
theme. Pantagruel accounts for Bridoye's good record thus
(xliii, 505): 'Et me semble qu'il y a je ne sçay quoy de Dieu qui
a faict . . . qu'à ces jugements de sort toutes les precedentes
sentences ayent esté trouvées bonnes . . .' The 'je ne sçay quoy'
can hardly be anything but grace in this context. Epistemon is
more explicit in his opinions and says (xliv, 508): '[Bridoye]
invocqueroit à son ayde la grace celeste.' Gargantua's farewell
speech to his son begins (xlviii, 516): 'Je loue Dieu, filz très-cher,
qui vous conserve en desirs vertueux,' and his letter in the *Quart
Livre* explains that his paternal affection is enhanced (iii, 569): 'par
l'esguard et reverence des graces particulières par election divine
posées [in Pantagruel]'. At every step man's weakness is strengthened by divine grace, and one text after another brings out the
continual dependence of man on God. If that were all, it might
not be unreasonable to wonder whether some sort of quietism
does not lie at the root of Rabelais's outlook. The counterpoise
can come only from free will, and his views on this matter are
therefore vital.

The number of unambiguous texts is disappointingly small and
virtually all those that count are from *Gargantua*. In more than
one connexion one can observe a disproportionate interest in this
book compared to the others, and whether the reason be external

(for instance, propaganda) or internal (a personal religious crisis) the emphasis on fundamental problems is a fact. Prayer, free will, pilgrimages are given far more attention in *Gargantua* than elsewhere.

The distinction between 'arbitre', 'vouloir' and 'volonté' is carefully preserved by Rabelais, but for convenience the texts which follow are given as they occur in the book. Rabelais speaks early on about (*Garg.*/IX, 153): 'les tyrans qui voulent leur arbitre tenir lieu de raison.' The next mention in fact concerns a particular tyrant, Picrochole, of whom Grandgousier writes, as we have already seen (XXIX, 112): 'Dieu eternel l'a laissé au gouvernail de son franc arbitre et propre sens, qui ne peult estre que meschant sy par grace divine n'est continuellement guidé.' Ulrich Gallet addresses Picrochole two chapters later (XXXI, 116): 'rien n'est ny saint ny sacré à ceulx qui se sont emancipez de Dieu et Raison pour suyvre leurs affections perverses.' Here the antitheses of the first two texts are resumed, a tyrant's will on the one hand and on the other God and reason. Gargantua in his harangue to the vanquished makes use of 'arbitre' in just the same way. By the people of the Canaries, defeated by his father (L, 165): 'feust decreté par consentement unanime que l'on offreroit entierement leurs terres, dommaines et royaulmes à en faire selon nostre arbitre.' As Gargantua and his father walk in the ways of God their 'arbitre' is not like that of the despotic tyrants mentioned above, but on the contrary leads them to outstanding magnanimity. A little later in the same harangue Gargantua speaks of his father: 'consyderant le franc vouloir et simplicité des Canarriens' and of the increasingly large tribute paid by them 'de franc vouloir'. This neatly marks the distinction between 'arbitre', essentially the instrument of decision, and 'vouloir', that of assent. Gargantua also declares: 'sans mon vouloir . . . estoit faicte ceste guerre.' By an accident of context all these texts have a political bearing, but the Thélème episode shows a wider— and more famous—use of the same ideas. The distinction between 'arbitre' and 'vouloir' appears in two texts (LVI, 178): 'Les dames au commencement de la fondation se habillèrent à leur plaisir et arbitre. Depuis feurent reformées par leur franc vouloir. . . .' The other text is probably the best known of all Rabelais's serious lines (LVII, 181): 'Toute leur vie estoit employée non par loix, statutz ou reigles, mais selon leur vouloir et franc arbitre' and as everyone knows their sole rule was 'Fay ce que vouldras'. Since there is no mention of grace (or, except for the private oratories, of religion) in the Thélème episode, this looks on the face of it like a complete contradiction of the phrase about free will in Grandgousier's letter. In fact there need be no inconsistency if the cardinal point be admitted that Rabelais is not always obliged to say everything he has in mind. Because he does not speak here of grace, it does not mean that even for the moment he has forgotten about it, and it is infinitely more probable that this text conforms with the others than that it opposes them.

It is Pantagruel who makes the distinction between 'arbitre' and 'volunté' in the Tiers Livre, oddly enough in a conversation with his father which recalls very closely the Erasmian inspiration of the earlier books. Of his marriage, Pantagruel says (XLVIII, 516): '. . . je m'en deportoys sus vostre bonne volunté et paternel commendement.' and a few lines on: 'Je n'ay jamais entendu que . . . ayt esté en arbitre des enfans soy marier non consentans, voulens et promouvens leurs pères, mères et parens prochains. Tous legislateurs ont ès enfans ceste liberté tollue, ès parens l'ont reservée.' The parental relationship of God to man obviously has close analogies with such a conception of liberty. Only one other remark from the Tiers Livre is worth quoting, and it is interesting as a reflection of the more precisely formulated Pantagruelism of the later books. Pantagruel asks about Panurge's proposed marriage (X, 383): 'N'estez-vous asceuré de vostre vouloir? Le point principal y gist: tout le reste est fortuit et dependent des fatales dispositions du ciel.' Our wills alone are completely in our power and once we have made them firm we can do no more to regulate our lives.

The comparative absence of discussion on human will, good or bad, free or restricted, does not mean that Pantagruel or the later books are indifferent to the question; it is simply approached from a different angle. The point is no longer the relationship between man's will and God, in any case a dangerous topic for prolonged debate, but between man and fate, and it is this formulation of the question which leads directly to Pantagruelism, the so-called 'stoicisme gai'. The real theme of the first part of the Tiers Livre, as has been often pointed out, is not so much marriage as the various methods of divination used to explore the question. Since all divination pre-supposes some degree of determinism (as

against pure chance) the direction of Rabelais's approach led him
naturally to consider man's position regarding fate. The two early
definitions of Pantagruelism in the Prologue and second chapter
of the *Tiers Livre* stress the good humour of a philosophy which
(357) 'toutes choses prenoit en bonne partie', but the Prologue to
the *Quart Livre* adds a more specific detail (544): 'certaine gayeté
d'esprit, conficte en mespris des choses fortuites.' Pantagruel's
advice to Panurge obviously refers to this: pure chance, 'les
choses fortuites', is beyond our control or prediction and we are
therefore better to ignore it altogether in deciding our attitude to
life. Homenaz himself is something of a Pantagruelist despite all,
for he claims for the reader of the Decretals (LI, 700) 'contemnement asceuré de toutes choses fortuites et terrestres.'

Besides blind hazard, fate in the sense of necessity must enter
into man's calculations and here scorn alone will not suffice.
Pantagruel speaks of everything beside our wills as 'fortuit et
dependent des fatales dispositions du ciel', and with this remark
he recalls the standard Aristotelian doctrine of hazard as modified
by the Scholastics. Paré[1] calls this conception of chance: 'l'inter-
section de deux causalités dont aucune fin ne détermine la
rencontre', but strictly speaking, 'pour le philosophe chrétien il
n'y a du hasard que par rapport aux causes secondes.' 'Les fatales
dispositions du ciel' are not only haphazard, however, and the
many texts quoted in this chapter which oppose various aspects
of judicial astrology must be completed by those few which
indicate how far astrology can be relied upon at all. Grandgousier's letter to his son has been quoted already in connexion
with free will and grace, but it begins with what looks like a quite
different tone (*Garg.*/XXIX, 112): 'Puisque telle est ceste fatale
destinée que par iceulx soye inquieté ès quels plus je me repousoie.'
Gallet in his speech asks Picrochole (XXXI, 115): 'Sont-ce fatales
destinées ou influences des astres qui voulent mettre fin à tes
ayses et repous?'—'Mais si ainsi estoit phée et deust ores ton heur
et repos prendre fin. . . .' Without the rest of the context, which
contains the Christian references already noted, these remarks
look exactly like the astrology that Rabelais condemns so often,
but one must be careful to make the distinction which Rabelais
puts in the mouth of Avicenna. Nobody in the Middle Ages
really doubted, as Paré says; 'Il y a dans le monde des causes

[1] Op. cit., p. 91.

nécessaires. De ce nombre sont les corps célestes. Ils effectuent toujours leurs rotations selon les mêmes lois et exercent constamment des influences de même nature sur le monde sublunaire.'[1] Gilson states a general truth thus: 'La volonté libre de l'homme mise à part, les philosophes et les théologiens s'accordent pour admettre un déterminisme astrologique universel.'[2] Grandgousier and Gallet, and Rabelais behind them, are offering as explanations of Picrochole's conduct something which everyone accepted as a fact. Free will, aided by grace as Rabelais insists, or chance, can apparently break the laws of this determinism, which otherwise were regarded as laws of nature like generation and corruption. The theme comes up again in the *Tiers Livre*. In his praise of the *braguette*, Panurge, newly proud of his philosophical knowledge, describes the end of the Golden Age (VIII, 377): 'presque tous animaulx par fatales dispositions se emancipèrent de luy [l'homme]' This comes in a purely pagan context but could apply equally well to Scholastic teaching. The juxtaposition of pagan and Christian ideas comes in a remark from Epistemon, commenting on Bridoye's case (XLIV, 507): 'Conjecturallement je refererois cestuy heur de jugement en l'aspect benevole des cieulx et faveur des Intelligences motrices.' An exceedingly complicated sentence follows, which, without its parentheses, says: 'Lesquelles . . . remueroient et tourneroient les déz . . .', but in between comes the reference already quoted to Bridoye invoking divine aid and guidance. In this case we are clearly in the realm of second causes, autonomous up to a point but not finally responsible for man's life.

A burlesque presentation of the familiar Greek poetic (as distinct from philosophical) view of fate can be seen in the agitated complaints of 'les Dieux Olympicques' faced with the marvels of Pantagruelion (LI, 531): '[Pantagruel] sera de brief marié, de sa femme aura enfans. A ceste destinée ne pouvonsnous contrevenir, car elle est passée par les mains et fuseaux des soeurs fatales, filles de Necessité.' Facetious as the passage is, it very well brings out the fundamental difference between the polytheism of the Greeks and the theology of Judaeo-Christianity: for the Greeks, poets and philosophers alike, God or the gods were variously defined, but were all without exception subject at all times to the blind laws of fate. A similarly burlesque treatment

---

[1] Ibid. [2] Gilson, *l'Esprit de la Philosophie Médiévale*, vol. ii, pp. 163–4.

has already been mentioned, where Frère Jan speaks of the consequences should Panurge try to contravene what is already (xxviii, 454) 'praedestiné'—'vouldroys-tu faire retrograder les planètes? . . . defiller les pelotons des Parces?' The idea is the same in the two texts; natural laws are made never to be broken, and if the course of the heavens is set to cause Panurge's *cocuage* (or, in the other case, Pantagruel's marriage) God alone can alter it.

Epistemon it is who once more gives the pagan theory with a Christian adaptation, in the *Quart Livre* just after the storm (xxiii, 628): 'Je consydère que si vrayement mourir est (comme est) de necessité fatale et inevitable en telle ou telle heure, en telle ou telle façon mourir est en la saincte volunté de Dieu.' The passage has already been quoted to illustrate Rabelais's constant emphasis on the omnipotence of God's will, but it is also interesting to see how the autonomy of natural laws is preserved and reconciled with Christianity. Our bodies are, in fact, the part which death affects, our corruptible and temporary homes, and it is in perfect conformity with medieval theories on physics to admit the influence of the heavens on the world of matter, but, wherever the soul is to be reckoned with, God's intervention has to be foreseen, in this instance to decide the manner of human death. The expression 'fatale necessité' is of course classical, but the sense of Epistemon's remarks makes it probable that Rabelais was just deliberately using words which were out of favour with the Scholastics because of their fatalistic associations, while really not diverging from normal teaching on the subject. As Paré puts it: 'Le destin est devenu l'ordre du monde prévu par un Dieu qui le connaît . . . Saint Augustin avait déjà appliqué au destin un sens analogue: la volonté même de Dieu prescrivant à la nature des lois qu'elle doit suivre et sauvegardant la liberté humaine.'[1] Unless one gives Rabelais credit for understanding standard teaching on fate and providence, such statements as this one by Epistemon are virtually meaningless.

Two more texts from the *Quart Livre* show how widely Rabelais's use of the idea of fate extended, from the conventionally literary to the deeply philosophical. A little later in the conversation after the storm Panurge is told by Frère Jan that he had no need to fear during the storm (xxiv, 630): 'Car tes

[1] Op. cit., p. 93.

destinées fatales ne sont à perir en eau.' The jest (which Shakespeare uses in a similar context in the *Tempest*) is richly developed
but rests none the less on the same pseudo-scientific theory as the
other remarks quoted above. The world of matter, with its
elemental compounds, is in every respect subject to invariable
laws (though not necessarily predictable ones) so that the ultimate
end of Panurge's body must be pre-determined in accordance with
these laws like any other material substance. The last example is
the famous affirmation by Pantagruel of his belief (xxvii, 639): 'Je
croy que toutes âmes intellectives sont exemptes des cizeaulx de
Atropos, toutes sont immortelles.' The expression 'cizeaulx de
Atropos' is no doubt chosen mainly as a literary embellishment,
and the *Briefve Declaration* tells us that it means only 'la Mort',
it serves to remind us too that the classically personified fates had
been replaced in Christian philosophy by divinely ordained laws,
and restricted in their activity to the world of matter. God alone
has power over souls and the rule of the fates is rightly rejected
by Pantagruel in this striking phrase.

Rabelais's dislike of astrology is explained equally as much by
these texts on fate as by the works actually dealing with the
subject directly, and few of his ideas are more coherent or force-
ful than these. Above all the absolute supremacy of God as first
cause, Creator, Preserver, Providence must be guaranteed and
respected. God's will and His grace are the factors which domin-
ate all human affairs, all the affairs of the created universe. In all
this, man's place is humble before God but not unworthy in the
world. Man's will is free, he can choose good or evil, and with
God's grace he will have the power to follow in the paths of
righteousness. For anyone who held so firmly to the doctrine of
personal responsibility for salvation (and in this we fully endorse
Febvre's view) no diminution of man's freedom could reasonably
be tolerated. Finally Rabelais recognizes as a philosophical fact
that God has pre-ordained the course of creation from all eternity,
and that he has set up a chain of second causes which produce
genuine but not independent effects. In the works on astrology
he quotes the theory of second causes from Avicenna, and elsewhere stresses that all these things are in the inscrutable will of
God. This is really the point at issue between the astrologers (or
rather *judicial* astrologers) on the one hand and on the other the
orthodox philosophers and theologians. Not for the first time we

find Rabelais on the side of the angels. By temperament he seems to have been allergic to the idea of determinism, and by religious conviction this antipathy was increased by his violent revulsion against those who presumed to lay down God's laws in their own name. Rabelais, one can be sure, would have made the same objection against Descartes's determinism as did Pascal. Whether the attempt was to prescribe the effects of celestial influences or to interpret God's election of the just and unjust, Rabelais utterly condemns it. Man and God are on different planes of existence and of understanding; it is neither our business nor our right to penetrate His secrets. There is, moreover, in Rabelais's case an additional factor which may be decisive: his frequent allusions to 'fiat voluntas tua' either explicitly or implicitly entail a submission to God's will which any attempt to forecast that will must tend to nullify. If a man wants to know the future it is not only for curiosity but so that he can try to circumvent his destiny, and this would seem still more reprehensible to Rabelais than the temerity of the merely inquisitive. The whole point of the long examination of methods of divination is that those tried are all ridiculed in their practice, but the examples of successful prophecy are all such that a communication from above accounts for them, not a man-made inquiry. The historic case of Langey, whose merit Rabelais so eloquently extols, shows the gulf which separates prophecy from astrology. As a key to his ethics, these views are also significant. Submission to the will of God and indifference to the hazards of second causes is Rabelais's message; such an attitude is already half-way to deciding the moral code of any sixteenth-century thinker.

17 : EPISTEMOLOGY AND PHILOSOPHY

IN a sense the whole of Rabelais's book is concerned with education. The first two books deal with the initial studies of their heroes, and the latter two with what one might call the post-graduate application of these studies. From this point of view the authenticity of the *Cinquiesme Livre* is a question of major importance, and if the spirit of its final chapter can ever be shown to derive from Rabelais himself, a very suitable conclusion to the whole work is thus provided. All learning is the pursuit of truth, whether in an absolute or purely pragmatic sense, and Rabelais's attitude to the methods of his day is directly dependent upon his broader conception of truth, which the later books do something to illustrate. For personal as well as polemical reasons Rabelais's treatment of these questions shows considerable evolution between the two groups of books, and whatever arbitrary divisions one cares to impose, the chronological distinction cannot be ignored.

The first two books are notable for their sustained and detailed attack on the Sorbonne and all it stood for, an attack which the transparent alterations of the 1542 edition do little to attenuate. The library of St. Victor and similar gibes scattered through the two books are plainly inspired by polemical motives, and perhaps a certain amount of personal rancour as well. There is little or no philosophical significance in these details; the ideas and persons attacked are for the most part those which all humanists disliked. The Reuchlin affair and the Dominicans concerned figure largely in the catalogue of St. Victor, most of the Franciscan authors find a place (but not, significantly, Bonaventura or the founder himself) and the best-known opponents of progressive ways are not spared, like Béda and le Quercu. The active hostility of these groups is sufficient reason for Rabelais's attitude, but personalities apart he devotes some space to criticizing their methods. The whole Janotus episode is a direct and obvious satire of pedantry and obscurantism at the Sorbonne, but it is at the same time precisely the sort of satire one would expect from a critical and intelligent student whether medieval or modern. Not logic nor

Latin, but bad logic and bad Latin are the butts of Rabelais's shafts. Janotus is the pedantic fossil which all systems seem to produce sooner or later, and he is not more typical of Scholasticism than of any other system. Thaumaste is a very different character, and the purport of his episode much more damaging than the other. He is neither a fool nor a pedant, and he comes in all sincerity to learn from Pantagruel. What is ridiculed in these chapters is the whole system of solemn disputation, an essential feature of Scholastic instruction. The broad farce of the episode depends largely on the assumption that Thaumaste takes seriously the gestures which Panurge and the reader know to be absurd. There is an undertone of anarchy in this, as in other scenes where the ignoble Panurge scores over characters whose worth is never in question. If one must not take the Thaumaste episode too seriously, two remarks of the Englishman himself express without any doubt Rabelais's own views (*Pant.*/xviii, 271): 'Je ne veulx disputer pro et contra, comme font ces sotz sophistes de ceste ville [Paris] et de ailleurs,' which Pantagruel applauds, saying that the proposed disputation by signs will put them: 'hors de ces frapements de mains que font ces badaulx sophistes quand on argue, alors qu'on est au bon de l'argument.' The second time Thaumaste says (275): 'Et, au regard de disputer par contention, je ne le veulx faire; aussi est-ce chose trop vile, et le laisse à ces maraulx sophistes lesquels en leurs disputations ne cherchent verité, mais contradiction et debat.'

Milder, but to the same effect, is the comment on Gargantua's feelings at the birth of his son and death of his wife (*Pant.*/iii, 203): 'D'un costé et d'aultre il avoit argumens sophisticques, qui le suffocquoient, car il les faisoit très bien in modo et figura; mais il ne les pouvoit souldre.' Rabelais's objection to the Scholastic disputation is the common one; it proves only which disputant is the most skilful in argument. As a means of arriving at truth Rabelais could never accept it and he seems to have had no use for it even as a mental exercise. The fervent study of gloss and commentary, equally dear to the Scholastics, was no less anathema to Rabelais. Personal opinions often three or four removes from the original text brought the reader no nearer the truth than disputes and provided a tedious and aesthetically unrewarding study.

Rabelais's answer to Scholastic methods is his theory of education, set out in Gargantua's letter to his son, and the actual programme accomplished a generation before by Gargantua himself. Insofar as humanism has concealed but persistent roots in the Middle Ages, it would not be hard to point out some parallels between Rabelais's ideas and those of—say—Albert the Great, but evidently the education of both the giants is far removed from contemporary Scholastic practice. The main features of these programmes are well enough known: for Gargantua, personal piety, physical fitness, oral instruction and object lessons from field-studies and so on, for Pantagruel, the same piety, philological training to enable study of all subjects, sacred and profane, arts and sciences, in the original texts, with encyclopaedic knowledge as the goal. The intellectual attitude typified by Pantagruel's proposed education is still quantitative first, qualitative second. The humanists of Rabelais's generation had not lost medieval habits of mind though they applied them in rather a different direction.

Much more illuminating than these conscious and obvious comments on the pursuit of knowledge, are the remarks scattered all over the work which bear witness to the persistence of technical Scholastic notions in Rabelais's philosophy and reveal clearly the degree of his dependence on ideas learned in his youth. Some of these remarks on epistemology have already been quoted in other connexions. There is the coincidence of Grandgousier's remark about his son (*Garg.*/xiv, 69), 'je congnois que son entendement participe de quelque divinité,' and the amplification of the same idea so long afterwards in the passage on dreams ('la sphaere intellectuale') but this is hardly enough to warrant a belief in Rabelais's thoroughgoing Platonic idealism. More conventional is Ulrich Gallet's suggestion that Picrochole's misguided behaviour is due to the fact that (*Garg.*/xxxi, 116): 'l'esprit calumniateur eust par fallaces espèces et phantasmes ludificatoyres mis en ton entendement . . .' Platonic but not very telling is Thaumaste's opening remark on meeting Pantagruel (*Pant.*/xviii, 270): 'Bien vray est-il, ce dit Platon, prince des philosophes, que si l'imaige de science et de sapience estoit corporelle et spectable ès yeulx des humains, elle exciteroit tout le monde en admiration de soy.' Curiously enough, the most explicit allusion to the Aristotelian theory of knowledge comes in the *Tiers Livre*, the most Platonic of the books, though it is true that Gargantua, who says it, is representative of older ways (xlviii, 517): 'par les fenestres de vos sens rien n'est on domicile de vostre esprit entré fors liberal sçavoir.' Also from the *Tiers Livre* is Pantagruel's explanation of why our ears are always open (XVI, 407): 'affin que continuellement puissions ouyr et par ouye perpetuellement aprendre: car c'est le sens sus tous aultres plus apte ès disciplines.' This accords very well with the insistence on oral work in *Gargantua* (though less well with modern psychology). As is so often the case with Rabelais, there seems to be no genuine contradiction between the Platonic theory of knowledge (reminiscence and participation in divine omniscience) as shown in the chapter on dreams and the Aristotelian 'nil in intellectu quod non prius in sensu.' Rabelais is not explicit here any more than he is on other similar questions, but he seems to have room for both theories of knowledge, the sensible in what concerns the material world and the spiritual in metaphysics. Such a synthesis is typical of his general habits, and since Pyrrhonism is so clearly rejected in the Trouillogan episode, no alternative solution would be very likely.

Whatever Rabelais's later reading may have been, he cannot have escaped a grounding in Aristotelian philosophy during his Franciscan training and the references to these studies are by no means all derogatory. The long and rather tiresome disquisition on the significance of white and blue begins with a quotation from the *Topics* (*Garg.*/x, 55): 'Aristoteles dict que, supposent deux choses contraires en leur espèce . . . si vous les coublez en telle façon qu'un contraire d'une espèce convienne raisonnablement à l'un contraire d'une aultre, il est consequent que l'aultre contraire compète avecques l'autre residu,' and this is elaborated at some length. Towards the end of the same chapter Rabelais writes: 'Si demandez comment par couleur blanche nature nous induict entendre joye et liesse, je vous reponds que l'analogie et conformité est telle.'

Besides the many burlesque uses of Scholastic terminology, there are some examples which seem to come almost naturally to Rabelais's pen. Thus (*Pant.*/II, 201): 'le Philosophe raconte en mouvant la question pourquoi c'est que l'eaue de la mer est salée' is only one instance of many which could be cited. A very late reminiscence of Aristotelian learning comes at the end of the *Quart Livre*, when Pantagruel says to Ponocrates (LXIII, 737): 'Par le decret des subtilz philosophes peripateticques nous est enseigné que tous problèmes, toutes questions, tous doubtes proposés doibvent estre certains, clairs et intelligibles.' The 'subtilz' seems to recall the Scotist teachers of Rabelais's early years, and the remark may derive from personal memories of logical training. Another odd item of logic is Pantagruel's rejection of the theory of a 'langaige naturel' (*TL*/xix, 418): 'les voix, comme disent les dialecticiens, ne signifient naturellement mais à plaisir.' If it is clear that the arid formalism of later Scholastic logic repelled Rabelais, these few references (with others not quoted) show that his training in this field had left some positive traces.

Besides the terms of formal logic, Rabelais shows himself familiar with the essential notions of Aristotelian philosophy and, what is more, appropriates them to his own use. The great problem of matter and form was not one in which Rabelais intended to become involved (*QL*/xi, 592): 'Il veult dire (respondit Epistemon) formes suyvantes la matière. Ainsi les nomme Averrois . . . Je vous diray (respondit Pantagruel) sans au problème proposé respondre, car il est un peu chatouilleux, et à peine y toucheriez-vous sans vous espiner.' The individuating factor in this composition, however, was a less dangerous subject. Immediately before Epistemon's remark just quoted, Rhizotome asks whether the natural attraction of monks to kitchens is due to: 'quelque vertus latente et proprieté specificque absconse dedans les marmites', and we have already seen that the definition of Pantagruelism is (*TL*/Prol., 349) 'une forme specifique et proprieté individuale'. Nature's role is to perpetuate her creatures (*TL*/viii, 376) 'sans jamais deperir les espèces, encores que les individuz perissent.' Rabelais uses Scholastic terms in these examples in such a way as to suggest his acceptance of the ideas behind them. The division of matter and form, the arrangement of substances by species and genera, even the technical Scotist theory of individuation are part of Rabelais's own mental equipment.

These indications, however slight, are useful to set against the Platonic references which occur rather frequently in the two later books. Apart from particular Platonic references, such as the chapter on dreams, Rondibilis's use of the *Timaeus* for opinions on women and numerous examples of neo-Platonic demonology from Plutarch, the theory to which Rabelais most often refers is naturally enough that of Ideas. The word '*idéé*' is evidently one that appealed to Rabelais for itself (like '*Servateur*'), and some examples of the way in which he uses it help to define the limits of his Platonism. In Panurge's praise of debt, just after a mention of (*TL*/III, 363) 'celle grande asme de l'univers, laquelle scelon les Academicques toutes choses vivifie,' comes 'repraesentez-vous en esprit serain l'idée et forme de quelque monde.' A little later the ideal world envisaged by him is compared to (IV, 366): 'l'idée des regions olympiques ès quelles toutes autres vertus cessent.' Pantagruel speaks of real married happiness as (X, 383): [semblant] reluire quelque idée et repraesentation des joyes de paradis,' and he himself is described as (LI, 528) 'l'idée et exemplaire de toute joyeuse perfection.' At Medamothi Epistemon buys a tapestry (*QL*/II, 565): 'onquel estoient au vif poinctes les Idées de Platon et les Atomes de Epicurus,' which the *Briefve Declaration* explains as (761) 'espèces et formes invisibles imaginées par Platon'. At the end of the Andouilles battle the monster which appears is described as (XLII, 676) 'l'Idée de Mardigras.' When Homenaz produces his sacred relic he says to the travellers (L, 696): 'Que vous semble de ceste imaige?' and goes on to explain that it is 'l'idée de celluy Dieu de bien en terre,' and a moment later 'le portraict', while the chapter heading calls the relic 'l'archetype d'un Pape.' In this one context, '*idée*' is used to describe a pictorial likeness as an alternative to '*imaige, portraict, archetype*'. A similar, but less obviously material, reference is a quotation from Petron (via Plutarch) who believed in a plurality of worlds, in the centre of which he said was (LV, 713) 'le manoir de Verité et le habiter les Parolles, les Idées, les Exemplaires et protraictz de toutes choses passées et futures.' This again gives '*exemplaires et protraictz*' apparently as synonyms for '*idées*', and though the passage is rather obscure, '*parolles*' seems also to have the same meaning here. These eight examples from the later books are typical of Rabelais's treatment of Platonism.[1] Except for Rabelais's last text, in any case a quotation, none of the others is specifically Platonic in fact, and in two cases '*idée*' is not used in a philosophical sense at all, but merely as an erudite alternative to '*imaige*'. Compared with his very precise use of Scholastic terms like '*forme specifique*' Rabelais's use of '*idée*' seems to be due to little more than verbal preference, prompted by philological motives. There is no

---

[1] Most Scholastic definitions of Ideas are taken from St. Augustine, from whom St. Thomas, for example, quotes the following: 'Ideae . . . formae principales quae divina intelligentia contineantur' and 'forma exemplaris in mente divina existens.' *Summa Theologica* 1. qu. 44.3 ad 3.

justification for assuming that he had any other view of matter and form than that taught by his Scholastic masters, and there is no text which shows conclusively that he had adopted more than a few of Plato's metaphysical doctrines to supplement or replace his original Scholastic grounding.

While Rabelais has a marked predilection for Plato in all matters concerning metaphysics, his practical, as distinct from technical, examples of epistemology are solidly based on the theory that knowledge enters the mind through the senses. Reference has already been made to the programme of Gargantua's education, in which field-studies, object lessons of all kinds, visits to craftsmen and specialists are given considerably more weight than book learning. Pantagruel's actual education is limited to academic studies in the first book, but Panurge makes in this connexion an important remark at the end of the *Tiers Livre* when a voyage to the Dive Bouteille is proposed (XLVII, 514): 'Je vous ay de longtemps congneu amateur de peregrinité et desyrant tousjours veoir et tousjours aprendre.' '*Longtemps*' is the operative word, as it shows that book learning did not long remain Pantagruel's main preoccupation. The letter and gifts sent back by Pantagruel from Medamothi are practical illustrations of this interest in knowledge for its own sake, and Pantagruel's words to the Macrobe reinforce this same impression (*QL*/xxv, 633): 'Une et seule cause les avoit en mer mis, sçavoir est studieux desir de veoir, apprendre, congnoistre, visiter l'oracle de Bacbuc.' Marichal quotes this,[1] without the last phrase (but, as he says, the suppression is perfectly legitimate) as describing Rabelais's general attitude; a good case could be made for separating the reference to the oracle from the preceding three verbs on linguistic grounds as well. In each one of the episodes (e.g. Macreons, Quaresmeprenant, Andouilles) it is Pantagruel who makes searching inquiry into the nature and customs of the place, and he usually has some opinion of his own to add to the newly won information. Even in the middle of travelling, however, he draws copiously from his stock of book learning. While Rabelais attaches due importance to the intellectual stimulus of new experiences and surroundings, he certainly never intended these purely practical measures to take the place of study, and classical rather than modern study at that, even in geography. Wisdom may, indeed must, be personally attained, but

[1] R. Marichal, *Quart Livre*, Introduction p. xxiii, n.4.

knowledge in the last analysis is for Rabelais a question of authority more than of experience. One recalls his own medical studies, his pride in presenting a philologically superior text, without any doubt a greater achievement in his eyes than the anatomical dissections for which modern science would be more inclined to honour him.

The question of authority in Rabelais's philosophy is really more important than any of the aspects so far considered. As regards method there are not very many indications of a technical nature, but those few which have any significance most probably reflect his Scholastic training. His philosophical language is precise and accurate, and he understands all the main problems of which he makes mention. His Platonism is extremely eclectic on the technical side, and his use of the word '*idée*' suggests propaganda more than conviction. Though the texts relevant to this subject are scanty and not of first importance, they are worth noting above all for their counterbalance to the more obvious and familiar attacks on Scholastics and their methods. For correcting an impression of unqualified hostility to things medieval, the slightest evidence is of some value, and taken as a whole the texts quoted add up to a not inconsiderable testimony. More important to a general appreciation of Rabelais's outlook is the stress he lays on direct observation and experience, during and after the years devoted to formal education.

There remains the overriding question '*pourquoi?*' to set beside the '*comment?*' The question of whether or not Christianity comes first in Rabelais's ideas is still hotly disputed. Even those who claim that he was an atheist do not deny that religion of an unequivocally Christian kind, and with definite Evangelical tendencies, takes the first place in the education of both the giants. Whatever sinister motives may be imputed to Rabelais in this, the fact remains and must have been taken literally by many more contemporaries than the partisans of his atheism seem to allow. As regards the later books, opinions are even more divided, and no proof will ever convince the believers either in Rabelais's atheism or his Christianity to change their opinions.

Some attempt has been made in other chapters to set out the arguments for believing that Rabelais was a Christian in the strict sense of the word in both the later books or more exactly that the impression given by the text is Christian, whatever secret views the author may have held. M. Febvre has done an immense service to students of the sixteenth century by stating so forcibly that incredulity, or thoroughgoing scepticism, is just not feasible in Rabelais's time, and that some positive alternative to Christianity must be supplied to support any charge of deviation. All that has been said in earlier chapters supports the belief that Rabelais was a Christian at all times, and that being so, held the truth of the Christian revelation to be absolute in the face of any rational attacks. The immediate corollary of this is that the Scriptures (and possibly more besides) take precedence over all other sources of wisdom; a Christian who believes he has an immortal soul (as Rabelais did) has both religious and philosophical reasons for holding spiritual wisdom to be supreme. The Platonizing tendencies of the later books only reinforce the initial conclusion: the truth, spiritual wisdom, derives from and is of God, either directly or through the Scriptures. If this is accepted, it necessarily follows that all other knowledge is of a lower order, having reference either to intellectual or material things subordinated to their Creator. The *fact* of subordination is not all, however, and for any sixteenth-century thinker the teleological conclusion inevitably follows. That any knowledge is always better than ignorance is an almost self-evident truth for men of an age which would have been astonished by Pope's *Essay on Man*,[1] and if pressed for a reason they would point to the essentially hierarchic arrangement of all things, whereby knowledge of even the humblest things is a stepping-stone towards knowledge of God, man's *raison d'être* on earth. It is, of course, true that many Christian scholars may not have sought consciously to explain the eternal significance of their academic studies, but without denying their religion they could not logically offer any other answer.

Thus far Rabelais may be said to subscribe to the notion 'philosophia theologiae ancilla', though his interpretation of theology was certainly not that of the Faculty represented at the Sorbonne. In a broad sense, these views were common to all Christians, Catholic or Reformed, but in Rabelais's case an additional factor is of great importance—the place of pagan authors. For many of the reformers the Catholic Church's greatest betrayal of the Christian truth was its acceptance of contamination

---

[1] Cusa, after St. Paul, showed that on the highest level the two were the same, as his title *De Docta Ignorantia* suggests, but this does not affect the issue.

by pagan philosophy, particularly Plato and Aristotle, but in that they were only following the party of extreme orthodoxy, represented in earlier ages by such men as SS. Peter Damian and Bernard, who had regarded all pagan writing as immoral in itself. The mass of opinion, both Catholic and Reformed, accepted the possibility of reconciling the best in paganism with Christianity. Erasmus's 'Sancte Socrates, ora pro nobis,' shocks only in its form; for centuries before Erasmus Plato had been 'the divine Plato', and Eusebius even speaks of him as a kind of Greek Moses.[1] The Platonic triad had from the earliest times been assimilated to the Trinity, and the work of St. Thomas in 'baptizing' Aristotle was only the logical extension of a process which had been going on for centuries. Except by extremists, it was generally agreed throughout the Middle Ages that the classical world had a considerable contribution to make to Christian culture. The educational and dogmatic developments of the later Middle Ages never wholly caused the rejection of that principle, but subordinated it to the growing and fatal cultivation of dialectic. For the generation of Erasmus and Budé, the great revival of classical learning in no way replaced Christianity, which remained the touchstone of all truth. Even 'Sancte Socrates' did not stop Erasmus criticizing the Church for admitting so many pagan ideas into its official teaching. Unlike Rabelais, Erasmus admitted pagan contributions only in the sphere of morals, not metaphysics. For him there was only one truth, and that was Christianity, supplemented by as much of pagan wisdom as could be fitted into a Christian framework.

The exaggerated cult of classicism, of which Rabelais was certainly no exponent, must be seen in the light of all this. When it comes to quoting authorities, Plato, Plutarch, an unbaptized Aristotle have Rabelais's favour to the exclusion of all Scholastic authors, and, in his book at least, of the Fathers too, but this authority is never set against Christianity. In all matters of faith, such as theology or metaphysics, where a clash is possible, Rabelais makes no attempt to present two points of view; in every case his chosen remedy is synthesis. In all other matters affecting human affairs, law, science, the arts, no doctrinal issue was involved, or, if it were, had already been assimilated by the Scholastics, so that

---

[1] 'What is Plato but Moses speaking Attic Greek?' Eusebius, *Praeparatio Evangelica.* XI, 10, p. 527a, following earlier writers.

the fundamental principle of a unique and Christian truth remained intact.[1] What Rabelais objected to was arbitrary institutional authority, as he saw it, such as that of the Popes or other dignitaries. The authority he accepted was that conferred by the tradition of centuries, by constant repetition and quotation, and visibly based on Scripture. The element of censorship and compulsion which came to be associated with Scholasticism was probably decisive in causing Rabelais to reject it. As for the fact of disagreement between the leading classical writers, which was so to worry Montaigne, Rabelais was unperturbed, for in synthesis he found a cure for all such ills.

Roger Bacon has a phrase which may be compared with Rabelais's outlook: 'Viri tam boni et tam sapientes sicut Pythagoras, Socrates, Plato et Aristoteles, et alii zelatores maximi sapientiae receperunt a Deo speciales illuminationes quibus intellexerunt multa de Deo.'[2] St. Thomas too, who in this may be taken as typical of all Scholastics, recognized that we attain knowledge of the truth in three ways: from God, from other men and from study, for which prayer, listening or reading and meditation are respectively necessary.[3] Rabelais seems to have accepted the views of his fellow friars on pagans as well as on the triple way to truth. 'Car tous philosophes et saiges antiques pour bien surement et plaisamment parfaire le chemin de congnoissance divine et chasse de sapience ont estimé deux choses necessaires: guyde de Dieu et compagnye d'homme.' (CL/XLVII, 911). Whether these are really Rabelais's own words or not (and they probably are) they aptly express the guiding principles of his philosophy. In the broad scheme of his thought Rabelais puts the purely human wisdom of the ancient world second only to the divine wisdom revealed in Scripture. Wherever there is truth it must come from God, wherever there is truth it must lead to God; such are the twin hinges of Rabelais's theory of knowledge, and thus far he seems to look back rather than forward.

---

[1] Cf. Gilson, *Héloïse et Abélard* passim, especially 'Moyen Âge et Naturalisme.'

[2] 'Such good and wise men as Pythagoras, Socrates, Plato and Aristotle, and other great lovers of wisdom received special illumination from God by which they understood many things about God.' In *Opus Tertium*, quoted Harris, *Duns Scotus*, vol. i, p. 125, n.1.

[3] St. Thomas, *Summa Theologica* 2.2 qu. 180.3 ad 4.

18 : ETHICS AND POLITICS

APART from the more or less obvious royal and patriotic propaganda with which much of Rabelais's work is filled there are certain more fundamental ideas about ethics, public and private, especially in the later books. In the sense that all ethics for the Christian are ultimately inseparable from religious belief, it is true that Rabelais's views on the duty of man to God form an integral part of his moral outlook, but it is convenient, and not unduly difficult, to make a distinction between religion and ethics which corresponds with a similar division in the book. Such serious moral thinking as there is in the first two books barely goes beyond the gospel injunction of the two greatest commandments to 'love God . . . and thy neighbour as thyself'. Thus the closing lines of Gargantua's letter to his son specifically remind him of his duty (VIII, 228): 'il te convient servir, aymer et craindre Dieu . . . Soys serviable à tous tes prochains et les ayme comme toy-mesmes.'

Although there is a good deal of political thought in these two books, problems of personal ethics do not really arise, partly because of the traditional framework on which the books are built and partly because Rabelais was not yet seriously concerned with ethics. Thélème is a good example of the very rudimentary approach to moral problems. Besides the question of human nature and free will, already discussed, the inscription on the gates suggests a very summary moral judgement between the sheep and the goats; summary because like the similar passage in *Aucassin et Nicolette*[1] it seems to be dictated by taste rather than principle. Moreover the brazenly immoral character of Panurge evidently ran away with its author at the beginning, and this perhaps indicates more clearly than anything else how far were serious moral ideas from Rabelais's mind when he composed the first two books. For these reasons, the ethics of these books hardly repay study, except in the political sphere, and while this is a pity from the historical point of view, the other two books offer some compensations.

[1] Compare chapter 5 where the same categories are denounced by the preachers for the same reasons.

After man's duty to God, which includes the religious concept of sin, man's duty to himself, not necessarily dependent on any religious teaching, is the starting-point for practical ethics and decides in large measure the wider question of his duty to his neighbour. In the later books a handful of texts give some idea of the qualities which Rabelais considered desirable. Pride of place inevitably goes to those making up Pantagruelism, of which the three definitions provide an adequate picture. From the Prologue to the *Tiers Livre* comes the first (349): 'une forme specifique . . . moiennant laquelle jamais en maulvaise partie ne prendront choses quelconques ilz congnoistront sourdre de bon, franc et loyal courage'. The second refers to the hero himself (*TL*/II, 357):

toutes choses prenoit en bonne partie, tout acte interpretoit à bien, jamais ne se tourmentoit, jamais ne se scandalizoit; aussi eust-il esté bien forissu du deificque manoir de raison . . . car tous les biens que le ciel couvre et que la terre contient . . . ne sont dignes d'esmouvoir nos affections et troubler nos sens et espritz.

The last and best-known is from the Prologue to the *Quart Livre* (545): 'c'est certaine gayeté d'esprit conficte en mespris des choses fortuites.' It is this last definition, incidentally, which Homenaz echoes in his praise of the Decretals through which men can win (*QL*/LII, 700) 'contemnement asceuré de toutes choses fortuites et terrestres.'

The two essential features of this Pantagruelism are neatly complementary: inwardly, a mild 'contemptus mundi', or at any rate an indifference to material and contingent events, outwardly, an optimistic view of human actions and tolerance towards everything save deliberate malice. The scorn of Fortune's caprices and earthly goods entails no sort of asceticism or even austerity, and only makes sense when seen against the eternal background as supplied by Rabelais's religious views. Stoic as it stands, this philosophy of life as practised by its inventor has closer affinities with the generous Platonism of such a Stoic as Cicero than the more austere doctrines of a Seneca or a Marcus Aurelius, but on the existing evidence it is better to avoid precise labels altogether.

Amplifying the first part of this philosophy, there is throughout a strong emphasis on the power of reason over passions, coupled with a highly developed sense of individual responsibility. Pantagruel is quite explicit on one important moral issue (*TL*/VII, 374):

'nos coeurs et pensées qui est l'officine de tout bien et tout mal.' Later, after the first series of consultations, Pantagruel gives as his opinion also that offered by Raminagrobis (XXIX, 456): 'en l'entreprinse de mariage chascun doibt estre arbitre de ses propres pensées et de soy-mesmes conseil prendre.' The power of reason and each man's responsibility for using it properly is balanced by the equal moral responsibility of each for physical actions to implement his decisions. Pantagruel's condemnation of Panurge's cowardice during the storm is on precisely these lines: (QL/XXII, 626): 'Si paour il a eu . . . pourveu que au reste il se feust evertué, je ne l'en estime un pelet moins', and Epistemon repeats his leader's words in describing the duty of the individual faced with danger (XXIII, 628): 'de nostre part convient pareillement nous evertuer, et comme dit le sainct Envoyé, estre cooperateurs avecques luy [Dieu].' The chain of personal duty from mind to body is thus established firmly, if not in very great detail.

With regard to the second part of Pantagruelism, a phrase which Rabelais uses at least three times in fairly serious contexts seems to reinforce his optimism and partly explain its nature. Epistemon proposes as an answer to the question of Bridoye's continued good fortune, that he has won the favour of the 'Intelligences motrices' (TL/XLIV, 507), 'en contemplation de la simplicité et affection syncère du juge Bridoye'; very similar is Rabelais's comment on the little Zacchaeus, whom God allowed to see Our Lord because of his (QL/Prol., 548) 'syncère et mediocre affectation', while the first phrase is repeated literally by Pantagruel explaining to the Macrobe how they escaped destruction in the storm (QL/XXV, 633): 'le hault Servateur avait eu esguard à la simplicité et syncère affection de ses gens.' The theme of simplicity is a very frequent one throughout the work, and more than once Rabelais describes how the devil abuses simple souls to their damnation. It is already a long step towards optimism to regard the evil in human actions as due largely to ignorance. As for the sincerity in the examples just quoted, Rabelais seems to rate this second only to positive virtue. Elsewhere he quotes with approval the verses from Magnificat 'He hath exalted the humble and meek', and whether his source was primarily scriptural or not this idea seems an integral part of his moral outlook. Malice is certainly not identified with cleverness in Rabelais's eyes, but there is something of a bias in his mind towards humble ignorance where superior wisdom is not attainable. Good intentions are essential whether realized or not, and one of the basic elements of Pantagruelism is to presume goodwill as far as possible and to cast no blame on shortcomings of performance. Naturally enough these views on the individual's duty to himself are closely bound up with the conception of how other people should be treated. What we have just called the external aspect of Pantagruelism is a part of this second problem, and probably the essential part, but there are various details to add for a complete picture. One or two general remarks provide the background for more specific texts. Thus Pantagruel cuts short Panurge's praise of debt with a quotation (TL/v, 369): 'Rien (dict le sainct Envoyé) à personne ne doibvez fors amour et dilection mutuelle' and follows with similarly relevant comment: 'Et suys d'opinion que ne erroient les Perses, estimans le second vice estre mentir, le premier estre debvoir. Car debtes et mensonges sont ordinairement ensemble ralliez.' He continues with a quotation from Plato's *Laws* describing how one may legitimately allow a neighbour to draw from ones well only when he has with negative results tried his own land, and ends: 'Ainsi est-ce grand verguoigne, tousjours, en tous lieux, d'un chascun emprunter plustout que travailler et guaigner.' This very outspoken attitude may be compared with Panurge's own illustration of 'Justice Commutative' (TL/II, 358): 'en achaptant cher (je diz à credit), vendant à bon marché (je diz argent comptant)', which precedes it by a few pages. Though the immediate context is financial, or at least material, Pantagruel's words are of much wider application in the sphere of morals. It is interesting that lies, which Rabelais specially abhorred, as we have seen in connexion with the devil, are linked with debt as the chief vices. Debt is the shifting of responsibility, in this case for honest toil or trading, from oneself to another, and the constant emphasis on personal responsibility in all spheres of action explains the violence of Pantagruel's attack.

The counterpart of this particular text is curiously enough one of the comparatively few where Rabelais mentions the Stoics by name (collectively). Writing back to his father from Medamothi, Pantagruel alludes to the Stoic belief concerning gifts (QL/IV, 571):

troys parties estre en benefice: l'une du donnant, l'aultre du recevant, la tierce du recompensant: et le recepvant très bien recompenser le

donnant quand il accepte volontiers le bienfaict et le retient en soub-
venance perpetuelle: comme, au rebours, le recepvant estre le plus
ingrat du monde qui mespriseroit et oubliroit le benefice.

Gratitude, in fact, is ample repayment, and by no means valueless
because it costs nothing. To this Stoic maxim may be joined
another, more commonplace, attributed to Seneca, perhaps the
most popular of all classical moralists at the time (*TL*/ix, 380):
'ce qu'à aultruy tu auras faict, soys certain que aultruy te fera',
which Pantagruel uses to jolt Panurge's conscience. Frère Jan
evidently regards this as an eminently just arrangement, for,
speaking of the friars whom Panurge is defending against the
heretical attacks of Raminagrobis, he says (*TL*/xxii, 428): 'Ilz
mesdisent de tout le monde: si tout le monde mesdit d'eulx, je
n'y pretends aulcun interest.' Apart from this example, the eye
for an eye principle is not much in evidence throughout the
work.

The duty of children to their parents and more specifically of
each of the giants to his father, is a frequent and important theme.
The unquestioning obedience as well as genuine affection shown
between each pair of father and son instructs by example rather
than precept, but one passage better than any other expresses
Rabelais's attitude on the subject. Before launching into his long
and violent attack on the parties concerned in irregular marriages
Gargantua hears his son accept in advance any paternal decision
on the matter (*TL*/xlviii, 517): 'Plustoust prie Dieu estre à voz
piedz veu roydde mort en vostre desplaisir, que sans vostre
plaisir estre veu vif marié.' Similarly there is no need to enlarge
here on the reciprocal duties of husband and wife, except to
reiterate that the subordinate position of the wife is to some
extent mitigated by the recognition both of a husband's responsibilities and of a wife's capacity for making her husband's life
more congenial.

More precise details are to be found in an examination of the
vices which Rabelais selects for attack. Twice he expresses his
disapproval of flogging boys (*QL*/xxi, 624): 'Si par fouetter
paouvres petitz enfanz, escholiers innocens, les pedagogues sont
damnez . . .', and Pantagruel's angry (*QL*/xlviii, 691): 'Si ne
desistez fouetter ces enfanz, je m'en retourne!' Apart from possible
memories of his own schooldays and perhaps the influence of

Erasmus, this dislike of corporal punishment (by no means universal even among the Humanists) accords well enough with Rabelais's general antipathy to exploitation of the weak by the strong. On the intellectual plane the same reaction can be seen with regard to the exploitation of simplicity and ignorance (*QL*/ LVIII, 720): 'Ilz [les Engastrimythes] estoient divinateurs, enchanteurs et abuseurs du simple peuple.' The same formulas reappear several times in similar contexts. Calumny is a vice of which quite a lot has already been said, and Rabelais's habitual use of '*Calumniateur*' for 'devil' speaks for itself. His definition of calumny as given in the *Ancien Prologue* to the *Quart Livre* shows that it is directly contrary to the practice of Pantagruelism (755): 'c'est quand on impugne le bienfaict, quand on mesdit des choses bonnes.'

As for the actual classes of people whom Rabelais condemns, the catalogue is traditional and obvious. His comment on the depraved habits of the Romans may be compared to the tone of his letters from Rome to Geoffroi d'Estissac, full of contemporary misdeeds (*QL*/XII, 593): 'A Rome, gens infiniz guaignent leur vie à empoisonner, à batre et à tuer.' The realities of Renaissance Italy fell rather short of its splendid theories. The same chapter (on the Chiquanous) gives the enemies of the nobles (and of Rabelais) as 'moine, prestre, usurier ou advocat.' The inscription on the gates of Thélème also excludes hypocrites, in the context meaning monks and clergy, lawyers and usurers, and adds jealous husbands and sufferers from the pox. The devil of Papefigue goes off to tempt (*QL*/XLV, 684): 'les nobles nonnains de Pettesec, les cagotz et briffaulx aussi,' and: 'les pillars chiquanous, desguyseurs de procès, notaires faulsaires, advocats prevaricateurs,' all of whom, however, have succumbed willingly before he arrives. Lucifer adds to the list (*QL*/XLVI, 686): 'marchands usuriers, apothecaires faulsaires, billonneurs, adulterateurs de marchandises,' and later, deceitful serving-maids. Personal dislike and traditional unpopularity go a long way to account for these attacks, but it is interesting that their moral basis seems in each case to be connected with the twin vices denounced by Pantagruel: falsehood and debt. The monks and clergy are upbraided above all for their hypocrisy, for the vices which their habit fails to conceal, the lawyers for their dishonesty and exploitation of the legal ignorance of their clients, usurers for profiting from others without labouring themselves, false traders for deception. Abuse of trust, exploitation of human simplicity and goodwill are the constant targets of Rabelais's shafts. Other vices and classes of evildoers are castigated from time to time, but hypocrites, lawyers and usurers come in for much the greatest number of attacks.

Most of the Seven Deadly Sins are dealt with by Rabelais; Lechery, in the person of Panurge and, to some extent Frère Jan, is not painted in flattering colours; Gluttony is severely condemned in the Gastrolatres, whose God is their belly; both Anger and Covetousness are expressly contrary to Pantagruelism but are not much emphasized in the work, except in Picrochole; Pride is the exact opposite of that simplicity which Rabelais so often praises; Sloth is just what Frère Jan condemns in his former brethren and later in Panurge; Envy is the besetting sin of *Antiphysie* and consequently of her unlovely offspring, the *Calumniateurs*. There is nothing particularly novel or interesting in Rabelais's treatment of these sins as such, and it cannot be said that he notably attenuates or emphasizes any of them. The most personal element is that dislike of falsehood and exploitation exemplified in so many of the episodes, and, from a positive standpoint, the insistence on personal responsibility for one's actions.

In the public sphere, ethics concern law and government. In his aversion to canon law, or more precisely to its contemporary abuse, Rabelais was at one with all the humanists and the royalist cause as well. The long and detailed attack on the Decretals is so obviously intended as propaganda that the theory underlying it is obscured; similarly the Baisecul and Bridoye episodes are both uncomplimentary to some aspects of civil law but cannot as they stand be taken to represent Rabelais's real opinions regarding the nature of laws. A formal profession of his belief in the natural origin of law comes in the Baisecul episode, when Pantagruel is railing at the ignorance and dishonesty of contemporary legists (*Pant.*/x, 238): 'Veu que les loix sont extirpées du milieu de philosophie moralle et naturelle, comment l'entendront ces folz qui ont, par Dieu, moins etudié en philosophie que ma mule?' Equally vital to their understanding are: 'les lettres de humanité et congnoissance des antiquitez et histoire.' The speech of Epistemon at the end of the Bridoye episode makes a similar distinction between jurisprudence and justice, and mentions with particular disapproval the authority of Tribunian (*TL*/xliv, 508) 'homme mescreant, infidèle, barbare, tant maling, tant pervers, tant avare et inique, qu'il vendoit les loix, les edictz ... à la partie plus offrante.' Though Bridoye himself does not accuse his colleagues on the bench of such flagrant venality, he recognizes the dominant role played by money in the administration of the law (*TL*/xlii, 500). 'Comme vous aultres, Messieurs, semblablement les sergens, huissiers etc. sugsants bien fort et continuellement les bourses des parties, engendrent à leurs procès teste, pieds....' This fact, true for all ages, is the inevitable source of the innumerable criticisms of lawyers throughout literature in general and Rabelais's work in particular, but it is no more an indictment of legal theory than the satire on the Decretals is a denial of the Church's right to temporal dues from the State.

The only text which goes right to the heart of legal theory is that in which Gargantua describes to his son the shameful practice whereby children can be married without their parents' consent. Pantagruel says first (*TL*/xlviii, 517): 'Je n'ay jamais entendu que par loy aulcune, feust sacre, feust prophane et barbare, ayt esté en arbitre des enfans soy marier, non consentans, voulens et promouvens leurs pères, mères et parents prochains.' This is the starting-point for Gargantua's attack on 'tant malignes et barbariques loigs', made by the clergy for their own advantage and to the detriment of the married pair: 'qui est cause suffisante pour les rendre suspectes comme iniques et fraudulentes.' The idea that the sanction of a law should be in the benefit to the subject and not to the legislator alone is clearly important. After the long diatribe against clandestine marriages, Gargantua tells of the priests who demanded of the secular arm exemplary punishment for those who had killed in vengeance the priests guilty of these crimes: 'Mais ne en aequité naturelle, ne en droict des gens, ne en loy imperiale quelconques, n'a esté trouvé rubricque,paragraphe, poinct ne tiltre par lequel fust poine et torture à tel fait interminé, raison obsistante, nature repugnante.' He continues: 'Ores est qu'un chascun trouvant le meurtrier sus le faict de homicide en la personne de sa fille ... le peut par raison, le doibt par nature occire sus l'instant et n'en sera par justice apprehendé.'

The connexion between reason, nature, justice is crucial and seems to point genuinely enough to Rabelais's own conception of the law. The successive antitheses are illuminating; 'loy sacre' is law based on divine authority, either the Decalogue or New Testament, 'loy prophane et barbare' is purely human law. This again has successive stages, *jus naturale* or *aequité naturelle*, *jus gentium* or *droict des gens*, and finally the codified law of the Roman Empire, *jus civile* or *loy imperiale*. The choice of terms is precise— *aequité*, *droit*, *loy*—and explains exactly whence Rabelais derived the authority of formal laws. As for the moral basis of *jus naturale* and *jus gentium*, the triple repetition of *nature—raison* provides the answer. The claims of nature and reason are paramount and laws must conform, if justice is to be done. The original tripartite division of law belongs to Justinian's *Digest*, where it was attributed to Ulpian,[1] and was classic throughout the Middle Ages.

Rabelais's emphasis on nature and reason in determining the course of justice represents no departure from long-established teaching. It had been held throughout the Middle Ages that justice and the rule of reason went together, and that human laws accord with the rule of reason to the extent that they derive from the natural law. Thus any human enactment which runs counter to the natural law ceases to be legal, and indeed becomes a corruption of law. Rabelais's objections to the Church's marriage laws, or rather to the way in which unscrupulous people kept within the letter while flagrantly violating the spirit, is in line with all responsible Scholastic teaching. The friars, some of whom had a particularly bad reputation for performing clandestine marriages, were also stern in denouncing the evil from the pulpit. Thus Maillard exclaims: 'Estis hic . . . domini ecclesiastici . . . qui ducitis mulieres in matrimonio de nocte sine sollenitate ecclesiae?'[2] and he is not the only one.

There is no doubt that the evil was widespread, but it is also true that parental pressure could produce a no less pernicious evil; parents could, and did, prevent their children both from marrying and entering religion, or, just as frequently, compel them to do so against their will (cf. the 'tropditeulx' of the *Cinquiesme Livre*). All that canon law could do was to lay down the right of free persons to decide their own future independently of their parents, and leave it to the conscience and good sense of all concerned to avoid abuses. The burden of Rabelais's argument here is that an

---

[1] See A. d'Entrèves, *Natural Law*, especially p. 42, for some Scholastic opinions on these points.

[2] 'Are you here you ecclesiastics . . . who lead women into marriage at night without the solemnities of the Church?' (Q/191 v.)

unjust law is no law, a legal system which coerces without rendering justice is not lawful. On this basis his criticism of both civil and canon law is easily explained. It is interesting that despite the great stress laid on God's will throughout the work, Gargantua does not here appeal to God's inscrutable justice, but to man's twin guides, nature and reason. Man has the ability, and thus the responsibility, to see that justice is done.

Built upon this traditional theory of law is Rabelais's view of government. The ideal rulers are the giants and their conduct of affairs can be taken as representing Rabelais's opinions on the subject. Particularly in the later books an attempt to justify French policy seems to lie behind much of the fiction, and it is certain that Rabelais's experiences in Piedmont with Guillaume du Bellay profoundly influenced his political thinking.

Rabelais recognizes man's duty to the body politic in Pantagruel's exposition of 'marié et non marié'. As a social animal, man must not (TL/xxxv, 478) 'laisser les offices qu'il doibt naturellement à sa patrie, à la republique, à ses amys . . . pour continuellement à sa femme complaire.'[1] These social duties come second only to the love of God, and the word 'naturellement' is thus significant. Similarly, Pantagruel's subjects (TL/i, 352) 'plus toust defauldroient de vie corporelle que de ceste première et unicque subjection *naturellement* deue à leur prince.' The same appeal to nature recalls Gargantua's speech cited above and Rabelais's solid belief in natural law in the traditional Christian sense. The loyalty of the giants' subjects in all the books sometimes parallels expressions of loyalty to the King of France, for instance Frère Jan's contempt for the 'fuyarts de Pavie' and Basché's preference (QL/xiii, 600) 'endurer en guerre cent coups de masse sus le heaulme au service de nostre tant bon roy qu'estre une foys cité par ces mastins Chiquanous', nor is the parallel an accident. For their part, the kings must earn loyalty and Rabelais's picture of the giants' rule is indeed attractive. The rustic patriarchal government of Grandgousier comes near enough the ideal of a small feudal lord, but the scale of action immediately expands in the *Tiers Livre* so that questions of provincial, not merely local, administration are at issue. The ideal remains above all one of personal rule. There is a glimpse of Gargantua coming out of his council and holding (TL/xlviii, 516) 'deux gros pacquets de

[1] Cf. Cicero, *De Officiis*, cap. vii.

requestes respondues et memoires de respondre.' The mention of
a council comes again when Pantagruel has to decide what action
to take against the Andouilles (*QL*/xxxvi, 660): 'Pantagruel
assembla son conseil pour sommairement leurs advis entendre'
and when he has given his opinion: 'la resolution du conseil feut
qu'en tout evenement ilz se tiendroient sus leurs gardes.' Monarchs, and as such solely responsible for their actions, the giants
do not act according to whim or as dictators, though nothing
remotely approaching democratic government was ever in
Rabelais's mind. They are not like the (*Garg.*/ix, 53) 'tyrans qui
voulent leur arbitre tenir lieu de raison.' Such tyrants as Nero,
Tiberius and Herod fill Pantagruel (*QL*/xxvi, 635) (and Rabelais)
with horror; force unsupported by right is a travesty of sovereign-
ty for him. Once more the theme of personal responsibility pre-
dominates in this view of kingship, once again reason is the
mainspring of men's behaviour, not will alone.

A detail of some interest is the relationship between ruler and
legislature as illustrated by Pantagruel's conduct on certain
occasions.[1] When he is consulted in the case of Baisecul v.
Humesvesne it is as a private person, who has just won a considerable reputation for learning, and his attitude to the court is
accordingly very different from that of the *Tiers Livre* when he
appears before the Parlement of Myrelingues. Invited by the
President of the Court to listen to the hearing of Bridoye's
defence, Pantagruel remains silent throughout, and when Trinquamelle invites his opinion he makes no attempt to impose his rank.
The context speaks of the Parlement as being 'souverain' and
there is no reason to suppose that the marquisate of Myrelingues
was a fief of Gargantua, though close contact between the two is
evidently of longstanding. However, Pantagruel is a superior
ruler and could obviously have demanded the fulfilment of his
wishes with the threat of force, or even as due to him for past
services rendered. In fact, he acts with remarkable modesty,
protesting that he has no judicial authority and submitting not a
judgement but a plea on Bridoye's behalf. Having lodged his
plea, he withdraws respectfully to join his companions, who have
been left outside, and goes home.

[1] Marichal, 'Rabelais et la réforme de la Justice', in *BHR* 1952, p. 185, for a most
valuable note on the changes between the editions of 1548 and 1552 of the *Quart
Livre*, which have the effect of putting Pantagruel 'au-dessus de l'humanité courante'.

A curious incident is that of the Chiquanous. Pantagruel has already expressed his disapproval of Panurge's story of Basché, in which the servants of the law are roughly handled. When the travellers land and treat the Chiquanous to a drubbing, it is a mild surprise to read (*QL*/xvi, 608): 'Pantagruel estoit resté en sa nauf et jà faisoit sonner la retraicte.' The sequel of this episode is that of the Chats Fourrez in the *Cinquiesme Livre*, more probably by Rabelais himself than any other part of that book, and it is noteworthy that Pantagruel once again takes no part in the conflict with the law. In these two cases there is no question of respecting the law even when unjust, let alone condoning the injustice; Pantagruel simply avoids a clash. These incidents, after all, do not take place in his own kingdom, and as a legislator, or at least a future legislator, he is in a particularly vulnerable position should he interfere with the laws of others, however iniquitous. If strictly speaking Pantagruel is above the law, *solutus legibus*, he has too much sense of responsibility to go openly against it. This seems to be the lesson of these episodes and it certainly enhances the dignity of kingship as Rabelais portrays it.

Finally in the sphere of politics comes the question of international relations. Here patriotism and support for French as against Imperial policy are ruling factors, but that does not alter the fact that the same moral arguments were used by both sides to prove the rightness of their cause; it is the nature of these arguments which concerns us here. The tone of the first two books is unmistakably that of humanists like Erasmus who utterly condemned war as inimical to culture and for whom pacifism is stronger than patriotism. Rabelais, always a good Frenchman, never took quite the same detached attitude as Erasmus, who owned loyalty to no country, least of all to his native Holland, and the fervour of the Prologue to the *Tiers Livre* is already foreshadowed in one or two of the passages in the early books, less high-flown as they are. It is hardly necessary to say that aggression is condemned in the strongest terms, as it has always been throughout the centuries, not least by the aggressors themselves. The development of the Picrocholine war shows that this was no mere lip-service in Rabelais's case. When Picrochole undertakes his first punitive expedition, actually unjustified but motivated by the injury suffered deservedly by his people, Grandgousier does not at once take up arms even in self-defence. First he sends

Gallet to remonstrate with Picrochole in the name of reason, then although (*Garg.*/xxxii, 117) 'sembla à tout son conseil que en toute force il se doibvoit defendre', he sends substantial reparations in cakes and cash to Marquet, and only when all these efforts have failed, does he resign himself to a defensive war.

At the end of the war, with victory achieved, Gargantua delivers a harangue to the defeated enemy in which he not only reiterates the humanitarian sentiments expressed by Gallet earlier, but puts them into practice. We have already seen Grandgousier send Toucquedillon back from captivity with a message for his king (XLVI, 155):

Le temps n'est plus d'ainsi conquester les royaulmes avec dommaige de son prochain frère christian. Ceste imitation des anciens Hercules, Alexandres, Hannibals, Scipions, Cesars et aultres telz est contraire à la profession de l'Evangile par laquelle nous est commandé guarder, sauver, regir et administrer chascun ses pays et terres, non hostilement envahir les aultres.

Such arguments based on Scripture were used by Joan of Arc, and similar motives inspired the preachers of the Crusades, whose task was as much to stop the leaders of Christendom from fighting each other as to range them against the infidel. When at the conclusion of hostilities the enemy is treated with exceptional magnanimity, only a handful of culprits being punished at all, Rabelais ensures that the lesson shall not be lost by referring directly to: 'les aultres roys et empereurs, voyre qui se font nommer catholiques'. By a curious irony, it was Charles V who undertook the abortive Crusade to North Africa, while Francis I was earning his title 'chrétien' in negotiations with the Sultan, but we are here concerned with Rabelais's theory, not with historical fact.

Closely bound up with this attitude to aggressive war is another commonplace of international propaganda in all ages—the sanctity of alliances, which all states admit and which the victims of aggression are inevitably accused of violating. The greater part of Gallet's harangue to Picrochole is on this theme, and one of the main grievances of Grandgousier is that a former ally should have attacked him without warning. The prompt and effective support of all his other allies and vassals gives a faithful picture of the old feudal idea in operation and contrasts with the faithlessness of

Picrochole. Contracts and alliances are not merely a legal device but morally binding, and for the Christian, as for the ancient Roman, even sacred.

The apparent change in the *Tiers Livre* is striking in itself but not genuinely contradictory. Once the giants in the first two books have embarked upon their defensive wars, Rabelais describes the military operations with enthusiasm. It is true that Gargantua's letter to his son denounces the invention of artillery as inspired by the devil, but his own exploits make use of all the ruses and stratagems of war. The Prologue of the *Tiers Livre* shows the author fired with admiration for things military, and reflects his feelings when the brothers du Bellay were busy preparing the defences of Paris and Turin. Even this praise of war is preceded by carefully chosen phrases (345): 'part à la fortification de sa patrie, et la defendre, part au repoulsement des ennemis, et les offendre.' Only a defensive war can be just and the joys of conquest for its own sake play not even a fictional role in Rabelais's work. Imperialism (in more senses than one) was an idea he utterly rejected.

The first chapter of the *Tiers Livre*, which continues the narrative of *Pantagruel* and belongs to the original scheme of the book, brings out the continuing moral bias of Rabelais's political views. Just like Gargantua's harangue to the vanquished, this chapter insists on the need for humane treatment of conquered peoples as against the ruthless repression (I, 354) 'de certains esprits tyranniques à leur dam et deshonneur.' The long series of classical references which follow all emphasize the duty of a king to treat his new subjects with justice, magnanimity and peace. 'Et plus en heur ne peult le conquerant regner, soit roy, soit prince ou philosophe, que faisant Justice à Vertus succeder. Sa vertu est apparue en la victoire et conqueste, sa justice apparoistra en ce que par la volunté et bonne affection du peuple donnera loix, publiera edictz, establira religions, fera droict à un chascun.' The conduct of Langey in Piedmont, not the views of Plutarch or Virgil, is the model for the whole chapter, but if Rabelais wanted theory to support his practice, he had no need to go back to the classics—the Schoolmen had taught no other lesson.

The last example in the work is the Andouilles episode in the *Quart Livre*, which shows that Rabelais's views on international relations had remained constant through twenty years, despite his

wide experience of practical diplomacy in the meantime. When
Pantagruel first hears of the conflict between the Andouilles and
Quaresmeprenant he at once offers to mediate (xxxv, 657): 'si
voyez que par quelque honeste moyen puissons fin à ceste guerre
mettre et ensemble les reconcilier, donnez m'en advis. Je m'y
emploiray de bien bon cœur et n'y espargneray du mien pour
contemperer et amodier les conditions controverses entre les
deux parties.' He learns, however, that an abortive attempt at
mediation has already been made by Xenomanes. Later, when
every indication warns them that the Andouilles are likely to take
hostile action, Pantagruel gives his orders to the company
(xxxvii, 664): 'leur feist une briefve remonstrance à ce qu'ilz
eussent à soy montrer vertueux au combat, si par cas estoient
constraincts (car encores ne povoit-il croire que les Andouilles
feussent si traistresses) avecques defense de commencer le hourt.'
The parenthesis shows Pantagruel faithful to his philosophy of
never thinking evil of anyone and the final clause insists again
that only a defensive battle is legitimate. The theme of alliances
also recurs and when the two armies are face to face, Pantagruel
sends Gymnaste to ask why (xli, 672): 'elles vouloient sans
defiance guerroyer contre leurs amys antiques.' and he cries out:
'Tous tenons de Mardigras vostre antique confaederé'. Finally the
situation described in Gargantua's harangue about the Canarriens
is repeated at the end of this war, when the queen of the Andouilles
offers homage on feudal terms, together with substantial tribute.
(xlii, 676) 'Pantagruel remercia gratieusement la royne, pardonna
toute l'offense, refusa l'offre qu'elle avoit faict et luy donna un
beau petit cousteau parguoys.' Even in this episode of high
fantasy, the serious theories are not forgotten and Rabelais is
consistent to the last.

It should be remembered that though Rabelais acts often enough
as apologist for royal policy, this did not by any means conform
with the standards represented in the book, nor could he seriously
have believed that it did. The appalling massacre of the Vaudois
(despite du Bellay's repeated and urgent pleas), the extremely
cavalier treatment of du Bellay himself by an ungrateful sovereign,
the constant attempts by French diplomats (including the du
Bellay brothers) to foment discontent and rebellion among the
princes of Germany, both Catholic and Protestant, against
Charles V, whom none could deny to be their rightful lord, are

only three examples of behaviour perfectly familiar to Rabelais and diametrically opposed to the principles of his fictional hero. The apologetic purpose of the book is important, but not to the exclusion of independent views on political morality. The very phrase 'political morality' prejudges the issue, but not without cause. In private ethics Rabelais had definite and constant theories concerning personal responsibility, tolerance of ignorance but not of evil, and of well-doing as well as right-thinking; in the wider sphere of public ethics these ideas are applied with equal force, and the conception of natural law outlined in Gargantua's speech in the *Tiers Livre* forms the essential link between the two spheres. This conception (incidentally according very well with the Platonism of the *Tiers Livre*) of an absolute standard of justice by which actual laws can be judged by the light of reason, at once puts all human relationships, private, public, national in the same perspective and enables us to speak with propriety of political morality. The appeal to nature and reason in Gargantua's speech was probably intended to set off the virtues of Roman civil law, based on these ideas, against the iniquities of later canon law, but the earlier appeal to the gospels (in Grandgousier's charge to Toucquedillon) shows that, unless a hidden change took place in Rabelais's attitude between these dates, the synthesis of sacred and profane authority underlying his legal concepts was essentially that of Scholastic theory (if not practice). It is natural to find the king bound on his higher plane by exactly the same moral code as the subject, with heightened powers heightening responsibility. Reason for the individual, council for the king, must be the guiding principles of all actions; both must assume the best of others until proved wrong; private falsehood or political duplicity are to be shunned above all else. In international relations still the same rules obtain; a treaty of alliance is as sacred as the individual's word of honour; defence is the only legitimate motive for hostile action; the king and his advisers as the leaders of the people are responsible for the conduct of affairs and they alone must pay the penalty for wrongdoing, not their innocent and misled subjects.

None of these ideas is peculiar to Rabelais, nor even the relative emphasis laid upon them, but they are on the whole old-fashioned for an age when classical antiquity was treated as modern. One marked feature of the whole system is that there is no trace of the exaggerated voluntarism of the Nominalists with whose doctrines

Rabelais would have been acquainted in his Franciscan days. Equally alien to his thought is the idea of expediency preached by Machiavelli. Granted that the evidence is regrettably sketchy, every sign points to an idealized form of feudal monarchy as being very much what Rabelais had in mind. If for no other reason, the directly personal responsibility of the ruler favoured such a conception. The moral, religious and social background of feudalism comes, indeed, nearer to the reality of Rabelais's fictional states than the Renaissance background of France, let alone Italy, or even the classical period in which he sometimes seems to see the Golden Age.

19 : MAN AS PORTRAYED IN THE CHARACTERS

WHILE all the theories and opinions expressed about man in general must carry great weight when it comes to assessing Rabelais's philosophy, a work of fiction such as his offers other, and perhaps more compelling, criteria. The actual characters of the work, with their strength and weakness, regarded above all through the eye of the ordinary reader and not of the moralist, are what must in the last analysis constitute one's impression of Rabelais's humanism. The comic style of the work, as well as the epic strain, inevitably distort the types of personality for literary effect, but without a norm no comedy is effective and it is seldom hard to decide what Rabelais distorts and what he upholds.

Granted that a major change of emphasis occurs after the first two books, when the gigantic theme is virtually abandoned, Pantagruel, Gargantua and Grandgousier stand in a privileged position in every sense. Not only are they beyond all criticism, but their example is meant to be followed. Near them is another group of characters, some fairly prominent, some merely episodic, who are also not criticized, but who for one reason or another are not held up as examples for all to follow. While Langey almost certainly belongs with the giants, the second group includes such characters as Epistemon, Hippothaddée, Rondibilis, Ulrich Gallet, Trinquamelle, Panigon, the Macrobe and others. To all of these respect is shown, and from their individual characteristics certain positive conclusions can be drawn. Another group consists of those who though '*sympathiques*' on balance are shown with obvious weaknesses, and who are certainly not meant to be imitated except in their particular redeeming virtue. Ramina-grobis, Bridoye, Basché and Frère Jan are among this company, and all in all it is probably with them that Panurge can be counted, though this is open to some doubt. If these characters are less virtuous than those mentioned before, they certainly gain in humanity and it may be that they are the most significant of all for a true appreciation of Rabelais's views. Last and most numerous come all the characters, major and minor, who represent Rabelais's personal parade of human folly. Like the crowded canvas of Erasmus, Rabelais's work teems with figures of every kind: Maître Tubal Holoferne, Janotus, Thaumaste, the Limousin, Trouillogan, Her Trippa, Homenaz, the Sibyl of Panzoult, Picrochole, the pilgrims, jostle one another in their antics, intellectual, political, religious, magical and the rest, which all go to show the follies of which man is so readily capable. Even with these, condemnation is not complete; ignorance is their greatest sin. For a perfectly symmetrical picture there should be some examples of absolute evil to balance the ideals of perfection, but, in fact, with the sole and uncertainly reliable exception of the *Isle Sonnante*, such characters do not appear in Rabelais's book. There are many references to evildoers—hints at the iniquity of Charles V, sinister gibes at the Sorbonne, memories of ancient tyrants, like Nero and Tiberius—but unless one includes such fantastic creatures as Loup-Garou, none takes shape as a living character. There is no individual villain, even if there is much dark villainy behind the scenes, inspired indeed by Satan, of whom we hear quite a lot, though he never appears in person. Naturally such categories as these are wholly artificial, and correspond only roughly with Rabelais's method of composition, but they help one to assess the relative importance of various qualities, good or bad, of human nature as portrayed in the work. Such a division is perhaps most justifiable on the grounds that it shades out the differences between Pantagruel (and his forbears) and the others, which is at first sight apt to be confusing.

In the case of the giants, and to some extent other characters as well, a distinction must be made between the first two books and the others. In the first books everything about Grandgousier, Gargantua and Pantagruel is gigantic; their physical and intellectual stature, but no less their moral qualities. The traditional model from which Rabelais was working inevitably casts an air of unreality over these fairytale figures, who cover an army with their tongues, pick up bells like rattles and swallow men with a gulp, but to this traditional source Rabelais adds so much realistic detail from life at La Devinière, that the giants live equally on the human and superhuman planes. With allowances for the difference in their age and situations, the three have much in common. Grandgousier plays very much the same role of aged ruler as his son adopts in the *Tiers Livre*; the two heirs apparent differ rather in their upbringing than their characters. The first and most obvious feature of these three models is that they belong to an essentially aristocratic conception of society. On closer inspection, it seems that a definitely feudal idea underlies these portraits, and not a monarchic conception of central government. The political references to France and the Empire are unambiguous, and in a general sense François I and Charles V can be identified with the giants and their respective enemies. At the same time, *Gargantua* in particular shows very clearly that the theory is national while the practice is local. Grandgousier recognizes his feudal obligations to his people (*Garg.*/xxviii, 111): 'Il faut que je preigne la lance et la masse pour secourir et guarantir mes pauvres subjectz. La raison le veult ainsi, car de leur labeur je suis entretenu et de leur sueur je suis nourry, moy, mes enfanz et ma famille.' Pantagruel calls on God's help before the battle with Loup-Garou and promises (*Pant.*/xxix, 313): 'par toutes contrées, tant de ce pays de Utopie que d'ailleurs, où je auray puissance et auctorité, je feray prescher ton sainct Evangile purement' but his grandfather recalls how he dealt with the 'cafard' at Cinais (*Garg.*/xlv, 153): 'depuis ce temps caphart quiconques n'est auzé entrer en mes terres, et m'esbahys si vostre roy les laisse prescher par son royaulme telz scandales.' The factual picture before Rabelais is of the Chinonais, the theory applies to France, to Christendom, but it is no more than theory. That being so, one should expect the archaism which is always typical of provincial or country ways, and in this light the feudalism of the giants seems perfectly natural. Though aristocratic, the world of the giants is patriarchal rather than courtly. Placed above their subjects by birth, the giants confirm their superiority by merit, but the relations between them and their subjects are inspired by the friendly spirit of country life, not the refined formality of the court. Mutual obligations govern their existence in the normal way of feudalism.

At home all three giants are shown as simple and unaffected; in fact as country gentlemen, not as great kings. Their rule is firm but tolerant. The affair of the *fouaces* is typical; Grandgousier's people are defended with all their king's might, but not until full restitution has been offered and refused. Prisoners are treated generously, but the war criminals are awarded due punishment.

In battle the giants are '*preux*', in Paris Gargantua and his son show themselves '*doctes*', everywhere they are devout. Courtliness is not much in evidence, though Pantagruel respects the conventions sufficiently to have serious qualms at leaving his lady in Paris without a farewell. Bons viveurs as they all are, the three giants are free from the vices of the flesh (at least, after Gargantua's change of régime). They command respect in every way and show themselves models of chivalrous virtues which are more human than gigantic.

There is no difficulty in matching their more sensational exploits with those of their legendary models, and this does not really tell us very much about Rabelais's humanism. A more useful comparison is between Rabelais's heroes in their human role and some of the historical figures of previous ages. The qualities which appealed to men of the Middle Ages varied according to individual taste and according to individual centuries, but as a generalization the 'medieval hero' is not so meaningless as most, and can at least be effectively contrasted with 'Renaissance man' as usually understood. There are not a few portraits of single heroes in medieval literature; excluding straightforward hagiography, there is Jocelyn's Abbot Samson, Gerald of Wales by himself, the great warriors and princes, like Gaston Phebus and Boucicault, but none is more specifically and exactly medieval than Joinville's St. Louis. In every material respect the comparison with the giants is admissible, and this single example may be more convincing than a multiplicity of others.

The famous picture of St. Louis dispensing justice beneath the oak at Vincennes (so famous that it finds a place even in the small *Larousse*'s brief account) is exactly that of Grandgousier or Gargantua in their own direct, paternal rule. It is historically true that St. Louis greatly strengthened the administrative organs of government and obviously could not, if he had wanted to, fail to delegate powers to others, but the feature on which Joinville insists and which caught the medieval imagination is that of direct rule. With this goes direct responsibility, and if Rabelais concentrated on this in his portrait of kingship we must not assume that he ignored the need for administrative bodies under the king. In the administrative field, again, Joinville lays much stress on the concern of St. Louis for his subjects' welfare, and his supervision of the royal officers. He seems indeed to have overstated the case with regard to Estienne Boileau in his attempt to demon-strate the king's enlightened government. In St. Louis's dealings with foreign powers, the very generous treaty with England, which aroused much chauvinist opposition in France, is given by Joinville as an example of the king's wisdom. These details may be fairly compared with the giants' treatment of their own conquered enemies (even if allusions to Charles V are also in-tended) and to the first chapter of the *Tiers Livre*. The martial exploits of St. Louis during the Crusade are, as one might expect, entirely worthy of him, combining skill with valour, and are perhaps the least distinctive feature of the account. The giants, St. Louis and the epic heroes all inevitably have similar exper-iences to which they react in similar ways.

In the religious sphere the comparison is particularly interesting. Joinville wrote after the canonization of St. Louis, and not un-naturally selected incidents to illustrate the nature of that sanctity. The king's interest in religion was fostered from childhood by his mother, he was probably a Tertiary of that same order to which Rabelais had belonged and the intensity of his religious life was unusual even for an age when attendance at religious service was a necessary and frequent part of every aristocrat's routine.[1] His religious life was regarded by his contemporaries as more ideal than normal, and it is therefore instructive to compare the revised system of education presented to Gargantua, in which devotional exercises play a part certainly more prominent than was usual in Rabelais's day. Granted that St. Louis follows the orthodox routine of Canonical Hours, Masses and so on, while Gargantua's prayers are almost aggressively Evangelical, they have in common that they practise an exceptional degree of genuine piety in the midst of all their manifold activities.

One particular incident affords a striking parallel between the heroes of Joinville and Rabelais. On the way from the Holy Land, the Crusaders' fleet ran upon rocks, from which they hardly dared hope for salvation. Joinville describes[2] how he found the king, deep in prayer before the reserved Sacrament, preparing for death. The king makes no attempt to direct operations, and indeed says that in such matters the experts are to be followed, but he shows

---

[1] See Maillard's reference to St. Louis's self-discipline quoted p. 31.
[2] Joinville, *Histoire de Saint-Louis*, p. 310, in *Historiens et Chroniqueurs du Moyen Âge*, Bibl. de la Pléiade.

no trace of the panic which medieval seafarers so often exhibited. Pantagruel is no sailor-king either, and admits after the storm that he thinks it folly to navigate unnecessarily, but like St. Louis he sets an example of piety at the approach of danger, he devoutly commends his soul to God and shows no trace of fear. Pantagruel, however, improves on St. Louis's conduct and by his personal exertions saves the company from shipwreck. Joinville, himself no lover of the sea, is content to show his hero brave and devout in the face of danger, and it is significant that Rabelais insists equally upon Pantagruel's piety and on his energetic actions.

St. Louis's moral attitude towards the Crusaders is another point which Joinville adduces as proof of the king's exceptional qualities. In an army of notorious immorality it was hard to impose absolute moral standards, and yet we find St. Louis delivering summary judgement against those convicted of theft, fornication and so on. In the same way, the disreputable practices of Panurge and Frère Jan would probably bring a smile rather than censure from most sixteenth-century readers, but we find Rabelais gratuitously showing Pantagruel reprove his companions for their excessive faults. St. Louis's campaign against gambling and blasphemy is well known. Apart from Joinville's account, Gringoire, a generation before Rabelais, devotes one whole episode to these details in his dramatized *Vie St. Louis*.[1] Precisely the same repugnance is shown by Pantagruel to these activities. One of the incidents which Joinville repeats several times to illustrate the king's sanctity is that in which he refuses to countenance financial dishonesty even with the Saracens; the same scrupulous attitude to money is shown by Pantagruel in his condemnation of Panurge's praise of debt.

The various foundations of St. Louis, the religious houses, the charitable institutions, most of all the Sorbonne, at first sight contrast directly with Rabelais's known antipathy to religious orders and to the Sorbonne, and yet in the thirteenth century the Mendicants were the vanguard of a learning as solid and triumphantly new as any that came with the Renaissance. The infant Sorbonne was for St. Louis what Gargantua's printing press was for him, the friars for him *were* 'les bons prescheurs evangeliques' through whom religion might be rejuvenated throughout his realm. The deformation of thirteenth-century institutions by

---

[1] Gringoire, *Vie Saint-Louis*, lib. VII.

succeeding centuries obscures the point that Joinville considered so important; that the king fostered with every means the cause of religion and godly learning, and regarded the religious and intellectual progress of his subjects as his own responsibility. Admittedly all enlightened monarchs in all ages have done the same, but the fundamental similarity between St. Louis and the kings of Rabelais remains closer than, for instance, that between François I and his saintly ancestor.

This comparison with St. Louis has been studied at some length because Joinville's biography is certainly the best example of the medieval ideal of a king, saint and warrior, seen from a historical, not a literary or imaginative point of view. Charlemagne enjoyed a similar reputation, indeed shows many points of similarity with St. Louis, and other medieval figures may embody the qualities extolled by Joinville, but none is so essentially a national figure as St. Louis. It is not suggested that Rabelais modelled his heroes on Joinville, though he cannot have failed to know the salient features of the king's life as repeated in numerous chronicles; all that we have tried to show is that a man writing around 1300 selected basically the same qualities to illustrate the exceptional character of his hero as Rabelais, composing an imaginative work more than two centuries later. Naturally many of the same qualities are admired in every age, but even a detailed comparison between St. Louis and Pantagruel (and to a lesser extent the other giants) shows a remarkable similarity, not easily paralleled elsewhere.

This point is emphasized by considering the brief references to Langey in Rabelais's work. Here we have to deal with an historical figure, acknowledged by friend and foe alike as possessed of exceptional qualities. Rabelais's mention of the 'chevalier preux et docte' and the 'âme heroique', with the little we know of his relations with Langey, suggest that his respect and admiration were of the same kind as Sleidan's,[1] for whom Langey was above all criticism. There is no doubt that experiences with Langey at Turin are the direct inspiration for the opening chapter of the *Tiers Livre*, and other episodes (the proposed mediation between the Andouilles and Quaresmeprenant, Papefigue and others) may also be distantly based on actual fact in which Langey was involved. The outstanding position of Langey in the long discussion on

---

[1] Sleidan, *Commentaires*, lib. xv, p. 552 (French trans. 1555).

immortality is the surest guide to Rabelais's feelings on the subject, but despite all this one cannot put Langey in the same class as Pantagruel—'l'idée et exemplaire de toute joyeuse perfection'—even though no other character comes so near. The reason is immediately apparent: Langey is the type of perfect gentleman, noble warrior and astute diplomat, but he fails to reach the highest place for the very good reason that he was always subject to orders from above, however great his personal responsibility. From that fact it is only a step to see why Rabelais could not take his portrait of perfection from real life around him: he must have known as well as we do that in the matter of virtue Langey far outshone his king, and since Charles V, the only other possible candidate, was the great enemy, his choice had to range elsewhere. Only a king, with the mystical prestige inherent in that office, could serve as the ideal, but one need not hesitate to put Langey in the highest place that his birth will allow. Tolerance and wisdom in government, courage and skill in warfare, patience and honesty in diplomacy, generosity and breadth of culture, and not least, a moral rectitude which led him to ruin himself by paying for corn to be imported into Piedmont in time of famine, and to intercede at some risk to himself in favour of the unfortunate Vaudois, such qualities are typical of the best men of the Renaissance, but more still of the chivalrous concepts of the Middle Ages. Guillaume, more than his brother Jean, follows a traditional pattern honoured already for centuries.

There may be some legitimate hesitation as to Langey's exact place in this scheme of things, but there need be none regarding the next group of characters. Kings come first, to be models for all their subjects, and a viceroy quite properly comes next, but after that there is no question of setting up models above other men. All the other characters in the work show man as he is, not as he ought to be. Some of these are too episodic to be of any great value to the present study. 'le bon roy ... sainct Panigon' (QL/x) is mentioned as it seems quite gratuitously, since he does virtually nothing but offer hospitality, and unless contemporaries could have recognized more easily than we a definite allusion, there seems little point in selecting such a lay figure for particular praise. The Macrobe is similarly treated with respect by Pantagruel, apparently because of his venerable age and bearing, but also perhaps to lend force to the arguments put into his mouth by Plutarch. Trinquamelle has been plausibly identified with Tiraqueau, but, as far as the book goes, stands only for the good and conscientious judge. Gallet is another personage drawn, it seems, from life and typifies the faithful counsellor and representative of his king. If these rather shadowy characters have any significance, it is above all to remind us that in Rabelais's work there is a middle way between idealism and satire.

Three members of this group with a recognizable individuality of their own are Epistemon, Hippothaddée and Rondibilis. These last two appear together on the same occasion and play comparable roles. One is 'bon theologien', the other a good doctor; they each give their advice and then go off, and but for Pantagruel's brief introductory remarks about one being married and the other celibate, we know nothing more about them. Once more fiction has been linked by critics with fact, but this does not help very much. The point is that neither of the two is criticized, except by Panurge, and that they may therefore be taken to exemplify qualities which Rabelais did not wish to ridicule in his book (or in fact either, probably). The theologian is old and above this world, his text is Pauline, he lives his religion. His acquiescence in God's will and his recognition that men and women have responsibilities no less than rights are substantially the views of Pantagruel. The doctor seems to speak more clearly with the voice of Rabelais himself. His learning is Classical, his religion is health, and nothing but professional competence matters in assessing his advice. His commendation of the 'preudes femmes' is one of the few non-technical sentences in his speeches; for the rest he shows a professional detachment towards human problems, until the moment when he pockets Panurge's fee. Scientific learning (that is, classical erudition) seems to be the chief justification for the respect shown to Rondibilis.

Epistemon is the most complete of the three, and in many ways a rather puzzling character. When he makes his first appearance, at Pantagruel's meeting with Panurge, Epistemon is no more than one of a company whose Greek names explain their characters (Eusthenes, Carpalim, Rhizotome) and at first he hardly distinguishes himself as a personality apart from the others, mere symbols. On appropriate occasions he lives up to his name 'knowing, skilful', and supplies erudite information, helps with the trap by which the enemy horsemen are destroyed, translates the Hebrew inscription on the mysterious ring sent to Pantagruel by his lady and so on. A passing remark during a discussion on the treatment to be accorded to the enemy's women shows him not averse to carnal pleasures, but the only incident in which he plays a major part is his miraculous healing after decapitation and his subsequent account of Hades. Even in this he is no more than the mouthpiece for Rabelais's own satire. Except for this last incident, it needs very careful reflection to produce any picture at all of Epistemon as portrayed in *Pantagruel*.

With the later books all this changes completely. With Frère Jan and Pantagruel himself, Epistemon is the only one of the original company to be asked for advice in Panurge's predicament. While the others fade away into utter insignificance, Epistemon takes shape as a real person increasingly interesting as the book progresses. His original role of the erudite scholar is maintained; his reappearance in the *Tiers Livre* is with a quotation from the Bible, and his comment is seldom lacking in any erudite discussion. To this he adds a notably critical attitude towards some of the episodes which the others accept more readily. He is much more incredulous (or intolerant) than Pantagruel; he doubts the wisdom of going to the Sybil of Panzoult, despite Pantagruel's encouragement; chosen once more to accompany Panurge, this time with Frère Jan, to Raminagrobis, he ridicules Panurge's panic and denies that the old poet meant any discourtesy to the Friars; more to humour Panurge than anything else he suggests the visit to Her Trippa, but only after scornfully rejecting Panurge's own proposal to visit the (TL/xxiv, 437) 'Isles Ogygies'— 'c'est abus trop evident et fable trop fabuleux.' Asked for his personal advice, Epistemon mentions Platonic theories, but admits that he does not recommend Panurge to follow them as he does not understand them himself and 'il y a de l'abus beaucoup'. He is equally sceptical about oracles, and, rather unexpectedly amid a wealth of classical references, speaks of 'celluy roy servateur' at whose coming all oracles fell silent. This positive statement of Christianity comes as quite a contrast to what one can almost call the rationalism of his other remarks, all definitely classical in spirit.

He gives little more hint of his religious views until the *Quart Livre*, when after the storm he reminds Panurge of the Pauline exhortation to co-operate with God. He too, alone of the company, finds the rhapsodies of Homenaz on the Decretals so intolerable that he has to go out for relief, which suggests a more complex psychology than appears at first. His conduct during the actual storm is also apparently contradictory; he initiates the very academic discussion on wills at the height of the danger, but when the worst is over has a hand badly cut because he had held so vigorously on to a cable. Pedantic as he often is, he is a man of action when necessary. Though far less broad-minded than Pantagruel, he does not extend his scepticism to the truths of Christianity.

The later development of his character gives every sign of being connected in some way with an actual model, just as Pantagruel's own qualities recall Langey more than once, and additional significance is given to Epistemon's character by some apparently gratuitous historical details. Already in the *Tiers Livre* he declares himself the personal friend of Bridoye, in whose son, a student at Toulouse, he takes a special interest. It is he who goes to fetch Bridoye and discovers his misfortune, and after Pantagruel's intervention it is he who makes the longest comment. He defends Bridoye for his moral rectitude and criticizes the defects of the legal system. Again it is Epistemon who claims to have been at the comedy in which Rabelais himself acted at Montpellier; in the *Quart Livre* he describes his (and obviously Rabelais's) visit to Italy some twenty years before, with the incident of Frère Lardon from Amiens. Later he recalls a specific incident at Saintes with Briand Vallée, du Douhet, a friend of Rabelais who died in 1544. Most interesting is the choice of Epistemon to describe the last moments of Langey, at which, of course, Rabelais was also present. None of the others is so closely identified with events in which Rabelais himself took part, and though present evidence can prove nothing, it is worth considering whether Epistemon may in fact represent the author. It may be significant in this connexion that the incidents in which he plays a part, except for Langey's death, belong to the period Rabelais was in Languedoc, already in the distant past at the date of composition. Certainly the mixture of erudition and action, classical and Christian, with its strongly critical vein, is in line with all we know of Rabelais's character. Nothing in Epistemon's character is very obviously censured, though his erudition seems at times to be overstressed, and it is hard to decide how far Rabelais approves of his character (the more so if one considers the possibility of a self-portrait). One thing seems certain: Epistemon is no abstraction, like the giants, nor primarily representative of a class of men, like Hippothaddée or Rondibilis, but a real person. He seems to belong more essentially to the first generation of the Renaissance than any of the characters so far discussed, and any attempt to explain him in terms of traditional inspiration can only be misdirected.

With the group we have called '*sympathique*', the weaknesses and the virtues are less evenly balanced, indeed the weaknesses are often the cause of our sympathy with a particular character. The bluff feudal lord Basché is very likable, but the disapproval of his rough justice expressed by both Pantagruel and Epistemon is important. Basché is generous and friendly to his dependents, loyal to his king and on good terms with his chaplain, but jealous of his noble rights and implacable towards the perversion of law practised by the prior and his like. In the particular instance described by Panurge, our sympathies are on Basché's side, but his primitive ideas of how to administer justice do not in themselves command much support.

Raminagrobis is in some ways similar. Previous remarks suggest that his past may have been slightly disreputable, but his edifying death is the impression which remains with us. The scarcely veiled attack on the Mendicants (*pace* Epistemon) takes much of its force from the contrast between their material preoccupations and the old poet's spiritual fervour.

Bridoye, Epistemon's old friend, is a little pathetic in his dotage, but his good qualities as stated by Pantagruel and Epistemon certainly outweigh his curious judicial practises. In these three cases of minor figures, redeeming features are emphasized so that the general faults of the character are forgotten. It is more than a coincidence that all the three are men of an older generation, and that their virtues are like their weaknesses traditional and familiar, and this serves to emphasize that part of Rabelais's inspiration which has its roots in the past.

In Frère Jan this tendency can be seen most clearly. His vices are the traditional monastic ones, ignorance, lechery, gluttony, but his chief virtue is that which his companions declare distinguishes him from his religious brethren: he is active and energetic. Indeed, in the later books this is the only favourable side to his character to receive any notice. His conviviality, his lack of prejudice ('il n'est point bigot'), his nonchalant observance of religious duties, which are all the subjects of praise or jest in *Gargantua*, compare very unfavourably with the sober habits of his new master in the later books. More than once he is reproved for his faults, and if he continues to hold our sympathy it is because he errs through no malice, but through very human weaknesses, and above all because his courage and resource never fail him. If he has any true religious feeling it is hard to see an trace of it in Rabelais's portrait (except perhaps for the early reference to the iniquity of those who betrayed Our Lord). His language is as free and easy as that of many medieval men of religion, and if the subjects of his irreverence and blasphemy are more often than not inessentials of the faith, every indication is that religion is for him an atavistic paganism overlaid with the completely formal or non-sacred 'matière de breviaire'. Pantagruel is patient with him as a companion who can be relied upon for help and good fellowship at all times, but for his shortcomings in themselves no excuse is offered. As an antinomy of a monk, Frère Jan is no longer effective once he begins to incur criticism; if he is more likable than his brethren, with their alleged hypocrisy, their killjoy attitude, their social uselessness, it cannot fairly be claimed that he is in any sense better than they. As we have seen, deceit, including hypocrisy, is for Rabelais chief of all the deadly sins, and on that score alone, Frère Jan, honest in every respect, escapes the worst condemnation, but he no longer occupies the favoured place with Pantagruel which seemed to be his with Gargantua. Frère Jan seems to come as near the margin of what can be tolerated and what must be rejected as any of Rabelais's characters, and as an example of human weakness he is finally saved only by his positive virtues, energy and honesty, both essential to Rabelais's notion of a worthy character.

After Pantagruel himself no character receives such detailed attention as Panurge, who more than once steps into first place, and yet the mass of information about him does not permit of a finally satisfactory estimate of this complex being. The development of his character from the almost heroic role in *Pantagruel* to his melodramatic discomfiture at the end of the *Quart Livre* has been noted by most critics, and the reasons, literary and psychological, put forward to explain it are on the whole convincing.

The obvious pleasure of the author in recounting the shameful exploits of Panurge in the first book is more than compensated by the many rebukes levelled at his head in the later books. In fact the complete immunity from reprisal which Panurge's cynical independence ensures at first is removed from him early in the *Tiers Livre* when he gets the flea in his ear. Thereafter he is himself open to all the misfortunes of his own erstwhile victims, with the added penalty of an uneasy conscience and anticipation of punishment well deserved. Like Frère Jan, Panurge is prone to all fleshly vices, unlike the monk he cannot be excused on grounds of ignorance, he is so full of wiles and malice. If he has the slightest consideration for the feelings of others he shows no sign of it; he is neither honest nor courageous; he is lazy and superstitious. Where Frère Jan's gospel in time of danger is expressed in action, Panurge seeks refuge in meaningless external acts of piety, which he promptly repudiates when the danger is over.

All this is familiar to every reader of Rabelais, but from it must be drawn the conclusions which will decide our final attitude to Rabelais's humanism. No one can hesitate to accept the giants as ideals, representing virtues which Rabelais regarded as sovereign, and the other characters, with their appropriate qualities, seem to belong to a reasonably normal outlook on life based on observation. With the character of Panurge there can be so many alternatives; to some extent he is a foil for Pantagruel's virtues, for instance in the opening chapters of the *Tiers Livre*, but the progressively more retiring role of Pantagruel makes the need for such a foil less imperative; to some extent he is a rascal whose very shamelessness is almost endearing and whose exploits are in a long popular tradition, but this is obviously only part of the truth. The projected voyage to the oracle would have given many writers the chance of converting Panurge from his evil ways at last, but Rabelais has no such moral intention. Panurge is too bad to stand for the average sinner, yet not bad enough to be dismissed as a thoroughgoing villain incapable of redemption. He is in fact redeemed by Pantagruel's continued toleration of him, though one cannot say how effectively, as the story stops too soon. His exaggerated orthodoxy serves a certain satirical purpose, but his worthlessness is the measure of how deceptive such satire can be.

Panurge is simply not typical of any one class, he is neither Iago nor Eulenspiegel, neither finally humiliated nor triumphant. There is in his character much of Patelin, of Villon, of Thersites too, and he is certainly not on the side of progress, but it would be idle to deny a certain actuality in his personality which owes no more to the Middle Ages than to any other period. The crux of the problem is the absence of a final verdict on Panurge, even a hint of hesitation on Rabelais's part to deliver such a judgement. At one time or another nearly all the other characters pass a moral judgement on Panurge, who remains impenitent. Perhaps the most satisfactory conclusion at which one can arrive is that in a work of infinite shades and variations, Panurge offers a fairly constant standard of immorality against which others can be compared, and which none the less remains too undistinguished to merit the name or opprobrium of evil.[1]

The peculiarly enigmatic character of Panurge seems even more so when compared with the other characters who are cast in the role of butts for Rabelais's wit. The parade of folly is perennial; as is fitting, false learning and empty pedantry are well represented —Janotus, Tubal, the Limousin scholar, Her Trippa, Trouillogan; Thaumaste is a genuine and sincere scholar, but his credulity qualifies him for admission to these ranks; Homenaz is too genial in his pomposity (except for his brief outburst against rebels and heretics) to be called evil rather than foolish; Picrochole is the victim alike of his humours and his vanity, flattered by his advisers. None of these, not even Picrochole, is coldly malicious like Panurge, and yet it is undeniable that they occupy a position much less favourable than his. Rabelais seems to prefer a knave to a fool, at least in literature, or to be more precise, he finds that folly is more monotonous than knavery and soon tires of its individual representation. In his choice of victims Rabelais is naturally not without polemical intentions, so that the Sorbonne and the Ultramontanes inevitably bulk large in his catalogue, but the caricatures are again perennial: for every age, the previous generation has its quota of snuffling pedants. From the moral point of view it should perhaps be added that all these kinds of folly are—theoretically—amenable to education and are far from presenting a gloomy picture of the human race.

The absence of thoroughly evil characters has already been

---

[1] A careful but rather unconvincing study of Panurge's character is L. Schrader, *Panurge und Hermes*.

mentioned, and links up with what has just been said. It is true
that there are in literature, as in life, few unmitigated villains, but
in Rabelais there are virtually none. The tyrants of old, Nero and
Herod, the reactionary tyrants of his own day, the Sorbonne and
the Inquisition, are only mentioned, none appears in person—
until the *Cinquiesme Livre*. That is not to say that Rabelais was
unwilling to admit the presence of evil, nor restrained by his
theme from introducing it if he had wished, for it would have
given Pantagruel a good opportunity for a heroic and virtuous
triumph. There seems no immediately obvious explanation for
this particular fact, though literary rather than psychological
motives are probably at the root of it, but it has the effect of
making Panurge the most sinful character in the book. This, in
its turn, seems to support the common view that Rabelais's book
breathes a general optimism, very different from the obsession
of the Middle Ages (not to mention Luther) with the sinfulness
of man, but this is an illusion. Because evil is thrust into the
background it is not forgotten, nor is Panurge a pretty picture of
the humanistic man which some people would have us seek in
Rabelais. The backcloth is well filled moreover with evil designs;
the prohibitions on the gates of Thélème, most of the Prologues,
Gargantua's speech on clandestine marriages are a few examples
of this. Besides the great number of fools whose misdeeds can
eventually be corrected by good learning, there is in Rabelais's
book a hard core of evil, against which no remedy save that of
brute force is proposed. His book has after all no explicit moral
purpose, though it is full of moral implications.

Nothing has been said here of the various allegorical figures,
Quaresmeprenant, Gaster and the rest, who play so large a part
in the *Quart Livre*. They belong rather to the field of theoretical
ethics than to its practical illustration, and they represent individuals no more than the old virtues and vices of the morality
plays. Nor has any attempt been made to examine an exhaustive
list of the many characters who make a brief, though sometimes
significant, appearance. The score or so mentioned above are
typical of the broader picture.

Striking is the predominantly Christian (in a formal sense)
complexion of the scene. Some are shown as specifically Evangelical, some as specifically Scholastic, but nearly all form part
of a contemporary religious background. With hardly any excep-

tions the characters who are favourably mentioned give verbal evidence of piety (Rondibilis is the most notable exception) and the others mostly belong to a society of which the form, if not the spirit, is conventionally Christian. Not a few of the characters are deliberately archaic, whereas very few stand for anything which in the sixteenth century could reasonably be called modern. Neither in the extent of their wisdom nor their folly, their virtues or their vices do the characters as a body stand out at all sharply from the tradition of previous centuries. The giants stand out in every sense from all the others, but as exceptional men they seem to follow rather the example of St. Louis than that of Plutarch's heroes.

The general view of man is certainly not one of despair, but no more is it the unbounded optimism of the chapters on Pantagruelion or Thélème. The limitations of humanity are constantly stressed as a fact and sometimes as a reproach, and it cannot be said that the example of Pantagruel comes any nearer the attainment of ordinary men as the book progresses. By the side of the more ambitious humanist manifestos to be found in several parts of the book, one must set these facts as being equally relevant to the impression acquired by a sixteenth-century reader, and perhaps to the personal belief of Rabelais as well. Man remains a creature full of imperfections, subject to the will of God and helpless without divine grace, with potentialities for good and evil alike. He can improve himself through education, and in this the wisdom of his pagan ancestors is to be respected, though not to the exclusion of his Christian heritage, which must always take first place.

20 : *LE CINQUIESME LIVRE*

IT is no part of the present work to try once more to assess the precise degree of authenticity of the last and posthumous book of the *roman de Pantagruel*. However, there are few critics who deny that whole chapters are in large measure consistent in style and content with the preceding books, and it seems only logical to round off this inquiry by applying just the same principles to the *Cinquiesme Livre* as to the others. It is not feasible to examine each chapter or group of chapters separately, and to analyse the texts quoted according to their distribution in the book could only be misleading in the present state of our knowledge. In fact, nearly all the main headings already discussed are applicable to this book, and only those chapters which are known to be close borrowings (e.g. from '*le Songe de Poliphile*)' prove quite barren. The mere fact that the intellectual background of the *Cinquiesme Livre* can or cannot be compared with that of the other four proves nothing final about its authorship; if anyone but Rabelais had written the book, it goes without saying that his background must have been very similar for the question of authenticity to have been raised at all, and from that point of view no new results can be expected from such a method as this. It is regrettable, but at present inevitable, that no confirmation of theories about the earlier books can legitimately be sought from this one; its opinions can only be stated to echo certain of Rabelais's ideas, or if such is the case, to clash with them.

In none of the books are there so few serious references to God as in this. The only titles used at all are 'Père paterne', 'seigneur' and 'souverain', each once. As against this, the definition given in the *Tiers Livre* is repeated in a very serious context; Bacbuc takes leave of the pilgrims with these words (XLVII, 910): 'Allez, amys, en protection de ceste sphère intellectuale, de laquelle en tous lieux est le centre et n'a en lieu aucun conference, que nous appelons Dieu.' The only other references to God's nature is in an earlier remark of Bacbuc (XLII, 901): 'ne dictes que à Dieu rien soit impossible—Onques (respondis-je) ne fut dict de nous; nous mentenons qu'il est tout puissant.' It must be said that, except for the chapters of the *Isle Sonnante*, the last book is notably pagan and mythological in its atmosphere, partly at least because of the very undigested state of its borrowings from classical or pseudo-classical sources, and this accounts for the paucity of references to God.

Much the same can be said of the spirit world, which is well enough represented by lists of pagan demi-gods, satyrs and so on, but all quite indiscriminately included without comment or explanation. Two of the former diabolical themes recur, however, in the early chapters; the Order of St. Michel is described as wearing (v, 783) 'le trophée d'un calomniateur', actually the defeat of the devil by the Archangel, and there is the familiar disapproval of gambling (x, 796): 'par le monde peu de joueurs sont qui ne soient invocateurs des diables [les vingt diables de hazart tant redoutés en noz pays]'. None of the other mentions is at all interesting, and the crowded world of daemons, heroes, angels and the rest is comparatively depopulated in the last book.

Psychology is no more prominent than diabology but one or two texts are worth noting. Despite Rabelais's very extensive borrowing from Plutarch, the doctrine of metempsychosis is almost ignored except in the *Cinquiesme Livre*. Panurge alludes to it as held by (xiii, 804) 'Pythagoras, premier amateur de sapience' and says to the Chats Fourrez: 'Si vous estiez hommes . . . après vostre mort, selon son opinion, voz âmes entreroient en corps de cossons.' By a procedure very familiar in the first four books, this doctrine is mentioned again in the following chapter by Frère Jan (xiv, 805): 'Les âmes d'iceulx, selon l'opinion de Grippeminault, après leur mort sont entrées ès sangliers, cerfs . . . et autres tels animaux.' This tells us nothing about Rabelais's opinion concerning metempsychosis, though there is not the slightest reason for supposing that he took it seriously, but it is interesting to see that what was a major omission of the other books is supplied in this. Another remark towards the end of the book recalls some of the discussions of the *Tiers Livre*; their guiding Lantern explains why the priest of Jupiter would not have passed beneath the arch of vines (xxxiv, 878):

Car y passant auroit le vin (ce sont les raisins) au-dessus de la teste . . . pour signifier que les pontifes et tous personnages qui s'adonnent et dedient en contemplation des choses divines doibvent en tranquilité leurs esprits maintenir, hors toute perturbation de sens, laquelle plus est manifestée en yvroignerie qu'en autre passion quelle que soit.

Medical knowledge is not forgotten in this any more than in the other books. The chapters on the Quinte contain an account of some of the cures effected by the Dame's officers, (xxi) and a discussion on the origin of Lent dwells on physiological details (xxix, 857): 'Caresme . . . la saison quand la chaleur naturelle sort du centre du corps auquel s'estoyt contenue durant les fredures et l'yver.' A parenthesis in a sentence by Bacbuc, concerning the fountain of the temple, again recalls a characteristic procedure (xlii, 899): 'Par la seule figure lymacialle que voyés bipartiente ensemble une quintuple infoliature mobile à chacune rencontre interieure (telle qu'est en la vène cave en lieu qu'elle entre le dextre ventricule du cueur) est ceste sacrée fontaine escoulée.'

The Dame de la Quinte is the only female character who plays any important and creditable role in the five books, but she can hardly be counted as a woman. In fact there is little about women in the book, apart from the usual disobliging references to nuns and other scabrous subjects. The association of the moon with woman has already been remarked, and Frère Jan reminds us of it (xxxiv, 879):

en la Revelation feut, comme chose admirable, veue une femme ayant la lune soubs ses pieds; c'estoit, comme m'a exposé Bigot, pour signifier qu'elle n'estoit de la race et nature des autres, qui toutes ont au rebours la lune en teste et par consequent le serveau tousjours lunaticq.

In its misogyny the last book follows the tradition of its predecessors.

The references to the animal and vegetable kingdoms show a much keener interest in these subjects than in those so far mentioned. These subjects were more widely known than more abstract ones, it is true, but there are certain indications from the way it is handled which cannot fail to recall the earlier books. The very definition of animals found in the *Tiers Livre* is repeated (xxvi, 844): 'Les chemins y sont animaulx [en l'isle des Odes] si vray est la sentence d'Aristoteles, disant l'argument invincible d'un animant estre s'il se meut de soy-mesmes'. The anecdote of 'le Baudet et le Roussin' is in the same popular tradition as the earlier fabliau 'le Renard et le Lion', and it is interesting to see the ass of Philemon reappearing after his first entry in the *Quart Livre* (xvii).

Old friends, too, are the two 'physetères' who provide a brief but dramatic diversion (XVIII, 821), curiously enough in the same paragraph which brings in again the Andouilles, on whose island the first 'physetère' was dismembered. Equally reminiscent is the use of an animal—or rather insect—simile in the first two chapters. Pantagruel compares the incessant ringing of the bells in the Isle Sonnante to a method of recalling bees (I, 773): 'Je doubte que là quelque compaignie d'abeilles ayt commencé prendre vol en l'air, pour lesquelles revocquer ce voisinage faict ce tremblement de poilles, chauderons, . . . de Cybelle, mère grand des dieux.' In the next chapter, Editus compares the Mendicants to the drones (II, 777): 'Tout ainsy toutesfois qu'entre les abeilles hantent les frelons, qui rien ne font fors tout manger et tout gaster, ainsi depuis trois cens ans . . . estoit advolé grand nombre de cagotz.' The old poet Raminagrobis in the *Tiers Livre* and Erasmus before him had also drawn on the insect world to describe the friars. Again, in the following chapter, Editus comes back to the bees (III, 778): 'des Clergaux naissent les Prestregaulx et Monegaulx sans compaignie charnelle comme se fait entre les abeilles.' This train of thought is very typical of the earlier books, where one mention almost invariably begets another. It may be quite unconnected with these three texts, but it is interesting to find bees appearing once again (from the *Georgics*, like the first reference) in the Oracle itself (XLIV, 903): 'de la Sacrée Bouteille yssoit ung bruit tel que font les abeilles naissantes de la chair d'un jeune thoureau occis et accoustré selon l'art et invention d'Aristeus.' The bird motif of the *Isle Sonnante* gives in itself ample opportunity for references to natural history, genuine or fantastic, and another whole chapter, the Pays de Satin (XXX), is devoted entirely to this theme. The treatment of this chapter is very much the same as that of the Medamothi and Gaster episodes in the *Quart Livre*, with the same personal reminiscences (of Lyons and Ligugé), and the same unicorn and chamelon, as well as other improbable creatures from Pliny and elsewhere.

Plants are not neglected in this last book, and the indifferent chapter on the Isle des Ferrements (borrowed from the equally indifferent *Navigations de Panurge*) is embellished with a quotation from Theophrastus, comparing trees to men (IX, 794): 'elles ont la teste, c'est le tronc, en bas,' followed by a typical list 'à leurs racines, caudices, gommes, nodulles.' The institution of Lent

gives Epistemon a chance to air his botanical and medical knowledge (xxix, 857): 'viandes . . . plus exitantes la personne à
lubricité . . . ; febves, poix, phaseoulx, chiches, oignons, noix . . .
salades toutes composées d'herbes veneriques, comme eruse,
nascitord, targon, cresson, berle, responces, pavot cornu, hobel-
lon, figues, riz, raisins.'

This list of natural history references is not exhaustive, but
shows that the same interest in the subject is reproduced in the
last book and that the knowledge is used in much the same way
as in the others. It is not therefore surprising that the theme of
Nature herself should also recall, sometimes textually, the earlier
books. The functions and limitations of nature are well expressed
in two phrases which have already been quoted; Editus, speaking
of the families too numerous to survive without sending some
members into religion says (IV, 780): 'qui à tous part feroit de
l'heritaige comme raison le veult, nature l'ordonne, et Dieu le
commande, la maison seroit dissipée,' and the other (IX, 795):
'Vray est comme en toutes choses (Dieu excepté) advient quelquefois erreur. Nature mesmes n'en est pas exempte, quand elle
produict choses monstrueuses et animaux difformes.' That sentiment had already been applied by Rondibilis to explain the
otherwise incomprehensible creation of women, and the other
text strongly recalls the antitheses of Gargantua between nature
and reason, in his attack on canon law as it affected marriage. An
additional aspect comes out in the episode of the Quinte, when
Dame Entelechie speaks of (xxiii, 834) 'Nature, ma royne'.
Entelechy is, in fact, a law of Nature, supreme as a law but still
subject to the rule of Nature herself.

Other standard ideas about Nature come in this book; her
infinite variety (II, 776): 'par l'ordre de nature (comme toutes
choses varient)'; her liking for certain numbers, already referred
to in connexion with Pantagruelion (xLII, 898): 'forme heptagone
(c'est nombre fort aymé de Nature)'; the mysterious law of
magnetism (cf. Gaster episode) (xxxvII, 885): 'Par donc la
rapacité et violence de l'aymant les lames d'acier, par occulte et
admirable institution de nature, pastissoient cestuy mouvement.'
In the fabliau of 'le Baudet' there is a subtle distinction between
the respective acts of God and Nature; the horse says to the ass
(vII, 788): 'Dieu t'a créé pour le service des humains . . . nous
autres, que Nature a produicts pour la guerre,' while the ass says

to himself a little later 'Nature ne m'a produict que pour l'ayde des pauvres gens.' The choice of words 'créé' and 'produict' is hardly accidental and though Nature is elsewhere spoken of as creating, properly that is the function of God alone. This same fabliau is an excellent example of Nature laying down a creature's proper station, to leave which is 'unnatural'. One omission from this picture of Nature is the great emphasis laid on her fertility in the other books, as on procreation in general, though Panurge and Frère Jan are there to ensure that the subject of sex is not forgotten.

In the field of physics and cosmology there is not a great deal. The last chapter of the book contains a scientific explanation by Bacbuc of the working of the elements (XLVII, 912): 'Par la rarefaction de nostre eaue dedans enclose, intervenant la chaleur des corps superieurs et ferveur de la mer salée, ainsi qu'est la naturelle transmutation des elemens, vous sera air dedans très sallubre engendré, lequel de vent clair, serain, delicieux vous servira; car vent n'est que air flottant et undoyant.' These ideas are familiar enough from the earlier books and represent scientific commonplaces of the day. By a suggestive coincidence, of a type very frequent in Rabelais, the reference to the important law of generation and corruption in this book seems to be an echo of the same passage of St. Paul which is suggested by the reference to the same law in the Papefigue episode. In the *Cinquiesme Livre*, Frère Jan says of the Chats Fourrez (XIV, 805): 'Ilz donques de corruptions vivent en generations periront,' in which Boulenger for one sees a reference to I Cor. xv. 42: 'So also is the resurrection of the dead. It is sown in corruption; it is raised in incorruption,' while in the Papefigue episode the peasant says (*QL*/XLVI, 685): 'Le grain que voyez en terre est mort et corrompu, la corruption de icelluy a esté generation de l'autre,' which seems to square with verse 36 of the same chapter: 'Thou fool, that which thou sowest is not quickened except it die.'

For the rest, none of the scientific allusions in the book is particularly interesting. Three astronomical references are worth mentioning; first Plato's famous music of the spheres (XVIII, 821): 'harmonie peu moindre que celles des astres rotans, laquelle dict Platon avoir par quelques nuits ouye en dormant,' an erroneous attribution found also in the *Tiers Livre*; then the movement of the planets is described, similar to the roads in the Isle des Odes (xxvi, 844): 'errans à la semblance des planettes, autres chemins passans, chemins croisans, chemins traversans,'; last, in the same chapter, a certainly unconscious allusion to the recently developed system of Copernicus: '[Pantagruel] nous dist que, selon son jugement, Philo, Aristacus et Seleucus avoient en icelle isle autrefoys philosophé et prins opinion d'affermer la terre veritablement autour des polles se mouvoir, non le ciel, encores qu'il nous semble le contraire estre verité.' It is instructive to see the reaction of Rabelais to what was to be the new theory, which he may have known to be current, and which he rejects as a hallucination like the moving roads. Equally instructive is the cautious, even sceptical attitude to the modern geographers classed with Herodotus and Hayton the Armenian (xxxi, 866)—'et tout pour Ouy-Dire.' If Rabelais is the true author of this part of the book, the more extravagant claims for his progressive outlook need to be revised.

The religious questions brought up in this book are not so easy to decide as in the others. The circumstances of publication, so long after Rabelais's death and unmistakably intended as Protestant propaganda, make the more extreme views suspect to some degree, but the existing evidence makes it illegitimate, indeed impossible, to point to *ad hoc* insertions by whoever gave the book to be published. The most immediately striking change from the other books is the violent, bitter and detailed satire on the religious orders in the *Isle Sonnante*. The comparatively good-humoured irony of Papimanie is far from the vehement tone of these chapters, where monastic and ecclesiastical institutions are sometimes savagely attacked. It is true that none of the arguments is new—idleness, lechery, cupidity—and that a specially virulent attack is directed at the Mendicants, always the favourite target, but the distinctive feature of the whole episode is its bitterness and detail. The very acid comment of Editus on the mothers of the land of Tropditeux, if by Rabelais, suggests very strongly a personal rancour (iv, 780): 'Je m'esbahis comment les mères de par de là les portent neuf mois en leurs flancs, veu qu'en leur maison elles ne les peuvent pastir neuf ans, non pas sept le plus souvent.' It would take subtle casuistry to find any loophole of defence for the religious in these chapters, and as they stand they represent an indictment of the religious life in all its phases. The unedifying episode of the Frères Fredons is infinitely less damaging, because openly farcical and restricted in scope. A remark of Frère Jan, though not inconsistent with his character throughout the work, reinforces the impression that the priesthood as such is under fire (xv, 807): 'Doncques vous m'avez compagnon pris pour en cestuy voyage messe chanter et confesser?' Probably no more than facetious, an odd remark at the end of a particularly pointless passage of the Isle des Ferrements adds to the generally negative impression of the book (ix, 795): 'C'est belle chose croire en Dieu.'

Despite the effect of these negative passages, there are one or two positive ones which sound the same note as that of the earlier books. The Apedeftes episode begins with a familiar phrase (xvi, 811): 'Après que le bon Pantagruel eut fait les prières et remercié le Seigneur de l'avoir sauvé de si grand danger . . .' A curious sentence, found only in the MSS., again sounds a positive note. At the end of the Isle des Odes (xxvi, 847): 'nous fust dict que Panigon sus ses derniers jours s'estoit en ung hermitage d'icelle isle retiré et vivoit en grand sainteté et vraye foy catholique, sans concupiscence, sans affection, sans vice, en innocence, son prochain aymant comme soy-mesmes et Dieu sur toutes choses; partant faisoit-il plusieurs beaulx miracles.' Some historical allusion is surely intended, but on the face of it the sentence seems a perfectly serious statement of religious principles, and in any event must have seemed that to many sixteenth-century readers. Most positive of all, and contrasting strongly with the opening chapters, are the last, especially when Bacbuc speaks. Of institutional religion there is no hint, but from the solemn recommendation of the company to 'ceste sphère intellectuale', and the statement that for true knowledge the two indispensable factors are 'guyde de Dieu et compaignie de homme' a very real religious belief seems to emerge, notably similar to that of the earlier books. This very mixed and inconclusive collection of texts is not exactly self-contradictory, but one has the impression of incoherence which anachronistic composition would explain. It seems almost incredible that all, or even the greater part, of the book could have been composed at the same time by the same person, whether Rabelais or another. An additional factor which makes the religious content hard to assess is the very subordinate role played by Pantagruel, on whom we come to rely more and more in the other books as Rabelais's authentic mouthpiece.

The questions of grace, free will and so on which had followed naturally the other religious themes of the early books are conspicuously absent. A few astrological references are to be found (III, 778): 'telle etoit l'institution première et fatale destinée des astres,' (IV, 782) 'par vertus de certaines constellations celestes,' (XI, 799) 'les conjunctions des planettes malefiques', and these are as ironic as those which occur so frequently in the other books. There is, however, no definite line in this book, and it is pointless to speculate why.

Allusions to formal philosophy, especially that of the Schools, are reasonably numerous, but follow no clear pattern. Apart from the chapters on the Quinte, naturally full of philosophical terms, there is still quite a varied selection in the book. The papal succession is described in Scholastic terms (III, 778): 'il y a en ceste espèce unité individue avecques perpetuité de succession, ne plus ne moins qu'un Phoenix d'Arabie.' Though the question of succession did not arise, the angels in Thomism provided another well-known example of a species formed by a single individual. One of the very few instances in the book of a term common in the others is the description of the Isle de Cassade as (X, 795) 'vraye idée de Fontainebleau.' Another rare example of a traditional pleasantry is Frère Jan's pun (XV, 808) 'Mais parlons un peu par escot, docteur subtil.' Other medieval figures are mentioned in various contexts (e.g. Albertus Magnus in *Ouy-Dire*) but none of the references is significant. Though Cornelius Agrippa reappears in this book as Hans Cotiral, the only reference to the occult which does not seem premeditated is Frère Jan's remark, when Panurge observes that the Frères Fredons forbear to process back into church by the door they had left (XXVII, 850): 'Ceste finesse est extraicte d'occulte philosophie.' As for the Quinte episode, the intrusion of Hebrew accompanies the familiar lists (XX, 827): 'categories, abstractions, secondes intentions . . . entités, metempsychosies, transcendans prolepsies.' Rather more meaningful is a reference to logic (XXII, 833): 'Plus nous fust dict que chose esloignée ne leur sembloit estre deux contradictoires vrayes en forme, en mode, en figure et en temps, chose pour laquelle les sophistes de Paris plustout se feroient desbaptiser que la confesser.'

As for the nature of true knowledge and the means of attaining it, the whole final episode of the Oracle is concerned with these problems. The interpretation of the allegory is not strictly relevant here, but it seems to reject any form of dogmatic philosophy in favour of a subjective approach. How near it comes to scepticism is a difficult question. More helpful than the Oracle itself are Bacbuc's closing words, which must represent the mature philosophy of their author, and are not inconsistent with what we know of Rabelais's own thought. After his reference to 'guyde de Dieu et compaignie de homme', Bacbuc gives some examples of the latter and concludes (XLVII, 911): 'Infailliblement aussi trouveront [les philosophes] tout le sçavoir et d'eulx et de leurs predecesseurs à peine estre la minime partie de ce qui est, et ne le savent.' This sounds more like a personally acquired outlook than the influence of any particular school of thought.

The few observations on morals reproduce most of the essential ideas of the earlier books. Stoic maxims reappear (XVIII, 819): 'la sentence du philosophe [Epictète] qui commandoit soubstenir et abstenir, c'est à dire temporiser', (XXVII, 850) 'la sentence de Ciceron et des Achademiques, lesquels veulent Vertus preceder, Fortune suyvre', and Bacbuc's words, which recall the sentiments expressed in Pantagruel's letter from Medamothi (XLVII, 909): 'nous establissons le bien souverain non en prendre et recevoir, mais en eslargir et donner.' More particular examples occur mostly in the Isle Sonnante chapters. When Panurge exhibits his usual cowardice at the Chats Fourrez, Frère Jan taunts him (XV, 808): 'bon coeur et franc, accompaignié de mains paralytiques,' (MS. reading) which is just the complaint of Pantagruel and Epistemon after the storm in the Quart Livre ('nous faut nous evertuer'). The list of evildoers has not changed either and is substantially that of Papefigue and the gates of Thélème (XI, 799): 'l'imposture des caphars, heretiques, faulx prophètes, la malignité des usuriers, faulx monnoyeurs, rogneurs de testons, l'ignorance et imprudence des medecins, chirurgiens, apothicaires, la perversité des femmes adultères, venefiques, infanticides,' immediately before these often quoted malefactors, are two other classes whose misdeeds are attacked no less often: 'les abus de la cour rommaine, les tyrannies des roys et princes terriens.' This catalogue is a negative one, since it is recited by the doorkeeper at the Guichet, for whom the evils of this world are in no way attributable to these causes but to the unspeakable iniquity of the Chats Fourrez, the lawyers whom Rabelais does not fail to attack in each of the books. There is no reference of any importance to politics in the book, except for the fact already mentioned that Pantagruel avoids conflict with the Chats Fourrez by staying in his ship, as he did in the Chiquanous episode.

As this brief summary indicates, there is much less metaphysical thought in this book than in the others, but most of the ideas scattered throughout the *Cinquiesme Livre* recall notions developed more fully in the earlier books. There are apparent discrepancies in composition, especially between the *Isle Sonnante* chapters and the final episode of the Oracle, and if the content of the book were such as to permit comparison with more passages of earlier books, more rather than less inconsistency would probably emerge under some of the headings. For all that, the intellectual background of the book, as revealed by its references as well as its ideas, is very much like that of Rabelais as seen in the first four books. The need is still acute for a really scientific examination of all the elements of this last book, from a linguistic, stylistic and philo- sophical point of view. It cannot be claimed that the evidence discussed in this chapter proves anything conclusive, but it is at least consistent with the theory of Rabelais's partial authorship.

PART III

THE SOURCES OF RABELAIS'S THOUGHT

21 : RABELAIS'S AUTHORITIES

(i) *Classical*

WHATEVER may be the final assessment between Scholasticism and Humanism respectively as influences in Rabelais's work and thought, it is hardly open to doubt that Rabelais himself wished to demonstrate to the full his proud title to the name of Humanist, and consequently to play down as much as possible the Scholastic training for which he professed so much contempt. In fact, hardly any Scholastic authorities are quoted by name except for purposes of ridicule; Nicholas of Cusa and Nicholas of Lyra are mentioned in passing, Duns Scotus, Ockham and Pierre d'Ailly are openly mocked. One must clearly distinguish between what Rabelais considered his authorities, the texts of antiquity, and what at best he might have admitted as distant influences, that is the works of the Schoolmen.

The sixteenth-century attitude towards authority and originality alike is so strikingly different from our own that it is only too easy to misinterpret the use made of classical writers by such men as Rabelais. What seems dishonesty, or at least laziness, today was universal practise then; plagiarism was no vice in an age when a man's erudition was measured by the quantity, not the quality, of his references. The importance of the innumerable compilations of *Antiquae Lectiones*, especially Erasmus's *Adages* and *Apothegmata*, cannot easily be overrated, but it must at the same time be remembered that all men of letters were equally aware of the short cuts available to those who wished to use them. Serious deception was not a possible, let alone a plausible, motive for having recourse to second-hand knowledge.

All this is of obvious and major importance in trying to decide what impression of himself Rabelais wished to convey, a question hardly less vital than that of his real learning. There are in effect three problems to be resolved, each of which may have a bearing on the others; first, what authors are actually named in quotations; second, what references or quotations are made without naming the author, either because they were so familiar as to need no explanation, or because of a deliberately esoteric appeal to the learned; third, what sources, direct or indirect, can most probably be suggested for given texts. It would be misleading to offer precise statistics based on a straightforward count through the work, because some references are wholly spurious, some apparently the result of a genuine error of memory and some, in fact very many, too vague and too generally repeated to be ascribed with any certainty to a particular author.

With these reservations, some interesting details emerge from a general survey of quotations and references scattered through the four books. In each book the name most frequently mentioned is that of Plato, quoted at least twice as often as any other author. One or two of these references are incorrect or very general, but the intention is unmistakable; not only in the *Tiers Livre* with its opening Platonic invocation, but in all the work Rabelais seeks to impress his readers with his enthusiastic Platonism. It is all the more striking that the two authors who are next on the list, named about equally often and between them just rivalling Plato's record, are Hippocrates and Galen, who for professional reasons might be expected to occupy a place of honour in a book by a doctor of medicine. The only other authors with anything like the same degree of prominence are again hardly unexpected—Pliny, Cicero and Aristotle. Besides Pliny's fund of stories, his great authority in natural history explains his place in a work where all branches of that subject receive special attention, and as for the other two, they had been throughout the Middle Ages the leading authorities in Latin and Greek respectively.

Leaving aside the two medical authors, one can see that Greece and Rome are equally represented, and that no departure from tradition is marked by this choice apart from the overwhelming preponderance of Platonism. No account has been taken of the poets, especially Homer, Virgil, Ovid, Horace, whose contributions are mainly literary and very much what one might expect from a man with pretentions to classical learning. Probably the most surprising thing about these results, based on an approximate count taken throughout the work on the most conservative principles, is that they offer no surprises. If the frequency of Plato's name is changed for that of Aristotle, the broad picture is one which medieval scholars would have found very familiar.

The special case of the *Briefve Declaration* in the *Quart Livre* is also worth noting; the explanations are mainly linguistic and parade rather more obviously than usual the author's satisfaction at his own erudition, but the results are much as before. Cicero is quoted seven times, with specific mention of six of his works, while Pliny runs him a close second. The remaining authors are a numerous and mixed collection, as they are in the four books themselves, and include all the main and many of the minor authorities. In a commentary on language the prominence of Cicero and Pliny is entirely natural, one the recognized master of Latin style, the other an unequalled authority on scientific and technical terms. As before, high authority is invoked for somewhat disproportionate ends: Cicero for the use of 'St, st, st' to impose silence, Pliny for an explanation of leap year.

The minor works add very little, since their quotations are mostly either scriptural or burlesque, but it is interesting to see in one of them, the *Almanach* for 1535, a reproduction in miniature of the distribution throughout the main work—the Old and New Testament are each quoted twice, Plato twice, and Aristotle and Hippocrates once each, all in the space of two pages.

The impression conveyed by all this must be supplemented by the equally important catalogue of authors less frequently cited. Plutarch, Strabo and Herodotus occur several times, especially in the two later books, but Lucian, with whose spirit Rabelais is so often identified, is hardly mentioned at all by name. There are literally dozens of other authorities, genuine and spurious, many of whom occur only in long lists culled from some index, but their effect is cumulative and was certainly intended by Rabelais to increase respect for his erudition. Some, like Cato, Hesiod and Heraclitus, sound so imposing that Rabelais omits to quote his real and always second-hand source, others, like Petron, are so obscure that their presence too is impressive until we discover that their only extant fragments are preserved by Plutarch or some equally accessible author. The argument by quantity, referred to so often before, is that most dear to Rabelais, as to most of his contemporaries, and explains the multiplicity of references, often trivial or even superfluous, in which he so clearly delights. There is a very definite method, however, in the presentation of this mass of knowledge. The great emphasis on Plato is in the nature of a manifesto, the numerous references to Galen and Hippocrates are meant as professional self-advertisement, while the others, Cicero, Pliny, Aristotle, are indispensable foundations for any classical culture, stylistic and scientific. The comparatively small number of references to Plutarch can be quite easily explained if one realizes that a large number of the quotations from other authors (including Plato) are taken from Plutarch, while the very modest position of Lucian, quite out of proportion to his real importance as a source, may well be due to reasons of prudence, since his reputation for impiety was widespread in the sixteenth century.

At the next stage, that is those identifiable references or quotations to which no name is attached, the question of trying to convey an impression is obviously less relevant, though still not negligible. The most immediately striking fact here is that in the *Tiers* and *Quart Livres* alone Plutarch is quoted anonymously at least as often as Plato (by name or not) in all the books put together. Even this is only part of the picture, for in the *Quart Livre*, for example, a whole group of chapters, culminating in the Pan story, embody paraphrases and even literal translations of two whole chapters from Plutarch (*De Defectu*). In such a case the source must have been familiar to many readers, but there are many others where another author's name disguises the true debt to Plutarch. Something similar, though on half the scale, is true of Pliny, whose name is mentioned about as often as not, and who in his turn supplies abundant material for whole episodes like Pantagruelion and Gaster. If these direct borrowings can be established with reasonable certainty, the inspiration of Lucian is much less explicit but comes next after that of Plutarch and Pliny. Plattard has shown how many phrases, allusions and general ideas can be traced more or less convincingly to Lucian, on whom a whole episode (Picrochole's dream of conquest), seems to be modelled. Apart from these three, and Cicero, to whom Rabelais does not always acknowledge his debt, it is hard to be sure from which of several possible sources Rabelais drew his material. Once again no account is taken of the poets, most of the numerous quotations from whom had been common property for centuries. For the rest there is no reason to suppose that Rabelais's readers could place his allusions with any more certainty than modern scholars when asked to decide between the rival claims of several minor authors.

The addition of Plutarch, Pliny and Lucian as anonymous contributors completely alters the appearance of the previous list.

Plutarch and Plato now tie for honours, with Pliny close behind, while the others gain hardly anything from the addition of anonymous references, except for Cicero, who still fails to approach the leaders. What this means in effect is significant: Plato and Aristotle are almost invariably quoted by name and not infrequently at second hand, Galen and Hippocrates, the twin pillars of medical wisdom, are also quoted by name in almost every case, but unlike the first two, apparently always first-hand and not infrequently from memory. Only Cicero of the great authors does not always figure by name, but many of the quotations from his works are known to be indirect. The deliberate and remarkable effacement of Plutarch's authority is no accident, but completely consistent with Rabelais's obvious intention of appealing wherever possible to the great *authors* of antiquity, in the medieval sense of *auctores* as against mere commentators or historians like Plutarch. The fact that this appeal to the primary authorities is often purely specious does not alter the situation. Plutarch, the favourite author of so many Renaissance writers, is the most conspicuous absentee from the medieval list of leading authorities and is precisely the one whose name is least emphasized by Rabelais.[1]

The last question is difficult to answer with anything more than a high degree of probability. The work of M. Plattard,[2] though over fifty years old, must still serve as a basis for any full inquiry into Rabelais's humanistic sources, an inquiry which lies outside the scope of the present study. Taken in conjunction with such special studies as those of Thuasne[3] and numerous articles in learned journals, Plattard's conclusions put into its proper perspective the impression of vast erudition which Rabelais's work at first tends to produce. The comparatively small number of spurious references and mistakes needs no further comment. The larger question is to know how far to take Rabelais's erudition at its face value and how far to explain it by his judicious use of the

---

[1] The actual figures based on a very approximate count, and including only explicit references by name or specific borrowings as indicated by the notes to the Boulenger edition, are as follows: by name, Plato 22(1), Hippocrates 11(1), Galen 10(1), Cicero 10(7), Pliny 10(6), Aristotle 9(1), Plutarch 6(2). The figures in parentheses refer to the *BD*, and are not included in the total. Anonymous references give these results, with the grand total in parentheses: Plutarch 23(29), Pliny 11(21), Cicero 6(16). If the *BD* figures are added the trend is still more marked. See also Marichal, 'Rabelais devant le néo-Platonisme', p. 184, for an excellent analysis of the slightly higher totals taken from Marty-Lavaux.

[2] J. Plattard, *L'Œuvre de Rabelais*.   [3] L. Thuasne, *Etudes sur Rabelais*.

innumerable and voluminous compendia at his disposal. That he made extensive use of these collections is no longer a matter for any doubt, but Plattard has shown how cautious one must be in explaining any particular display of erudition simply in terms of borrowing from any one book:[1] 'Nous ne relevons pas dans son œuvre de séries d'exemples ou de cas singuliers qu'il ait constitué lui-même de toutes pièces, mais nous n'en trouvons pas non plus qu'il n'ait grossies et enrichies.' The works of Caelius Rhodiginus, Ravisius Textor, Baptista Fulgosa and, above all, Erasmus, contain a high proportion of Rabelais's erudition, while the more original works of such men as Budé and Agrippa are full of detailed references of the kind which Rabelais could, and did, annex for his own use. At the same time classical writers like Aulus Gellius and Plutarch are a treasure-house of other men's wealth. Besides these contemporary and antique sources, Rabelais had access to early Christian apologists like Eusebius, to whom we owe an immense number of classical fragments preserved by him alone, as well as very long passages from classical authors followed by a Christian commentary, in itself a fruitful and provocative form of literature for such a writer as Rabelais. For particular questions, like those of dreams and marriage, Rabelais seems to have drawn much from contemporary treatises, in these two cases J. C. Scaliger and Tiraqueau, and new discoveries are constantly being made which establish previously unidentified intermediaries between him and the original sources of antiquity.

That is not to say that Rabelais had not read the authors whose names he quotes with such pride, but for the purposes of his book it has been shown, for instance, that his professed and recognized enthusiasm for Plato did not deter him from going to Erasmus or Plutarch or any other convenient source for his quotations. The comic effect of much of his erudition corresponds with Rabelais's intentions and one must not be surprised if he chooses the most economical way of achieving this effect. If Rabelais says nothing by way of acknowledgement to his second-hand sources (C. Rhodiginus, it is true, is twice quoted in connexion with a ventriloquist), this is neither unusual nor ungrateful. Authors, not compilers, are quoted, and the others expect and receive no acknowledgement for the work they make available to all.

The greatest difficulty which arises from this is not so much the

[1] Op. cit., p. 275.

determining of a particular source for a text, really of secondary importance, but the possibility that opinions and comments following the text may also come from some source other than Rabelais himself. The Pan legend is a good case in point, and is only one of many. Plattard's conclusions may appropriately be recalled:[1] 'les moralistes et philosophes lui fournissent moins d'idées et de théories que de sentences et d'exemples: leur contribution à son œuvre ne diffère point, pour une grande part, de l'érudition qu'il emprunte aux grammariens anciens et modernes, aux recueils d'adages, de "mots dorés" et d'apothegmes.' If one admits this hardly contestable statement, the risk one takes in assuming Rabelais's expressed opinions to be his own is increased by the impossibility of ascribing them to identifiable authors.

Even when one has allowed for borrowing on the most generous scale, the residue of genuine erudition left in Rabelais's work bears out the many contemporary tributes to his learning from such weighty men as Budé and Tiraqueau. This brief discussion of the impression he tries to convey by his selection of authors to be named or to remain anonymous, and his methods of compilation from second-hand sources, shows Rabelais to have been both a scholar and an opportunist, profiting by skill in extracting impressive authorities from easily accessible catalogues to give an impression of erudition at once more extensive and of a somewhat different nature from what is really the case. An important question is raised by Plattard's statement quoted above: if Rabelais uses the moralists and philosophers more for examples than for ideas and theories, what attitude does he adopt towards these ideas and theories on the occasions when he cannot avoid them?

Of the six authors most frequently quoted, three, Pliny, Galen and Hippocrates, are more concerned with phenomena than ideas, while another three, Plato, Plutarch and Cicero, deal with systems of thought. As for Aristotle, he can hardly be treated outside the context of Scholasticism, because Rabelais had become acquainted with the Scholastic interpretation of Aristotle long before he could have studied that author on his own account; he cannot therefore be regarded in the same light as the others. From the three authors just mentioned all the main tenets of both Platonism proper and Stoicism must have come to Rabelais's notice whatever other

---

[1] Ibid., p. 266.

sources he may have used. We know that much of Cicero, and to a lesser extent Plutarch, came to Rabelais at second-hand from sixteenth-century compilations, but it is fair to assume that the philosophical problems they raised were familiar to him in the original.

In view of the great emphasis on Plato and Platonism in his work, it is particularly important to see what becomes of the main doctrines of that system at his hands. Plattard's judgement is not an encouraging start to such an inquiry: 'Rien dans son roman n'indique qu'il ait étudié avec une ferveur particulière celui que tous les humanistes contemporains eussent appelé, comme lui, "le prince des philosophes".'[1] As far as Rabelais's text goes, the quotations from the Republic, Symposium, Phaedo and Timaeus do not even prove that Rabelais had read the books in question, but unless it is admitted that his studies included these four at least, his professions of Platonism, confirmed by evidence external to his book, must be dismissed as mere bluff. It is true, of course, that any number of Platonic theories of a general kind in Rabelais's work can be, and probably are to be, explained by indirect influences but that is not at present the point at issue. From whatever sources he finally selected the doctrines reflected in his work, it must remain a fundamental hypothesis of Rabelaisian criticism that he had at some time made contact with the original text, any deviations from which cannot be regarded as accidental and demand an explanation.

Superficially the most obvious concession to Platonism is the philosophical debate to be found in all the books, especially the Tiers Livre, where the detailed discussion of particular problems lends itself very well to the Socratic method. It would be unwise to push the resemblance too far; the dialogue form had become popular in the Renaissance (and before) apart from any Platonizing tendency, and Erasmus's Colloquia are alone enough to account for Rabelais's literary choice. All the same, in a revolt against all Scholastic influences, the first victim is naturally formal logic, and literary preferences apart, it is probably safe to assume that Rabelais accepted the Platonic pattern as the best means of exposition and discussion.

More fundamental to the system of Plato is his epistemology, and here literary questions are definitely subordinated to philo-

---

[1] Ibid., p. 225. On all this see Marichal, art. cit.

sophical ones. Two great doctrines are concerned: that of Ideas and that of reminiscence. Once again, any revolt against Scholasticism would tend to encourage those theories which challenged Aristotle's authority in this field, but the situation is somewhat complicated by the Augustinian and Platonic strain so characteristic of Franciscan thought. Even this strain, still marked in Bonaventura, had eventually undergone the rigid formalizing treatment of the Schools, and when Rabelais came upon Platonic idealism in the original he cannot have been unaffected by the contrast it made with his Scotist studies. In fact, he goes out of his way to use the word '*idée*' as often as possible, and in such a way as to suggest almost polemical rather than philosophical motives. The chapter on Rabelais's philosophy has tried to show that his idealism is Platonic more in its expression than its content. He may well have accepted, and understood, the doctrine, but the evidence of his book suggests something less than deep conviction. While the theory as such is not distorted or misrepresented, its deeper implications seem on the face of it to have escaped Rabelais. The two later books in particular present such a detailed picture of vigorous empiricism, that the contemplation of eternal truths, though not ignored, is quite secondary.

The doctrine of reminiscence, with its cognate teaching about the soul's immortality and divine origin, receives very different treatment. It was for one thing self-contained in a way in which the other was not and its implications could be considered independently. The *Tiers Livre*, with its many chapters on divination, afforded an excellent opportunity for Rabelais to state his views on the subject and it is quite striking how far he goes in appreciating and understanding this theory. The long speech of Pantagruel on dreams (including the 'sphaere intellectuale'), the discussion about dying men as prophets, and, in the *Quart Livre*, the discussion of immortality, all show a thorough grasp of the problems involved and a consistency altogether lacking in the treatment of Platonic Ideas. Granted the limited context of these discussions, they are still examples of genuine Platonic theories being incorporated into Rabelais's work, intelligently and sympathetically.

The doctrine of immortality in itself (that is, considered without reference to theories of knowledge) is an essential feature of Platonism, but one which no Christian could approach with an

open mind. Since neither the Church nor the temper of the age
permitted much latitude in this basic matter, it goes without saying that the belief in immortality expressed in the *Phaedo*, though
distinctively Platonic, could be adopted without indicating any
necessary Platonic influence. It happens that Rabelais refers
directly to the *Phaedo* in this connexion, but it can hardly be
doubted that his beliefs about the soul came to him from traditionally Christian sources and were scarcely affected by subsequent
acquaintance with Plato. No doubt Rabelais, like so many of his
contemporaries, as well as men of the Middle Ages, was glad to
establish the conformity of the 'divin Platon' with Christian teaching, but there can be no question as to which took precedence in
his mind.

A much more cogent argument in favour of Platonic influence
can be based on the relationship described between body and soul,
which has a prominent place in the later books. Here again,
Christian doctrine prevented complete freedom of speculation,
unless, like Pomponazzi, the speculator was able to resort to some
kind of 'double truth' defence, but within the circle of absolute
orthodoxy there was still plenty of room for manœuvre. Already
in Plato's works there is a strong tendency to regard the body as
a temporary and restrictive abode for the soul, which can and
should even in this life seek liberty through contemplation,
dreams and so on. This tendency became preponderant in the
neo-Platonists, Christian and pagan, and gave powerful inspiration to a mysticism based on the belief that the body is a hindrance
to spiritual perfection. The Manichean excesses in this direction
show one logical outcome of such a view, but far more common
was the type of spirituality which became the hallmark of Renaissance Platonism and was exemplified in Marguerite de Navarre
and her group. Those for whom technical problems of philosophy,
whether epistemology or even ethics, presented small interest
found in this spiritual bias the main attraction of Platonism, and
Rabelais shows throughout his work that no other Platonic
doctrine appealed to him so much. It is relevant to recall that
Plato himself offers no incentive for the type of negative asceticism
which succeeding generations of Christians regarded as necessary
for subduing the lower instincts of the body, and in the *Republic*,
for instance, lays much stress on physical fitness. Socrates was
himself, as we know, of exceptionally robust physique, and while

indifferent to bodily pleasures could on occasion show that he had no need to fear their domination. Such later Platonists as Marguerite tend to stress devotional activity to the exclusion of all physical demands, and it is interesting to see how Rabelais was able to combine a faithful representation of Platonic spirituality with a balanced outlook on the body, essential to his medical profession and at the same time perfectly consistent with genuine Platonism. The resultant balance may not be due to Plato at all, but is important as showing that Rabelais's enthusiasm for spirituality is tempered by a moderation which is more Platonic than neo-Platonic.

The remaining elements of Plato's metaphysics reflected in Rabelais are his theology and demonology, but one reference ('l'intellectuale sphaere'), which is medieval, is all that comes out of the first, and in the other there is no doubt that the more highly developed version of Plutarch is that which Rabelais follows. As far as it goes, then, it may be said that Rabelais is in sympathy with the broad lines of Plato's metaphysics, whose theories he reproduces very faithfully in some cases, though at other times his familiarity with them appears somewhat superficial. When we turn to more concrete questions the results are a little different.

On the subject of love and the relationship between the sexes in general Plato has a good deal to say, not all of it consistent. The *Symposium* offered in its Androgyne myth a fruitful source of much pseudo-Platonism among poets of the Renaissance, and Rabelais makes a direct reference to the theory. Nowhere in his work, however, is there the slightest concession to the romantic conception of love suggested by it. Ironically enough, it is another Platonic dialogue, the *Timaeus*, which furnishes Rabelais (or at least Rondibilis) with his most effective anti-feminist weapon, though double-edged as has been shown.[1]

Neither the neglect of the *Symposium* nor the telling but almost certainly second-hand reference to the *Timaeus* is so significant as the treatment of the *Republic*. Rabelais goes out of his way in his first two books to quote from this dialogue by name, and it seems very likely that he had it in mind when he came to compose the chapters on Thélème. There, as in the *Republic*, high-born women enjoy rights equal (indeed, almost superior) to those of their male companions, but this equality is short-lived and is only

---

[1] M. A. Screech, 'Rabelais, de Billon and Erasmus'.

faintly echoed in Hippothaddée's respect for a wife's rights,
Rondibilis's grudging admission that a few 'preudes femmes'
must be excepted from the general condemnation deserved by
their sex, and perhaps Gargantua's thought for wives and daughters in his speech on marriage at the end of the *Tiers Livre*. These
later examples fall far short of the principle of equality laid down
in the *Republic* and accepted at Thélème. This equality, based on
social, not spiritual, values, is no less essential a part of Plato's
Utopia than the theory of the family into which it fits. The com-
munal possession of mates—one can hardly say wives—the complete disruption of the family by the immediate separation of
parents from their children, henceforth to be bound to one
another by no ties at all, and the consequent dictatorship by the
state over all human relationships are the essential features of this
ideal society; the first few pages of the *Timaeus* which resume the
argument of the previous day (i.e. of the *Republic*) make this quite
clear. Rabelais's constant emphasis on filial duty, on the significance of heredity and all family ties is completely at variance with
such ideas, and he had every reason to reject them, but nowhere
is there any hint that he had come across these theories or intends
to discuss them. This omission is negative evidence almost
amounting to proof, and at least makes very suspect Rabelais's
professed enthusiasm for the *Republic*.

In the four Platonic dialogues under discussion the chief remaining theory, expounded at greatest length in the *Timaeus*, is
the cosmology. This need not be dealt with in any detail here.
Aristotle had begun the process of criticism which continued
unceasingly throughout the Middle Ages, when for so long the
Timaeus was regarded as all the Plato to be known, or at any rate
to be seriously considered. There are certainly references to its
theories in Rabelais—to the World Soul, for example—but none
which had not been examined and re-examined by scores of
commentators. As far as cosmology is concerned anything
Platonic in Rabelais is not directly due to Plato.

Perhaps as important as all these factors put together is the
person of Socrates. Erasmus had set the fashion with his 'Sancte
Socrates, ora pro nobis', and those who had grown weary of
Aristotle's impersonal authority, not to speak of its handling by
the Schoolmen, quite naturally turned with delight to a figure as
human and inspiring as that of Plato's master. There are several

features of his character which reappear in that of Pantagruel—his indifference to women, to bodily hardship, his ability to drink more heavily than any of his companions or not at all, his contempt for all this world could do to him in comparison with the joys that awaited him hereafter, his special antipathy for the Sophists who deceived the unlearned and brought the name of philosophy into disrepute. All these qualities are not peculiar to Socrates, and belong to a type of hero not uncommon in the ancient world. The comparison between Socrates and Pantagruel can, admittedly, be pushed too far; Pantagruel is as much Alexander the great captain as Socrates the great philosopher. It may, however, be well to consider two small points of detail from the later books which suggest that the person of Socrates was very much in Rabelais's mind. First is the edifying death of Raminagrobis, which though explicitly Christian, and even Evangelical, is preceded by direct allusions to the *Phaedo*; second, the two mentions of the 'demon de Socrates' which in the *Quart Livre* Pantagruel admits having himself. Other pointers, such as Pantagruel's leadership of the discussions in the later books, are less precise, but all in all Socrates's character can be claimed to have influenced Rabelais more decisively than any more abstract Platonic theories, such as that of Ideas. Even the allusion to Socrates as a Silenus box, though borrowed from Erasmus, stands in so prominent a position at the very beginning of the Prologue to *Gargantua* as to lend support to this claim.

All these considerations taken together suggest some reservations concerning Rabelais's Platonism. To describe it as eclectic, like that of a Ficino, may be misleading; Rabelais's omission of ideas basic to Plato's main works is probably due not so much to ignorance as to reliance on intermediary sources. If these omissions were really deliberate, the emphasis on *'idées'* and the bare mention of the World Soul, the acceptance of the sexual equality proposed in the *Republic* (at least for Thélème) and complete absence of comment on the more radical theory of society offer paradoxes hardly compatible with genuine Platonism. There are several hints pointing to a solution of the problem. The frequent citations of Plutarch and Cicero, both generous borrowers from Plato, the marked interest in the person of Socrates, the emphasis on the spiritual rather than the epistemological side of Platonism, all indicate the same line of approach. Relations between the

Academy and the Stoa had always been close, and the description of Socrates as the 'patron saint of all Stoics'[1] may show the way to putting Rabelais's Platonism in a truer perspective. Faguet's happy phrase 'un stoïcisme gai' was originally applied to one side of Rabelais's philosophy, the active philosophy of Pantagruelism, 'mespris des choses fortuites', but it can in fact be greatly extended. The moral significance of Stoicism often overshadows the rest of its doctrines, and one is apt to forget that for a considerable period Stoicism was a complete and vigorous system, constantly evolving, which incorporated, and even on occasion challenged, those of Plato and Aristotle.

The moral theories of Stoicism were more or less common to all its writers, and Rabelais seems to have found them mostly in Cicero and Plutarch, whose teaching he accepts and reproduces on many important points. In our chapters on 'Providence' and 'Ethics' an attempt has been made to establish the pattern of Rabelais's thought on these matters and link it where appropriate with Stoic theories. It is now time to ask whether his Platonic metaphysics and admiration of Socrates should not be explained by reference to the same source.

To go no further than Cicero, whom Rabelais must have known outside the compendia of the sixteenth century, a combination of Stoic ethics with Platonic metaphysics appears in all his main works. Cicero constantly supports Platonic theories while professing general acceptance of the Stoic position, and in cosmology and metaphysics, for instance, he offers no solutions alien to Platonism. Perhaps it is going too far to say that 'Stoic' was almost as general a term in Cicero's time as 'Christian' in the Middle Ages, but the difference between extreme rigorists like Seneca and Marcus Aurelius on the one hand and more liberal thinkers like Cicero on the other can still be accommodated under the same general heading. Cicero's adaptation of Platonism offered an example which succeeding generations of Stoics, and then of Christians, were not slow to follow. The synthesis between the Stoic ethic, with its characteristic conception of nature and law, and Platonic metaphysics was enduring and popular. In such a synthesis the position of Socrates is obviously central, and could lead the inquiring mind equally well to either aspect of the system. The Renaissance saw a revival of much ancient thought dis-

---

[1] B. Russell, *History of Western Philosophy*, p. 276.

entangled from the medieval commentaries, and in this revival Plato and the Stoics held a leading place. Some of the humanists left Stoicism as it was, others deliberately adapted it to Christianity more or less successfully. In this process Platonism played a vital role: '[Le platonisme] est en quelque sorte l'intermédiaire qui permettra une adaptation plus complète du stoïcisme au christianisme.'[1]

The avidity of sixteenth-century writers (and readers) for moral sentences made the works of Cicero and Plutarch immensely popular. The parade of heroes in Plutarch, the moral and political reflections of a great statesman like Cicero, the practical ethic of the Stoic emperor Marcus Aurelius, would always appeal to the general public more than the abstract theories which lay behind them. That Rabelais should have followed the practice of his age in quarrying extensively from these authors is entirely natural. The reason for the comparative prominence of Socrates and the misleadingly exact allusions to the *Republic* is surely to be found in the fact that practical moralists used practical texts. Indeed, when one reads *De Officiis*, *De Senectute*, *De Natura Deorum*, *Somnium Scipionis*, there seems more and more cause to consider Rabelais's Platonism (in his book at any rate) as pre-selected— even pre-digested. The strong neo-Platonic element in his demonology comes beyond all doubt from Plutarch, so that applying Ockham's razor to the question a good case could be made for limiting Rabelais's Platonism solely to what he had found in Cicero and Plutarch, ignoring for the moment possible Scholastic intermediaries. It is noteworthy, for example, that Cicero's enthusiasm for Plato does not prevent him abandoning the communistic theory of society for a family feeling no less ardent than Rabelais's own.

This analysis is only intended to show how little direct acquaintance with Plato *need* be assumed from Rabelais's work. It does not mean that he followed Cicero and Plutarch to the letter any more than Plato—he has no use for the theory of metempsychosis, essential to Plutarch, and less still for Cicero's prim attitude towards natural functions[2]—nor that he had no intermediaries to interpret these authors in their turn. What he says of heroic souls is very clearly inspired by Stoic teaching, and his attitude to

---

[1] L. Zanta, *La Renaissance du Stoïcisme*, p. 135.
[2] Cicero, *De Officiis*, cap. xxix, xxxv.

nature and law may profitably be compared with Stoic ideas, but the medieval assimilation of these ideas was so thorough that there is no point here in conducting another detailed analysis of Rabelais's treatment of Stoic ideas. Any attempt to fix a permanent label on Rabelais, be it 'Stoic', 'Platonic' or anything else can lead only to infinite regress, and is not at all helpful. Most fruitless of all is the kind of criticism which points out that Pantagruel's 'mespris des choses fortuites' is foreshadowed in Budé's title *De Contemptu Rerum Fortuitarum*.[1] There is no reason to suppose that Budé, any more than Epictetus or any other Stoic, was the only begetter of such a commonplace idea. When notions so general are in the air, it is dangerous to expect tidy and precise attributions. The one thing that can be stated with assurance is that Rabelais wished his ideas to be associated with classical sources as distinguished as possible, regardless of their immediate provenance and regardless very often of their intrinsic triviality.

In his relations with Platonism, so proudly proclaimed throughout the work, as with Stoicism, equally influential if less publicized, Rabelais shows an eclecticism founded on what seems to be no more than the principle of economy, and therefore quite different from that of a Ficino or a Budé. We are not here concerned with Rabelais's private philosophy, only with his treatment of original texts, and the difference is fundamental. Plato and Platonists, Cicero and Stoics, are named in the work for reasons of prestige, independently of what they say, and the most convenient source for the greatest number of doctrines is always that which he chooses. The fundamental system of thought underlying the work inevitably modifies the impact of these borrowed texts and ideas. As Plattard so rightly says, Rabelais goes to his classical writers not for ideas but for examples. This seems to explain the apparent contradiction between Rabelais's reputation for learning and his actual performance. The perusal of Plato's works is no light task, apart from any linguistic difficulties, and there is no inconsistency in supposing Rabelais unable or unwilling to find examples from his own reading as convenient to his purpose as those which he could extract from more accessible intermediaries. If, as he claims and as seems in any case so probable, Rabelais's main object in his book is to please, it would serve no useful purpose to be a purist in selecting quotations. From what has

[1] J. Bohatec, *Budé und Calvin*, p. 116.

just been said, it appears most unlikely that Rabelais was indebted
to classical authors for his mental habits, though one need not
question his familiarity with their works. The main thing is that
the authorities are there to answer by name in his work, and if
they do no more than signify *acte de présence*, that is because
Rabelais wanted them to do no more.

(ii) *Scriptural*

As an authority in a special sense, the Bible must be considered
in the same way as the sources of classical antiquity. The use of
scriptural authority was, of course, nothing new, either in serious
or in comic works, but any account of Rabelais's methods would
be incomplete without an examination of the way in which he
treated sacred texts. The subject has already been dealt with by
Plattard with his customary thoroughness.[1] Many of his conclusions have been familiar for a long time, especially Rabelais's
predilection for St. Paul, but a close analysis of scriptural references from Plattard's list (one or two are too vague to be included,
and one at least is omitted by Plattard, no doubt inadvertently) is
still surprisingly revealing.

The number of references is remarkably stable through the
four books; some twenty-two in each of *Gargantua* and *Pantagruel*,
twenty-five in the more erudite *Tiers Livre*, and a rather unexpected
drop to nineteen in the *Quart Livre*. The *Cinquiesme Livre* does not
concern us here, but in fact, as Plattard points out, it is exceptionally barren of such references, with only eight in all. Very interesting is an analysis of the parts of Scripture which Rabelais chooses
for inclusion in his work. A large number, probably the majority,
of the scriptural references are either facetious or positively dis-
respectful in their particular context, while a smaller number,
none the less considerable, are perfectly serious, or at any rate
with no suggestion of irreverence. To the latter category belong,
as one would expect, the quotations from St. Paul, hardly any of
them open to mockery, and the greater number of other New
Testament references. These together come to about thirty, of
which ten each occur in the first two books alone. Mention has
already been made more than once of the markedly religious
atmosphere of *Gargantua*, and in this book, alone of the four, New

---

[1] J. Plattard, 'L'Ecriture Sainte dans Rabelais' in *RER* 1910.

Testament (and thus serious) references outnumber those from the Old Testament by two to one. The Psalms have been treated separately throughout, since, although strictly speaking scriptural, they were better known in their daily context as 'matière de breviaire'. Even in *Pantagruel*, where religion is somewhat less prominent, New and Old Testament references are about equal. In the two other books the Old Testament is quoted much more often than the New. One point which has engaged the attention of all commentators is that when later editions suppressed certain references (mostly New Testament), apparently to avoid giving gratuitous offence, the three which seem supremely blasphemous to modern readers are left in; of Our Lord's words on the Cross, three occur in facetious, even unseemly contexts: the 'lama, lama sabacthani' in *Pantagruel*, 'Sitio' in *Gargantua* and the final cry 'Consummatum est' in the *Tiers Livre*. Nothing could more effectively warn us against applying modern standards of reverence to Rabelais. Most of the other New Testament references are comparatively anodyne; the illustrations of 'albus', probably from a concordance, as Plattard shows, the incident of Zacchaeus and so on. These are used in exactly the same way as classical texts, to provide examples and high authority for particular observations.

The Psalms are treated very differently, and since Frère Jan is so often the one to proclaim some familiar verse with his war-cry 'matière de breviaire', the primarily comic effect hardly needs emphasizing. Whether it be tags like 'ad te levavi' or 'jusqu'aux vitulos', a lengthy jest like Lasdaller's exposition of the Psalm or simply the chanting of Marot's setting to 'Hors d'Egypte', the Psalms are not used to confer authority on a particular statement, nor to illustrate Rabelais's erudition, but as a source of texts, serious or comic, which would be almost as familiar to his readers as a popular refrain. This very familiarity makes the question of irreverence hardly applicable, though the Reformers at least could not approve the bad taste which they were bound to see in such use of sacred texts.

The rest of the Old Testament (including three references from the Apocrypha, all from Tobit) accounts for the greatest number of Rabelais's scriptural references, some forty-four in all. Very few of these are used in any but a facetious way, but obvious and deliberate irreverence is rare. For this reason it is particularly interesting to see from which parts of the Bible Rabelais most often selects his texts. With the sole exception of *Gargantua* (exceptional in several ways when it comes to religion) the Pentateuch, and specially Genesis, accounts for the majority of these texts. Most of the others come from the Books of Solomon, Proverbs or Ecclesiastes, or from Kings; there is hardly a single reference to a prophetic book, though Isaiah and Daniel come in once each. The usual application of these texts is either to support some purely erudite piece of information, especially in the *Tiers Livre*, where Leviticus, Deuteronomy and Numbers are invoked as authorities for Jewish customs, or to amuse, with such stories as Adam and Eve and the Flood. The early books of the Old Testament are naturally those which can be regarded as less intimately bound up with the essentials of the Christian faith, and which at the same time had provided innumerable themes for popular art and drama throughout the Middle Ages. In this way it can be said that Rabelais used the Old Testament for two distinct purposes, both of which apply equally to his use of classical authors; for authoritative support of learned information and as a source of semi-mythology. In this connexion, the three mentions of Tobit (quoted again in the Almanach for 1535) bear out Rabelais's interest in those books which tell a story, and which for that reason had become most familiar in the Middle Ages.

Plattard's conclusions can scarcely be challenged after all these years; despite the number and variety of scriptural references in Rabelais, it cannot be said that he shows more than normal professional knowledge for a man whose adult life was mainly spent in ecclesiastical company. The two or three mentions of Lyra, and to the 'cabalistes et massorètes' suggest that memories of scriptural glosses were still with him, but the single passage where the version of Erasmus seems to be specifically invoked is not enough evidence of any close or scientific study of the Bible on Rabelais's part. Alike in his adequate, but undistinguished knowledge of the Bible and the liberties he took with it, Rabelais remains in the old tradition: 'dans les facéties dont le texte biblique est le thème, il ne dépasse pas en audace les docteurs et moines des générations précédentes.'[1] This is not the place to return to a discussion of Rabelais's religious motives for treating

[1] Ibid., p. 339.

Scripture as he did, but if one considers the Bible in the same way as the other authorities, Plato, for instance, the conclusion is inescapable that he wished his readers to form a certain impression which closer scrutiny seems to belie. Much of the biblical atmosphere derives from absolute commonplaces, notably Genesis and the Psalms, many of the more erudite references may quite well be due to a concordance, and making the most generous allowances, one finds no evidence from his work that Rabelais had any knowledge at all of a very substantial part of the Old Testament. The Bible had always been accepted as the supreme authority, and the revival of biblical studies brought about by such men as Erasmus made it impossible for Rabelais to maintain his position as a man of learning without calling frequently upon biblical allusions. Despite this, on balance the evidence shows that the Bible was for him an authority rather than an influence, with the important exception of the Pauline Epistles, which he seems to have studied with some care and which can properly be considered as both an authority to quote and an influence to inspire.

In his admirable conclusion to the article quoted above, Plattard points out that there is a complete absence of Patristic reference in Rabelais's work. At first sight this omission, which we may well believe extended to his reading as to his writing, is a little surprising in one who professed such admiration for Erasmus, editor of a monumental series of Patristic works. The explanation of this apparent contradiction can almost certainly be seen in the way he treated his classical and biblical sources. His first aim in quoting, whether by name or not, was to impress, and all indications are that he used the simplest and most economical means at his disposal in every case to achieve this end. Compilations, concordances, indexes, second-hand sources like Plutarch, are all used in preference to the original texts. Moreover, Rabelais's normal reading would keep him in touch with these sources, whereas with the Fathers a new and ponderous mass of material awaited him, unless he were content to rely on the Scholastic works which served preachers and popular theologians. This latter course ran counter to his intention of appearing the enlightened humanist, apart from any intrinsic apathy it may have roused in him. It is probably for these reasons that Augustine, Jerome, Ambrose and the others do not figure in the work. This is not to say that Rabelais had escaped the considerable element of Patristic learning embodied in every Scholastic work of any substance, but which is quite distinct from a study of the Fathers for themselves. To put the matter in its simplest form, Rabelais does not call upon the Fathers because the possible increase in prestige which might accrue from doing so was heavily outweighed by the certain extra burden of work it would entail.

22 : FRANCISCAN DOCTRINES AND THEIR INFLUENCE

To balance the influence of those classical and scriptural sources which Rabelais so proudly acknowledged, or which can otherwise be identified, one must consider the effect of the Franciscan training to which Rabelais never alludes, except to mock generally at Scotists, and which presents certain difficulties of identification. No detailed programme of Franciscan studies for the period in question has survived, and even if it had one would have to make allowances for local variations, nor are there any Scholastic works bearing Rabelais's *ex libris*. The best one can do is to reconstruct from the evidence available what studies he most probably pursued and then see how they are reflected in his work, if at all.

Though much of the formal training received by young friars was theoretical rather than practical, the sermons offer by no means negligible evidence of the way in which it was practically applied. It would not be reasonable to expect preachers to display much formal intellectual talent in the popular pulpit, and neither metaphysics nor speculative theology are ever likely to bulk very large in sermons. On moral and pastoral theology, however, the preachers have a good deal to say, and this sometimes leads them into discussion of more abstract themes. On the related topics of sin and salvation, faith and works they are positive and specific, and in view of the importance of these topics in the theological debates of the sixteenth century it is useful to consider the teaching that people were accustomed to hear from friars (and others) up to and even after the time of Luther. What follows is taken from sermons which simply expounded a doctrinal norm, free of any polemical context, though already in Messier's day debate on these matters was accompanied by heresy and schism.

Treating the question of original sin Maillard is in a long line of theologians who associate the Fall with sexual sin. If his hearers wonder why an adult is ashamed to show his private parts, Maillard affirms (A/40 v.) that this is because they are harmful, and that those who feel no shame are thus called innocent (a play on 'nocentes-innocentes'). Similarly he says that the reason why animals great and small are turned against us is again original sin. Classical ideas about a lost Golden Age included the same belief in a previous harmony between man and beast, lion and lamb, and Panurge refers to this in his burst of erudition early in the *Tiers Livre* (VIII).

The preachers constantly impress on their hearers that if the fault is always man's and man's alone the saving grace is always God's. Thus at the beginning of Lent Menot (T/3) warns the people of Tours of their perilous state, saying that we are all in danger of eternal damnation unless we recover lost grace through the merits of Christ's Passion. He goes on with a succinct statement of how the economy of salvation works:

A man of most evil life, renieur de Dieu, looks well in the evening and in the morning is found dead. What do you say about that, Mesdames? Is it reprobation or predestination for him? Scotus says that if anyone is eternally predestined this is due to the pure grace of God, though none is reprobated by God unless his true deserts demand it. Bonaventura says that no cause lies in the person reprobating, but a most effective cause in the person reprobated.[1]

Maillard conveys the same message through a simple image: 'The sun cannot enter the house of a man who closes his windows.'[2]

Many more examples in the same strain could be quoted, all stressing that the total responsibility for sin and damnation lies with man, but that God has freely made the gift of grace available to all through Christ. The preachers are firmly opposed to any doctrine of irresistible grace or of predestination to damnation. While theirs is ultimately a message of hope, they do not offer salvation on easy terms and constantly point out how few are actually saved. There is, though, all the difference in the world (and in the next) between a doctrine which says that salvation is difficult and one that says it is impossible for most of us. Their statistics are not meant to encourage facile optimism, but they

---

[1] 'Erit in hac villa homo pessimae vitae, renieur de Dieu. De sero facit bonum vultum: de mane invenitur mortuus. Quid dicitis de hoc, dominae? Est sua reprobatio, vel praedestinatio? Scotus . . . dicit quod si aliquis sit aeternaliter praedestinatus, hoc est ex mera Dei gratia. Nullus tamen est a Deo reprobatus, nisi suo exigente demerito. Bonaventura . . . dicit quod nulla est causa in reprobante; est tamen causa efficacissima in reprobato.' (T/5)

[2] 'Sol non potest intrare domum suas fenestras claudentis.' (F/126)

are not meant either to promote despair. We have already seen[1] that according to legend St. Bernard came back to report that only three were saved out of 35,000 who died on the same day as he. Maillard points out that even the irreproachable Carthusians have scruples about their unworthiness and Menot admits that he does not feel assured of salvation, even wearing the habit of St. Francis and faithfully observing his rule. All the threats are meant as spurs to amendment; there is always something to be done about it.

There are 40,000 priests in Hell, as many merchants, as many nobles, as many rich men and oppressors of the poor, who did not deserve damnation as much as you do. Are there not many in this company who have done more to earn damnation than wicked Dives? You hear me well, you ecclesiastics . . .[2]

Maillard's statistics are fanciful (representing, on St. Bernard's showing, less than a week's intake into Hell) but the argument is clear and direct: without charity the fate of Dives will be the fate of all. The practical lesson is meant to be practically applied, and while the preachers quite often discuss theory it is never long before they bring discussion down to earth. Some people lull their consciences with convenient texts, and put off effective repentance, backed by the scriptural assurance that a man may repent on his deathbed and yet be saved. Menot warns them that it is most unwise to count on this last chance, and quotes Scotus in support.[3] Even outwardly good works will not satisfy God, who looks into the hearts and minds of men to see what good fruit they bring forth.

The words with which Maillard opens one of his series sum up Franciscan, and indeed Scholastic teaching in general, on the themes of grace, faith, works and salvation, which Luther and then Calvin were soon to make so bitterly controversial: 'Messieurs, will many of you be found who have grace and faith informed by charity?'[4]

[2] 'Sunt xl milia sacerdotes in inferno, tot mercatores, tot nobiles, tot divites et pauperum oppressores qui non tantum demeruerunt damnationem sicut vos. Nonne multi sunt in ista societate qui melius meruerunt damnari quam malus Dives? Auditis me bene, domini ecclesiastici . . .' (Q/220 v.)
[3] 'Paenitentia quae fit in extremis vix est sufficiens ad efficaciam salutis.' (P/459). He devotes the entire second part of the sermon to this one question.
[4] 'Domini, an plures invenientur de vobis qui habent gratiam et fidem formatam caritate?' (s/87)

The theology implied in the phrase 'fides formata caritate' was to be of critical importance throughout the century, but long before it became the subject of doctrinal dispute it had for centuries been the basis of exhortation. Maillard is certainly not using the phrase as a shibboleth, but almost as a cliché, and when some thirty years later Rabelais wrote of 'foy formée de charité' he knew very well what he was doing.

The saving grace of *caritas* is the indispensable counterbalance to the preacher's endless talk of sin. The Christian life is not just something to talk about, and certainly not inaccessible to the ordinary man, but it demands effort and action. Damnation can be earned only too easily, simply by letting human nature go its own way. Pharisaical good works, encouraging complacency and pride, will not deceive God, though they may momentarily deceive man. Through Christ we have hope of grace, and though we can never work our passage alone, nor earn salvation as of right, God's commandments are no secret, and no man is prevented by his nature from obeying them unless he rejects God's helping hand. This is the robust and positive doctrine which the preachers' verbal excesses sometimes obscure, and though the demands of the popular pulpit do not permit much technical detail, there is a mass of theological authority to which they can turn for support. It is more helpful in the first instance to compare what Rabelais has to say about Christian life and salvation, and what is implied by the conduct of Pantagruel, with the normative teaching of the sermons rather than with the later doctrines of the Reformers. On that basis he does not seem to have strayed far from the Franciscan fold over the years.

The task of the preachers was to exhort and instruct, and to this end they raised questions of general relevance to daily life, usually involving legal, moral, or perhaps devotional points susceptible of more than one interpretation. These questions are invariably treated in terms of authorities for or against a particular opinion, and the preacher's task is to select and present his authorities, not to advance theories on his own account. Naturally enough, numerous questions of great importance to philosophers and theologians never arise in the sermons because they are too technical for popularization and of no immediate relevance to problems of daily life. To this extent any statistics based on frequency of authorities cited must be treated with some reserve if they are to be used as the sole guide to the reading habits of the preachers. At the same time very few writers of the class likely to be adduced as authorities confined their work to a single field, and the fact that a preacher quotes a given name is presumptive evidence of his familiarity with the writer's general ideas. It is certainly safe to assume that the training received by Rabelais followed the same general pattern as that revealed by the leading men of his order in his time, though variations in detail are only to be expected.

With this minor reservation, and subject to the suspicion which all statistics must arouse, an analysis of the modern index to Menot's sermons reveals some interesting facts. The four great Latin Fathers, SS. Ambrose, Augustine, Gregory and Jerome, together with St. John Chrysostom for the Greeks, account for 123 references. With the addition of St. Bernard, who though much later enjoyed the same prestige as the early Fathers and is often counted as the last of the great Latin Fathers, this group of six occurs 150 times in the index, and St. Augustine alone accounts for one-third of the references. The next group consists of five Franciscan doctors, Alexander of Hales, Bonaventura, Nicholas of Lyra, Richard of Middleton and Scotus, and collects about one hundred references, of which one-third go to Bonaventura. Finally St. Thomas and Aristotle are mentioned just under twenty times each. No other author or group of authors reaches double figures, except the purely literary trio of Juvenal, Ovid and Seneca, with less than thirty all together. Out of about three hundred references in all to philosophers and theologians it is noteworthy that Augustine easily outstrips the rest with forty-seven, followed by Bonaventura with thirty-two, with all the others in a bunch much closer together.[1]

These figures are undigested and approximate, but the relative frequency seems to be confirmed by the other preachers. Since there is no proper index to their works one must rely on impression and a rough check. On that basis the only significant additions to the list are St. John Damascene for the Greek Fathers, St. Anselm, the Benedictine doctor, and Bacon for the Franciscans. Ockham's name is barely mentioned by any of them,

---

[1] The actual figures are, in order of frequency: Augustine 47, Bonaventura 32, Scotus and Gregory 26, Jerome 23, Alexander of Hales and Bernard 22, Aristotle 19, Thomas 18, Ambrose 15, Chrysostom 12, Nicolas of Lyra 11, Richard of Middleton 7.

and then only in passing. Certain other writers, like Landulph the Carthusian and a former Patriarch of Jerusalem, are regularly quoted as giving details of the life of Christ, numerous canonists are quoted on points of law, but for the rest outsiders are virtually ignored and Menot's distribution seems to be typical.

The broad conclusions from all this are obvious: the preachers base their teaching above all on the five great Latin Fathers, especially Augustine, and almost invariably go to the accepted doctors of their own order when further opinion or commentary is required. They make an exception to this rule only in the case of St. Thomas, already recognized throughout the Church as holding a privileged position, but even he has to take his place after Bonaventura, Scotus and Alexander of Hales. It is, of course, certain that many of the patristic references came via a medieval author, and in terms of actual books read and hours spent in study by friars of the sixteenth century the Fathers must fall far behind the medieval writers from Peter Lombard onwards who collected and commented on their opinions. The situation is in this respect exactly comparable with that of the classical authors quoted by Rabelais; the man whose name comes up most often is the one with most prestige.

This pronounced loyalty of the preachers for doctors of their own order corresponds closely to the instructions, quoted earlier, [1] given by the Minister-General, Lychetus, to the Paris house of studies. Scotus's commentaries on the *Sentences*, as presented by Lychetus himself, were to be the basis of study in theology. The fact that Lychetus did not mention Bonaventura must certainly not be taken to imply any disapproval of the Seraphic Doctor. On formal points it was probably felt that Scotus had the last word, but the sermons are sufficient evidence of the unrivalled prestige enjoyed by Bonaventura as a master of spirituality. It is significant in this connexion that rather later in the century the Pope recognized the complementary, not contradictory, roles of the two great Franciscan doctors by approving new constitutions for the Conventuals, under which they were to have two regents in theology, one expounding Bonaventura and the other Scotus. [2] For all these reasons it is abundantly clear that Rabelais was trained on a specifically Franciscan diet of Scotus and Bonaventura, and whatever other doctrines he may have encountered,

---

[1] See p. 16.   [2] In 1568. Gilson, *Jean Duns Scot*, p. 660.

Thomism for example, would always have been treated as less reliable than Franciscan teaching.

It is not for nothing that Scotus is known as the Subtle Doctor, and all modern interpreters of his thought agree that it is exceedingly complex.[1] Until quite recently there was disagreement about the authenticity of some of his works, a problem of which the men of the sixteenth century were already aware, and in some ways we are better equipped today to understand what Scotus really wrote and thought than were Rabelais's contemporaries. Happily all that is necessary here is to consider the broad lines of Scotist teaching, regardless of authenticity in the canon of Scotus's works and of precise textual comparisons, with the ideas expressed by Rabelais on the same subjects.

It must be said at once that though both philosophers and theologians regard Scotus as being one of themselves, he himself emphatically claimed to be a theologian. In other words, it was as a Christian to whom truth has been revealed that he approached problems which pagan philosophers had attempted to solve by unaided reason. This does not mean that he denied the power of reason to grasp the truth, indeed rather the contrary is the case; he simply denied that the philosophers in question had attained it. Apart from other considerations, only a Christian (or a Jew) could properly appreciate how man's original nature, including his reason, had been altered by the Fall. The practical effect of Scotus's claim to be a theologian derives from the aim, as he saw it, of theology: to bring men nearer to salvation and thus to the beatific vision. It is well to remember that in the midst of his admittedly rebarbative subtleties Scotus was not playing a peculiarly complicated and pointless intellectual game, but striving towards the common goal of all Christians—for himself and others too. It follows from this that God's word, as revealed in Scripture, is final, and any solution of a problem which fails to take Scripture into account, let alone contradicts it, is quite simply false. That being said, it remains true that Scotus's methods are not necessarily the best, or even, for very many people, at all effective

---

[1] The most authoritative modern treatment is by Gilson, op. cit. though he quite deliberately considers only Scotus's principal ideas. The book by C. S. R. Harris, *Duns Scotus*, is rather fuller, and perhaps clearer, but he accepts as authentic certain works vital to his argument which have subsequently been proved not to be by Scotus, and this unfortunately weakens his case. The summary which follows is mainly based on Gilson.

means of reaching the end desired. Whatever his personal spiritual life, it can hardly be said that his work conveys a feeling of devotional warmth and urgency, as Bonaventura's unquestionably does.

It is generally agreed that the key to Scotus's thought lies in his attitude to being, 'esse', which he regarded as the proper object of philosophical thought. The most characteristic feature of Scot ism in this respect is the so-called 'univocity of being', that is the idea that 'esse' wherever it may be manifested is the same. In this he ran counter to Thomism, which established a system of analogies between the 'esse' of God and that of His creatures. It has been said that much of the difference between Scotus and Aquinas is purely terminological, and that when one or the other attributes this or that property to 'esse' or 'essentia' they are not using the same word in the same sense. This is of first importance from a historical point of view, but as far as the disputants on each side in the sixteenth century were concerned it is beside the point. Disagreement on definitions had become disagreement on prin-ciples, and Scotists and Thomists were clear enough that they stood for opposing ideas.

This doctrine of univocity momentarily exposed Scotus to the dangers of pantheism, and he took special care to define the difference between God, source of all being, and His creatures in terms which would make it absolutely clear that the creature in no way participated in the Creator.[1] One difference is that God's essence is infinite being. He *is* being, and thus totally distinct from the finite being possessed by creatures. Another lies in the relationship between God and His world. Scotus ensures that everything outside God should be seen to fall into the realm of the contingent by teaching that the decisive act by which the possible becomes the existent is accomplished by the divine will, 'le décret d'une suprême liberté'.[2] God has from all eternity in His intellect ideas of all possible essences, but it is only by a free act of will that He chooses these rather than those to be actualized. This act is not necessary in the sense that it confers on God some quality which was essential to His nature, for the creation adds no perfection to the Creator, nor is it determined by God's

---

[1] 'Il faut faire intervenir un acte séparateur pour assurer la contingence du possible.' Gilson, *La Philosophie au Moyen Âge*, p. 598.
[2] Ibid.

intellect, which presents to His will all the possibilities out of which only a specific part will come into existence. He could will any, or none, of the Ideas present in His intellect. Scotus thus ensures separation between the one infinite being and finite creatures, as well as the 'contingence du possible'.

The effects of this doctrine of the divine will are far-reaching. By ascribing to a perfectly free act of God's will the cause whereby all creatures have being, and by rejecting any system of analogies between various forms of being, Scotus eliminates the need for any genuinely causal links in the created world. God, as first cause, alone remains autonomous and immutable by changeless decree, and so-called second causes are in constant and direct dependence on His will. When Scotus attacks 'the philosophers' (i.e. Aristotle and the Arabs) it is above all for the necessitarism into which their theological ignorance inevitably led them. God's absolute freedom and the absolute dependence of everything else on His will are fundamental principles which Scotus is not prepared to modify in the slightest degree.

As a matter of practical experience certain effects do always follow certain causes, not only in the field of physical sciences but also in that of morals, and indeed human understanding of these subjects would not otherwise be possible, but Scotus strenuously distinguishes between what always in fact is seen to happen and what must necessarily happen. In this connexion miracles illustrate the distinction, for they are no more and no less dependent on the intervention of the divine will than what we regard as the natural order, once it is recognized that the autonomy of second causes is permissive, not essential. Similarly in the field of morals God is not bound to observe any necessary causal connexion between the accomplishment of particular good works and salvation. Election is purely gratuitous, and certainly no matter for human prediction. Scotus makes the point in regard to the Decalogue that the first three commandments, referring as they do to relations between Creator and creature, and thus inseparable from God's essence, are binding in a different way from the other seven, which deal with relations with one's neighbour, and from which God has on several occasions recorded in Scripture dispensed individuals. Neither the first table of the law nor the second is to be disobeyed by man, for disobedience carries inescapable consequences, but, as the New Testament shows, mere compliance with the letter of the law may be less pleasing in the sight of God than true obedience to its spirit. Scotus plainly states that eternal truths are decreed by God and dependent on His will: 'Réserve faite du principe de contradiction et de son immutabilité, la volonté de Dieu est donc maîtresse absolue du choix et de la combinaison des essences; elle n'est pas soumise à la règle du bien, c'est au contraire la règle du bien qui lui est soumise.'[1]

Such voluntarism in the hands of a pagan philosopher could easily lead to despotism and anarchy, but Scotus was writing with the assurance of a Christian who knows what sort of God created the world and maintains it in being. It is wholly to falsify his position to postulate imaginary consequences such as would follow from granting absolute liberty to a non-Christian God. Physics, therefore, is a possible and proper study for men, because it deals with the settled order of the world as it is, but if the physicists try to conclude from their study that there are laws of nature which cannot be changed they are exceeding their brief. Similarly, in the economy of salvation God is no oriental despot, no blind fate playing with men as 'flies to wanton boys', and though our incurable anthropomorphism may sometimes tempt us to see injustice in His acts of judgement, this cannot be, for His whole essence is good and cannot, by the principle of contradiction, include injustice.

It is in some ways misleading to speak of the primacy of God's will over His intellect in Scotism, for in the divine essence the two faculties are identical in perfection, though our creatural state may make us more aware of the omnipotence exercised by His will. When it comes to man there need be no such hesitation. Gilson says at the beginning of his analysis of the contrasting positions of Scotus and Aquinas: 'Dans l'ordre de la noblesse il est exact que Duns Scot ait reconnu un primat de la volonté.'[2] Such assertions as this, and such formulas as 'Nihil aliud a voluntate est causa totalis volitionis in voluntate'[3] reinforce the misgiving which the word 'voluntarism' has come to inspire since Scotus's time. If one tries to remove what Scotus has to say of the human will from its theological context misgiving, and misunderstanding, is inevitable. Gilson concludes his section on

[1] *La Philosophie au Moyen Âge.*, p. 599.
[2] Gilson, *Jean Duns Scot*, p. 594.
[3] *La Philosophie au Moyen Âge*, p. 601.

the Scotist doctrine of the will with a masterly statement of the whole position:

Entre *sapientia* et *caritas* certains théologiens donnent la palme à la sagesse et c'est même pourquoi ils tiennent l'intellect pour plus noble que la volonté. Ils se réclament d'ailleurs en cela d'Aristote. 'Sed contra hoc arguit alius philosophus noster, scilicet Paulus, qui dicit quod caritas excellentior est'. Voila donc qui est réglé, et, du même coup, explique l'esprit même du scotisme, car du primat de la charité sur la sagesse découlent celui de la volonté sur l'intellect, et de la liberté sur la nature finie, donc aussi le rejet du nécessitarisme des 'philosophes'.[1]

When all the philosophical formalities and 'isms' have been debated the bedrock of Scotist teaching is as solidly scriptural as that of the humblest preacher. A briefer formulation of Scotus's view sheds all technicality: 'La fin suprême de l'homme est dans l'amour, c'est-à-dire dans la volonté.'[2] This doctrine of love, *caritas*, has always been fundamental to the Franciscan spirit, whether manifested in the simple life and words of St. Francis himself or in the intellectual intricacies of the Scotists, and no matter what differences may have divided individuals or groups within the order one from another they have through the centuries always agreed on this. One sees at once the relevance of *caritas* if one substitutes for the Christian God of love the philosophers' God of omnipotence. Voluntarism based solely on power is all its opponents decry, but based on love its whole aspect changes. God created the world not because of some inscrutable whim but because of His love for what is good, He sent His Son to redeem fallen man not because He had to, but freely out of His love. If we ask that His will should be done it is not in fatalistic acceptance of what must be, but because He necessarily (in the proper sense of the word) wills what is good. So one can go through the whole chain of effects. This is why faith is only true when it is 'foy formée de charité'. This again is why humble ignorance can in God's sight be preferable to intellectual brilliance.

No Christian would question the excellence of charity against the authority of St. Paul, but very many did not accept a conclusion such as that of Scotus, putting the will above the intellect. The doctrine of *caritas* may have other possible consequences, but Scotus's doctrine of the will had no other possible cause. It should not be thought that he in any way deprecated the dignity of intellect, or disparaged the use of reason; indeed the whole point of his consideration of philosophical problems would have been lost if such had been his attitude. Here, as in most other questions of the kind, the differences between one thinker and another are over definitions and emphasis rather than aims and essentials.

From a technical point of view the outstanding contribution of Scotus was his doctrine of individuation, which is both more original and more difficult to follow than what has so far been discussed. The standard view of those who, like St. Thomas, followed Aristotle was that a substance consists in a union of matter and form, in which matter constituted the principle of individuation. For several reasons, notably his own peculiar theory of matter, Scotus did not accept this view, and he had particularly at heart to rehabilitate the individual in epistemology. In general in his time knowledge of the individual was regarded as a negation of knowledge of some universal, a limitation imposed on a class, and one individual differed from another of the same species through the quantitative determination conferred by matter. This was not good enough for Scotus, who thought: 'The individual as such exists by virtue of something positive which makes it just exactly what it is and nothing else. This positive entity he calls the *Haecceitas*.'[1] This, the ultimate reality in nature, is what our minds actually perceive in the concrete before they begin the work of abstraction. This doctrine has certain technical advantages, it makes the status of matter less passive, for example, and obviates the need for the clearly unsatisfactory theory of quantitative determination, which in the case of the angels had led to some very odd theories. It cannot be pretended that Scotus solved the problem of the universals, but he made a serious attempt to do so with this notion of *Haecceitas*. The difficulty of his theory lies in the very complex classification of matter, form and their union into which Scotus—or his followers—was led, but this does not concern us now. A modern critic finds a latent suspicion of anarchy in 'ces éléments discrets dont on ne voit pas du tout qu'ils forment un système',[2] but this may be reading history backwards, through the distorting glass of Ockham's Nominalism. At all events, emphasis on the individual, not only in theology, where Christianity had left no alternative, but also

[1] Harris, op. cit., vol. ii, p. 94.   [2] Bréhier, op. cit., p. 391.

in epistemology is one of the most characteristic and important features of Scotism. This emphasis may be connected with his resistance to the idea that any laws or classifications other than those directly promulgated by God are necessary or autonomous, but whatever its cause, Scotus's theory of individuation forced men to reconsider more traditional approaches. An interesting, and entirely predictable, consequence of this doctrine is his violent onslaught on the impious Averroes who tried to read into Aristotle his own deplorable doctrine of the universal soul, which was incompatible with personal immortality. In the view of Scotus there is no need to be a Christian, with the revealed certainty of personal survival, to arrive by unaided reason at the correct solution.

For internal reasons Scotus never produced a system or *summa* as St. Thomas had done, but his main works, that is his courses on the *Sentences* given in Oxford and Paris, as well as other commentaries, have something to say on most of the questions debated in his day. He seems to have been competent in mathematics and science, as well as theology and philosophy, and anyone who had studied his works would be very well informed on a wide range of topics. Much, perhaps most, of what he taught was common ground with Schoolmen from whom he differed on the sort of issue just discussed. While Scripture remained the acknowledged repository of truth there was only a limited area over which men could disagree in comparison with the ideological battleground of later centuries. Their disagreement was as bitter as philosophical polemics will always be, but while there is nothing artificial about Scotus's antipathy for Averroes (whom he would certainly have condemned to the flames if history had allowed such a confrontation), it is obviously in a different category of disagreement from that which he expressed with Aquinas, whom he respected and often praised. The medieval method of debate led him to state what he conceived to be the views of his various opponents before proceeding to refute them (or perhaps to accept them on particular points), and the attitude to authority is reflected by the copious references to Scripture and the Fathers with which Scotus supports his own arguments. Though Scotus does not make agreeable reading, he does provide a detailed discussion of the views of his predecessors, Greek, Arab and Christian, on nearly all the problems he discusses.

As an example of what would no longer be regarded as a vital question, or even a topic of conceivably useful discussion, it is worth mentioning his teaching on angels. Scripture guaranteed their existence and described some of their functions, and they also figured under various names in the works of Greek and Arab philosophers. As pure spirits, separate intelligences, they had to be accounted for in any discussion of matter and form and their nature had to be distinguished from that of man, with which it has obvious affinities. Though empirical data was rare, but not wholly lacking, discussion went into considerable detail and has been satirized in the supposed debate about how many angels can dance on the point of a pin. Two statements of Scotus show the sort of problem he tried to solve: 'Il n'est pas contradictoire à sa nature [d'ange] d'être présent en plusieurs lieux à la fois, au moins par la puissance divine . . . ni même que deux anges soient simultanément dans le même lieu, toujours par la puissance divine.'[1] ('Lieu' is to be taken here in the Euclidean sense of a geometrical point.) Scotus was, of course, not unique or exceptional in thus dealing with angels, but he was probably more thorough than most. His extraordinarily complex teaching about the hylomorphic composition of angels (that is the idea that to their form was added matter, but of a non-quantitative kind) and the principle of their individuation certainly led him into intricacies of argument which it would be hard to surpass, and anyone brought up on Scotism would be ideally equipped for any subsequent study of classical demonology.

While Scotus provided the formal basis of instruction in the Franciscan order, an element of at least equal importance was (and still is) contributed by Bonaventura. His thought was in some respects incorporated into Scotus's own commentaries, and in others superseded or modified, but for all their differences of temperament and outlook they both remain in the same Franciscan tradition. Bonaventura is best known for his devotional and mystical strain, and apart from his famous *Vita Christi* his most celebrated work is the *Itinerarium mentis ad Deum*. Gilson goes so far as to say: 'toute la pensée bonaventuréenne est concentrée dans l'*Itinéraire de l'Âme à Dieu*, dont les sept chapitres condensent la matière de plusieurs volumes.'[2] It would be difficult to find a

[1] Gilson, *Jean Duns Scot*, p. 412, n. 1.
[2] 'La Philosophie Franciscaine' in *S. François d'Assise* 1226-1926, p. 152. For a complete account of Bonaventura's thought see Gilson. *La Philosophie de Saint-Bonaventure*.

work of comparable brevity which presented so complete and coherent a system of thought, at least until the *Discours de la Méthode*.

The framework of this little book[1] is based on the ecstatic vision of St. Francis on Monte Alverna, where he received the stigmata, and the six wings of the seraph who appeared there are used by Bonaventura to symbolize the six stages of the soul's ascent towards God. These stages are, like the wings, in pairs. The first two start from the realm of nature, and we must seek to contemplate God through the signs He has left in the world ('per vestigia ejus in universo') and then in the world accessible to our senses ('in vestigiis suis in hoc sensibili mundo'). These two chapters deal very briefly with a characteristic feature of Bonaventura's thought, the vast and complex system of analogies between natural and supernatural things which he sometimes carries to extraordinary lengths. The second chapter contains an interesting reference to the Macrocosm (nature) entering the Microcosm (man) through the senses, and also an identification of the 'Intelligentiae' of the philosophers (Rabelais's 'Intelligences motrices') with the angels of Christian theology. Here we already see dim reflections of the divine nature; thus Bonaventura compares the images engendered by things in men's minds with the generation of the Son by the Father.

The next two stages are in the soul itself, imprinted in its natural powers with God's own image ('per suam Dei imaginem naturalibus potentiis insignitam') and conscious of this through seeing in its own processes analogies with God's nature; thus the three faculties of *memoria* (the faculty by which ideas are stored, not that which recalls them) *intelligentia* and *voluntas* reflect the relationship between the Father, the Son and the Spirit. In the next stage when grace has restored to the soul the blurred outlines of God's image ('in sua imagine donis gratuitis reformata') man can see his soul restored to its original likeness with God through the mediation of Christ. Here Bonaventura shows how sense preoccupations hold us back from our journey to God.

Finally comes contemplation of God in His unity of being ('divinae unitatis per ejus nomen primarium, quod est esse'). In this chapter v, the most relevant to the present study, we read of the successive steps upward to knowledge of God, who should

[1] In *Opera Omnia*, vol. vii, pp. 125–34.

be contemplated in His signs in the outside world, in His image in our souls and in light above ('contingit contemplari Deum . . . extra nos per vestigium, intra nos per imaginem, et supra nos per lumen.') Shortly afterwards come successively the text from Exodus, 'Ego sum qui sum', and the definition of God as 'sphaera intelligibilis, cujus centrum est ubique et circumferentia nusquam.' The last stage accessible to reason is contemplation of the Trinity of goodness ('beatissimae Trinitatis in ejus nomine, quod est bonum.') There, faced with the abyss between man's finite and God's infinite natures, man seems to have no way of completing the journey, but in reality the bridge is always there: Christ, God and man, Mediator and Redeemer.

A seventh chapter sets the mystical crown on the work of reason, and tells of the ecstasy which releases mind and understanding to be united with God ('de excessu mentali, et mystico, in quo requies datur intellectui, effectu totaliter in Deum per excessum transeunte.') The work concludes on a note of deepest devotion and spiritual exaltation, and Bonaventura makes it clear that human reason can advance only so far, but alone can never bring final mystic union of the soul with God.

In such a system the mystic gift of *caritas* far surpasses *sapientia*, which only allows us to embark on the initial stages of our pilgrimage. Side by side with the Christian and devotional implications of Bonaventura's mysticism it is plain enough to see the Platonic elements which had inspired mystics for centuries. The search for a higher truth beyond the shadowy and distorted world of created things, the inward search through self-knowledge for this truth, even the contemplation of God in his twin attributes of being and goodness, are features of all neo-Platonism, and are not even exclusively Christian. Obviously the final leap, the mediation of Christ, is the step which Bonaventura regards as most vital, and which at the same time owes nothing to Plato.

These ideas can be found considerably amplified in the rest of Bonaventura's work, where his Platonic epistemology leads him, for example, to say that God has the Ideas of all individuals from all eternity and knows as present and simultaneous all things to come.[1] In the present state of our knowledge of late Scholasticism and of Franciscan instruction it is not possible to say how far an individual, like Rabelais, would be free to choose between the

[1] Quoted in *Jean Duns Scot*, p. 309, n. 3.

teaching of Scotus and Bonaventura on points where they dis-
agreed, but all that matters is that we know for certain that the
works of both were studied; there can be no doubt as to which
Rabelais preferred.

A word should be said on the formal presentation of Scotism,
for to this rather than to its content one should probably ascribe
Rabelais's revulsion. One cannot be sure of the actual editions
Rabelais may have studied, but in this respect they do not differ.
The leading Paris Scotist in Rabelais's day was Pierre Tartaret,[1]
whose commentaries on the whole of Aristotle were published in
1514 and may very well have been in Rabelais's hands, for he is
remembered in the library of St. Victor. Early in the volume a
phrase occurs in a commentary on the *Summulae Logicales* of
Petrus Hispanus:[2] 'Dialectica est ars artium, scientia scientiarum,
ad omnium methodorum principia viam habens,' and Tartaret
bears this out. For folio after folio he expounds Aristotle's philosophy by taking each question and dividing it into 'Sciendum 1,
2, 3, Dubitandum 1, 2, 3, Conclusio'. Within each sub-division
the same symmetrical pattern is preserved, and the monotony of
this inexorable rhythm soon becomes intolerable. It is rare for a
method to be at once so systematic and so repellent, and the
contrast with the ease and warmth of the *Itinerarium* underlines
the diversity of influences to which Franciscan students were
exposed. At the same time Tartaret's work leaves no doubt that
what the student learnt, however unwillingly, he was unlikely to
forget. This indeed is true of Scholastic methods in general.

This training is reflected in Rabelais's work above all in the
unmistakable pattern underlying the many references thrown out
in so many contexts throughout a work written over a period of
twenty years. Such a pattern betokens long familiarity and firm-
ness of touch, and it is beyond reasonable doubt that it derives in
the first instance from Scholastic training. The hierarchical conception of the universe, extending from God through spirits to
man and the world of matter, is that to which Rabelais invariably
refers. There are no gaps in the chain of being, and the question
of communication between the different levels is one in which
Rabelais takes particular interest. Virtually all educated men of

---

[1] Or Tateret. 'Pierre Tateret, du diocèse de Lausanne, recteur de l'Université en
1490 . . . devenait le représentant le plus autorisé du scotisme parisien.' Renaudet
Pré-Réforme . . . , p. 95.   [2] Originally published in 1494.

the sixteenth century accepted the idea of a hierarchy, whatever their training might have been, so that the critical test is to see how Rabelais chooses between available alternatives and how he assimilates into his thought ideas which do not seem to have originally belonged to it. No problem arises in the case of scientific subjects, where one can only speak of Franciscan influence in such limited examples as that of Roger Bacon, but in theology, metaphysics, epistemology, ethics, in fact all the subjects discussed by Bonaventura and Scotus, one can judge whether or not influence is detectable.

The first, and easily the most important, choice of alternatives before Rabelais was between what Scotus habitually calls the 'philosophers and theologians'. If Rabelais had ignored metaphysical questions, and had relied for his theology on the Bible and the Fathers, restricting philosophical inquiry to moral issues, he would have been following Erasmus, his master in so many things, whose 'Philosophia Christiana' was on those lines. Erasmus explicitly reproached the Scholastic authors for having contaminated the teaching of the gospels with the speculations of pagans, especially Aristotle, and many of the Reformers took the same view. Another alternative before Rabelais was to follow such men as Dolet, who concentrated their attention on classical thought, especially that of Plato, and left theology to the professionals. Sometimes this course might lead to a sort of fideism, or even to the radically anti-Christian rationalism of Pomponazzi and his school, but common prudence enabled many humanists to steer clear of any clash. Critics of the past quarter century have put forward their case for enrolling Rabelais in each of these alternative schools (though no one has yet claimed that he belonged to both) and in between these extremes of the critical spectrum every shade of moderate opinion has found a place. There is also the third choice, which Scotus himself represents, and which is opposed, though not equally, to both Erasmus and Pomponazzi. Before Erasmus there had been such men as Peter Damian, before Pomponazzi there had been Averroes and the medieval Averroists. If the word 'Scholastic' can properly be used to cover both Thomists and Scotists it is largely because all the Schoolmen, of whatever persuasion, rejected these two extremes, the first as unrealistic, the second as pernicious. Though Rabelais repudiates Scholastic methods, and personally disliked those who practised them, his work establishes beyond a peradventure where he stands on this issue.

There are in the entire work of Rabelais only two formal definitions of God, one in each of the later books. In the *Tiers Livre* (XIII), when he writes of 'ceste infinie et intellectuale sphaere', Rabelais invokes the authority of Hermes Trismegistus, but wherever he had most recently found this favourite text of Renaissance (following medieval) neo-Platonism, he had seen it first in the *Itinerarium*, where the Christian context gives it full meaning. The sole definition in the *Cinquiesme Livre* (XLVII) is again the 'sphere intellectuale', this time without Hermes, and the coincidence must be taken as evidence in favour of this final chapter being largely authentic. In the *Quart Livre* (XLVIII) the definition is 'celluy qui est', based on the 'Ego sum' text of Exodus, which more than any other single text lies at the foundation of all Scholastic thought. The proximity of these two definitions on successive pages of the *Itinerarium*, and the fact that out of all the possible definitions he could have chosen Rabelais selected only these, should by now need no further comment. If one adds to formal definitions the names of God to which Rabelais gives special prominences the picture is complete. The difference between the Creator *ex nihilo* in Genesis and the prime mover and first cause of the Greeks is basic to theology and metaphysics, and even to physics for Scotus, while the concept of God as Saviour is what distinguishes Christianity from all other religions. Rabelais's consistency in stressing God's active attributes, and especially 'createur' and 'servateur', may be compared with Maillard's use in a single sermon[1] of 'Dieu le Createur' thirteen times and 'Nostre Saulveur' six.

The long sentence about the 'intellectuale sphère' goes on to speak of God's simultaneous knowledge of past, present and future, again in terms strongly reminiscent of Bonaventura, but the emphasis in all Rabelais's work, including the opuscules, is all on the divine will rather than the divine intellect. Whether Rabelais be upbraiding Calvin or the astrologers for their presumptuous folly in trying to predict God's inscrutable will, whether it be Hippothaddée gently reminding Panurge that all things, including success in marriage, are in God's hands or Pantagruel submitting himself in the midst of mortal danger to

[1] That preached at Bruges on Passion Sunday 1500. In *Œuvres Françaises*.

God's will, the theme 'fiat voluntas tua' recurs constantly. In a few cases the context is vaguely Stoic, when for example there is talk of 'fatalles destinées', but the great majority of references to God's will are unequivocally Christian. More than that, they are wholly consistent with Scotist training. The first brief chapter of the *Pantagrueline Prognostication* justifies one in going further, for, after a fervent tribute to God who has created and now maintains all things in being, Rabelais specifically quotes Avicenna (920) (almost the only serious quotation from an Arab in a work full of burlesque references) in rejecting the idea that second causes have any autonomy. Scotus examines Avicenna's views very carefully in formulating this essential point of his teaching. Not only does Rabelais know, he follows Scotus on this crucial issue. He too is utterly opposed to any idea of necessitarism, and in view of his close interest in Stoicism this is significant.

Enough has by now been written about Rabelais's use of the Scholastic formula 'foy formée de charité', but the role of *caritas* in his work is not confined to this single reference, important as it is. Here too Rabelais faced a variety of choices, corresponding to the variety of experience and book learning he had acquired, and his final decision again brings him into line with his former masters. Neither good cheer, nor massive learning, nor Stoic ataraxia are the whole of Pantagruelism in its final form, though they are all components of it. The primacy of the will in man is as marked in Rabelais as it is in Franciscan teaching, and partly no doubt motivated his attraction to Stoicism, but mere strength of will is not an end in itself, any more than wisdom ('science sans conscience . . .'). Though Pantagruel is explicitly stated (*TL*/11) to have attained ataraxia, he does not stop there, but uses his own moral strength as an example to others and in the service of God and his neighbour. The various definitions of Pantagruelism stress the duty to love (though the word is not actually used) one another as well as one's duty to desire God's will, not merely to submit to it passively. In word and deed Pantagruel is the living embodiment of *caritas*. This is, of course, not a Franciscan monopoly, and plenty of people who have never read a line of Scotus, nor perhaps heard of St. Francis, might well strive towards some such ideal, but it is quite another matter to develop it in such detail as Rabelais did and fit it into a coherent and consistent system. A suitable test of Franciscan influence is to ask whether

Rabelais would join Bonaventura and Scotus in subordinating intellect to will, and in accepting that 'la fin suprême de l'homme est dans l'amour'. In this connexion the Pan episode is clearly relevant. The fact that Rabelais echoes an exemplum familiar throughout the Middle Ages in a chapter which expresses his profoundest religious feeling shows how firm a hold his past had on him. The emotion evoked in this confession of faith is simply Christian, man's love for the God who died out of love for him, and is not peculiar to any group or sect, but it is well to ponder these solemn words of Rabelais before trying to decide which influence made his religion what it was. A comparison with the last chapter of the *Itinerarium* is suggestive.

These are the really important elements in Rabelais's theology and philosophy, but there are plenty of others where points of contact can readily be established with Franciscan teaching. On the question of individuation, for example, Rabelais's subsequent wide reading had not made him forget Scotus's doctrine of *Haecceitas*, and when he comes to define Pantagruelism in the Prologue to the *Tiers Livre* he uses the formula 'forme specifique et proprieté individuale' which distinctively belongs to Scotism, and this on an occasion surely calling for some care in the choice of words. Similarly, Rabelais's great interest in demonology and his treatment of Plutarch's theories on the subject show how thoroughly he knew Scholastic teaching about angels, and other spirits. Details of vocabulary, expression, references and analogies too numerous to repeat here all prove Rabelais's familiarity with Scholastic ways. Item by item the evidence may be inconclusive, but taken cumulatively all that has been considered in the preceding chapters adds up to a strong case.

A final point specifically concerns the influence of Bonaventura. As one can see in the *Itinerarium*, because it is so concentrated, but also in his other works, Bonaventura is advancing views which are completely Christian and mainly Platonic. In metaphysics and epistemology, in writing of God, spirits, man and their relationship, Bonaventura discusses at length all the main positions of Platonism as they affect Christianity. The coherence of his thought, and the attractive quality of the man, make him a natural master for a young friar of genuine intellectual distinction and religious convictions. The features of Platonism on which Rabelais dwells are those which Bonaventura had made familiar to him, those he omits or treats perfunctorily are almost always those which Bonaventura does not discuss. Resemblance is not the same as causality, and it is not necessary to claim that Rabelais's lifelong enthusiasm for Plato is solely due to Bonaventura. All the same, it is incontrovertible that Bonaventura was the first cause of this enthusiasm, because it was through him that Rabelais became initiated into Platonic thought, and on this point anyone is free to agree or disagree with Avicenna on the role of second causes.

Franciscan influence is not represented just by chance references but by a whole cast of mind. Though Rabelais never admitted this influence, we can see how it decisively shaped that of the classical authorities to whom he pays such generous tribute.

CONCLUSION

THE first part of this book has drawn attention to the relevance of Rabelais's early training in fitting him for speedy success as a popular author. A study of the sermons which were in use as models during Rabelais's time as a friar brings out very clearly the standards of language, religion and morality set by Franciscans who were in constant contact with an audience largely identical with the reading public to which Rabelais later addressed himself. With practice his skill improved, but the training which had ensured the success of his initial literary experiments remains a factor to be considered throughout his career as an author. It is only too easy to discuss his irreverence or grossness, his habits of style or targets of attack, without reference to Franciscan training or preaching, but to ignore such vital evidence is to invite errors as conspicuous as they are widespread.

In the second part of this book the primary aim has been to present a comprehensive analysis of Rabelais's thought and attitudes over a very wide range of topics. The question of how his ideas evolved from one book to another has not been examined in any detail, but the changing distribution of quotations on particular subjects is usually obvious enough to need no comment. It is interesting to find that the greater intellectual density of the later books barely, if at all, affects the consistency of Rabelais's thought over twenty years. His interests change, as one would expect, and his attitude to certain moral and religious issues evolves, largely as a result of a changing world and his personal experience, but the intellectual infrastructure remains substantially the same. One may conclude from this that his early training had provided Rabelais with mental equipment and a store of ideas which were to persist throughout adult life in a recognizably constant form, despite the considerable variety of authors and examples chosen from time to time to support particular theories.

This claim rests on the belief that Rabelais's world-picture remains systematic, comprehensive and consistent from 1532 to 1552, that the formal instruction he had received as a friar provided such a world-picture, and that Ockham's razor makes it unnecessary to seek additional or alternative causes for a phenomenon already fully explained. The technical knowledge which may have come to him through his medical studies is an exception which does not invalidate the general rule. Rabelais's ideas about God, spirits and man are more highly developed than the ostensible nature of his book would lead one to expect, and the last two chapters have considered how these ideas can be related to classical and Scholastic sources respectively. The Platonism of Bonaventura and the voluntarism of Scotus are outstanding examples of how permanently Franciscan teaching had marked Rabelais's mind. Neo-Platonism and Plutarch, Stoicism and Cicero left marks no less profound and no less lasting, but in time they came second. If Rabelais's treatment of classical ideas showed no clear pattern, but were just a hospitable synthesis of any thoughts that came drifting his way, or if on the other hand he had firmly accepted a given body of doctrine, be it Platonic, Stoic or anything else, it could be argued that his early training had been superseded or forgotten. The facts of the case are, however, quite different, and correspond closely to common educational experience. The plainest fact of all is that Rabelais had been well taught, and whether he liked his masters or not, they had affected him for life.

The signs of a man who has been well taught are familiar enough, at least to those who teach. Above all they appear in an ability to ask the right questions, to see just where new ideas fit into an existing framework and to assimilate fresh knowledge so that consistency never becomes mere stagnation. The characteristics of those who have been badly taught, or not taught at all, are perhaps even more familiar and are revealed in the two extremes of rigidity and confusion. Rabelais had a lively and capacious mind, but it is hard to believe that it was tidy by nature, still less through spontaneous self-discipline. The numerous brief references to Scholastic teaching show that Rabelais's memory had retained some of the lessons of his youth, but the work as a whole shows that his intellect continued to draw life and strength from his receding past.

If early reactions against Scotus led Rabelais to appreciate Bonaventura more, they did not prevent him from accepting, perhaps unwittingly, a number of Scotist doctrines. Thus we find him in later years emphasizing the primacy of will over intellect, rejecting the efficacy of second causes and showing a constant preoccupation with the individual rather than the universal. From Bonaventura, appropriately called the Seraphic Doctor, Rabelais first learned how the spirit can ascend to higher things, mounting the rungs of the Platonic ladder from the created world to God. From Bonaventura, too, he would have learned that angels have a part to play not only on the points of Scotist pins, but in true mystical experience. There is no reason to doubt that Rabelais's first acquaintance with the real Plato through his humanist friends at Fontenay thrilled him with a sense of discovery, but sober truth compels the admission that, judged solely on the evidence of his book, he does not seem to have learned very much from Plato himself that he would not already have learned of Platonism from Bonaventura.

Rabelais's later attraction to Stoicism, modified by whichever adjective one may prefer, was of incontrovertible importance in determining his attitude to many questions, but before he knew of Stoicism he had been brought up in the peculiarly Franciscan tradition of *caritas*. Rabelais's personal experience within the order may well have disillusioned him about the way in which certain Friars Minor followed the ideal of their founder, but this is no reason for supposing that he was at all disillusioned about the ideal itself. It is only too easy to forget that the arid distinctions of Scotus and the jeremaiads of the sermons were ultimately intended to further the cause of charity, but this is what the Franciscans have always claimed to stand for. In practice the ideal of *caritas* has been served by the friars' distrust and dislike of barriers between men, whether social, economic or intellectual, by an appeal which has often touched the hearts of the mighty but is primarily aimed at the masses and by a sometimes ferocious insistence on poverty as the surest protection against the world of material preoccupations which keep men back from truly loving God. The definitive version of Pantagruelism no doubt owes as much to Rabelais's temperament as to his training, but a comparison with what Erasmus, Loyola or Calvin, to name three very diverse contemporaries, have to say on similar themes reveals no such affinity with *caritas* as can hardly be missed in Rabelais. It is fair to say that all three are as far from the ideal of St. Francis as they are from Pantagruelism, and it is surely fair to add that a man who has once been attracted to St. Francis is being quite consistent if he ends up as a Pantagruelist.

It is an open question how far Rabelais deliberately drew on his early training for the purposes of his book. In his original bid for money and popular success it seems almost certain that he made the most of preaching techniques which he could never have expected to exploit once he had left the order. It has been pointed out in an earlier chapter that Rabelais's public standing in 1532 did not seem likely to gain lustre from his experiment in popular authorship, and that he was probably not at first disposed to devote more than minimal effort to creating for himself a style adequate to his money-making purpose. Certain chapters in the first two books on matters of education, religion and politics show that he was not content with mere fun even at the beginning, but his motto was and remained 'jusques au feu exclusivement'. In these first books there is a latent tension between Rabelais the man, daily pursuing interests and taking risks for which he was accountable, and the pseudonymous Nasier, whose similar risks and interests could always be disavowed on the pretext of comic invention or distortion (though the disavowal might not have turned away official wrath). The element of fantasy heavily outweighs that of reality, partly because the heroes are giants and also because of the improbable exploits of Panurge and Frère Jan, partly because of the use of reminiscence to recreate a lost world, to which both childhood and the *années de moinage* belong. One has only to compare Rabelais's natural style as it can be seen in his correspondence with that of the four books to realize that his Wonderland involved the creation of a special language as well as fictitious events and characters, side by side with those of real life. He is in his book, and at the same time apart from it.

When the success of the first two books convinced Rabelais that profitable popularity was not only assured but compatible with prestige, there was less need for him to keep the respected and erudite doctor at a distance from the intellectually less ambitious popular author. With his own name on the title page Rabelais enters into a new relationship with his creation. From the opening dedication to Marguerite right to the end the *Tiers Livre* is frankly pretentious, and aimed far above the heads of the public whose favour he had first solicited. The *Quart Livre*, dedicated to a cardinal, comes nearer a point of balance between popular and erudite, but the simple fun of the early books is now interspersed with passages of great complexity, and Rabelais shows off his learning unashamedly. Above all the fairy-tale giants of the first books are now reduced in physical stature, but morally exalted in the highest degree. Pantagruel is a real hero, 'l'idée et exemplaire de toute joyeuse perfection', whom we are meant to follow because he is a man like us, not a being in another dimension.

Apart from Rabelais's phenomenal literary success, which he can scarcely have anticipated, the publication of his second book coincided with a decisive change both in his own fortunes and in the world around him. By entering the service of the du Bellay brothers Rabelais became acquainted with a world of high-level diplomacy and government of which he can previously have had only the haziest notions, and during the same period, 1532-46, the Placards, Calvin's emergence, Dolet's execution and the opening of the Council at Trent marked successive stages on a road leading inexorably to civil war. The signs which men, Messier for example, had failed to read as late as the year before *Pantagruel* had now been fulfilled. The men of Rabelais's generation could look back in 1546 and recognize that they had passed the point of no return, though they probably could not have said just when. For Rabelais another point of no return had been passed, and one that can be located with precision. The premature death of Guillaume du Bellay in 1543 robbed Rabelais of more than a friend and protector, and his capacity for hero-worship, successively applied to Erasmus and Budé, found total satisfaction in the contemplation of his dead master. From the very first chapter of the *Tiers Livre*, when Pantagruel is dealing with the conquered Dipsodes, he bears unmistakable imprints of Langey's influence. Pantagruel is, of course, more than Langey, but in drawing his fictional hero Rabelais is taking a model from life. The new authority of Pantagruel in everything he does and says is the surest guide to Rabelais's intentions in the later books. The early giants had been either father-figures, doubtless modelled on Rabelais's own family life, or projections of Rabelais's wish fulfilment for himself, but the later Pantagruel is set above author and reader alike.

The practical consequences of Langey's influence on the ideal Pantagruel and of world events on Rabelais's creation are very complicated. In the first place the new form of the work entails the successive presentation of theories, characters and experiences to Pantagruel, whose reactions are meant to indicate the right way. All the other characters are judged by reference to him, which is not the case in the earlier books, and all fall short. Then, Rabelais is intellectually and personally committed in his later books and frequently propounds views (usually through Pantagruel) which are clearly meant to be taken seriously and which cover almost every major problem of human life. Finally, the fictional age of Pantagruel makes the intrusion of the past a very different thing from the natural evocation of childhood memories associated with the giants' childhood, while the open problems of 1532-4 have been so overtaken by events that speculations about an all too ominous future have little or no point after 1546.

All these facts, as well as the passage of the years after Rabelais left Fontenay, would make one expect far less sign of Franciscan influence, whether by direct reminiscence or in habits of mind and speech. Popular appeal is no longer the paramount need, nor has Rabelais to conceal himself behind an assumed persona; the religious and intellectual movements of the 1520's have come to fruition; years of reading and discussion have deposited layer upon layer of classical erudition upon the bedrock of Scholastic training, long since repudiated. The actual evidence of the later books confounds expectations. The two Bonaventuran definitions of God occur respectively in the *Tiers Livre* and *Quart Livre*, a verbal reference to the technical Scotist doctrine of individuation comes in the *Tiers Livre* Prologue, the *Quart Livre* is the one to mention Frères Maillard and Bourgeois (of fifty years before), the only two references to Amy come in the *Tiers Livre* and in a probably authentic chapter of the *Cinquiesme Livre*, the debt to Scholasticism is proved in the crucial Pan chapter of the *Quart Livre*, and so on and so on. To be brief and categorical, the 'temps perdu', including the *années de moinage*, is nowhere more in evidence than in the later books. Erasmus's influence on whole episodes, notably the death of Raminagrobis in the *Tiers Livre* and the storm in the *Quart Livre*, is outstanding, and this at a time when everything he had stood for was being distorted or destroyed. When we find Rabelais condemning Calvin and Putherbe in the same sentence of the *Quart Livre* of 1552, a few chapters after his most solemn and dangerous affirmation of Christian belief, it is no wonder that the lost promises of the past attract him more as his life draws to a close than twenty years before when there still seemed to be a future. Instances could be multiplied of references in the later books to the quite remote past, and such identifications as those of Hippothaddée with Lefèvre d'Etaples, Raminagrobis with Crétin (or Jean Lemaire de Belges) and Rondibilis with Rondelet have won general acceptance. The case for seeing the last books as a sort of 'Recherche du Temps Perdu', probably to have been 'Retrouvé' in a final version of the oracle of the Dive Bouteille, is more than just plausible and must involve the années de moinage as much at least as the rest of the past.

As to why this should be so, several answers are possible. It could perhaps be argued that in the later books, despite the higher intellectual content, Rabelais is still exerting himself as little as possible, using short cuts to erudition like indexes and compendia, and exploiting memory when invention fails. On these grounds persistence of Scholastic habits of mind could be attributed to mere economy of effort, when it does not represent deliberate parody. An alternative explanation would be his sheer inability to escape from well-taught ideas which he was too lazy or unintelligent to replace and too hostile to acknowledge. There may be a little truth in both these views, but that which is now proposed is that when experience of life and books had taught Rabelais all he could learn, he came to realize (as the oracle perhaps hints) that his early training had left him with profound convictions, which he had been able to enrich and diversify from later learning, but which he had not been able to discard with his friar's habit. In his refusal to cast aside his frock, Frère Jan may for once stand as a symbol of Frère François.

However unwilling Rabelais would have been to admit his debt to the Franciscans, and however remote he may have felt himself from their training, the unprejudiced observer may feel better qualified to judge than he was. The last point is really the first: in their official list of writers, a substantial volume in no need of padding, the Franciscans have since the seventeenth century acknowledged Rabelais as one of their own, albeit with caution and this book has sought only to justify their inclusion of 'Franciscus Rabelesius, Scriptor Ordinis.'

BIBLIOGRAPHY

All works actually referred to are listed, with the usual exceptions of the Bible, Shakespeare and some classical texts. The principal works consulted with profit are also included, except that works on Rabelais have only been listed when they have been referred to in the text. This is not intended in any way as a select bibliography on Rabelais.

Place of publication is Paris unless otherwise stated.

1. Patristic

EUSEBIUS, *Chronicorum Canonum*, Latin trans. by St. Jerome, Basle, 1529.

—— *Praeparatio Evangelica*, ed. and trans. E. H. Gifford, Oxford, 1903.

ISIDORE OF SEVILLE, *Etymologiarum Libri xx*, ed. W. M. Lindsay, Oxford, 1911.

2. Medieval and Scholastic

ROGER BACON, *Opus Tertium* (part) ed. A. G. Little, Aberdeen, 1912.

BONAVENTURA, SAINT, *Itinerarium Mentis ad Deum*, in *Opera*, 7 vols. in 4, Mainz, 1609.

PETRUS COMESTOR, *Historia Scolastica*, 1513.

CUSANUS (NICOLAS OF CUSA), *De la Docte Ignorance*, ed. and trans. E. Molinier, 1930.

JOINVILLE, *Histoire de Saint Louis*, in *Historiens et Chroniqueurs du Moyen Âge*, Bibl. de la Pléiade, 1942.

Liber Exemplorum, British Society for Franciscan Studies, Aberdeen, 1908.

GUILLAUME DE LORRIS and JEAN DE MEUNG, *Roman de la Rose*, ed. E. Langlois, SATF, 1914.

Monumenta Franciscana, 2 vols. in Rolls Series, London, 1882.

SACROBOSCO (JOHN OF HOLYWOOD), *De Sphaera*, with commentaries by Pierre d'Ailly, Lefèvre d'Etaples, Michel Scot, Venice, 1518.

JOH. DUNS SCOTUS, *Quaestiones in Sententias*, 2 vols., ed. H. Cavellus, Antwerp, 1620.

PIERRE TARTARET, *Expositio in Summulas Logicales* . . . *cum Commentariis in Aristotelem*, Basle, 1514.

THOMAS AQUINAS, SAINT, *Opera*, 16 vols. Rome, 1881–1948.

—— *Selected Political Writings*, ed. and trans. A. d'Entrèves, Oxford, 1948.

VINCENT DE BEAUVAIS, *Speculum Naturale*, Douai, 1620.

3. Sermons

ANTOINE FARINIER, *Sermones xxi de Peccatis*, A. du Roy, Lyon, 1518.

OLIVER MAILLARD, *Sermones de Adventu, Quadragesimales* . . . S. Gueygnard, Lyon, 1503 (Bibl. Nat. D 5197).

—— *Sermones de Stipendio Peccati*, P. Pigouchet, 1500.

—— *Œuvres Françaises* (incl. *Carême de Nantes, Sermon de Bruges, Chansons*), ed. A. de la Borderie, Nantes, 1877.

MICHEL MENOT, *Sermons Choisis* (incl. *Carême de Tours* and two *Carêmes de Paris*), ed. J. Nève, 1924.

ROBERT MESSIER, *Sermones de Quadragesima*, A. Boucard, 1531.

4. Rabelais

FRANÇOIS RABELAIS, *Œuvres*, ed. H. Clouzot (Garnier) n.d.

—— *Œuvres*, ed. A. Lefranc and others, vols. i–v, 1913–.

—— *Œuvres*, ed. J. Boulenger, Bibl. de la Pléiade, 1934.

—— *Pantagruel*, ed. V. L. Saulnier, 1946.

—— *Quart Livre de* 1548, ed. J. Plattard, 1910.

—— *Quart Livre*, ed. R. Marichal, 1947.

—— *L'Isle Sonnante*, ed. J. Boulenger, 1905.

5. Sixteenth Century

H. CORNELIUS AGRIPPA, *De Occulta Philosophia*, Antwerp, 1531.

A. DE BEATIS, *Voyage du Cardinal d'Aragon* (1517–18), ed. and trans. M. Havard de la Montaigne, 1913.

G. BIGOT, *Christianae Philosophiae Praeludium*, Toulouse, 1549.

A. BOUCHARD, *De l'Excellence et Immortalité de l'Âme*, Bibl. nat. MS. Fr. ancien 1991 fonds.

G. BUDÉ, *Epistolae Latinae* in *Opera*, 2 vols., Basle, 1557.

—— *Epistolae Graecae*, Latin trans. A. Pichon, 1574.

J. Calvin, *Institution Chrétienne* (1541 text), ed. J. Pannier, 4 vols., 1956.

P. Crinitus, *De Honesta Disciplina*, Lyon, 1543.

Epistolae Obscurorum Virorum, ed. H. G. Stokes, London, 1925.

Erasmus, *Colloquia*, Delft, 1729.

—— *Enchiridion*, French trans. attributed to L. Berquin, Lyon, 1542.

—— *Stultitiae Laus*, Basle, 1676.

H. Estienne, *Apologie pour Hérodote*, 1572.

M. Ficino, *Theologia Platonica*, 1559.

Folengo, *Histoire Maccaronique de Merlin Coccaie*, ed. P. L. Jacob, 1876.

P. Gringoire, *Vie Saint Louis*, in *Œuvres*, Bibl. Elzevirienne, 1858.

Marguerite de Navarre, *L'Heptaméron*, ed. M. François, 1943.

—— *Théâtre Profane*, ed. V. L. Saulnier, 1946.

P. Mexia, (or Mejia) *Silva de Varia Leccion*, Soc. Bibliofilos Esp., Madrid, 1938.

—— *Collection of Histories*, English trans. of above by T. Fortescue, London, 1571.

G. Postel, *De Orbis Terrae Concordia* . . . , 1543.

—— *De Etruriae Regionis Originibus*, Florence, 1551.

J. Sleidan, *Commentaires touchant l'estat de la religion et de la republique . . . sous Charles V*, 1555.

A. Turnèbe, *Plutarchi Opera* (Latin Trans.), Strasbourg, 1600.

Polydore Vergil, *De Inventoribus Rerum*, Basle, 1544.

P. Ronsard, *Œuvres*, 2 vols., Bibl. de la Pléiade, 1938.

6. Modern

G. Atkinson, *Les Nouveaux Horizons de la Renaissance Française*, 1935.

E. Auerbach, *Mimesis*, New York, 1957.

J. Barnaud, *Jacques Lefèvre d'Etaples*, Cahors, 1900.

I. Boberg, *Sagnet om den store Pans Død*, Copenhagen, 1934.

J. Bohatec, *Budé und Calvin*, Graz, 1950.

A. de la Borderie, *Œuvres Françaises d'Olivier Maillard*, Nantes, 1877.

V. L. Bourrilly, *Guillaume du Bellay*, 1904.

W. J. Bouwsma, *Concordia Mundi, Career and Thought of G. Postel*, Harvard, 1957.

E. BREHAUT, *An Encyclopaedist of the Dark Ages, Isidore of Seville*, New York, 1912.

E. BRÉHIER, *La Philosophie du Moyen Âge*, 1937.

H. BUSSON, *Sources du Rationalisme au XVIe Siècle*, 1922.

R. C. CHRISTIE, *Etienne Dolet*, London, 1880.

M. COURTECUISSE, *Tables Capitulaires des Frères Mineurs de l'Observance . . . de Bretagne*, 1930.

R. CUDWORTH, *An Intellectual System of the Universe*, London, 1845.

M. DE GRÈVE, *L'Interprétation de Rabelais au XVIe Siècle*, Geneva, 1961.

A. D'ENTRÈVES, *Natural Law*, London, 1951.

L. DELARUELLE, *Guillaume Budé*, 1907.

—— *Répertoire de la Correspondance de G. Budé*, 1907.

Etudes Rabelaisiennes, I; see also SCREECH, Geneva, 1956.

L. FEBVRE, *La Religion de Rabelais*, 1942.

Saint François d'Assise 1226–1926, see also GILSON, 1927.

E. GILSON, *Etudes de Philosophie Médiévale*, Strasbourg, 1921.

—— 'Quelques Notes Médiévales sur le TL', in *RHF*, ii, 1925.

—— *La Philosophie de Saint Bonaventure*, 1925.

—— 'La Philosophie Franciscaine' in *Saint François* above.

—— *Les Idées et Les Lettres*, 1932.

—— *L'Esprit de la Philosophie Médiévale* (Gifford Lectures), 2 vols., 1932.

—— *Héloïse et Abélard*, 1938.

—— *La Philosophie au Moyen Âge*, 2nd ed. 1945.

—— *Jean Duns Scot*, 1952.

C. S. R. HARRIS, *Duns Scotus*, 2 vols. Oxford, 1927.

C. H. HASKINS, *The Renaissance of the Twelfth Century*, Cambridge, 1927.

H. HAUSER et A. RENAUDET, *Les Débuts de l'Âge Moderne*, 1927.

D. HAY, *Polydore Vergil*, Oxford, 1952.

J. HUIZINGA, *Erasmus*, London, 1924.

—— *The Waning of the Middle Ages*, London, 1937.

L. KARL, 'Sur la Mort de Pan dans Rabelais' in *Mélanges Picot*, 1913.

R. KLIBANSKY, *The Continuity of the Platonic Tradition*, London, 1939.

M. D. KNOWLES, *The Religious Orders in England*, 3 vols., Cambridge, 1948–59.

A. J. KRAILSHEIMER, 'Rabelais et Postel' in *BHR*, 1951.

ABBÉ LACURIE, *Histoire de l'Abbaye de Maillezais*, Fontenay-le-Comte, 1852.

C. V. LANGLOIS, *La Vie en France au Moyen Âge*, 1908.

—— *La Connaissance de la Nature au Moyen Âge*, 1911.

A. LEFRANC, *Les Navigations de Pantagruel*, 1905.

—— *Grands Ecrivains Français de la Renaissance*, 1914.

M. MANN, *Erasme et les Débuts de la Réforme Française*, 1933.

LECOY DE LA MARCHE, *La Chaire Française au Moyen Âge*, 1880.

R. MARICHAL, 'Rabelais devant le néo-Platonisme' in *François Rabelais* below.

—— 'Rabelais et la Réforme de la Justice' in *BHR*, 1952.

A. MÉRAY, *Les Libres Prêcheurs, Devanciers de Luther et de Rabelais*, 1860.

—— *La Vie au Temps des Libres Prêcheurs*, 1878.

H. MEYLAN, 'Sur la Mort de Lamy' in *François Rabelais* below.

R. MORÇAY, *L'Abbaye de Thélème*, 1934.

G. R. OWST, *Preaching in Mediaeval England*, Cambridge, 1926.

—— *Literature and Pulpit in Mediaeval England*, Cambridge, 1933.

G. PARÉ, *Le Roman de la Rose et la Scolastique Courtoise*, 1941.

J. PLATTARD, *L'Œuvre de Rabelais*, 1909.

—— 'L'Ecriture Sainte dans Rabelais', in *RER*, 1910.

A. PROST, *H. Corneille Agrippa*, 2 vols., 1881.

François Rabelais 1553–1953, see also MARICHAL, MEYLAN, Geneva, 1953.

S. REINACH, *Cultes, Mythes, Religions*, vol. iii, 1913.

A. RENAUDET, *Pré-Réforme et Humanisme à Paris*, 2nd ed. 1953.

B. RUSSELL, *History of Western Philosophy*, London, 1946.

V. L. SAULNIER, *Maurice Scève*, 2 vols., 1948.

—— 'Dix Années sur Rabelais' in *BHR*, 1949.

A. SAMOUILLAN, *Oliver Maillard, sa Prédication, son Temps*, Toulouse, 1891.

L. SCHRADER, *Panurge und Hermes*, Bonn, 1958.

M. A. SCREECH, 'Rabelais, de Billon and Erasmus' in *BHR*, 1951.

—— 'The Death of Pan and Heroes' in *BHR*, 1955.

—— 'Some Stoic Elements in Rabelais's Religious Thought' in *Etudes Rabelaisiennes, I*, Geneva, 1956.

—— *L'Evangélisme de Rabelais*, Geneva, 1959.

—— *The Rabelaisian Marriage*, London, 1958.

A. DE SÉRENT, 'Les Pères Gardiens du grand Couvent de Paris' in *La France Franciscaine*, iii, 1914–20.

A. DE SÉRENT, 'Les Statuts des Quatre Provinces Françaises des Cordeliers', in *RHF*, vii, 1930.

F. DE SESSEVALLE, *Histoire Générale de l'Ordre de Saint François*, vol. ii, 1937.

B. SMALLEY, *English Friars and Antiquity in the Early Fourteenth Century*, Oxford, 1960.

G. SOURY, *La Démonologie de Plutarque*, 1942.

L. THUASNE, *Etudes sur Rabelais*, 1904.

—— *Villon et Rabelais*, 1911.

E. M. TILLYARD, *The Elizabethan World Picture*, London, 1945.

P. IMBART DE LA TOUR, *Les Origines de la Réforme*, vol. i, 1948; (2nd ed.), vol. ii, 1946; (2nd ed.), vol. iii, 1914; vol. iv, 1935.

L. WADDING, *Annales Minorum*, 30 vols., 2nd ed., Quaracchi, 1931–51.

—— *Scriptores Ordinis Minorum*, Rome, 1651.

M. DE WULF, *Philosophy and Civilisation in the Middle Ages*, Oxford, 1920.

—— *Histoire de la Philosophie Médiévale*, 1936.

L. ZANTA, *La Renaissance du Stoïcisme au XVIe Siècle*, 1914.

7. *Periodicals*

Archivum Franciscanum Historicum, 1908–

Bibliothèque d'Humanisme et Renaissance, 1941–

Humanisme et Renaissance, 1934–40.

Revue d'Etudes Rabelaisiennes, 1903–12.

Revue d'Histoire Franciscaine, 1924–31.

Revue du Seizième Siècle, 1913–34.

GENERAL INDEX

The index does not include references to fictitious characters in Rabelais's work, nor to episodes other than that of Thélème. A separate index to quotations from Rabelais has seemed the best way of dealing with these points.

INDEX LOCORUM

This index lists by chapters all those passages in Rabelais's work which are actually quoted or to which direct reference is made. It does not include more vague or general references to characters, episodes or groups of chapters. It should be pointed out that multiple references to a particular chapter do not necessarily indicate that the same passage of the chapter is in every case that which has been used.

It is perhaps worth pointing out that the comparatively small number of chapters against which a blank entry stands indicates how truly representative is the sample of Rabelais's thought and expression which this book has attempted to analyse.